How to Form a Corporation in Pennsylvania

Rebecca A. DeSimone
Attorney at Law

SPHINX® PUBLISHING
AN IMPRINT OF SOURCEBOOKS, INC.®
NAPERVILLE, ILLINOIS
www.SphinxLegal.com

First Edition, 2003

Published by: **Sphinx® Publishing, An Imprint of Sourcebooks, Inc.**®

<u>Naperville Office</u>
P.O. Box 4410
Naperville, Illinois 60567-4410
630-961-3900
Fax: 630-961-2168
www.sourcebooks.com
www.SphinxLegal.com

This publication is designed to provide accurate and authoritative information in regard to the subject matter covered. It is sold with the understanding that the publisher is not engaged in rendering legal, accounting, or other professional service. If legal advice or other expert assistance is required, the services of a competent professional person should be sought.

From a Declaration of Principles Jointly Adopted by a Committee of the
American Bar Association and a Committee of Publishers and Associations

This product is not a substitute for legal advice.

Disclaimer required by Texas statutes.

Library of Congress Cataloging-in-Publication Data
DeSimone, Rebecca A., 1963-
  How to form a corporation in Pennsylvania / by Rebecca A. DeSimone.--
1st ed.
     p. cm.
  Includes index.
  ISBN 1-57248-358-X (alk. paper)
  1. Incorporation--Pennsylvania--Popular works. I. Title.
KFP213.5.Z9 D47 2003
346.748'06622--dc22
                              2003019181

Printed and bound in the United States of America.
VHG Paperback — 10 9 8 7 6 5 4 3 2 1

Acknowledgment

I wish to extend an enormous debt of gratitude to my parents for their unshakable constancy, to F. Clifford Gibbons, Esquire for his ever present faith and guidance, and to Marya Kopacz and Becky Moran for their unwavering support and encouragement.

CONTENTS

USING SELF-HELP LAW BOOKS

Before using a self-help law book, you should realize the advantages and disadvantages of doing your own legal work and understand the challenges and diligence that this requires.

The Growing Trend

Rest assured that you won't be the first or only person handling your own legal matter. For example, in some states, more than seventy-five percent of the people in divorces and other cases represent themselves. Because of the high cost of legal services, this is a major trend and many courts are struggling to make it easier for people to represent themselves. However, some courts are not happy with people who do not use attorneys and refuse to help them in any way. For some, the attitude is, "Go to the law library and figure it out for yourself."

We write and publish self-help law books to give people an alternative to the often complicated and confusing legal books found in most law libraries. We have made the explanations of the law as simple and easy to understand as possible. Of course, unlike an attorney advising an individual client, we cannot cover every conceivable possibility.

Cost/Value Analysis   Whenever you shop for a product or service, you are faced with various levels of quality and price. In deciding what product or service to buy, you make a cost/value analysis on the basis of your willingness to pay and the quality you desire.

When buying a car, you decide whether you want transportation, comfort, status, or sex appeal. Accordingly, you decide among such choices as a Neon, a Lincoln, a Rolls Royce, or a Porsche. Before making a decision, you usually weigh the merits of each option against the cost.

When you get a headache, you can take a pain reliever (such as aspirin) or visit a medical specialist for a neurological examination. Given this choice, most people, of course, take a pain reliever, since it costs only pennies; whereas a medical examination costs hundreds of dollars and takes a lot of time. This is usually a logical choice because it is rare to need anything more than a pain reliever for a headache. But in some cases, a headache may indicate a brain tumor and failing to see a specialist right away can result in complications. Should everyone with a headache go to a specialist? Of course not, but people treating their own illnesses must realize that they are betting on the basis of their cost/value analysis of the situation. They are taking the most logical option.

The same cost/value analysis must be made when deciding to do one's own legal work. Many legal situations are very straight forward, requiring a simple form and no complicated analysis. Anyone with a little intelligence and a book of instructions can handle the matter without outside help.

But there is always the chance that complications are involved that only an attorney would notice. To simplify the law into a book like this, several legal cases often must be condensed into a single sentence or paragraph. Otherwise, the book would be several hundred pages long and too complicated for most people. However, this simplification necessarily leaves out many details and nuances that would apply to special or unusual situations. Also, there are many ways to interpret most legal questions. Your case may come before a judge who disagrees with the analysis of our authors.

Therefore, in deciding to use a self-help law book and to do your own legal work, you must realize that you are making a cost/value analysis. You have decided that the money you will save in doing it yourself outweighs the chance that your case will not turn out to your satisfaction. Most people handling their own simple legal matters never have a problem, but occasionally people find that it ended up costing them more to have an attorney straighten out the situation than it would have if they had hired an attorney in the beginning. Keep this in mind while handling your case, and be sure to consult an attorney if you feel you might need further guidance.

Local Rules   The next thing to remember is that a book which covers the law for the entire nation, or even for an entire state, cannot possibly include every procedural difference of every jurisdiction. Whenever possible, we provide the exact form needed; however, in some areas, each county, or even each judge, may require unique forms and procedures. In our state books, our forms usually cover the majority of counties in the state, or provide examples of the type of form which will be required. In our national books, our forms are sometimes even more general in nature but are designed to give a good idea of the type of form that will be needed in most locations. Nonetheless, keep in mind that your state, county, or judge may have a requirement, or use a form, that is not included in this book.

You should not necessarily expect to be able to get all of the information and resources you need solely from within the pages of this book. This book will serve as your guide, giving you specific information whenever possible and helping you to find out what else you will need to know. This is just like if you decided to build your own backyard deck. You might purchase a book on how to build decks. However, such a book would not include the building codes and permit requirements of every city, town, county, and township in the nation; nor would it include the lumber, nails, saws, hammers, and other materials and tools you would need to actually build the deck. You would use the book as your guide, and then do some work and research involving such matters as whether you need a permit of some kind, what type and grade of wood are available in your area, whether to use hand tools or power tools, and how to use those tools.

Before using the forms in a book like this, you should check with your court clerk to see if there are any local rules of which you should be aware, or local forms you will need to use. Often, such forms will require the same information as the forms in the book but are merely laid out differently or use slightly different language. They will sometimes require additional information.

Changes in the Law   Besides being subject to local rules and practices, the law is subject to change at any time. The courts and the legislatures of all fifty states are constantly revising the laws. It is possible that while you are reading this book, some aspect of the law is being changed.

In most cases, the change will be of minimal significance. A form will be redesigned, additional information will be required, or a waiting period will be extended. As a result, you might need to revise a form, file an extra form, or wait out a longer time period; these types of changes will not usually affect the outcome of your case. On the other hand, sometimes a major part of the law is changed, the entire law in a particular area is rewritten, or a case that was the basis of a central legal point is overruled. In such instances, your entire ability to pursue your case may be impaired.

Again, you should weigh the value of your case against the cost of an attorney and make a decision as to what you believe is in your best interest.

INTRODUCTION

Many people dream of starting their own business but fear that complicated rules and expensive procedures will pose insurmountable hurdles to their entrepreneurial visions. Perhaps you have considered breaking from your current employment or work environment and venturing into a new enterprise in which you may create the type of company or business you have always imagined. Indeed, your dreams and imaginings need not be illusory. This book is designed with the aspiring corporate novice in mind. Put aside your trepidation and peruse the pages of this guide as you discover that the dream of starting your own business is well within your reach.

This book will lead you on a journey through the corporate set-up process. You will learn the way in which a business entity is formed. Various types of business entities will be explained, and you will discover their unique characteristics and requirements. Overviews, as well as in-depth discussions will be provided about an assortment of substantive business topics. Each will offer insights and deeper understanding of the questions and concerns helpful to the new entrepreneur.

In this modern world of ever-changing careers, layoffs, reorganizations and workplace challenges, it is often the case that the idea of a starting a new business manifests itself. This book will illuminate your path as you explore the corporate start-up process. You will find instructions for setting up your business, as well as the necessary forms to make your objectives a reality.

As you follow the incorporation process on a step-by-step basis, you will find that your vision of beginning your own business may be easier that you first thought. The book is replete with forms for filing, Pennsylvania Statutes for reference, and a handy glossary of terms to aid in your more complete understanding and comprehension of all things corporate.

I | BUSINESS ENTITIES

Incorporating your business, protecting your *assets*, and limiting your potential liabilities are likely your top concerns if you have taken the first step of reading this book. The chapters that follow will be of assistance in your overall understanding of the business set-up process and the incorporation procedures.

You have many options from which to choose regarding your *business structure*. Before forming your corporation, you should be aware of the various classifications of corporate forms you can take. Not all forms are discussed equally. This book focuses on the small business set-up. A small business can form as a *C corporation*, the corporate form that all corporation take unless some other *election* is made, or one of the other types discussed. The "S" election for small corporations may be the most common and is discussed throughout the book.

The type and composition of the corporate form that you will choose will be affected by various liability, tax, and protective considerations. This chapter addresses the distinctions between and among the most common corporate forms–C corporations, *S corporations*, and *Professional corporations*, as well as addressing *Foreign corporations* and *Not-for-Profit corporations*.

In evaluating the material with the objective of choosing the proper corporate structure for your business, you should give thoughtful consideration to the following issues.

- How will the owners of the business be compensated?

- Are instant financial gains necessary or is your business willing to wait for cash to insure more positive tax results?

- Will your business have employees?

- Do you wish to have tax advantages as perks or benefits to your employees?

- How will you finance your business?

- Will investors in the business receive or share in gains from the business?

- Should the business lose money or fail, will you be protected from tax consequences from the losses that will follow?

- If you realize a profit, how, and to whom will the profit be paid and taxed?

- Do you require flexibility to alter the nature of your business as it develops?

- Will the owners or principals be responsible for the obligations and conduct of the business entity?

C Corporations

A *general corporation*, also known as a C corporation, is the most common corporate type, but is generally used by larger corporations. A C corporation may have an unlimited number of *stockholders*. A C corporation is normally chosen by those businesses that are planning to have more than thirty shareholders or planning a large, public stock offering.

The C corporation usually pays taxes at two levels. First, the corporation is required to pay taxes based on the corporation's profits. Additionally, the owner or shareholder is taxed when the corporation distributes profits, known as *dividends*, to the individual.

Smaller businesses can form as a C corporation, and if they fail to take additional steps in their formation process, they will be classified as C corporations. However, smaller business usually are formed under S corporation status, a term that is often used interchangeably with the term *close corporation*. A close corporation or closely held corporation usually limits the number of shareholders or owners to no more than thirty. Additionally, the transfer of ownership or shares of stock are restricted and most of the shareholders are actively involved in the management of the business. Shares of a close corporation (S corporation) are therefore not normally traded on a stock exchange.

S Corporations

Most readers of this book will choose to make the *"S" election* when forming their corporation. The desirability of selecting S corporation standing is highly-regarded among business organizers. Some advantages of electing S corporation status are as follows:

- limited liability is preserved to shareholders because of the corporate form;

- avoidance of double taxation is achieved, allowing monies to be withdrawn by owners with payment of tax once, instead of twice at the corporate and individual levels;

- cash basis method of accounting is permitted;

- S corporation status allows a start-up company to pass initial losses through to its shareholders to the extent of its losses;

- corporations are exempt from accumulated earnings tax; and,

- corporation status tends to eliminate unreasonable compensation problems for executive officers.

However, there are some limitations that should be considered *before* electing "S" status. Some of the limitations include:

- ✪ only one class of *stock* is permitted;

- ✪ the number of shareholders is limited as well as the types of entities eligible to become shareholders;

- ✪ the possible forms of *debt financing* are restricted, since certain kinds of debt of an S corporation can be considered equity, thus creating two classes of stock and threatening termination of S corporation status;

- ✪ S corporation status restricts freedom of choice if a non-December 31 tax year is desired; and,

- ✪ an S corporation can easily and inadvertently terminate its favorable tax status.

Tax Advantages

One of the main reasons for making the "S" election is the favorable tax advantages the owners of this type of corporation receive. A non-S corporation generally is taxed on its earnings by both the federal and state governments, while its shareholders are basically taxed on any profits distributed to them, usually in the form of dividends. When a corporation has few shareholders and the earnings are substantially distributed to them, this can be a significant tax disadvantage.

A corporation electing S corporation status is treated for income tax purposes similarly to a *partnership*, but retains the corporate advantage of limited liability relative to its shareholders. The principal tax advantage for S corporation election is to escape double taxation and to gain overall lower taxation.

An S corporation pays no tax on its earnings and files annually an informational return, while the individual shareholders are subject only to the individual tax rates. In essence, the S corporation is viewed as a pass-through entity like a partnership, meaning it passes through income and losses separately to its shareholders. The S corporation generally is not subject to any corporate tax on these items.

Tax Disadvantages

However, there are a few potential problems that you should analyze if an S corporation is planned. Internal Revenue Service auditors look very closely at the salary that the business owners of the S corporation pay, or fail to pay themselves. Often, S corporation income, losses, deductions, credits, and the like pass through the business to the actual business owners and must be reported upon their own individual income tax returns. Corporation distributions are not subject to FICA withholding taxes, however, the S corporation business owner is required to withhold taxes for FICA. Such taxes are considerable and can amount to approximately 7.65 percent on a current $87,000 salary. It is problematic that some S corporation owners may be inappropriately tempted to issue to themselves an unnaturally low salary and thus lessen the amount they owe in Social Security and Medicare payroll taxes.

To steer clear of this problem with the IRS, it is critical to be honest and forthright on all documentation. Take pay that is reasonable and check with other firms or businesses as to the salaries that they utilize in the industry as reasonable. Bear in mind that salaries are more justifiable if they are approved by the corporate Board of Directors.

Professional Corporations

This corporate form has only become available to practicing professionals within the last twenty years. Traditionally, professional practitioners have not been permitted to avail themselves of the use of the corporate form because their professional skills are considered personal; the relationship of clients or patients is confidential; and, professional qualities are required that cannot be attributed to a corporation. Now most states have adopted special acts permitting professionals to incorporate. Pennsylvania has adopted the *Professional Corporation Law* that permits various persons in certain regulated professions to engage in the practice of their professions through the use of a corporate structure.

Professional Corporation Defined

The *Professional Corporation Law* has defined a profession to include the performance of any type of personal service to the public that requires a license, admission to practice, or other legal authorization. These are regulated professions in which a professional relationship is established between the professional and his or her client requiring confidentiality and where a potential liability can arise out of the professional services rendered. In preserving that relationship, the corporate form will not shield the professional against personal liability that may arise from the performance of services.

Restrictions on Professional Corporations

In professional corporations, only a person who holds a license to practice his or her profession may serve as a shareholder, officer or director, and shares may be issued or voluntarily transferred only to a licensed persons. Employees who render professional services must also be licensed. The corporate form of practice does not in any way affect any laws applicable to the relationship between the professional and his or her client or patient, including laws on confidentiality and liability for negligence. Shareholders of professional corporations may not enter into voting trust agreements or any other type of agreement granting any other person other than the shareholder the right to exercise any voting rights of any shares issued by the professional corporation.

A professional corporation may be formed only for the purpose of rendering the particular professional services and may not engage in any business other than the rendering of these professional services. It may, however, invest its funds in real estate, *mortgages*, stocks, *bonds* and any other type of investment and may own real estate or personal property necessary or appropriate for rendering its professional services.

A professional corporation must acquire a **STATEMENT OF ELECTION OF PROFESSIONAL CORPORATION STATUS** from the state board regulating that particular profession. (see form 9, p.144.)

Not-for-Profit Corporations

Not-for-Profit Organizations fall outside the general business set-up in that they possess very specific and decidedly unique requirements that must conform to government regulations and policies. Not-for-Profit corporations are usually formed for charitable purposes. Specific filing requirements establish that the business entity exists as a Non-Profit or Not-for-Profit organization. That is not to say that the owners, officers, and directors go without financial compensation. Those individuals are generally well rewarded in the form of a regular salary paid from the corporate account. The critical and distinguishing aspect between a Not-for-Profit corporation and that of a For-Profit corporation is that the profits (or proceeds) generated by the Not-for-Profit business are not shared by the owners, officers, and/or directors as they can be in a For Profit business entity.

Foreign Corporations

Foreign corporations are business entities established in one state, yet doing business in another state. For the purposes of this book, foreign corporations will not be explored in-depth. The basic legal requirements for a foreign corporation doing business in Pennsylvania are discussed in Chapter 4.

2 | CHOOSING A NAME

Before formally incorporating your business and filing the necessary documentation, some preliminary considerations must be made. One of the most important is selecting a name for the corporation.

Selection of Corporate Name

An obtainable and allowable name for a proposed corporation must be chosen in order to file its *Articles of Incorporation* with the Corporation Bureau of the Department of State. The proposed corporate name may be reserved for 120 days by paying the appropriate fee and filing the appropriate form with the Corporation Bureau. Before taking any action, examine the records of the Corporation Bureau concerning corporate names, and, before filing any documents, seek guidance and advice directly from the Corporation Bureau on the current filing fee, the proper form, and the availability of your proposed name.

The *Business Corporation Law* of 1988 mandates the following be included in the corporate name:

- ✪ the word corporation, company, incorporated, or limited, or an abbreviation of one of these words;

- ✪ the word association, fund, or syndicate; or,

- ✪ words or abbreviations having similar meanings in a language other than English.

Duplicate Names

The *Business Corporation Law* mandates that a corporate name may not be the same as, or confusingly similar to:

- ✪ the name of any other Pennsylvania corporation, whether in existence or whose *Articles of Incorporation* have been filed, but have not become effective;

- ✪ the name of any foreign corporation that is either authorized to do business in Pennsylvania or has filed an application for a certificate of authority that is still pending; or,

- ✪ any name exclusively registered or reserved for the use of another person.

Notwithstanding the foregoing prohibitions, a corporation may use a name that is the same as or confusingly similar to another name by obtaining the written consent of the entity holding the name or if the name becomes available by operation of law.

Written consent for same or confusingly similar name. To use the same name of another corporation, the other entity must:

- ✪ state in writing that it is in the process of changing its name; it is about to cease doing business; or that its business is being wound up; or, that it is about to withdraw from doing business in Pennsylvania;

- ✪ execute the official Corporation Bureau form **CONSENT TO APPROPRIATION OF NAME/CONSENT TO USE OF SIMILAR NAME** (form 1, p.119); and,

✪ file both the written statement and official form with the Department of State.

To use a confusingly similar name of another corporation, the other entity must:

✪ execute the official Corporation Bureau form **CONSENT TO APPROPRIATION OF NAME/CONSENT TO USE OF SIMILAR NAME** (form 1, p.119) and

✪ file it with the Department of State.

NOTE: *The **CONSENT TO APPROPRIATION OF NAME** and the **CONSENT TO USE SIMILAR NAME** have been combined by the Pennsylvania Department of State into one form.*

Operation of law. The Business Corporation Law mandates the use of a name which is the same as or confusingly similar to that of another entity under the following circumstances:

✪ the other entity has filed a certificate with the Department of Revenue stating that it is out of existence;

✪ the other entity has failed to file with the Department of Revenue for three successive years a report or return required by law and the Department of Revenue has certified this failure to the Department of State;

✪ the other entity has abandoned its name by amending its *Articles of Incorporation*, or by a *merger, consolidation*, division, expiration, dissolution or otherwise, and no successor in any such corporate action has adopted the name; or,

NOTE: *The Corporation seeking to use the name is required to provide the Department of State with an official certified record of the fact of the abandonment.*

✪ the other entity has caused the termination of the use of its name owing to its failure to make required decennial filings.

NOTE: *The corporation seeking to use the name must prepare a verified statement, affirming that at least thirty days prior written notice was given to the name's prior holder at its registered office and that the applicant believes that the prior holder is out of existence.*

Prohibited Words

The *Business Corporation Law* lists words that either may not be used in a corporate name or that may be used only if the corporation has satisfied certain conditions. Generally prohibited words include words which are known to be used by other entities such as "Burger King" or "Pepsi." Other words that are prohibited are those that indicate a type of entity classification that is not factual. For example, if your business is established as an S corporation and you place the LLP designation after your corporate name.

Fictitious Name Registration

A corporation conducting business in Pennsylvania under a name other than its corporate name as set forth in its *Articles of Incorporation* is required generally to register that other non-corporate or fictitious name with the Department of State. An application must be made to the Corporation Bureau for the registration of a fictitious name. The application is made on the official Corporation Bureau form **APPLICATION FOR REGISTRATION OF FICTITIOUS NAME.** (see form 2, p.121.)

This application must contain the following information:

- ✪ the fictitious name;

- ✪ a brief statement concerning the character or nature of the business or other activity to be carried on under or through the fictitious name;

- ✪ the address of the principal place of business (a post office box is not acceptable);

- ✪ the name and address, including street and number, if any, of each individual interested in such business or other activity. (Where a participant in a business or activity is a partnership or other organization composed of two or more parties, it is only necessary to name such partnership or other participating organization. Where the application for registration relates to a trust or similar entity, only the trustees or governing body thereof need be named.);

✪ with respect to each entity, other than an individual, interested in such business or other activity:

✪ the name of the entity and a statement of its form of organization;

✪ the name of the jurisdiction under the laws of which it is organized;

✪ the address, including street and number. if any, of its principal office under the laws of its domiciliary jurisdiction; and,

✪ the address, including street and number, if any, of its registered office, if any, in this Commonwealth. (A post office box is not accepted.)

✪ a statement that the applicant is familiar with the provisions of Section 332 (relating to effect of registration) and understands that filing under the *Fictitious Names Act* does not create any exclusive or other right in the fictitious name;

✪ The application may designate one or more parties who shall be authorized to execute amendments to, withdrawals from or cancellation of the registration on behalf of all then existing parties to the registration; and,

✪ the application must be signed by each individual, corporation (one officer), partnership (by a partner), trust (by the trustees) or other entity (one officer) interested in the business or activity; or by any attorney-in-fact.

Name Restrictions
A *fictitious name* may not contain a corporate designator (corporation, incorporated, limited, etc.) unless at least one entity named on the application for registration of the fictitious name is a corporation. A corporate applicant may utilize the term company as part of its fictitious name. There is no requirement that a corporation utilize a corporate designator in its fictitious name.

Duplicate Names
Certain words may not be used as part of a fictitious name unless the corporation has satisfied certain other conditions. Names implying that the entity is an educational institution, bank or trust company, or engaged in engineering or surveying, must be approved for use by the Department of Education, Department of Banking or State Registration Board for Professional Engineers, Land Surveyors and Geologists, respectively. The word *cooperative* can only be used if the entity was formed under the applicable law.

A corporation's fictitious name must not be the same as or confusingly similar to the name of any other domestic corporation or any foreign corporation authorized to do business in Pennsylvania, or the name of any association registered with the Department of State, unless the name is made available for use under the provisions described in the above section. Also, the fictitious name must not be the same as or confusingly similar to the name of any limited partnership organized in Pennsylvania, or any administrative department, board or commission, or other agency of Pennsylvania.

Legal Advertisement

If the application for fictitious name registration includes an individual, then the *Notice of Registration* must be officially published in two newspapers, one of general circulation and the other a legal newspaper, in the county in which the registrant's principal place of business is or will be located.

Advertising requirements. One must advertise the filing or intention to file one time in two newspapers, one of general circulation, the other a legal newspaper, if any, in the county where the registered office is located stating:

✪   the name of the proposed corporation and

✪   a statement that the corporation is to be or has been organized under the provisions of the *Business Corporation Law of 1988*.

Exemption

Certain activities and organizations are exempt from the fictitious name registration. These activities are described broadly as nonprofit or professional activities and activities expressly or impliedly prohibited by law from being conducted under a fictitious name. The organizations are unincorporated associations, electing partnerships, and limited partnerships registered with the Department of State. Despite the exemption, the above-mentioned entities may voluntarily register their fictitious names.

The failure to register a fictitious name does not affect the validity of any act or contract of the corporation using the fictitious name; however, the corporation may not maintain an action in Pennsylvania arising out of any transaction in which the corporation used an unregistered fictitious name unless the corporation first pays a civil penalty of $500 to the Department of State.

3 INITIAL CORPORATE DOCUMENTS

This chapter will focus upon the completion of the *Articles of Incorporation*, and starting your corporation. The *Articles of Incorporation* are the set of documents that are required by the Pennsylvania Department of State to officially incorporate your business entity. *Bylaws*, the governing document of the corporation, are also discussed along with adopting them at your first organizational meeting.

Articles of Incorporation

The **ARTICLES OF INCORPORATION** (form 3, p.125) and the fee requirements associated with filing your **ARTICLES OF INCORPORATION** may be ordered directly from the Pennsylvania Department of State. Legally, the **ARTICLES OF INCORPORATION** are the documents that inform the Department of State as to the nature of the business you are establishing. The forms provide your business address, your new corporate name, your organizers/owners, and various pertinent information as to your set-up designation.

Articles of Incorporation must be filed with the Pennsylvania Department of State and be signed by all incorporators. The following information must be filed:

✪ *name*—the name of the corporation (See Chapter 2 for the requirements for corporate names and procedures for reservation of corporate names.);

✪ *location and address*—of initial registered office. The address must include street and number, if any. (A post office box is not acceptable.);

✪ *statement that the corporation is incorporated* under the provisions of the Business Corporation Law of 1988;

✪ *period of existence*—the period during which the corporation shall continue in existence, if not perpetual;

✪ *authorized shares*—the number of shares that the corporation has authority to issue or that the corporation is organized upon a non-stock basis;

✪ *incorporators*—the names and addresses of the incorporators. One or more persons (or corporations) may act as incorporators by signing and delivering to the Department of State the *Articles of Incorporation* for the corporation. Incorporators need not be directors, officers, shareholders or employees of the corporation.

Articles of Incorporation are not required by law to be prepared by an attorney, however, because of a number of complex matters that need consideration in organizing a corporation including tax considerations, it is advisable for the incorporators to seek legal assistance to assure that all important matters receive timely consideration. Publication of either the intent to file or the filing of the *Articles of Incorporation* must be made in two newspapers of general circulation, with one being a legal journal. (See *Legal Advertisement* and *Docket Statement* later in this chapter.)

Persons desiring to do business in Pennsylvania as a corporation must file the documents with the Secretary of the Commonwealth. Through the Corporation Bureau, the Secretary of the Commonwealth files documents evidencing various kinds of business transactions.

Corporation Bureau   The Corporation Bureau is open from 8:00 a.m. to 5:00 p.m., Monday through Friday. Documents may be submitted for filing by bringing them directly or mailing them to:

Corporation Bureau
P.O. Box 8722
Harrisburg, PA
17105-8722

A fee is charged for filing documents. Payment of fees must be made by check or money order when the documents are presented for filing. No cash is accepted. If you desire a copy of the document you are filing, please enclose an extra copy of the document along with your request and a self-addressed stamped envelope. If you need assistance, the staff of the Corporation Bureau is available to answer questions and provide help. They can answer filing questions. They cannot answer legal questions.

Non-Obligatory Provisions

Examples of provisions that the corporation might find desirable to adopt and include in its *Articles of Incorporation*, or provisions that the corporation may adopt specifically to relax or supersede other provisions, are as follows:

- ✪ *limited purpose*—A corporation may restrict its purpose in its *Articles of Incorporation*;

- ✪ *limited term of existence*—A corporation may restrict its term of existence, overriding the presumption of perpetual existence;

- ✪ *deferred effective date*—A corporation may permit an incorporator to designate an effective date, other than the filing date, of the *Articles of Incorporation*. (A designated effective date will only be valid if it is later than the filing date.);

- ✪ *initial directors*—A corporation may permit the naming of the initial Board of Directors in the corporation's *Articles of Incorporation*. If directors are named, they must have consented in writing to serve as directors and are required to hold the organization meeting;

- ✪ *denial of cumulative voting*—a corporation may deny or modify cumulative voting rights in its *Articles of Incorporation;*

- ✪ *preemptive rights*—If a corporation desires to provide for preemptive rights for its shareholders, it must do so in its *Articles of Incorporation;*

✪ *indemnification*—broad flexibility is permitted in drafting indemnification clauses either for insertion in the corporation's *Articles of Incorporation* or bylaws;

✪ *limited personal director liability*—Section 1713 of the *Business Corporation Law* of 1988 permits a limitation of a director's personal liability for money damages if provided either in the corporation's *Articles of Incorporation* or bylaws;

✪ *partial written consent*—a provision is permitted in a corporation's *Articles of Incorporation* or bylaws permitting shareholder action by partial written consent;

✪ *amending articles*—the corporation's *Articles of Incorporation* can modify the majority vote requirement necessary to amend, alter, repeal, or adopt any of the *Articles of Incorporation*;

✪ *proxy expenses*—Section 1757(c) of the *Business Corporation Law* of 1988 authorizes a corporation to restrict in its *Articles of Incorporation* the payment of reasonable expenses for solicitation of votes, proxies, or consents of shareholders by or on behalf of the board of directors;

✪ *shareholder distribution rights*—a corporation may insert in its *Articles of Incorporation,* specifically enforceable shareholder rights as to the declaration and payment of dividends, the redemption of shares, or the making of any other form of distribution;

✪ *shareholder meetings*—corporations may modify in its *Articles of Incorporation* the statutory requirement of an annual meeting of the shareholders to elect directors. The corporation may modify in its *Articles of Incorporation* the right of shareholders holding 20% or more of the votes to call a special meeting of the shareholders;

✪ *uncertificated shares*—a corporation may provide in its *Articles of Incorporation* for uncertificated shares;

✪ *standard of care for officers*—a corporation may modify in its bylaws or *Articles of Incorporation* the statutory standard of care required of corporate officers;

✪ *share classification*—the corporation's *Articles of Incorporation* may authorize the Board of Directors, generally, to divide authorized and unissued shares and classes and to establish voting rights, designations, preferences, limitations and special rights. (If this provision is adopted, then the board may easily create classes and rights by amending the *Articles of Incorporation* without shareholder approval.);

✪ *shareholder proposals amending articles*—a corporation may change by a provision in its *Articles of Incorporation,* the general rule that its shareholders have a statutory right to propose amendments to the *Articles of Incorporation*; and,

✪ *other clauses*—provisions may be inserted in the *Articles of Incorporation* required by statute to be stated in the articles, bylaws, or in any agreement or instrument. The insertion possibilities for the draftsperson of the *Articles of Incorporation* become endless and the *Articles of Incorporation* could become quite detailed. Consideration should be given, however, to the ease of amending the bylaws versus the *Articles of Incorporation.*

Unalterable Provisions   There are a number of provisions that *cannot* be modified, eliminated, relaxed or made inconsistent by provisions in the *Articles of Incorporation.* Examples include the following:

✪ corporate records and inspection rights;

✪ liability of directors for unlawful dividends and other distributions;

✪ furnishing of financial reports;

✪ rights of dissenters;

✪ shareholder rights to receive notice;

✪ *fiduciary duties* of directors;

✪ mandatory indemnification; and,

✪ appointment of a custodian of a corporation in the event of shareholder deadlock or other causes.

Legal
Advertisement
and
Docket
Statements

The notice of intention to file or the filing of *Articles of Incorporation* must be officially published. *Officially published* entails being published in English in two newspapers of general circulation, one of which is to be the legal newspaper in the county where the corporation's registered office is or will be located. The advertisement must disclose the corporate name and make a statement that the corporation is being, or was, incorporated under the statutory provisions of Pennsylvania.

In addition, a **DOCKETING STATEMENT** (form 4, p.128) must accompany the **ARTICLES OF INCORPORATION** (form 3, p.125). The **DOCKETING STATEMENT** acts as a cover sheet identifying the type of entity being registered along with other general information about the entity. It must be submitted in triplicate, so that the Department of Revenue and Department of Labor and Industry, in addition to the Department of State, will have information regarding the corporation, for contacting you regarding the required tax reports.

Bylaws

The corporation should adopt a set of bylaws to manage and regulate its internal corporate affairs. In general, it is permitted that bylaws allow any provision regarding corporate governance that is not inconsistent with applicable laws or the corporation's *Articles of Incorporation.*

Generally, small business start-up companies formulate their own individualized bylaws. There is no specifically required form or format to create a bylaw for a business entity. The goals and objectives of the business entity are articulated in a line-by-line guide that constitutes the outline for the proper and intended functioning of the business. Often, a mission statement will precede the bylaw section, setting forth the idealized vision for the company. From that point, a section entitled "Bylaws" enumerates the operating rules of the entity and the rights of the company's Board of Directors, Officers, and employees.

Bylaws are not always created (S corporations often choose to ignore the creation of bylaws) and business entities can exist in the absence of formal bylaws. It is recommended that some basic bylaw instruction be provided specifically with regard to the scheduling of annual meetings, financial record keeping structure, and hiring/firing policies.

Registered Agents

A *Registered Agent* (or *Registered Office*) is required to be listed or filed with the Department of State Corporation Bureau. Every business corporation shall have and continuously maintain in this Commonwealth a registered office which may, but need not, be the same as its place of business. Thus, the incorporator must list with the Department of State the address of the business entity and the actual place of business. A post office box is not acceptable. The address is needed to provided contact data for the Department of State, Corporation Bureau.

Organizational Meeting

After the corporate existence begins, an organization meeting of the incorporators must be held for the purposes of, among other things, adopting bylaws and electing directors. If the directors are named in the *Articles of Incorporation*, the director and not the incorporators would hold the organizational meeting. If the organization meeting is to be held by the incorporator, his or her role is largely to accept the *Articles of Incorporation*, adopt the bylaws, elect the Secretary of the corporation, and elect the directors. The incorporator may act in person, by written consent or by proxy.

The Board of Directors of a corporation are permitted to take action without a meeting, if prior to or subsequent to their action, they unanimously consent in writing. These consents must be filed with the Secretary of the corporation. If the directors are to hold the organization meeting, a common practice is to have the members of the Board of Directors execute a unanimous consent in lieu of an organization meeting and consent to a series of resolutions adopting bylaws, electing or appointing officers, authorizing the officers to utilize corporate funds to purchase stock books, minute books, and books of account as well as to pay all fees and expenses associated with the incorporation and organization of the corporation.

Other matters generally included are to approve the form of the capital stock certificate and corporate seal (if one is desired), to file foreign qualification applications, to open bank accounts and to authorize withdrawals, to grant authority to contract and issue capital stock, to approve shareholder agreements, and authorize S corporation status.

4 SPECIFIC TYPES OF CORPORATIONS

This chapter will provide information about various types of corporate entities. Most particularly, this section will focus upon the S corporation, providing explanation of what is required to form an S corporation and further detailing the essence of what it means to become and S corporation. Additionally, this chapter will address the foreign business corporation and the professional corporation in an effort to better familiarize you with some specific set-up aspects of each.

Electing S Corporation Status

S corporations may be formed by filing **ARTICLES OF INCORPORATION** on the same forms prescribed by the Department of State for the incorporation of general business corporations (C corporations). Section 1361 of the Internal Revenue Code (United States Code, Chapter 26 Sec. 1361) sets forth the requirements for election S corporation status. The corporation meeting the eligibility requirement must elect S corporation status within a strict time period and all of its beneficial shareholders must consent to the election.

In addition, other factors should be considered that are specific to the corporation and shareholder considering an S election. There are numerous ongoing requirements to maintain S corporation status. The individual shareholder tax situation should be carefully examined with respect to:

- ✪ contemplated gifts of stock;

- ✪ availability of tax free distributions to shareholders;

- ✪ likelihood of the length of time the corporation would operate at a loss;

- ✪ whether shareholders desire losses;

- ✪ realization of specific income, losses, deductions, or credits attributed to shareholders; and,

- ✪ their specific estate and financial plans.

To elect S status you must file **ELECTION BY A SMALL BUSINESS CORPORATION (IRS FORM 2553)**. (see form 5, p.129.)

Pennsylvania S Corporation Act

Pennsylvania recognizes any corporation that has a valid federal S corporation election in effect and does not derive passive investment income in excess of 25% of its gross receipts. Under the *Pennsylvania S Corporation Act*, shareholders are taxed at the individual rates on all income realized by the corporation and deemed to have been distributed to them. The income is considered exempt from Pennsylvania corporate net income taxation.

There are some minor differences between the Pennsylvania and federal S corporation acts. A tax adviser should be consulted. The S corporation election under federal and state law should be given serious consideration after a careful review and examination of each shareholder's tax situation and how the potential tax advantages impact their future tax, estate, and gift planning.

Termination of S Corporation Status

Termination of an S corporation may be required in certain circumstances. Section 1362 of the United States Code provides that an S corporation election may be terminated by the corporation's ceasing to qualify, receiving excess passive income, or by shareholder revocation. In order to discontinue or to dissolve your S corporation, it is suggested that you notify the Corporation Bureau of the Department of State. **ARTICLES OF DISSOLUTION (DOMESTIC)** (form 16, p.173) should be filed to conclude the existence of the S corporation. This simple process will wrap-up or conclude the life of the corporate entity and will provide notification to the Department of State Corporation Bureau that the business is no longer operating within the Commonwealth of Pennsylvania.

Foreign Business Corporations

A foreign corporation is a corporation formed in another state (other than Pennsylvania) doing business within the Commonwealth of Pennsylvania. No foreign corporation may do business in Pennsylvania without receiving a *Certificate of Authority* from the Secretary of the Commonwealth. To receive a *Certificate of Authority*, a foreign business corporation must file with the Department of State an **APPLICATION FOR CERTIFICATE OF AUTHORITY** (see form 6, p.135), signed by one duly authorized officer of the corporation containing the following information:

✪ *name*—the name of the corporation;

✪ *state or country of incorporation*;

✪ *principal office*—the address of the principal office in the state or country of incorporation. Must include street and number, if any. (A post office box is not acceptable.);

✪ *registered office*—the address of the proposed registered office in the Commonwealth of Pennsylvania must include street and number, if any. (A post office box is not acceptable.); and,

✪ *purpose*—a statement that the purpose of the corporation involves pecuniary profit, incidental or otherwise, to its shareholders.

A **DOCKETING STATEMENT** (form 4, p.128) must also be filed in triplicate so that the departments of Revenue, Labor, and Industry can have your desired mailing address, to contact you regarding the required tax reports.

The *Business Corporation Law* requires that the corporation shall advertise its intention to file or the filing of the application for a *Certificate of Authority*. Proofs of publication of such advertising should not be delivered to the Department of State, but should be filed with the minutes of the corporation.

Amended Certificate of Authority

Subsequent to the issuance of the *Certificate of Authority*, a foreign authorized corporation may wish to change its name as a result of *amendments* to its charter or mergers with other corporations. In order to change its name, the corporation must file with the Secretary of the Commonwealth an **APPLICATION FOR AMENDED CERTIFICATE OF AUTHORITY** (form 7, p.138) signed by one duly authorized officer of the corporation containing the following information:

- ✪ *name*—the name under which the corporation received a *Certificate of Authority* to do business in Pennsylvania;

- ✪ *state or country of incorporation*;

- ✪ *principal office*—address of principal office in state or country of incorporation. (A post office box is not accepted.);

- ✪ *registered office*—the address of the corporation's present registered office in Pennsylvania; and,

- ✪ *the change*—including a statement that the change has been effected or authorized under the law of the domiciliary state.

No corporation shall be issued an *Amended Certificate of Authority* with a name the same as or confusingly similar to the name of any Pennsylvania corporation or any other foreign corporation authorized to do business in Pennsylvania.

Application for Termination of Authority

An authorized foreign corporation may wish to withdraw from doing business in Pennsylvania. The corporation may withdraw by filing with the Department of State an **APPLICATION FOR TERMINATION OF AUTHORITY (FOREIGN CORPORATION)** (form 8, p.141) signed by one duly authorized officer of the corporation, setting forth and containing the following information:

- ✪ *name*—the name of the corporation must be exactly as it appears on the **APPLICATION FOR CERTIFICATE OF AUTHORITY** or the latest amendment;

- ✪ *state or country of incorporation*;

- ✪ *date of Authorization of Authority*;

- ✪ *the date the original Certificate of Authority was issued*;

✪ statement that the corporation surrenders its *Certificate of Authority* to do business in this Commonwealth; and,

✪ address where *service of process* can be sent.

The following clearances must be filed with the application.

✪ A notice of clearance issued by the Pennsylvania Department of Revenue that all Pennsylvania taxes have been paid by the corporation or that the corporation is not subject to such tax, must be attached to the **CORPORATE DISSOLUTION OR LIQUIDATION** (form 17, p.177). Clearance forms may be acquired by contacting:

Pennsylvania Department of Revenue
Bureau of Corporation Taxes
Business Clearance Section
7th Floor, Strawberry Square
Harrisburg, Pennsylvania 17128-0702
717-787-4883

✪ A notice of clearance issued by the Pennsylvania Department of Labor and Industry. Clearance forms may be acquired by contacting:

Office of Employment Security
Department of Labor & Industry Building
Harrisburg, Pennsylvania, 17121
717-783-8418

✪ *Proof of Publication* of such advertising should not be delivered to the Department but should be filed with the minutes of the corporation.

Professional Corporations

Professional corporations may be formed by filing **ARTICLES OF INCORPORATION** (form 3, p.125) on the same forms prescribed by the Department of State for the incorporation of business corporations. The **ARTICLES OF INCORPORATION** must contain a heading stating the name of the corporation and that it is a Professional Corporation. The professional officers license number must be included on the **DOCKETING STATEMENT**. (see form 4, p.128.)

Name   The incorporators of a professional corporation may adopt any corporate name that is not contrary to law, the ethics of their profession, or any applicable rule or regulation of any governmental agency. The requirements as to corporate names set forth in Chapter 2 are not applicable to a professional corporation name if the name is restricted to the full or last name of any individual or individuals currently or formerly associated with the organization or any predecessor with the option to add:

✪   Associates;

✪   and Associates; or,

✪   PC.; but,

✪   PA. is not permitted.

5 | CORPORATE DIRECTORS, OFFICERS, AND COMMITTEES

This chapter will detail information about the leadership of your business entity. It will provide an outline and discussion of the types of oversight and duties of the governing bodies of each specific entity.

Board of Directors

A *Board of Directors* is required for all corporate entities. Even an S corporation must name a Board of Directors albeit a small board of only two persons is required. The minimum required Board of Directors must consist of a President and a Treasurer.

The Board of Directors is the official governing body of the business entity. They offer business decisions, conduct meetings, and direct the overall functioning and goals of the business entity.

Credentials   A director of a business entity must be an individual who is at least 18 years old. Corporate directors are not required to be stock owners in their corporate business.

Choice of Directors   Directors are usually selected by virtue of a shareholder election process. Sometimes, the primary Board of Directors can be set forth in the *Articles of Incorporation* documentation or they can be chosen by the business incorporators. Openings that come up in the Board may be filled by a vote of the majority of the serving directors.

Number   Generally, the number of directors is stated within the corporate *bylaws* or within the *Articles of Incorporation*. The Board of Directors must contain at least one director. If the bylaws and/or the *Articles of Incorporation* fail to establish the quantity of directors, it is customary to set three as the operating amount.

Often, the number of directors is specifically set in the *bylaws* as opposed to the *Articles of Incorporation* since amendment of the bylaws may be made more simply and without delay. The *bylaws* can be written to provide that the exact number of directors be established on a yearly basis by the Board. Directors may indicate that the Board may consist of not less than a definite minimum number of directors, or not more than another specific maximum number of directors. Such indication is set forth in the bylaws. Such documentation should be written at least sixty days before the annual meeting of the shareholders.

Term   Corporate directors act for the specific *term* set forth within the *bylaws*. This term is usually one year or until the successor has been selected and qualified.

Majority and Quorum   Generally, a majority of the Board of Directors in office is required to comprise a *quorum*. Rulings of the majority of the quorum present and voting shall constitute an act of the board. Unless constrained by writing within the *bylaws*, any conduct permitted to be undertaken at a meeting of the Board of Directors may be undertaken without a Board meeting, if, all directors file with the Corporate Secretary a consent in writing.

Authority   Generally, the corporate Board of Directors assigns authority to its officers and agents unless provided specifically by statute or in a bylaw adopted by the shareholders. Corporate controls set forth by statute are implemented by a Board of Directors.

Duties   Fiduciary responsibility to the corporation and its shareholders is required. The Board of Directors must conduct themselves in good faith and in a way reasonably thought to be in the paramount business interest of the corporation. Directors must conduct themselves with evident concern, proficiency, and due diligence, in a manner that a reasonable person would deem appropriate if put in the situation.

Good faith acts of the Board of Directors include acting upon judgments, news, information, or accounts assemble and/or put forth by the following:

- ✪ attorneys;

- ✪ CPAs/public accountants;

- ✪ experts;

- ✪ corporate officers;

- ✪ business employees; and,

- ✪ any Board established committee.

Business Judgment Rule   Generally, an act of the Board of Directors is assumed to be made in the best interest of the corporation. Such act must be undertaken absent a breach of corporate fiduciary duty, self-dealing, or lack of good faith.

Directors' Personal Liability   Personal liability to a corporation for monetary damages may be claimed against a Board of Director for any action taken in his or her role as director. A bylaw may provide that a corporate director will not be personally liable to the corporation for monetary damages. Nevertheless, no clemency from personal liability for directors to the corporation can occur in the following cases.

- ✪ The director has failed to perform the duties of his or her corporate office in a manner that constitutes *breach* of corporate fiduciary duty, self-dealing, or lack of good faith.

- ✪ The director has violated criminal federal, state, or local statutes or federal, state or local tax laws.

Corporations may offer protection for directors either through the *bylaws*, an agreement, or an independent vote of the shareholders or directors. No protection may be made in cases where the director's conduct is determined by a court to have constituted willful misconduct or recklessness.

Board of Directors' Committees

The Board of Directors or the *bylaws* of a corporation may set up certain committees comprised of one or more corporate directors. Committees may possess the authority of the full Board of Directors, but committees shall not have any authority to carry out the following:

- ✪ submissions to shareholders of any action requiring approval of shareholders;

- ✪ establishment or filling of openings on the Board of Directors;

- ✪ adoption, modification, or rescinding of the *bylaws*; or,

- ✪ amendment or repeal of any resolution of the Board which by its terms is amendable or rescindable only by the board itself.

Committees are utilized to effect special objectives or missions of the business entity. For example, a committee may be established to evaluate employee work habits to seek more corporate efficiency.

Often, *committees* (or *collaborating groups*) are needed to aid the proper and effective functioning of the business entity. Such committees may be established by a vote of the Board of Directors or may be established more decisively in the corporate bylaws. Committees are typically formed to address specific or developing goals of the business entity. A common example of a committee used in the regular course of a business entity is that of a hiring committee. A committee of such nature will review and assess the qualifications of the potential employees. *Standing committees* may be described and enumerated in the *bylaws* to address routinely needed committee functions.

Officers

Corporations must possess a President, a Secretary, and a Treasurer. The President and Secretary must be actual individuals, but the Treasurer may be a corporation. Any number of offices may be held by the same person, however, it is recommended that the President not be the same person as the Treasurer, in order to avoid the appearance of impropriety. A corporation does not want any suggestion of the possibility of monetary co-mingling or access to corporate funds, making it good policy that the President and Treasurer positions must be occupied by different individuals.

Roles

The President directs the overall goals, objectives, and mission of the business entity. The Vice President assists in this objective. There may be multiple Vice President positions to advance the goals of the President. The Secretary of the business entity keeps all corporate or business records, maintains the minutes of meetings and documents correspondences made on the part of the business entity. The Treasurer keeps records of all finances associated with the business and tracks profits and losses.

Term, Removal, and Salary

The usual term of office is for a period of one year, unless specifically provided in the *bylaws*. An officer of a corporation may be removed with or without cause.

Salaries vary and can be set by the Board of Directors (by vote) or established in the *bylaws* of the business entity,

Duty of Care

An officer shall perform his her corporate duties in good faith, in a method reasonably believed to be in the best interest of the corporation, and with such care, including reasonable inquiry, skill and diligence, as a person of ordinary prudence would use under similar circumstances.

6 | ISSUING STOCK

This chapter will explore what is involved in the *stock issuing process*. You will discover the meanings of certain terms applicable to stock and learn the way in which stock shares are used, exchanged and classified. Stockholders (shareholders) possess certain rights that will also be explored in this chapter.

Capital Stock

Stock shares are the units into which the rights of the shareholders to participate in the control of a corporation, in its profits, or in the distribution of its assets are divided. The division of ownership can be made in several different ways with different classes of stock being issued to reflect the different ownerships rights an individual may have. The two most typical classes are *common* shares and *preferred* shares.

Common stock owners generally possess the voting rights of the corporate shareholders, thus possessing the ability to elect the directors of the corporation. Preferred stock owners generally do not possess voting rights, but instead are given a preference over common stock holders for dividend payments, and in liquidation rights. Dividing the shares of stock into classes if generally done for financial reasons and is beyond the conduct of most new small businesses.

Pennsylvania corporations usually have at least one class of shares, the *common shares*, which quite often represents the only authorized shares. Pennsylvania corporations may have *preferred* or *preference shares*. If preferred shares are to be issued, seek the advice of an attorney experienced in these matters for further guidance.

Authorization of Shares

Every business corporation has the power to create and issue the number of shares stated in its *Articles of Incorporation*. A corporation may only issue shares that are authorized by its *Articles of Incorporation* or in an amendment to its *Articles of Incorporation*. Authorized shares are the shares of all classes that the corporation is authorized to issue. The Board of Directors may be granted sole authority to amend the articles in this regard and designate the class and terms of each issue of stock, unless a bylaw adopted by the shareholders provides otherwise.

While the dividing of corporate stock into multiple classes is beyond the scope of this book, you should be aware that the original *Articles of Incorporation*, or an amendment thereof, may be drafted to authorize the corporation's Board of Directors to make the divisions of classes and to determine their respective rights and preferences.

Section 1522 of the Pennsylvania Business Statutes addresses the issuance of shares in classes and Board of Director action. The general rule is that the division of shares into classes or into series within any class, the determination of the designation and the number of shares of any class or series, and the determination of the voting rights, preferences, limitations and special rights, if any, may be accomplished by the original articles or by any amendment to those *Articles of Incorporation*.

Unless otherwise restricted in the *Articles of Incorporation*, authority is granted to the Board of Directors to determine the number of shares issued. This power includes the power to increase the previously determined number of shares to a number not greater than the aggregate number of shares that the corporation is authorized to issue by the *Articles of Incorporation*. Unless otherwise restricted in the *Articles of Incorporation*, if no shares are outstanding, the Board of Directors may amend the designations and the voting rights, preferences, limitations and special rights, if any, of the shares.

Before any shares issue, the corporation shall file in the Department of State a statement with respect to shares executed by the corporation, setting forth:

- ✪ the name of the corporation;

- ✪ the resolution of the Board adopting its action with respect to the shares;

- ✪ the aggregate number of shares of the class or series;

- ✪ any other provision of the resolution;

- ✪ the date of the adoption of the resolution; and,

- ✪ its effective date if different from the adoption date.

Consideration   Except as otherwise restricted in the *bylaws*, shares of a business corporation may be issued at a price determined by the Board of Directors, or the board may set a minimum price or establish a formula or method by which the price may be determined.

The corporation's Board of Directors determines the price of issued shares, except as restricted by the corporation's bylaws. In lieu of a specific bylaw provision, the Board is free to establish a minimum price per share, or a formula or method by which the price can be determined, as well as dictate the payment terms.

Unless restricted in the *bylaws*, *consideration* for shares can take the form of money, obligations (including a shareholder's obligation), services performed (whether or not the services were contracted for), contracts for future services, or other tangible or intangible property.

In the absence of a bylaw provision restricting such authorization, the Board of Directors, in the context of effectuating stock dividends or stock splits, may issue, without consideration, the corporation's shares on a *pro rata basis* to all shareholders or to shareholders of one or more classes or series, provided the relative rights of the stockholders of the class or series are not adversely affected. When a stock dividend or stock split occurs, the percentage of ownership of each shareholder stays the same, even though the number of shares owned changes.

Preemptive Rights Except as set forth in its *Articles of Incorporation*, a corporation may issue shares, option rights, or securities having conversion or option rights, or obligations, without first offering them to its shareholders. This is called *preemptive rights* of the corporation.

Miscellaneous Rights There are additional rights and powers the Board of Directors possess in regards to shares of stock. These additional rights include granting stock options, issuing fractional shares, issuing un-certificated shares, and restricting the transfer of shares.

Stock Certificates *Stock certificates* are official documents created and issued by a corporate entity that indicate a particular investor or stockholder (shareholder) owns a share (or a piece) of the business entity. The corporate Board of Directors determines whether or not stock certificates will be offered. Most small S corporations elect not to issue stock, and thus, no certificates are required or generated.

Pennsylvania Securities Issues

It is unlawful for any person to offer or sell any *security* in Pennsylvania unless the security is registered or the security or transaction is exempt from registration. All securities offered or sold by a newly formed Pennsylvania business corporation then, must either be registered or subject to an exemption from registration. Exemptions are based either on the nature or type of the security or the nature or type of the transaction in which the security is offered and/or sold.

Exempt Transactions Numerous types of transactions are exempt from the registration requirements. The Pennsylvania Securities Commission has issued regulations increasing the list of exempt transactions. The issuance of shares by a newly organized Pennsylvania non-registered business corporation will normally qualify as some exempt transaction, not subject to the registration requirements. Careful research into the registration requirements and the exemptions from registration must be conducted to determine which exemption, if any, is available under the facts and circumstances.

Securities Act The *Securities Act* is a federal law that generally prohibits the offering or sale of any security by the use of the mails or other means or instruments of interstate commerce, unless the security or transaction is exempt from registration or the security is registered in compliance with the *Securities Act.*

The federal *Securities Act* as amended (15 U.S.C. Secs. 77a through 77aa) also requires that shares be registered. However, the following exemptions from registration under the *Securities Act* may be available to a newly formed Pennsylvania non-registered business corporation.

✪ Section 3(a)(11)—*intrastate offerings.* Section 3(a)(11) of the *Securities Act* exempts from registration securities offered and sold only to persons resident in a single state, where the issuer is incorporated by and doing business within that state.

✪ Section 4(2)—*public offering.* Section 4(2) of the *Securities Act* exempts from registration requirements transactions by an issuer not involving any public offering.

✪ Regulation D—*safe harbors.* The Securities and Exchange Commission (SEC) published Regulation D pursuant to Section 3(b) of the *Securities Act,* which consists of six rules (Rules 501-506) that are a series of safe harbor provisions available only to issuers. Reliance upon these Rules is considered more certain by securities practitioners than reliance on Section 4(2) of the *Securities Act.* Each rule deals, generally, with the dollar amount of the offering, number of purchasers, the information to be disclosed and concurrent compliance with state securities requirements.

✪ Regulation A—*$5,000,000 within a twelve-month period.* Pursuant to Section 3 (b)of the *Securities Act,* the SEC issued Regulation A consisting of Rules 25 1-263. In general, Regulation A exempts securities offerings up to $5,000,000 within a twelve-month period after deducting the dollar amount of securities sold twelve months before the start of, and during, the offering period.

Distributions

Corporate *distribution* is the direct or indirect transfer of assets or the indebtedness of the corporation respecting its shareholders by dividend or by purchase, redemption, or other attainment of shares. *Cash dividends, property dividends,* repurchases of corporation's own shares of stock are considered distributions. To be clear, stock dividends and stock splits (shares that have split in value) are not measured as distributions since they fail to remove corporate assets from the corporation's holdings.

The corporate Board of Directors may authorize distributions unless otherwise restricted in the corporate *bylaws*. Corporate distributions are forbidden unless:

✪   the corporation will remain solvent after the distribution and

✪   the total liabilities of the corporation exceed assets.

These two factors are known as the *equity insolvency analysis* and the *balance sheet analysis*.

Equity Insolvency Analysis
The corporation is prohibited from issuance of distributions if production of the distribution results in the corporation being incapable of paying its obligations, debts, and liabilities in the usual course of business. This means that the shareholders get paid last. All other obligations must be met before dividends can be issued.

Balance Sheet Analysis
The corporation is prohibited from issuance of distributions if such distribution results in the total assets of the corporation becoming less than the total liabilities, including the funds required, if needed, to dissolve the corporation.

Valuation
Corporate Directors are permitted to make use of any reasonable method of *valuation* or any of the following corporate valuation systems:

✪   value the assets and liabilities of the corporation as set forth in the records of the corporation;

✪   value the unrealized *appreciation* and *depreciation* of the corporate assets and liabilities; or,

✪ value the current assets and liabilities of the corporation either separately, in segments, or as an entity of an operating business.

Under some of the valuation techniques, you may not be able to make a distribution, while under another, you can. If any allow it, a distribution can be made. The idea, again, is that the shareholders get paid after all other obligations of the corporation are covered (not necessarily paid, but funds available.)

Distribution Date The corporate Board of Directors may state any given date as the date for measuring the distribution result. However, the distribution must occur within 125 days of the given date. If no date is specifically set by the corporate board, the distribution is to be calculated as of the *distribution date*.

Illegal Distributions Corporate Directors who authorize an illegal distribution are responsible and wholly liable to the corporation. If multiple Directors are involved, they will be deemed to be *jointly and severally liable* for the amount of the distribution in excess of the distribution amount that could have been issued absent breach of the corporate rules. Directors are held harmless in situations wherein they have authorized unlawful distribution if reasonable reliance involved good faith upon information supplied by corporate officers, employees, legal counsel, certified public accountants, or the Board of Directors.

Corporation's Right to Re-acquire Its Own Shares

A corporation may acquire its own shares. A corporation may generally repurchase or redeem its own shares in a manner not inconsistent with its *bylaws* or *Articles of Incorporation.*

The *repurchased shares* are considered issued, but not outstanding, unless the corporation's *Articles of Incorporation* state the acquired shares may not be reissued. In the latter case, the result is that the authorized shares of the class representing the acquired shares must be reduced by the number of reacquired shares. To acquire its issued and outstanding shares, a corporation could issue debt either under redemption or purchase.

7 SHAREHOLDERS

The discussion of shareholders is further developed in this chapter. It will provide a more comprehensive analysis of the meetings, notices, and records required in the shareholder process.

A corporation is owned by the shareholders. If you incorporate your business, it is possible that you may be the only shareholder in the corporation. You may also be a Director, the President, and even the janitor. Wearing these many different hats can be confusing. However, you must act and record your actions in the different roles appropriately. Failing to do a required action can result in the loss of corporate status and possibly subject you to personal liability. One of the actions that must be taken is an annual shareholder meeting.

Shareholder Meetings

Regular shareholder meetings are established in the *bylaws* and they set the number of meetings to be held each year and the time at which those meetings will occur. At least one shareholder meeting must be held in each calendar year.

Annual Meetings

Except as otherwise provided in the *Articles of Incorporation*, at least one meeting of the shareholders is to be held in each calendar year for the election of directors. Shareholders may participate in meetings by conference telephone or similar communications equipment provided all persons participating in the meeting can hear one another. Every corporation shall keep minutes of all meetings of shareholders. In the absence of a bylaw provision to the contrary, all shareholder meetings shall be held in Pennsylvania at the corporation's registered office. The failure to hold an annual meeting will not warrant a dissolution or affect otherwise valid acts of the corporation. When an annual meeting is not called and held within six months after the designated time, any shareholder may call the meeting.

Special Shareholder Meetings

At any meeting electing directors, the *adjournment* may be only on a day-to-day basis or for longer periods not exceeding fifteen days each, as the shareholders present and entitled to vote shall direct.

Additional shareholder meetings may be convened at any time in the following manner:

✪ as called by the corporate Board of Directors;

✪ as called by the shareholders entitled to cast at least 20% of the votes that all shareholders are entitled to transmit at the certain special meeting; or,

✪ by such corporate officers as provided in the corporate bylaws.

Notice of Meetings

For the meetings to be valid, notice of every meeting must be in writing and shall be issued at the command of the corporate Secretary to each shareholder permitted to cast a vote at the meeting. Written notice must be issued ten days before the stated date set for a meeting that will consider a elemental change or five days before the stated date set for the meeting.

Notice of regular meetings must indicate the time, place, and date of the meeting. Notice of any special meeting shall specify the place, day, and hour of the meeting, and the general nature of the business to be transacted at the meeting.

Notice may be delivered in person, sent via US mail, or delivered by telegram, delivery courier service, or via facsimile (fax).

Special Notice Necessities   Supplementary information shall be enclosed within the shareholder meeting notice for any and all special meetings when the following are to be addressed:

✪   changes to the corporate bylaws;

✪   articles to be amended;

✪   issues addressing rights of corporate dissenters;

✪   corporate merger;

✪   exchange of shares, asset transfers, or dissection of the corporate entity;

✪   corporate dissolution; or,

✪   particular resolutions.

Waiver of Notice Requirements   The notice requirement can be waived. A signed *Waiver of Notice* executed by the individuals entitled to be served with notice is valid and any such waiver may be executed prior to, or subsequent to, the time of the meeting. Having attended the meeting suggests and establishes waiver of notice. This can be a important exception to the family-run corporations or other corporations with few shareholders. It allows for faster decision making through the meeting process without having to strictly follow the notice requirements.

Date of Record

The date of record sets and determines the time to establish those shareholders entitled to notice of and to cast their vote at the shareholder meeting. The record date shall not be set in excess of ninety days before the date of the shareholder meeting except in adjournments. The record date sets a cut-off to determine who is entitled to make decision at the shareholder meeting. In a small corporation, this may not be of great concern, but in larger corporations with millions of issued shares, it is necessary to pick a specific date to determine who are the actual shareholders for meeting purposes.

Quorum

Shareholder meetings shall not be convened to transact corporate business without a *quorum*. A quorum at a shareholder meeting is established by the shareholders present who are entitled to cast at least a majority of the votes. If a quorum is established, the shareholders present at the meeting can transact business until adjournment, despite the fact that the departure of certain shareholders results in less than a quorum. Thus, once a quorum was established, the withdrawing shareholders *cannot* prevent the remaining shareholders from conducting corporate business.

Voting Rights

Unless otherwise provided in the *Articles of Incorporation*, each shareholder is afforded the right to one vote for every share in the shareholder's name on the corporation's books. Cumulative voting is permitted and consists of multiplying the number of votes a shareholder is entitled to vote by the number of Directors being elected and entitling the holder to cast all his or her votes for one director candidate or distribute the votes among the several candidates.

Proxies

Shareholders who are entitled to vote at a shareholders meeting may give permission to another individual to cast his or her vote by *proxy*. A proxy must be in writing, signed by the shareholder (or by his or her attorney in fact/agent), and properly filed with the corporate Secretary. A proxy may be revoked. Revocation may be done despite any provision to the contrary. The revocation of proxy, however, is not valid until notice in writing has been issued to the corporate Secretary. Three years from the date of its execution, a proxy automatically becomes null and void unless a specifically lengthier period of time is expressly stated in the proxy.

Consent

Unless restricted by the corporation's *bylaws,* any action required or allowed to be taken at a meeting of shareholders may be taken without a meeting if, prior or subsequent to the action, the consent of all shareholders entitled to vote at the meeting is filed with the Secretary of the corporation. If the *bylaws* authorize it, an action required or permitted to be taken at a meeting of the shareholders may be taken without a meeting upon the written consent of the shareholders. These shareholders would have been entitled to cast the minimum votes necessary to authorize the action at a meeting at which all shareholders were present and voting, provided such consents were filed with the Secretary of the corporation. For such partial written consent to be effective, ten days prior written notice of the action taken thereby must be given to all shareholders who have not consented.

Inspection Rights

Corporate shareholders possess the right to inspect and scrutinize the share register, books, account records, and minutes of proceedings. Shareholder may perform the examination in person, by agent, or by retained counsel.

A corporate shareholder's request to inspect the share register, books, account records, and minutes of proceedings must be made in writing, stating the purpose of the inspection. A proper purpose, defined as a purpose reasonably related to the interest of the person as a shareholder, must be established by the shareholder wishing to inspect.

Shareholders may apply to the court to obtain an order to *Compel the Inspection* in situations where the corporation declines permission for examination of share register, books, account records, and minutes of proceedings.

Shareholders' Receipt of Financial Records and Information

Shareholders must receive (from the corporation) annual financial statements that are comprised of a year end balance sheet and an income and expense statement for the year. The balance sheets and income and expense statements must be sent to the shareholders 120 days after the close of each fiscal year.

Financial Information
The corporation must prepare *financial statements* for the fiscal year. Such financial statements examined by a certified public accountant should be attended by the prepared report of the CPA. The person responsible for preparing the corporate financial statements is sometimes not a professional in the accounting field. Private persons or corporate members preparing such financial statements must supply a report supplementary to the financial statements that sets forth information as to whether or not the accompanying financial statements were arranged with commonly customary principles of accounting.

8 | REPORTS, RECORDS, BOOKKEEPING, AND FILING REGISTRATIONS

Reports, records, books, and filing issues will be analyzed in this chapter. The complexities of record keeping and filing is vast in the business entity world.

Records and Reports

Minutes are the written records of meetings held by the corporate entity. Minutes are generally overseen and administered by the corporate Secretary. They typically comprise a fully set forth statement of the events, discussion, votes, and objectives of all meetings held by the board of directors or held in otherwise established meetings critical to the operating of the business.

Corporations must retain:

✪   inclusive and truthful records of bookkeeping and accounting;

✪   details of events and meetings of the incorporators, share-holders, and board members; and,

✪   share list that sets forth general personal information of each of the shareholders, as well as the number and class of shares each holds.

Tax Records   Records and filings pertaining to taxes must be kept sufficient to show and to establish income, deductions, and other tax items. Employers must retain precise account of employment taxes or reports sufficient to show and to support exemptions if applicable. Tax records must be retained in an accessible and secure place and must be on hand for inspection. (Treasury Regulations. Sec. 31.6001-1 (e)(1); 61 Pa. Code Sec. 117.15.)

Share Register   A share register must be retained and must be kept at the business office, used as the principal place of business, or the office of the registered agent. In an action to enforce a request for inspection, courts my compel any reports, books, papers, and/or business records for review.

Format   Reports, records, books, and papers kept by a corporation may be retained in any format that can be converted into reasonably legible written form within a reasonable time that accurately portrays the record. Tax records must be retained in a format that allows the IRS to determine whether there is responsibility for tax liability and must show the quantity of such tax responsibility. (Treasury Regulations. Sec. 31.6001-1(a).)

Retaining information and records in computer format requires caution. Security questions could arise as well as the possibility of disaster and destruction. Backup copies and emergency procedures need to be put into place. The up-keep and maintenance of computer systems must also be maintained.

Email   The growing technological burst of activity has led to widespread use of email. Corporate issues or records that may bear certain confidential property and intellectual property (copyright or patent information, trade secrets) might not serve as an appropriate subject for email.

Sending, cataloging, and preserving email raises specific care issues related to confidentiality responsibilities. Further, a propensity exists for emailers to make use of relaxed, chatty, unconstricted tone. Such situations create an unprofessional appearance or may generate certain indistinctness that appear questionable. Small corporations should consider discussing use of email with their associates or employees and perhaps require a condition that an email sender or recipient preserve and maintain hard document photocopies.

Litigation Papers   It is understood that all business entities should maintain clear, accurate, and honest business records, papers, and business related documents. Steer clear of the appearance of impropriety that may suggest the business information may have been ruined or purged in anticipation of litigation or investigation. A periodic removal of documents can and should take place on a regular course of business schedule.

NOTE: *Do not destroy documents that are or can potentially become necessary in a litigation matter.*

Attorney-client confidentiality is usually considered commencing at an initial communication with a clients. Recent case law has held that attorneys may wish to discuss with the business client related concerns that effectuate an unintentional waiver of the privacy or privilege in consultations about operational issues. Historically, courts have held that records and paperwork prepared by attorneys or in anticipation of litigation may be removed from litigation discovery.

The complexities of record keeping and filing is extensive in the business entity realm. The more information that is kept and maintained relative to your clear business objectives, the more beneficial the result. Documenting business objectives, financial outlays and income, and overall transaction, will serve your business well in the long term.

9 TAX REQUIREMENTS

Although this book is not designed to address tax consequences of the business entity structure, there are a few tax issues to consider in your business start-up. It is strongly suggested that you consult with an accountant or tax advisor to protect your tax interests associated with forming and operating your business entity. General tax issues are outlined in this chapter in order to provide insight into some tax consequences and concerns

Taxpayer Identification Numbers

Business owners who must withhold taxes, must submit an application for an *employer identification number (EIN)* as required by the Internal Revenue Code (IRC) Sec. 6109. This is done by filing an **APPLICATION FOR EMPLOYER IDENTIFICATION NUMBER (IRS FORM SS-4).** (see form10, p.147.)

Federal Income Tax Filings

Corporations file annual federal income tax returns on Form 1120 or 1120-A. S corporations are required to remit taxes only to cover benefits of timing of payments between the entity and the owners when a special fiscal year is used that is not justifiable, and, in the case of S corporations, on certain passive income. Most S corporations taxable issues are passed through the business entity to the partners, members, and/or shareholders who include and reflect the taxed items upon their own personal income tax returns.

Quarterly Estimated Taxes

C corporations and individuals are subject to a penalty if estimated income taxes are not paid. (IRC Secs. 6654, 6655.) If subject to income tax as an entity, S corporations must remit estimated quarterly tax payments.

FICA

FICA or the lesser known *Federal Insurance Contributions Act* is set forth under IRC Sec. 3101. Employers and employees each pay 7.65% into the social security fund. Of that amount, 6.2% is established and set aside for old age, survivor, and disability insurance; 1.45% is reserved for hospital insurance. The tax is assessed up to a maximum amount of annual wages and the business employer must withhold an employees' segment. The employer is liable for it if not paid.

Federal Unemployment Tax Act

The *Federal Unemployment Tax Act (FUTA)* as set forth by IRC Sec. 3301 provides that *unemployment insurance* be regulated as a joint federal and state program. Federal tax is assessed upon employers who pay employee wages of $1500 or more in any calendar quarter or employ one or more individuals for some portion of a day in each of twenty or more calendar weeks. Employers receive credit for up to 90% of their federal tax liability for payments of state tax.

Withholding

The payroll period designates the amount of employee wages employers are required to withhold for income taxes. Exemptions and allowances can be claimed by the employee on Form W-4. Withholding amounts can be determined by percentage and taxable bracket. FICA and income taxes withheld should be reported quarterly. The total amount of taxes withheld related directly to deposit requirements to be deposited monthly on or before the 15th day of the following month. Employers must supply W-2 Forms. The employer submits a summary W-3 Form, *Transmittal of Income and Tax Statements* with copies of W-2 Forms on the last day of February to the Social Security Administration. FUTA is reported annually.

State Tax Requirements

In addition to the federal taxation issues a corporation faces, the Commonwealth of Pennsylvania also imposes certain tax obligations on corporations and its owners. These various tax implications are associated with forming a business entity. It is advisable to seek the aid of a qualified tax professional in all matters related to creating your own business entity as this book is a general guide and it is not designed to supply tax advice.

Corporate Income Tax

Corporate net income tax is a tax on the income of domestic corporations and on foreign corporations that do business, carry on activities, have capital or property employed or used in, or own property in the state. The tax is based on federal taxable income with some modifications.

Personal Income Tax

Personal income tax holds that residents and nonresidents who have income from sources within the state, including an individual's distributive share of S corporation income, are subject to personal income tax.

S corporations are not taxed as entities. Instead share-holders are taxed on their share of income and gain. S corporations file an information return due thirty days after its federal tax return.

Withholding

Withholding establishes that an employer that maintains an office or transacts business in the state must withhold personal income tax for each payroll period from compensation payments to a resident individual or to a nonresident individual who performs services on behalf of the employer in the state. Withholding returns are made quarterly during the year and deposits of withheld taxes are made quarterly, monthly, or semimonthly, depending on the total amount expected to be withheld. The employer is liable for tax not withheld or deposited.

Unemployment Taxes

Unemployment compensation law holds that business employers are liable for tax at rates based on their unemployment claims experience up to a certain amount of wages paid to each employee. Employers withhold the employees' portion of the tax. Reports are due and tax is paid quarterly.

10 | CHANGES TO THE CORPORATION

Changes to the corporation include amending the *Articles of Incorporation*, mergers and consolidations, share exchanges, and/or sale of corporation assets.

Adjustments and changes to the corporate structure are often required after the business has been established. Once a business entity has functioned for a time, adjustments may be needed to make the business run more smoothly. Such changes to the corporate structure or business entity can be effectuated by filing an **ARTICLES OF AMENDMENT (DOMESTIC CORPORATION).** (see form 11, p.155.) It is likely that you will not need to address this aspect of the corporation process until your business has operated for a substantial period of time.

Articles of Amendment

The corporation may choose to make amendment to its **ARTICLES OF INCORPORATION** in order to:

- ✪   adopt a new name;

- ✪   change its term of existence;

✪   alter its business objectives;

✪   completely reword the articles; or,

✪   affect the rights of the shareholders.

Proposal   An *Amendment to the Articles of Incorporation* may be proposed in one of two ways. It may be put forth by the acceptance of a Board of Directors' resolution or by the petition of shareholders.

Notice   A notice of the meeting at which the amendment will be discussed and acted upon must be written such that shareholders are aware that they may act on a proposed amendment. (See Chapter 7 for notice requirements for meetings.)

Adoption   *Amendment to the Articles of Incorporation* is approved by a vote of the majority of the shareholders or by a majority vote in each share class unless the *Articles of Incorporation* require a larger quantity vote. **ARTICLES OF AMENDMENT (DOMESTIC CORPORATION)** (form 11, p.155) needs to be filed with the Department of State. In addition to the filing fee, two copies of a completed **DOCKETING STATEMENT (CHANGES)** (form 12, p.158) and any necessary copies of the **CONSENT TO APPROPRIATION OF NAME/CONSENT TO USE OF SIMILAR NAME** (form 1, p.119) shall accompany **ARTICLES OF AMENDMENT (DOMESTIC CORPORATION)** effecting a change of name and the change in name shall contain a statement of the complete new name.

Dissenters   The shareholder has no right to halt any proposed plan or amendment to the *Articles of Incorporation* unless there is a showing of fraud.

Mergers and Consolidations

Merger entails a situation wherein one corporation is absorbed by another and then ceases to exist. *Consolidation* entails a situation wherein all the combining corporations are viewed as dissolved and all lose their individual identity into a new corporate entity thereby assuming all properties, rights, privileges, and liabilities of the ingredient corporations.

A plan of merger or consolidation must be prepared when corporations merge or consolidate. Written notice of a meeting of shareholders must be given to each shareholder of record (see Chapter 7) of each corporation that is a party to the merger or consolidation in all cases wherein there is a desire to move forward on a proposed merger or consolidation plan. A merger or consolidation plan is implemented upon receiving a positive vote of the shareholder majority.

ARTICLES/CERTIFICATE OF MERGER (form 13, p.160) will need to be filed with the Department of State along with two copies of a completed **DOCKETING STATEMENT (CHANGES)** (form 12, p.158), one copy of a completed **DOCKETING STATEMENT** (form 4, p.128) with respect to the new corporation resulting from a consolidation, and any necessary copies of the **CONSENT TO APPROPRIATION OF NAME/CONSENT TO USE OF SIMILAR NAME** (form 1, p.119).

Dissenters   Any shareholder of a corporation that is party to a merger or consolidation may raise objection to the proposed merger or consolidation and such shareholder is entitled to the rights of dissenting shareholders provided by statute.

Exchange of Shares

All of the outstanding shares of one or more classes or series of a domestic corporation may be acquired by any person through an exchange of all of the shares pursuant to a plan of exchange. An *exchange plan* must be arranged and drafted and such plan must take in matters required by statute. An exchange plan may be set forth, accepted, altered subsequent to acceptance, and terminated by the substitute corporation in the basically similar method as the merger plan. A summary of the plan and a copy of the statute relating to rights of potential dissenters must be enclosed with meeting notice to the shareholders.

Upon the exchange plan becoming effective, shares to be converted either no longer exist, or are exchanged. The former holders of the shares are thereafter entitled to only the shares, securities, cash, or property into which they have been converted or exchanged. The *Articles of Incorporation* of the exchanging corporation are then altered as set forth in the plan of exchange.

Articles of Exchange   Upon adoption of a plan of exchange, **ARTICLES OF EXCHANGE (DOMESTIC BUSINESS CORPORATION)** (form 14, p.165) must be executed by the exchanging corporation. Any necessary copies of the **CONSENT TO APPROPRIATION OF NAME/CONSENT TO USE OF SIMILAR NAME** (form 1, p.119) shall accompany the **ARTICLES OF EXCHANGE** effecting a change of name. The change in name shall contain a statement of the complete new name.

Corporate Asset Transfer

Disbursement of all, or significantly all of the property and assets of a corporate entity, when made in the regular course of business, or for the purpose of relocating the business, may be authorized by the Board of Directors. Consent of the shareholders is not required for such a transaction, unless otherwise provided in the *bylaws*. However, if such transfer is not made in the regular course of business, the transfer may be made only pursuant to a plan of asset transfer.

Policies and regulations regarding plans of asset transfer and rights of the dissenters in asset transfers do not apply to the disposition of all of the assets of a corporate entity if:

✪   they directly or indirectly own all of the outstanding shares of another corporation to the other corporation if the voting rights are not distorted by the transfer of assets;

✪   they are made in association with the dissolution or liquidation of the corporation; or,

✪   the assets transferred are simultaneously leased back to the corporation.

Asset Transfer Plan   The *asset transfer plan* must set forth the conditions of the asset transfer or the plan may permit the Board of Directors to set the terms, including the value to be received by the corporation. An asset transfer plan may be projected and accepted in largely the same fashion as a merger plan, except that the statutory requirements relating to acceptance by the corporate Board of Directors are inapplicable. A summary of the asset plan and, if appropriate, a copy of the statute relating to rights of the dissenters must be enclosed with the notice of the shareholder meeting.

Dissenters. If a corporate shareholder in a business entity that accepts an asset transfer plan rejects the plan and complies with statutes pertaining to rights of the dissenters, the shareholder is entitled to the rights and resolutions of dissenting shareholders provided in the statute. Such rule does not apply to a sale of assets pursuant to a court order or a sale for money where all net proceeds of sale are required to be distributed to shareholders in accordance with their respective interests.

Corporate Division

A corporate entity may subdivide into separate and self-determining corporation entities. The corporate entity prompting the division, is chosen as the surviving corporation. The surviving corporation and the new corporation (or corporations) are jointly appointed as the resultant corporate entities.

Division Plan   A *division plan* must be set forth listing the items required by statute. Further, *Articles of Incorporation* including all requisite statements for each newly formed corporation resulting from the division must be included in, or attached to, the division plan.

A division plan is put forth and accepted in the same fashion as established for the proposition and acceptance of a merger plan, except that statutes relating to acceptance of the merger plan by the Board of Directors are inapplicable. A division plan that fails to alter the state of incorporation, provide for special treatment, or amend its articles does not require the acceptance and approval of the shareholders of the corporation under the following circumstances.

✪   The dividing corporate entity possesses only one class of stock and the stock of each resulting corporate entity is disbursed pro rata to the corporate shareholders of the dividing corporate entity.

✪   The dividing corporate entity survives the division, and all of the stock of the new corporations are solely owned by the surviving corporate entity.

✪ The asset transfer effected by the division, if through means of sale, lease, exchange, or other disbursement, would not require shareholder approval.

A summary of the division plan and a copy of the statute relating to rights of the dissenters must be enclosed with the notice of the shareholder meeting. A shareholder of a corporation that adopts a plan of division, who objects to the plan and complies with the provisions of the statute, is entitled to the rights and remedies of dissenting shareholders.

Division Articles

Upon acceptance of a division plan, **ARTICLES/CERTIFICATE OF DIVISION** (form 15, p.168) must be established by the corporate entity providing all required statutory information. **ARTICLES/CERTIFICATE OF DIVISION** must then be filed with the Department of State. Division is generally effective upon filing.

The following, in addition to the filing fee, shall accompany the **ARTICLES/CERTIFICATE OF DIVISION:**

✪ two copies of a completed completed **DOCKETING STATEMENT (CHANGES)** (form 12, p.158);

✪ one copy of a separate completed **DOCKETING STATEMENT** (form 4, p.128), with respect to each new corporation resulting from the division;

✪ any necessary copies of the **CONSENT TO APPROPRIATION OF NAME/CONSENT TO USE OF SIMILAR NAME** (form 1, p.119);

✪ any necessary governmental approvals; and,

✪ tax clearance certificates evidencing payment of all taxes and charges payable to the Commonwealth are required from the Department of Revenue and the Bureau of Employment Security of the Department of Labor and Industry if the dividing corporation will not survive the division.

Consequence of Corporate Division

Corporations created through division are answerable to their own liabilities. The division plan may forgive some of the resulting corporations from debts of the dividing corporation to the extent specified in the division plan, as long as there is no creditor fraud or breach of voting rights. Further, the forgiveness from debt must not be legally violative and must comply with the law. Before using division to resolve corporate debt, see Chapter 13 on bankruptcy.

II | FINANCING

Every new business needs financing. Whether it is to get started, to make purchases, or for growth and expansion, securing funding is critical. Luckily resources are available.

Sources Of Financing

The following are some sources of financing that you may explore to capitalize your business entity.

- ✪ Family, friends and employees—ask a friend, relative, or associate to go in the business with you.

- ✪ Personal borrowing—borrow from a bank by obtaining a personal loan.

- ✪ Employee stock option plan—capitalize your business by asking employees to invest in the business thereby issuing stock to them in exchange for their investment.

✪ Private offering—offer your business interest to a limited or exclusive group of investors.

✪ Commercial lending—seek a commercial line of credit as a form of start-up capital. Banks are eager to assist small business. Check with your local commercial bank and make inquiry as to any special rates for corporate borrowers.

✪ Small Business Administration (SBA) Loan Guaranty Program—loans are made to any qualifying small business, independently owned and operated, not dominant in its field and which meets employment or sales standards developed by the SBA using Standard Industrial Classification Codes.

✪ Pennsylvania Industrial Development Authority and/or Ben Franklin Partnership—programs designed to offer start-up aid and funding sources to new Pennsylvania businesses. Both agencies focus upon the small business owner and each exists for the benefit, growth, and development of the entrepreneurial enterprise. Creative financing and unique sources of financing options as well as more traditional or standard funding opportunities are offered through these programs.

✪ Pennsylvania Minority Business Development Authority—provides low-interest, long-term loans and guarantees and guarantees of surety bonds.

✪ Venture capitalists—privately-owned organizations that invest in small growth businesses. Investment may be in equity or debt, but will involve substantial protections for the venture capitalist.

Small Business Administration

The U.S. *Small Business Administration (SBA)* is an independent Federal Agency, created by Congress in 1953 to assist, counsel, and champion the efforts of America's small businesses. SBA's Loan Guaranty Programs have helped thousands of small companies get started, expand, and prosper. The goal of this program is to increase the amount of capital available to small business through the commercial banking community and some non-bank lending institutions.

Your first step in securing SBA loan guaranty assistance is talking to your banker. Only a participating commercial lender may apply for an SBA loan guaranty.

Any new business presents a considerable risk to a potential lender. A SBA guaranty can help the lender reduce the risk and approve a business loan that is based on a solid business plan. Oftentimes, the lender can extend a loan on more favorable terms when a SBA guaranty is given. This improves the cash flow position of the new business and the likelihood of success. SBA guaranteed loans are made by private lenders, usually banks, and guaranteed up to 90%, by the SBA.

The Process
There are three principal parties to a SBA guaranteed loan—the small business loan applicant, the lender, and the SBA. The lender plays the central role in the loan delivery system. The small business loan applicant submits the loan application to the lender, who makes the initial review, and, if approved for submission to the SBA, forwards the application and analysis to the SBA office with an application for a loan guaranty. If approved by the SBA, the lender closes the loan and disburses the funds. SBA, in essence, becomes an insurance policy for the lender.

Eligibility Requirements
The SBA defines a small business as one that is independently owned and operated, not dominant in its field, and meets employment or sales standards developed by the Small Business Administration. In general, the following criteria are used by the SBA in determining if a concern qualifies as a small business:

✪ wholesale—not more than 100 employees;

✪ retail or service—annual sales or receipts of not more than $3.5 million. (If the business does not fit the size criteria, it may contact the SBA for a specific ruling.);

✪ manufacturing—not more than 500 employees (numerous exceptions). (If the business does not fit the size criteria, it may contact the SBA for a specific ruling.); and,

✪ constructions—annual sales or receipts of not more than $7.0 million. (If the business does not fit the size criteria, it may contact the SBA for a specific ruling.)

The type of business is also a criteria for approval. SBA approval cannot be granted if the applicant is engaged in certain activities, including the following:

- ✪ newspaper, book, and magazine publishing (and other opinion forming media);

- ✪ gambling or speculation; or,

- ✪ financing real estate held for sale or investment.

Purpose of Loan   An SBA loan guarantees may be granted for one or more of the following business purposes:

- ✪ to finance the purchase of land or buildings, to cover new construction as well as expansion or conversion of existing facilities;

- ✪ to finance the purchase of equipment, machinery, supplies, or materials;

- ✪ to supply working capital; or,

- ✪ short term seasonal financing, contract financing, and construction financing.

Credit   The Small Business Administration general credit criteria requires that a loan
Requirements   applicant must:

- ✪ have sufficient capital in the business so that when combined with the items applied for in the loan application, he or she can operate on a sound financial basis;

- ✪ show that the proposed loan is of sound value;

- ✪ show that the past earnings records and/or future prospects of the firm indicate ability to repay the loan and other fixed debt, if any, out of profits; and,

- ✪ be able to provide from his or her own resources sufficient funds to have a reasonable amount at stake to withstand possible losses, particularly during the early stages, if the venture is a new business.

Amount and Terms The actual amount of the SBA's guaranty will vary with the intended use of loan proceeds. It cannot exceed 90% or $750,000 (whichever is less) of the bank's loan to the small business.

The SBA expects all loans to be repaid as soon a possible. Generally the maturity will vary with the proposed purpose of the loan. For example, the maturity date will be up to seven years for working capital, up to ten years for machinery and equipment and up to twenty years for purchase or construction of plant facilities. Repayment is usually on a monthly installment basis, principal and interest. Variations may be negotiated to meet seasonal cycles of business activity.

The interest rates on SBA guaranty loans are negotiated between the applicant and lender based on the credit merits of the application. The SBA establishes a maximum that banks may charge depending on the maturity of the loan. For loans with a maturity of less than seven years the maximum rate is the prime rate plus 2.25%. For loans with a maturity of seven years or more, the rate can be up to the prime rate plus 2.75%.

The time involved for the SBA to process a loan is directly related to the quality of the application received. If the loan package submitted to the SBA by the bank is complete, the SBA will usually have a decision for the institution within two weeks.

Collateral While *collateral* is not a prime consideration, the SBA requires that all business assets be pledged to secure the loan. In addition, the personal guarantees of the principals, secured by specific personal assets, may be required.

12 TRAINING AND COUNSELING TOOLS

In addition to providing financial assistance to businesses, the *Small Business Administration's (SBA) Business Development Division* manages a statewide network of free small business counseling and low-cost training resources designed to meet the needs of the existing business owner as well as the new business start-up.

Business Development Assistance

A complete line of small business management aids and publications is available from the Business Development Division. For a low cost, it provides guidance and insight in the following topical areas:

- ✪ finance;

- ✪ management;

- ✪ general management and planning;

- ✪ crime prevention;

- ✪ marketing;

- ✪ personnel; and,

- ✪ new products/ideas/inventions.

A directory and order form for publications and videos can be obtained by calling 412-644-2780.

Service Corps of Retired Executives

Perhaps the best known SBA sponsored resource is *SCORE*, the *Service Corps of Retired Executives*. SCORE is an independent, national, non-profit organization of retired business men and women who volunteer their time to provide free counseling and low-cost training to small business owners and prospective entrepreneurs.

SCORE's primary market consists of the thousands of people thinking about or who recently started their own business. Through a series of monthly workshops and direct one-on-one counseling, SCORE provides the novice entrepreneur a solid base of knowledge for launching a new business venture. Existing business owners can benefit from the experience of retired business owners who have operated their own successful enterprises and have faced the same problems you face today.

Some of the workshop topics presented by SCORE chapters include:

- ✪ business planning;

- ✪ business insurance;

- ✪ record keeping;

- ✪ business taxes;

- ✪ Marketing;

✪   financing a new venture;

✪   legal aspects of starting a business; and,

✪   federal taxes.

SCORE Offices   **EASTERN PENNSYLVANIA**

Lehigh Valley SCORE
Rauch Building 37
Lehigh University
621 Taylor St.
Bethlehem, PA 18015-3117
610-758-4496

Harrisburg SCORE
c/o West Shore
Chamber of Commerce
4211 Trindle Road
Camp Hill, PA 17011
717-761-4304

Cumberland Valley SCORE
c/o Chambersburg
Chamber of Commerce
75 South 2nd Street
Chambersburg, PA 17201
717-264-2935

Bucks County SCORE
c/o Chamber of Commerce
409 Hood Boulevard
Fairless Hills, PA 19030
215-943-8850

York SCORE - Satellite Office
c/o Hanover Chamber of Commerce
146 Carlisle Street
Hanover, PA 17331
717-637-6130

Eastern Montgomery SCORE
Baederwood Office Plaza
1653 The Fairway
Suite 204, 2nd Floor
Jenkintown, PA 19046
215-885-3027

Lancaster SCORE
313 W. Liberty Street
Suite 231/Liberty Place
Lancaster, PA 17603
717-397-3092

Lebanon SCORE - Satellite Office
c/o Chamber of Commerce
PO Box 899
252 North 8th Street
Lebanon, PA 17042
717-273-3727

Philadelphia SCORE
1315 Walnut Street
5th Floor
Philadelphia, PA 19107
215-790-5050

Pottstown SCORE
244 High Street
Suite 302
Pottstown, PA 19464
610-327-2673

Reading SCORE
c/o Chamber of Commerce
601 Penn Street
Reading, PA 19601
610-376-3497

Sunbury PA SCORE - Satellite Office
Central Susquehanna
Chamber of Commerce
PO Box 10
Shamokin Dam, PA 17876
570-743-4100

Monroe County SCORE
556 Main Street
Stroudsburg, PA 18360
570-421-4433

Main Line SCORE - Satellite Office
Main Line Chamber of Commerce
175 Strafford Avenue
Suite 130
Wayne, PA 19087
610-687-6232

Chester County SCORE
Government Service Center
601 Westtown Road, Suite 281
West Chester, PA 19380
610-344-6910

Wilkes-Barre SCORE
Stegmaier Building - Room 403
7 North Wilkes-Barre Blvd
Wilkes-Barre, PA 18702
570-826-6502

North Central PA SCORE
Executive Plaza - Suite 305
330 Pine Street
Williamsport, PA 17703
570-322-3720

York SCORE
Cyber Center
2101 Pennsylvania Avenue
York, PA 17404
717-845-8830

WESTERN PENNSYLVANIA

Altoona-Blair
3900 Devorris Center
for Business Development
Altoona, PA 16602
814-942-9054

Central Pennsylvania
Industry and Technology Center
2820 E. College Avenue - Suite E
State College, PA 16801
814-234-9415

Clearfield SCORE Location
650 Leonard Street
Clearfield, PA 16830
814-765-8987

Erie
120 West Ninth Street
Erie, PA 16501
814-871-5650

Huntingdon Branch Office
Hunt Tower - 500 Allegheny Street
Huntingdon, PA 16652
814-643-3126

Johnstown Branch Office
111 Market Street
Johnstown, PA 15901
814-535-2650

McKeesport Location Office
301 Fifth Avenue
McKeesport, PA 15132
412-664-1219

Meadville Branch Office
628 Arch Street, Box A201
Meadville, PA 16335
814-337-5194

Mon Valley
Mon Valley Business
Development Center
435 Donner Avenue
Monessen, PA 15062
724-684-4277

Pittsburgh
Room 1314 Federal Building
1000 Liberty Avenue
Pittsburgh, PA 15222
412-395-6560 X-130

Uniontown
140 North Beeson Avenue
Uniontown, PA 15401
724-437-4222

Westmoreland
Saint Vincent College
2nd Floor - Placid Hall
300 Fraser Purchase Road
Latrobe, PA 15650
724-539-7505

Small Business Institutes

The *Small Business Institute* program allows the SBA to contract long-term consulting services from area colleges and universities to provide in-depth consulting and technical assistance to small businesses, free of charge. For the existing business owner, this program can provide valuable assistance with business and marketing planning, financial and management analysis, and overall business troubleshooting. A team of students work under the guidance of a faculty coordinator with the client small business for a six to eight weeks duration. Case assignments are made in coordination with the beginning of the Fall semester, (August/September) and the Spring semester (January).

Pennsylvania Small Business Development Center Network

The *Pennsylvania Small Business Development Center Network (PAS-BDC)* is rapidly becoming the focal point for all small business assistance programs. The PASBDC program is a joint venture of the U.S. Small Business Administration and the Pennsylvania Department of Commerce. The program is designed to provide comprehensive management and technical assistance to the small business community. Small businesses are counseled and trained in areas of concern such as accounting, advertising, marketing, government procurement, personnel management, and bank relations. The centers also offer basic start-up assistance including help in preparing financial statements and loan applications. Consulting services are provided free and training programs are low or no cost.

For Pennsylvania small business owners, the *Small Business Development Center Network* is your one stop shop for accessing programs and resources of the Small Business Administration, State of Pennsylvania and the numerous local government and private supported initiatives that serve small business.

Small Business Innovation and Research Program

The *Small Business Innovation Research (SBIR) Program* came into existence with the enactment of the *Small Business Innovation Development Act* of 1982. Under SBIR, agencies of the Federal Government with the largest research and development budgets are mandated to set aside a legislated percentage each year for the competitive award of SBIR funding agreements to qualified small business concerns. The SBA has unilateral authority and responsibility for coordinating and monitoring the government-wide activities of the SBIR program and reporting on its results annually to Congress.

Firms interested in participating in SBIR should contact the SBA Office of Innovation, Research, and Technology in Washington, D.C. at 202-205-7777 to be placed on the mailing list for quarterly pre-solicitation announcements.

Procurement Automated Source System

To develop an inventory of small businesses interested in performing federal contracts and subcontracts, the SBA has developed the *Procurement Automated Source System (PASS)*. This national database lists the names of small businesses and their capabilities, so that federal procurement officers and private prime contractors can readily identify small firms which are potential contractors and subcontractors. Many federal agencies and some of the nation's largest prime contractors access the system when searching for small companies to meet their procurement needs.

Minority Business Assistance

The *SBA Minority Small Business Division* works closely with SBA Lending and Business Development officials, Small Business Development Centers, banks, and Economic Development and Procurement officials to help focus programs on the special needs of minority owned small businesses. Training programs are jointly developed and offered throughout the year to any minority small business owner interested in developing business management abilities and exploiting procurement opportunities in the state, federal and private sectors.

SBA Business Opportunity Specialists serve as the clearinghouse for minority business owners seeking specific management or contract assistance by tapping into the extensive minority and small business assistance programs available throughout the state.

.

Federal Contract Assistance

The *8(a) Contracting and Business Development Program* is named for the section of the *Small Business Act* from which it derives its authority. Through the program, existing small businesses owned by socially and economically disadvantaged persons may obtain federal contracts to support a carefully planned program designed to strengthen the competitive viability of the firm. Prospective applicants for participation in the SBA 8(a) program must meet a number of eligibility requirements including, but not limited to:

✪   an established track record of at least two full years of revenue producing business operation as demonstrated by federal tax returns;

✪   socially and economically disadvantaged;

✪   ownership, control, and operated full-time by a disadvantaged applicant; and,

✪   a reasonable potential for success through participation in the 8(a) program.

The 8(a) program can be an effective tool for assisting the minority business entrepreneur. Anyone interested in learning more about the SBA 8(a) program is encouraged to contact the *Minority Small Business Division* of your local SBA office. To locate an office near you, go to the SBA website at:

www.sba.gov

International Trade Assistance

One of the primary objectives of the SBA is to encourage small businesses to consider the global marketplace. Through a range of educational and outreach programs, the SBA is encouraging more small businesses to participate in international trade and assist those currently exporting to expand their markets. Export assistance is available through:

✪ export marketing publications and resource guides;

✪ Matchmaker Trade Missions, co-sponsored with the U.S. Department of Commerce that arrange direct contacts for American firms with potential partners in new international markets; and,

✪ counseling, through SCORE and the Pennsylvania Small Business Development Center Network, in cooperation with the Pennsylvania Office of International Development.

13 ECONOMICALLY DISTRESSED CORPORATIONS

A corporate entity encountering serious economic trouble may be compelled to reorganize the entity or halt business. Corporate reorganization can come in the manner of an out of court workout or a court managed reorganization, under *Chapter 11 Bankruptcy* provisions. (11 U.S.C. beginning with Sec. 1101.) Total liquidation, which will result in dissolution of the corporate entity, occurs through *Chapter 7* of the Bankruptcy Code. (11 U.S.C. beginning with Sec. 701.)

Out-of-Court Workout Rehabilitation

A corporate entity may enter into contracts or agreements with creditors to release debts at settled amounts. An out-of-court workout bears similarity to a Chapter 11 filing, however there is no court involvement. Like a Chapter 11 filing, a realistic business plan covering at least one year of the debtor's future operations should be created. An out-of-court workout does not provide Chapter 11 protection, but does avoid the costs associated with Chapter 11 procedures.

The out-of-court rehabilitation option is often a desirable choice to those entities that wish to reduce their fiscal cost outlays associated with court processes. Court costs, delay, and all aspects of court related redress and remedies can create mounting fiscal concerns for a troubles business. Out-of-court rehabilitation provides a way in which to avoid these significant expenditures.

Besides cost savings, other advantages that an out-of-court workout may have over Chapter 11, include cases where:

- a stigma attached to filing may significantly affect the corporation;

- the creditors are few or not representative of a wide range of various debtors;

- the corporation can begin paying debts promptly; or,

- the corporation possessed additional collateral to offer in place of cash.

Chapter 11 Rehabilitation

Chapter 11 may be a more favorable alternative than an out-of-court workout in situations such as:

- litigation matters pending against the corporation are numerous;

- a buyer desires a purchase of assets free of all indebtedness and liens;

- a lender seeks benefit of Chapter 11 debtor-in-possession financing;

- lenders refuse to accept reasonable conditions;

- the corporation does not wish to reorganize, however, fails to pay debts;

- the corporation seeks tax avoidance or tax forgiveness on income by proceeding under Chapter 11; or,

- significant government claims must be paid first outside of bankruptcy and would receive no priority in bankruptcy filing.

Pros and Cons to Filings Under Chapter 11

Determining whether to pursue reorganization under Chapter 11 requires careful review of the pros and cons of reorganization under Chapter 11.

Advantages.

- ✪ Pending and threatened litigation for damages or equitable relief is stayed.

- ✪ The corporation will continue the operation of its business in most cases.

- ✪ The corporation may obtain financing from new lenders by granting them equal or priming liens, over the objection of existing secured lenders.

- ✪ Lenders are often more willing to lend under court supervised terms and conditions.

- ✪ A Chapter 11 debtor has the benefit of a favorable statute, the Bankruptcy Code.

Disadvantages.

- ✪ Filing for Chapter 11 relief may present a negative stigma.

- ✪ Only 20% to 25% of all Chapter 11 filings result in a successful reorganization.

- ✪ A Chapter 11 debtor is required to promptly demonstrate a positive income flow.

- ✪ A Chapter 11 filing increases expenses of the corporation (cost of counsel, accountants, and experts associated with the case).

Chapter 7 Liquidation

Chapter 7 involves stopping business operations, disbursing business assets to satisfy liabilities and ultimately terminating and dissolving the corporate entity. This procedure is administered by a trustee approved by and overseen by the Bankruptcy Court. Discharged debts are ordered because the corporate entity halts existence. Chapter 7 bankruptcy sets forth a methodical liquidation wherein liabilities significantly surpass assets and maintaining business functioning is not possible.

Other Remedies

When a business entity is insolvent or anticipates financial trouble, the corporate Board of Directors may, through resolution, and without consent of the corporate shareholders, authorize and designate the officers of the corporation to execute a deed of assignment for the benefit of creditors. They may also choose to file a voluntary bankruptcy petition as discussed above, or file to obtain appointment of a receiver upon a complaint filed by creditors.

Dissolution

A corporation must file **ARTICLES OF DISSOLUTION (DOMESTIC)** (form 16, p.173) when it wishes to terminate its existence. Tax clearance certificates from the Department of Revenue and from the Bureau of Employment Security of the Department of Labor and Industry evidencing payment of all taxes and charges payable to the Commonwealth must also be filed with the **ARTICLES OF DISSOLUTION (DOMESTIC).**

The IRS form required to report a corporate dissolution is **CORPORATE DISSOLUTION OR LIQUIDATION (IRS FORM 966).** (form 17, p.177.) The form is also available at www.irs.gov. If you go to the small business section, it has a checklist for closing a business. That may help you make sure that all other required tasks have been completed.

14 HIRING AN ATTORNEY

By purchasing this book you have probably decided that you are going to incorporate your business yourself or you want to be well informed when you met with an attorney to prepare the paperwork for you. However, there are many occasions that occur doing the course of a business where you will need to decide if hiring an attorney is the best course of action for you and the business. Beyond the initially filings, there will be future corporate filings that the corporation must do to stay in existence, the corporation may be sued or what to sue another organization, and the corporation may want to endeavor into projects needing the expertise and advice of an attorney.

It may be possible for an officer or director of a corporation to represent the company in a small claims actions, but generally, a corporation must be represented by an attorney for any legal matters requiring a court appearance. For legal matters not involving court appearances, such as corporate filings and other registrations, a corporate officer or employee may be able to handle the matter.

Costs

One of the first questions you will want to consider, especially in the early stages of the corporation's existence is the cost of an attorney. Attorneys come in all ages, shapes, sizes, sexes, racial, and ethnic groups-and also price ranges. For a very rough estimate, you can expect an attorney to charge anywhere from $250 to $20,000 for business law matters. Lawyers usually charge an hourly rate for contested business law matters, ranging from about $100 to $300 per hour. Most new (and therefore less expensive) attorneys would be quite capable of handling a simple business matters, but, if your situation became more complicated, you would probably prefer a more experienced lawyer. As a general rule, you can expect costs to be more than what you think it will be at the beginning of the matter.

Advantages and Disadvantages to Hiring A Lawyer

The following are some advantages to hiring a lawyer.

- ✪ You can let your lawyer worry about all of the details. By having an attorney, you need only become generally familiar with the contents of this book, as it will be your attorney's job to file the proper papers in the correct form, deal with the courts, and to deal with your opponent and your opponent's attorney.

- ✪ Lawyers provide professional assistance with problems. In the event your case is complicated, or suddenly becomes complicated, it is an advantage to have an attorney who is familiar with your case. It can also be comforting to have a lawyer to turn to for advice and answers to your questions.

On the other hand, there are also advantages to representing yourself such as:

- ✪ saving the cost of a lawyer and

- ✪ selecting an attorney is not easy.

You may want to look for an attorney who will be willing to accept an hourly fee to answer your questions and give you help as you need it. This way you will save some legal costs, but still receive some professional assistance. You will also establish a relationship with an attorney who will be somewhat familiar with your organization or a particular case in the event things become complicated and you need a full-time lawyer.

Selecting a Lawyer

Selecting a lawyer is a two-step process. First, you need to decide with which attorney you will make an appointment, then you need to decide if you wish to hire (retain) that attorney.

Ask a Friend

A common, and frequently the best, way to find a lawyer is to ask someone you know to recommend one to you. This is especially helpful if the lawyer represented your friend in a business law matter.

Lawyer Referral Service.

You can find a referral service by looking in the Yellow Pages phone directory under *Attorney Referral Services* or *Attorneys*. This is a service, usually operated by a bar association, that is designed to match a client with an attorney handling cases in the area of law the client needs. The referral service does not guarantee the quality of work, nor the level of experience, or ability of the attorney. Finding a lawyer in this manner will at least connect you with one who is interested in business law and business law matters, and probably has some experience in this area.

Yellow Pages

Check under the heading for *Attorneys* in the yellow pages phone directory. Many of the lawyers and law firms will place display ads indicating their areas of practice, and educational backgrounds. Look for firms or lawyers that indicate they practice in areas such as *Incorporations, Small Business,* and *Business Law.* Big ads are not necessarily indicative of expertise. Keep in mind that some lawyers do not need to advertise.

Ask Another Lawyer

If you have used the services of an attorney in the past for some other matter (for example, a real estate closing, traffic ticket, or a will), you may want to call and ask if he or she could refer you to an attorney whose ability in the area of business law is respected.

Evaluating Lawyers

From your search, you should select three to five lawyers worthy of further consideration. Your first step will be to call each attorney's office, explain that you are interested in seeking representation and aid in business law matters, and ask the following questions.

✪ Does the attorney (or law firm) handle this type of matter?

✪ What is the fee range, and what is the cost of an initial consultation? *(Do not expect to get a definite answer on a business law fee, but the attorney may be able to give you a range or an hourly rate. You will probably need to meet with the lawyer for anything more detailed.)*

✪ How soon can you get an appointment? *(Most offices require you to make an appointment.) Once you get in contact with the attorney at the appointment, ask the following questions.*

  ✪ How much will it cost?

  ✪ How will the fee be paid?

  ✪ How long has the attorney been in practice?

  ✪ How long has the attorney been in practice in Pennsylvania?

  ✪ What percentage of the attorney's cases involve business law cases or other business law matters? (Do not expect an exact answer, but you should get a rough estimate that is at least twenty percent.)

✪ How long will it take? *(Do not expect an exact answer, but the attorney should be able to give you an average range and discuss things that may make a difference.)*

If you get acceptable answers to these questions, it's time to ask yourself the following questions about the lawyer.

✪ Do you feel comfortable talking to the lawyer?

✪ Is the lawyer friendly toward you?

✪ Does the lawyer seem confident in himself or herself?

✪ Does the lawyer seem to be straight-forward with you, and able to explain issues so you understand?

If you get satisfactory answers to all of these questions, you probably have a lawyer with whom you will be happy to work. Most clients are happiest with an attorney with whom they feel comfortable.

Working with a Lawyer

In general, you will work best with your attorney if you keep an open, honest, and friendly attitude. Also, also consider the following suggestions.

Ask Questions

If you want to know something or if you do not understand something, ask your attorney. If you do not understand the answer, tell your attorney and ask him or her to explain it again. You should not be embarrassed to ask questions. Many people who say they had a bad experience with a lawyer either did not ask enough questions or had a lawyer who wouldn't take the time to explain things to them. If your lawyer isn't taking the time to explain what he or she is doing, it may be time to look for a new lawyer.

Give Complete Information

Anything you tell your attorney is confidential. An attorney can lose his or her license to practice if he or she reveals information without your permission. So do not hold back. Tell your lawyer everything, even if it does not seem important to you. There are many things that seem unimportant to a non-attorney, but can change the outcome of a case. Also, do not hold something back because you are afraid it will hurt your case. It will definitely hurt your case if your lawyer does not find out about it until he or she hears it in court from your opponent's attorney. But if your lawyer knows in advance, he or she can plan to eliminate or reduce damage to your case.

Accept Reality Listen to what your lawyer tells you about the law and the system. It will do you no good to argue because the law or the system does not work the way you think it should. For example, if your lawyer tells you that the judge cannot hear your case for two weeks, do not try demanding that he or she set a hearing tomorrow. By refusing to accept reality, you are only setting yourself up for disappointment. And remember—it is not your attorney's fault that the system is not perfect, or that the law does not say what you would like it to say.

Be Patient The advice to be patient applies both to being patient with the system (which is often slow), as well as being patient with your attorney. Do not expect your lawyer to return your phone call within an hour. Your lawyer may not be able to return it the same day. Most lawyers are very busy. It is rare that an attorney can maintain a full caseload and still make each client feel as if he or she is the only client. Despite the popular trend toward lawyer-bashing, you should remember that many lawyers are good people who wish to aid and assist the public.

Talk to the Secretary Your lawyer's secretary can be a valuable source of information. Be friendly and get to know the secretary. Often he or she will be able to answer your questions, and you will not get a bill for the time you talk to the secretary.

Your Opponent It is your lawyer's job to communicate with your opponent, or with your opponent's lawyer. Let your lawyer do his or her job. Many lawyers have had clients lose or damage their cases when the client decides to say or do something on their own.

Be On Time The advice to be on time applies to both appointments with your lawyer and to court hearings.

Keep Your Case Moving Many lawyers operate on the old principle of the squeaking wheel gets the oil. Work on a case tends to be put off until a deadline is near, an emergency develops, or the client calls. There is a reason for this. Many lawyers take more cases than can be effectively handled in order to earn the income they desire. Your task is to become a squeaking wheel that does not squeak too much. Whenever you talk to your lawyer, ask the following questions.

- ✪ What is the next step?

- ✪ When do you expect it to be done?

- ✪ When should I talk to you next?

Call your lawyer if you do not hear anything when you expect. Do not remind your lawyer of the missed call. Just ask how things are going.

Firing Your Lawyer

If you can no longer work with your lawyer, it is time to either go it alone or get a new attorney. You will need to send your lawyer a letter stating that you no longer desire his or her services and are discharging him or her from your case. Also state that you will be coming by his or her office the following day to pick up your file. The attorney does not have to give you his or her own notes or other work he or she has in progress, but he or she must give you the essential contents of your file (such as copies of papers already filed or prepared and billed for, and any documents that you provided). If the lawyer refuses to give you your file, for any reason, contact the Pennsylvania Bar about filing a complaint, or grievance, against the lawyer. Of course, you will need to settle any remaining fees charged.

GLOSSARY

A

accounts payable. Bills that are owed.

accounts receivable. The amounts of money due or owed to a business or professional by customers or clients.

action. A lawsuit in which one party (or parties) sues another.

addendum. An addition to a completed written document.

adjusted basis. In accounting, the original cost of an asset adjusted for costs of improvements, depreciation, damage and other events that may have affected its value during the period of ownership.

advance. A payment which is made before it is legally due, such as before shipment is made, a sale is completed, a book is completed by the author, or a note is due to be paid.

affidavit. Any written document in which the signer swears under oath before a notary public or someone authorized to take oaths (like a County Clerk), that the statements in the document are true.

agency. The relationship of a person (called the agent) who acts on behalf of another person, company, or government, known as the principal.

agent. A person who is authorized to act for another (the agent's principal) through employment, by contract or apparent authority.

agreement. Any meeting of the minds, even without legal obligation.

amend. To alter or change by adding, subtracting, or substituting.

antitrust laws. Acts adopted by Congress to outlaw or restrict business practices considered to be monopolistic or which restrain interstate commerce.

apparent authority. The appearance of being the agent of another (employer or principal) with the power to act for the principal.

appreciate. To increase in value over a period of time through the natural course of events, including inflation, greater rarity, or public acceptance.

asset. Generally any item of property that has monetary value.

assignment for benefit of creditors. A method used for a debtor to work out a payment schedule to his or her creditors through a trustee who receives directly a portion of the debtor's income on a regular basis to pay the debtor's bills.

association. Any group of people who have joined together for a particular purpose.

attorney. An agent or someone authorized to act for another.

attorney of record. The attorney who has appeared in court and/or signed pleadings or other forms on behalf of a client.

attorney-client privilege. The requirement that an attorney may not reveal communications, conversations and letters between himself or herself and his or her client, under the theory that a person should be able to speak freely and honestly with his or her attorney without fear of future revelation.

attorney-in-fact. Someone specifically named by another through a written power of attorney to act for that person in the conduct of the appointer's business.

audit. An examination by a trained accountant of the financial records of a business, including noting improper or careless practices, recommendations for improvements, and a balancing of the books.

auditor. An accountant who conducts an audit to verify the accuracy of the financial records and accounting practices of a business.

authority. A right coupled with the power to do an act or order others to act.

B

business. Any activity or enterprise entered into for profit.

C

carrying on business. Pursuing a particular occupation on a continuous and substantial basis.

doing business. Carrying on the normal activities of a corporation on a regular basis or with substantial contacts-not just an occasional shipment.

certificate of incorporation. A document which some states issue to prove a corporation's existence upon the filing of articles of incorporation. In most states the articles are sufficient proof.

certified check. A check issued by a bank which certifies that the maker of the check has enough money in his/her account to cover the amount to be paid.

charter. The name for articles of incorporation in some states, as in a corporate charter.

check. A draft upon a particular account in a bank, in which the drawer or maker (the person who has the account and signs the check) directs the bank to pay a certain amount to a payee .

civil law. A generic term for non-criminal law.

civil liability. A potential responsibility for payment of damages or other court-enforcement in a lawsuit, as distinguished from criminal liability, which means open to punishment for a crime.

civil penalties. Fines or surcharges imposed by a governmental agency to enforce regulations such as late payment of taxes, failure to obtain a permit, etc.

claim. To make a demand for money, for property, or for enforcement of a right provided by law.

close corporation. A corporation which is permitted by state law to operate more informally than most corporations (allowing decisions without meetings of the board of directors) and has only a limited number of shareholders. Usually a close corporation's shareholders are involved in the actual operation of the business and often are family members.

collateral. The property pledged to secure a loan or debt, usually funds or personal property as distinguished from real property.

collusion. Where two persons (or business entities through their officers or other employees) enter into a deceitful agreement, usually secret, to defraud and/or gain an unfair advantage over a third party, competitors, consumers or those with whom they are negotiating.

commingling. The act of mixing the funds belonging to one party with those of another party, or, most importantly with funds held in trust for another.

common law. The traditional unwritten law of England.

common stock. The stock in a corporation in which dividends are calculated upon a percentage of net profits, with distribution determined by the board of directors.

complaint. The first document filed with the court by a person or entity claiming legal rights against another.

conflict of interest. A situation in which a person has a duty to more than one person or organization, but cannot do justice to the actual or potentially adverse interests of both parties.

consideration. Something of value exchanged for the performance or promise of performance by the other party in a contract.

corporation. An organization formed with state governmental approval to act as an artificial person to carry on business (or other activities), which can sue or be sued, and (unless it is non-profit) can issue shares of stock to raise funds with which to start a business or increase its capital.

counter offer. An offer made in response to a previous offer by the other party during negotiations for a final contract.

creditor. A person or entity to whom a debt is owed.

D

damages. The amount of money which a plaintiff (the person suing) may be awarded in a lawsuit.

depreciate. To reduce the value of an asset each year theoretically on the basis that the assets (such as equipment, vehicles or structures) will eventually become obsolete, worn out and of little value.

dissolution of corporation. A termination of a corporation, by either a) voluntarily by resolution, paying debts, distributing assets and filing dissolution documents with the Secretary of State or b) by state suspension for not paying corporate taxes or some other action of the government.

E

expense. In business accounting and business taxation, any current cost of operation, such as rent, utilities and payroll, as distinguished from capital expenditure for long-term property and equipment.

express contract. A contract in which all elements are specifically stated (offer, acceptance, consideration), and the terms are stated, as compared to an "implied" contract in which the existence of the contract is assumed by the circumstance.

F

face value. In shares of stock, the original cost of the stock shown on the certificate, or *par value*.

fiduciary. A person (or a business like a bank or stock brokerage) who has the power and obligation to act for another (often called the beneficiary) under circumstances which require total trust, good faith and honesty.

fiduciary relationship. Where one person places complete confidence in another in regard to a particular transaction or one's general affairs or business.

foreign corporation. A corporation which is incorporated under the laws of a different state or nation.

full disclosure. The need in business transactions to tell the *whole truth* about any matter which the other party should know in deciding to buy or contract.

G

good faith. An honest intent to act without taking an unfair advantage over another person or to fulfill a promise to act, even when some legal technicality is not fulfilled.

J

joint and several. A debt or a judgment for negligence, in which each debtor (one who owes) or each judgment defendant (one who has a judgment against him/her) is responsible (liable) for the entire amount of the debt or judgment.

joint enterprise. A generic term for an activity of two or more people, usually (but not necessarily) for profit, which may include partnership, joint venture or any business in which more than one person invests, works, has equal management control and/or is otherwise involved for an agreed upon goal or purpose.

joint liability. When two or more persons are both responsible for a debt, claim or judgment.

joint venture. An enterprise entered into by two or more people for profit and for a limited purpose.

judgment creditor. The winning plaintiff in a lawsuit to whom the court decides the defendant owes money.

jurisdiction. The authority given by law to a court to try cases and rule on legal matters within a particular geographic area and/or over certain types of legal cases.

L

limited liability. The maximum amount a person participating in a business can lose or be charged in case of claims against the company or its bankruptcy.

limited partnership. A special type of partnership common when people need funding for a business, or when they are putting together an investment in a real estate development.

liquidate. To sell the assets of a business, paying bills and dividing the remainder among shareholders, partners or other investors.

litigation. Any lawsuit or other resort to the courts to determine a legal question or matter.

M

merger. The joining together of two corporations in which one corporation transfers all of its assets to the other, which continues to exist.

minutes. The written record of meetings, particularly of boards of directors and/or shareholders of corporations, kept by the secretary of the corporation or organization.

O

obligation. A legal duty to pay or do something.

offer. A specific proposal to enter into an agreement with another.

P

partner. One of the co-owners and investors in a partnership.

partnership. A business enterprise entered into for profit which is owned by more than one person.

pierce the corporate veil. to prove that a corporation exists merely as a completely controlled front (alter ego) for an individual or group, so that in a lawsuit the individual defendants can be held responsible (liable) for damages for actions of the corporation.

preferred dividend. A payment of a corporation's profits to holders of preferred shares of stock.

preferred stock. A class of shares of stock in a corporation which gives the holders priority in payment of dividends (and distribution of assets in case of dissolution of the corporation) over owners of common stock.

principal place of business. The location of the head office of a business where the books and records are kept and/or management works.

Q

quasi corporation. A business which has operated as a corporation without completing the legal requirements, often in the period just before formal incorporation.

R

register. The record of shareholders, and issuance and transfer of shares on the records of the corporation.

S

shareholder. The owner of one or more shares of stock in a corporation. Also called a stockholder.

shareholders' agreement. An employment agreement among the shareholders of a small corporation permitting a shareholder to take a management position with the corporation without any claim of conflict of interest or self-dealing against the shareholder/manager.

shareholders' derivative action. A lawsuit by a corporation's shareholders, theoretically on behalf of the corporation, to protect and benefit all shareholders against the corporation for improper management.

shareholders' meeting. A meeting, usually annual, of all shareholders of a corporation to elect the board of directors and hear reports on the company's business situation.

stock. A share in the ownership of a corporation. Also called shares.

stock certificate. A printed document that states the name, incorporation state, date of incorporation, the registered number of the certificate, the number of shares of stock in a corporation the certificate represents, the name of the shareholder, the date of issuance and the number of shares authorized in the particular issue of stock, signed by the president and secretary of the corporation. On the reverse side of the certificate is a form for transfer of the certificate to another person.

stock option. The right to purchase stock in the future at a price set at the time the option is granted.

stockholder. A shareholder in a corporation.

U

unissued stock. A corporation's shares of stock that are authorized by its articles of incorporation, but have never been issued (sold) to anyone.

V

voting trust. A trust that solicits vote proxies of shareholders of a corporation to elect a board of directors and vote on other matters at a shareholders' meeting.

W

winding up. The liquidating of the assets of a corporation, settling accounts, paying bills, distributing remaining assets to shareholders, and then dissolving the business.

Appendix A Pennsylvania Corporate Statutes

Included in this appendix are *selected* Pennsylvania Corporate Statutes concerning general provisions; corporate powers, duties and safeguards; nonstock corporations; and, professional corporations.

CORPORATIONS—TITLE 15
CHAPTER 11 GENERAL PROVISIONS

Sec. 1101. Short titles.

(a) Title of subpart.-This subpart shall be known and may be cited as the Business Corporation Law of 1988.

(b) Prior law.-The act of May 5, 1933 (P.L. 364, No. 106) shall be known and may be cited as the Business Corporation Law of 1933.

Sec. 1102. Application of subpart.

(a) General rule.-Except as otherwise provided in this section, in the scope provisions of subsequent provisions of this subpart or where the context clearly indicates otherwise, this subpart shall apply to and the words "corporation" or "business corporation" in this subpart shall mean a domestic corporation for profit. See section 101(b) (relating to application of title).

(b) Coordination with other laws.-Where any other provision of law contemplates notice to, the presence of or the vote, consent or other action by the shareholders, directors or officers of a business corporation, without specifying the applicable corporate standards and procedures, the standards and procedures specified by or pursuant to this subpart shall be applicable.

(c) Exclusions.-This subpart shall not apply to any of the following corporations, whether proposed or existing, except as otherwise expressly provided in this subpart or as otherwise provided by statute applicable to the corporation:

1. A banking institution.

2. A credit union.

3. A savings association.

(d) Cooperative corporations.-This subpart shall apply to a domestic corporation for profit organized on the cooperative principle only to the extent provided by Subpart D (relating to cooperative corporations).

(e) Business corporation ancillaries.-The domestic corporation provisions of this subpart shall apply to any of the following corporations, whether proposed or existing, except as otherwise expressly provided by statute applicable to the corporation:

1. A business development credit corporation.

2. Any other domestic corporation for profit incorporated under or subject to a statute that provides that the corporate affairs of the corporation shall be governed by the laws applicable to domestic business corporations.

Sec. 1104. Other General Provisions.
The following provisions of this title are applicable to corporations subject to this subpart:

Section 101 (relating to short title and application of title).

Section 102 (relating to definitions).

Section 103 (relating to subordination of title to regulatory laws).

Section 104 (relating to equitable remedies).

Section 105 (relating to fees).

Section 106 (relating to effect of filing papers required to be filed).

Section 107 (relating to form of records).

Section 108 (relating to change in location or status of registered office provided by agent).

Section 109 (relating to name of commercial registered office provider in lieu of registered address).

Section 110 (relating to supplementary general principles of law applicable).

Section 132 (relating to functions of Department of State).

Section 133 (relating to powers of Department of State).

Section 134 (relating to docketing statement).

Section 135 (relating to requirements to be met by filed documents).

Section 136 (relating to processing of documents by Department of State).

Section 137 (relating to court to pass upon rejection of documents by Department of State).

Section 138 (relating to statement of correction).

Section 139 (relating to tax clearance of certain fundamental transactions).

Section 140 (relating to custody and management of orphan corporate and business records).

Section 152 (relating to definitions).

Section 153 (relating to fee schedule).

Section 154 (relating to enforcement and collection).

Section 155 (relating to disposition of funds).

Section 162 (relating to contingent domestication of certain foreign associations).

Section 501 (relating to reserved power of General Assembly).

Section 503 (relating to actions to revoke corporate franchises).

Section 504 (relating to validation of certain defective corporations).

Section 505 (relating to validation of certain defective corporate acts).

Section 506 (relating to scope and duration of certain franchises).

Section 507 (relating to validation of certain share authorizations).

Sec. 1105. Restriction on equitable relief.
A shareholder of a business corporation shall not have any right to obtain, in the absence of fraud or fundamental unfairness, an injunction against any proposed plan or amendment of articles authorized under any provision of this subpart, nor any right to claim the right to valuation and payment of the fair value of his shares because of the plan or amendment, except that he may dissent and claim such payment if and to the extent provided in Subchapter D of Chapter 15 (relating to dissenters rights) where this subpart expressly provides that dissenting shareholders shall have the rights and remedies pro-

vided in that subchapter. Absent fraud or fundamental unfairness, the rights and remedies so provided shall be exclusive. Structuring a plan or transaction for the purpose or with the effect of eliminating or avoiding the application of dissenters rights is not fraud or fundamental unfairness within the meaning of this section.

Sec. 1108. Limitation on incorporation.
A corporation that can be incorporated under this subpart shall not be incorporated except under the provisions of this subpart.

Sec. 1109. Execution of documents.
(a) General rule.-Any document filed in the Department of State under this title by a domestic or foreign business corporation subject to this subpart may be executed on behalf of the corporation by any one duly authorized officer thereof. The corporate seal may be affixed and attested but the affixation or attestation of the corporate seal shall not be necessary for the due execution of any filing by a corporation under this title.

Sec. 1110. Annual report information.
The Department of State shall make available as public information for inspection and copying the names of the president, vice-president, secretary and treasurer and the address of the principal office of corporations for profit as annually forwarded to the department by the Department of Revenue pursuant to section 403(a)(3) of the act of March 4, 1971 (P.L. 6, No. 2), known as the Tax Reform Code of 1971.

CHAPTER 15. CORPORATE POWERS, DUTIES AND SAFEGUARDS

Sec. 1501. Corporate capacity.
Except as provided in section 103 (relating to subordination of title to regulatory laws), a business corporation shall have the legal capacity of natural persons to act.

Sec. 1502. General powers.
(a) General rule.-Subject to the limitations and restrictions imposed by statute or contained in its articles, every business corporation shall have power:
1. To have perpetual succession by its corporate name unless a limited period of duration is specified in its articles, subject to the power of the Attorney General under section 503 (relating to actions to revoke corporate franchises) and to the power of the General Assembly under the Constitution of Pennsylvania.
2. To sue and be sued, complain and defend and participate as a party or otherwise in any judicial, administrative, arbitrative or other proceeding in its corporate name.
3. To have a corporate seal, which may be altered at pleasure and to use the seal by causing it or a facsimile thereof to be impressed or affixed or in any other manner reproduced.
4. To acquire, own and utilize any real or personal property, or any interest therein, wherever situated.
5. To sell, convey, mortgage, pledge, lease, exchange or otherwise dispose of all or any part of its property and assets, or any interest therein, wherever situated.
6. To guarantee, become surety for, acquire, own and dispose of obligations, capital stock and other securities.
7. To borrow money, issue or incur its obligations and secure any of its obligations by mortgage on or pledge of or security interest in all or any part of its property and assets, wherever situated, franchises or income, or any interest therein.
8. To invest its funds, lend money and take and hold real and personal property as security for the repayment of funds so invested or loaned.
9. To make contributions and donations.
10. To use abbreviations, words, logos or symbols upon the records of the corporation, and in connection with the registration of, and inscription of ownership or entitlement on, certificates evidencing shares in or other securities or obligations of the corporation, or upon any notice such as the notice provided by section 1528(f) (relating to uncertificated shares), and upon checks, proxies, notices and other instruments and documents relating to the foregoing, which abbreviations, words, logos or symbols shall have the same force and effect as though the respective words and phrases for which they stand were set forth in full for the purposes of all statutes of this Commonwealth and all other purposes.
11. To be a promoter, partner, member, associate or manager of any partnership, enterprise or venture or in any transaction, undertaking or arrangement that the corporation would have power to conduct itself, whether or not its participation involves sharing or delegation of control with or to others.

12. To transact any lawful business that the board of directors finds will aid governmental policy.

13. To continue the salaries of such of its employees as may be serving in the active or reserve armed forces of the United States, or in the National Guard or in any other organization established for the protection of the lives and property of citizens of this Commonwealth or the United States, during the term of that service or during such part thereof as the employees, by reason of that service, may be unable to perform their duties as employees of the corporation.

14. To pay pensions and establish pension plans, pension trusts, profit sharing plans, share bonus plans, share option plans, incentive and deferred compensation plans and other plans or trusts for any or all of its present or former representatives and, after their death, to grant allowances or pensions to their dependents or beneficiaries, whether or not the grant was made during their lifetime.

15. To conduct its business, carry on its operations, have offices and exercise the powers granted by this subpart, or any other provision of law in any jurisdiction within or without the United States.

16. To elect or appoint and remove officers, employees and agents of the corporation, define their duties, fix their compensation and the compensation of directors, to lend any of the foregoing money and credit and to pay bonuses or other additional compensation to any of the foregoing for past services.

17. To enter into any obligation appropriate for the transaction of its affairs, including contracts or other agreements with its shareholders.

18. To accept, reject, respond to or take no action in respect of an actual or proposed acquisition, divestiture, tender offer, takeover or other fundamental change under Chapter 19 (relating to fundamental changes) or otherwise.

19. To have and exercise all of the powers and means appropriate to effect the purpose or purposes for which the corporation is incorporated.

20. To have and exercise all other powers enumerated elsewhere in this subpart or otherwise vested by law in the corporation.

(b) Enumeration unnecessary.-It shall not be necessary to set forth in the articles of the corporation the powers enumerated in subsection (a).

Sec. 1503. Defense of ultra vires.

(a) General rule.-A limitation upon the business, purposes or powers of a business corporation, expressed or implied in its articles or bylaws or implied by law, shall not be asserted in order to defend any action at law or in equity between the corporation and a third person, or between a shareholder and a third person, involving any contract to which the corporation is a party or any right of property or any alleged liability of whatever nature, but the limitation may be asserted.

Sec. 1504. Adoption, amendment and contents of bylaws.

(a) General rule.--Except as otherwise provided in this subpart, the shareholders entitled to vote shall have the power to adopt, amend and repeal the bylaws of a business corporation. Except as provided in subsection (b), the authority to adopt, amend and repeal bylaws may be expressly vested by the bylaws in the board of directors, subject to the power of the shareholders to change such action. The bylaws may contain any provisions for managing the business and regulating the affairs of the corporation not inconsistent with law or the articles. In the case of a meeting of shareholders, written notice shall be given to each shareholder that the purpose, or one of the purposes, of a meeting is to consider the adoption, amendment or repeal of the bylaws. There shall be included in, or enclosed with, the notice a copy of the proposed amendment or a summary of the changes to be effected thereby. Any change in the bylaws shall take effect when adopted unless otherwise provided in the resolution effecting the change.

(b) Exception.--Except as otherwise provided in section 1310(a) (relating to organization meeting), or in the articles to the extent authorized by section 1306(b) (relating to other provisions authorized), the board of directors shall not have the authority to adopt or change a bylaw on any subject that is committed expressly to the shareholders by any of the provisions of this subpart. See:

Subsection (d) (relating to amendment of voting provisions).

Section 1521 (relating to authorized shares).

Section 1713 (relating to personal liability of directors).

Section 1721 (relating to board of directors).

Section 1725 (relating to selection of directors).

Section 1726 (relating to removal of directors).

Section 1729 (relating to voting rights of directors).

Section 1756 (relating to quorum).

Section 1757 (relating to action by shareholders).

Section 1765 (relating to judges of election).

Section 2105 (relating to termination of nonstock corporation status).

Section 2122 (relating to classes of membership).

Section 2124 (relating to voting rights of members).

Section 2302 (relating to definition of minimum vote).

Section 2321 (relating to shares).

Section 2322 (relating to share transfer restrictions).

Section 2325 (relating to sale option of estate of shareholder).

Section 2332 (relating to management by shareholders).

Section 2334 (relating to appointment of provisional director in certain cases).

Section 2337 (relating to option of shareholder to dissolve corporation).

Section 2923 (relating to issuance and retention of shares).

(c) Bylaw provisions in articles.--Where any provision of this subpart or any other provision of law refers to a rule as set forth in the bylaws of a corporation, the reference shall be construed to include and be satisfied by any rule on the same subject as set forth in the articles of the corporation.

(d) Amendment of voting provisions.--

1. Unless otherwise provided in a bylaw adopted by the shareholders, whenever the bylaws require for the taking of any action by the shareholders or a class of shareholders a specific number or percentage of votes, the provision of the bylaws setting forth that requirement shall not be amended or repealed by any lesser number or percentage of votes of the shareholders or of the class of shareholders.

2. Paragraph (1) shall not apply to a bylaw setting forth the right of shareholders to act by unanimous written consent as provided in section 1766(a) (relating to unanimous consent).

Sec. 1505. Persons bound by bylaws.
Except as otherwise provided by section 1713 (relating to personal liability of directors) or any similar provision of law, the bylaws of a business corporation shall operate only as regulations among the shareholders of the corporation and shall not affect contracts or other dealings with other persons unless those persons have actual knowledge of the bylaws.

Sec. 1506. Form of execution of instruments.
(a) General rule.-Any form of execution provided in the articles or bylaws to the contrary notwithstanding, any note, mortgage, evidence of indebtedness, contract or other document, or any assignment or endorsement thereof, executed or entered into between any business corporation and any other person, when signed by one or more officers or agents having actual or apparent authority to sign it, or by the president or vice president and secretary or assistant secretary or treasurer or assistant treasurer of the corporation, shall be held to have been properly executed for and in behalf of the corporation.
(b) Seal unnecessary.-The affixation of the corporate seal shall not be necessary to the valid execution, assignment or endorsement by a corporation of any instrument or other document.

Sec. 1507. Registered office.
(a) General rule.-Every business corporation shall have and continuously maintain in this Commonwealth a registered office which may, but need not, be the same as its place of business.
(b) Statement of change of registered office.-After incorporation, a change of the location of the registered office may be authorized at any time by the board of directors. Before the change of location becomes effective, the corporation either shall amend its articles under the provisions of this subpart to reflect the change in location or shall file in the Department of State a statement of change of registered office executed by the corporation setting forth:

1. The name of the corporation.

2. The address, including street and number, if any, of its then registered office.

3. The address, including street and number, if any, to which the registered office is to be changed.

4. A statement that the change was authorized by the board of directors.

(c) Alternative procedure.-A corporation may satisfy the requirements of this subpart concerning the maintenance of a registered office in this Commonwealth by setting forth in any document filed in the department under any provision of this subpart that permits or requires the statement of the address of its then registered office, in lieu of that address, the statement authorized by section 109(a) (relating to name of commercial registered office provider in lieu of registered address).

Sec. 1508. Corporate records; inspection.

(a) Required records.- Every business corporation shall keep complete and accurate books and records of account, minutes of the proceedings of the incorporators, shareholders and directors and a share register giving the names and addresses of all shareholders and the number and class of shares held by each. The share register shall be kept at either the registered office of the corporation in this Commonwealth or at its principal place of business wherever situated or at the office of its registrar or transfer agent. Any books, minutes or other records may be in written form or any other form capable of being converted into written form within a reasonable time.

(b) Right of inspection.-Every shareholder shall, upon written verified demand stating the purpose thereof, have a right to examine, in person or by agent or attorney, during the usual hours for business for any proper purpose, the share register, books and records of account, and records of the proceedings of the incorporators, shareholders and directors and to make copies or extracts therefrom. A proper purpose shall mean a purpose reasonably related to the interest of the person as a shareholder. In every instance where an attorney or other agent is the person who seeks the right of inspection, the demand shall be accompanied by a verified power of attorney or other writing that authorizes the attorney or other agent to so act on behalf of the shareholder. The demand shall be directed to the corporation at its registered office in this Commonwealth or at its principal place of business wherever situated.

(c) Proceedings for enforcement of inspection.-If the corporation, or any officer or agent thereof, refuses to permit an inspection sought by a shareholder or attorney or other agent acting for the shareholder pursuant to subsection (b) or does not reply to the demand within five business days after the demand has been made, the shareholder may apply to the court for an order to compel the inspection. The court shall determine whether or not the person seeking inspection is entitled to the inspection sought. The court may summarily order the corporation to permit the shareholder to inspect the share register and the other books and records of the corporation and to make copies or extracts therefrom, or the court may order the corporation to furnish to the shareholder a list of its shareholders as of a specific date on condition that the shareholder first pay to the corporation the reasonable cost of obtaining and furnishing the list and on such other conditions as the court deems appropriate. Where the shareholder seeks to inspect the books and records of the corporation, other than its share register of list of shareholders, he shall first establish:

1. That he has complied with the provisions of this section respecting the form and manner of making demand for inspection of the document.

2. That the inspection he seeks is for a proper purpose.

Where the shareholder seeks to inspect the share register or list of shareholders of the corporation and he has complied with the provisions of this section respecting the form and manner of making demand for inspection of the documents, the burden of proof shall be upon the corporation to establish that the inspection he seeks is for an improper purpose. The court may, in its discretion, prescribe any limitations or conditions with reference to the inspection or award such other relief as the court deems just and proper. The court may order books, documents, and records, pertinent extracts therefrom, or duly authenticated copies thereof, to be brought into this Commonwealth and kept in this Commonwealth upon such terms and conditions as the order may prescribe.

(d) Certain provisions of articles ineffective.-This section may not be relaxed by any provision of the articles.

Sec. 1521. Authorized shares.

(a) General rule.-Every business corporation shall have powers to create and issue the number of shares stated in its articles. The shares may consist of one class or be divided into two or more classes and one or more series within any class thereof, which classes or series may have full, limited, multiple or fractional or no voting rights and such designations, preferences, limitations and special rights as may be desired. Shares that are not entitled to a preference, even if identified by a class or other designation, shall not be designated as preference or preferred shares.

(b) Provisions specifically authorized.-

1. Without limiting the authority contained in subsection (a), a corporation, when so authorized in its articles, may issue classes or series of shares:

i. Subject to the right or obligation of the corporation to redeem any of the shares for the consideration, if any, fixed by or in the manner provided by the articles for the redemption thereof. Unless otherwise provided in the articles, any shares subject to redemption shall be redeemable only pro rata or by lot or by such other equitable method as may be selected by the corporation. An amendment of the articles to add or amend a provision permitting the redemption of any shares by a method that is not pro rata nor by lot nor otherwise equitable may be effected only pursuant to section 1906 (relating to special treatment of holders of shares of same class or series).

ii. Entitling the holders thereof to cumulative, non cumulative or partially cumulative dividends.

iii. Having preference over any other shares as to dividends or assets or both.

iv. Convertible into shares of any other class or series, or into obligations of the corporation.

2. Any of the terms of a class or series of shares may be made dependent upon:

Facts ascertainable outside of the articles if the manner in which the facts will operate upon the terms of the class or series is set forth in the articles.

i. Terms incorporated by reference to an existing agreement between the corporation and one or more other parties, or to another document of independent significance, if the articles state that the full text of the agreement or other document is on file at the principal place of business of the corporation and state the address thereof. A corporation that takes advantage of this subparagraph shall furnish a copy of the full text of the agreement or other document, on request and without cost, to any shareholder and, unless it is a closely held corporation, on request and at cost, to any other person.

3. The articles may confer upon a shareholder a specifically enforceable right to the declaration and payment of dividends, the redemption of shares or the making of any other form of distribution if the distribution is at the time of enforcement then not prohibited by section 1551(b)(2) (relating to limitation). Such a right shall not arise by implication, but only by either an express reference to this section or another express reference to specific enforceability of a distribution.

(c) Additional restrictions upon exercise of corporate powers.-Additional provisions regulating or restricting the exercise of corporate powers, including provisions requiring the votes of classes or series of shares as conditions to the exercise thereof, may be specified in a bylaw adopted by the shareholders.

(d) Status and rights.-Shares of a business corporation shall be deemed personal property. Except as otherwise provided by the articles or, when so permitted by subsection (c), by one or more bylaws adopted by the shareholders, each share shall be in all respects equal to every other share.

Sec. 1522. Issuance of shares in classes or series; board action.

(a) General rule.-The division of shares into classes and into series within any class, the determination of the designation and the number of shares of any class or series and the determination of the voting rights, preferences, limitations and special rights, if any, of the shares of any class or series of a business corporation may be accomplished by the original articles or by any amendment thereof. The amendment may be made by the board of directors as provided in subsection (b).

(b) Divisions and determinations by the board.-An amendment of articles described in subsection (a) may be made solely by action of the board if the articles authorize the board to make the divisions and determinations. Unless otherwise restricted in the articles, authority granted to the board to determine the number of shares of any class or series shall be deemed to include the power to increase the previously determined number of shares of the class or series to a number not greater than the aggregate number of shares of all classes and series that the corporation is authorized to issue by the articles and to decrease the previously determined number of shares of a class or series to a number not less than that then outstanding. Upon any such decrease under this section, the affected shares shall continue as part of the aggregate number of shares of all classes and series that the corporation is authorized to issue. Unless otherwise restricted in the articles, if no shares of a class or series are outstanding, the board of directors may amend the designations and the voting rights, preferences, limitations and special rights, if any, of the shares of the class or series.

(c) Statement with respect to shares.-Whenever the board acts under subsection (b), it shall adopt a resolution setting forth its actions. Before any business corporation issues any shares of any class or any series of any class with respect to which the board has acted under subsection (b), the corporation shall file in the Department of State a statement with respect to shares executed by the corporation, setting forth:

1. The name of the corporation.

2. The resolution of the board required by this subsection.

3. The aggregate number of shares of the class or series established and designated by:

i. The resolution.

ii. All prior statements, if any, filed under this section or corresponding provisions of prior law with respect thereto.

iii. Any other provision of the resolution.

4. The date of the adoption of the resolution.

5. If the resolution is to be effective on a specified date, the hour, if any, and the month, day and year of the effective date.

(d) Effect of filing statement.-Upon the filing of the statement in the department or upon the effective date specified in the statement, whichever is later, the resolution shall become effective and shall operate as an amendment of the articles, except that neither the filing of the statement nor the integration of the substance of the resolution into the text of the articles by means of a restatement of the articles as permitted by this subpart or otherwise shall prohibit the board of directors from subsequently adopting resolutions authorized by this section.

(e) Termination of proposal.-Prior to the time when a resolution required by subsection (c) becomes effective, the amendment to be effected thereby may be terminated by the board or pursuant to the provi-

sions therefor, if any, set forth in the resolution. If a statement with respect to shares has been filed in the department prior to the termination, a statement under section 1902 (relating to statement of termination) shall be filed in the department.

Sec. 1523. Pricing and issuance of shares.

Except as otherwise restricted in the bylaws, shares of a business corporation may be issued at a price determined by the board of directors, or the board may set a minimum price or establish a formula or method by which the price may be determined.

Sec. 1526. Liability of subscribers and shareholders.

A subscriber to, or holder or owner of, shares of a business corporation shall not be under any liability to the corporation or any creditor thereof with respect to the shares other than the personal obligation of a shareholder who has acquired his shares by subscription to comply with the terms of the subscription.

Sec. 1529. Transfer of securities; restrictions.

(a) General rule.-The transfer of securities of a business corporation may be regulated by any provisions of the bylaws that are not inconsistent with 13 Pa.C.S. Div.8 (relating to investment securities) and other provisions of law.

(b) Transfer restrictions generally.-A restriction on the transfer or registration of transfer of securities of a business corporation may be imposed by the bylaws or by an agreement among any number of security holders or among them and the corporation. A restriction so imposed shall not be binding with respect to securities issued prior to the adoption of the restriction unless the holders of the securities are parties to the agreement or voted in favor of the restriction.

(c) Restrictions specifically authorized.-A restriction on the transfer of securities of a business corporation is permitted by this section if it:

1. obligates the holder of the restricted securities to offer to the corporation or to any other holders of securities of the corporation or to any other person or to any combination of the foregoing a prior opportunity, to be exercised within a reasonable time, to acquire the restricted securities;

2. obligates the corporation or any holder of securities of the corporation or any other person or any combination of the foregoing, to purchase the securities that are the subject of an agreement respecting

the purchase and sale of the restricted securities;

3. requires the corporation or the holders of any class of securities of the corporation to consent to any proposed transfer of the restricted securities or to approve the proposed transferee of the restricted securities; or

4. prohibits the transfer of the restricted securities to designated persons or classes of persons and the designation is not manifestly unreasonable.

(d) Subchapter S restrictions.-Any restriction on the transfer of the shares of a business corporation for the purpose of maintaining its status as an electing small business corporation under Subchapter S of the Internal Revenue Code of 1986 or a comparable provision under state law shall be conclusively presumed to be for a reasonable purpose.

(e) Other restrictions.-Any other lawful restriction on transfer or registration of transfer of securities is permitted by this section.

(f) Notice to transferee.-A written restriction on the transfer or registration of transfer of a share or other security of a business corporation, if permitted by this section and noted conspicuously on the face or back of the security or in the notice provided by section 1528(f) (relating to uncertified shares) or in an equivalent notice with respect to another uncertificated security, may be enforced against the holder of the restricted security or any successor or transferee of the holder, including an executor, administrator, trustee, guardian or other fiduciary entrusted with like responsibility for the person or estate of the holder. Unless noted conspicuously on the security or in the notice provided by section 1528(f) or in an equivalent notice with respect to another uncertificated security, a restriction, even though permitted by this section, is ineffective except against a person with actual knowledge of the restriction.

Sec. 1530. Preemptive rights of shareholders.

(a) General rule.-Except as otherwise provided in the articles, a business corporation may issue shares, option rights or securities having conversion or option rights, or obligations without first offering them to shareholders of any class or classes.

(b) Cross references.-See sections 1525(e) (relating to shares subject to preemptive rights) and 2321(b) (relating to preemptive rights.)

Sec. 1531. Voting powers and other rights of certain security holders and other entities.

The power to vote in respect to the corporate affairs and management of a business corporation and other shareholder rights as may be provided in the articles may be conferred upon:

1. Registered holders of obligations issued or to be issued by the corporation.

2. The United States of America, the Commonwealth, a state, or any political subdivision of any of the foregoing, or any entity prohibited by law from becoming a shareholder of a corporation.

CHAPTER 21. NONSTOCK CORPORATIONS.

Subchapter A. Preliminary Provisions

Sec. 2101. Application and effect of chapter.

(a) General rule.--This chapter shall be applicable to:

1. A business corporation that elects to become a nonstock corporation in the manner provided by this chapter.

2. A domestic corporation for profit subject to Subpart D (relating to cooperative corporations) organized on a nonstock basis.

3. A domestic insurance corporation that is a mutual insurance company.

(b) Application to business corporations generally.-- The existence of a provision of this chapter shall not of itself create any implication that a contrary or different rule of law is or would be applicable to a business corporation that is not a nonstock corporation. This chapter shall not affect any statute or rule of law that is or would be applicable to a business corporation that is not a nonstock corporation.

(c) Laws applicable to nonstock corporations.-- Except as otherwise provided in this chapter, this subpart shall be generally applicable to all nonstock corporations. The specific provisions of this chapter shall control over the general provisions of this subpart. In the case of a nonstock corporation, references in this part to "shares," "shareholder," "share register," "share ledger," "transfer book for shares," "number of shares entitled to vote" or "class of shares" shall mean memberships, member, membership register, membership ledger, membership transfer book, number of votes entitled to be cast or class of members, respectively. Except as otherwise provided in this article, a nonstock corporation may be simultaneously subject to this chapter and one or more other chapters of this article.

Sec. 2102. Formation of nonstock corporations.

(a) General rule.--A nonstock corporation shall be formed in accordance with Article B (relating to domestic business corporations generally) except that its articles shall contain:

1. A heading stating the name of the corporation and that it is a nonstock corporation.

2. The provisions required by section 2103 (relating to contents of articles and other documents of nonstock corporations.)

(b) Initial members.--Upon the filing of articles of a nonstock corporation, the subscribers to the minimum guaranteed capital of the corporation, if any, and the incorporators shall be the initial members of the corporation.

Sec. 2103. Contents of articles and other documents of nonstock corporations.

In lieu of required statements relating to shares or share structure, a nonstock corporation shall set forth in any document permitted or required to be filed under this subpart the fact that the corporation is organized on a nonstock basis. A nonstock corporation may, but need not, have a minimum guaranteed capital which shall be furnished by the subscribers thereto in such proportions as they may agree.

Sec. 2104. Election of an existing business corporation to become a nonstock corporation.

(a) General rule.--Any business corporation may become a nonstock corporation under this chapter by:

1. Adopting a plan of conversion providing for the redemption by the corporation of all of its shares whether or not redeemable by the terms of its articles and adjusting its affairs so as to comply with the requirements of this chapter applicable to nonstock corporations.

2. Filing articles of amendment which shall contain, in addition to the requirements of section 1915 (relating to articles of amendment):

 i. A heading stating the name of the corporation and that it is a nonstock corporation.

 ii. A statement that it elects to become a nonstock corporation.

 iii. A statement that the corporation is organized on a nonstock basis.

 iv. Such other changes, if any, that may be desired in the articles.

(b) Procedure.--The plan of conversion of the corporation into a nonstock corporation (which plan shall include the amendment of the articles required by subsection (a)) shall be adopted in accordance with the requirements of Subchapter B of Chapter 19 (relating to amendment of articles) except that:

1. The holders of shares of every class shall be entitled to vote on the plan regardless of any limitations stated in the articles or bylaws on the voting rights of any class.

2. The plan must be approved by two-thirds of the votes cast by all shares of each class.

3. If any shareholder of a business corporation that adopts a plan of conversion into a nonstock corporation objects to the plan of conversion and complies with the provisions of Subchapter D of Chapter 15 (relating to dissenters rights), the shareholder shall be entitled to the rights and remedies of dissenting shareholders therein provided. There shall be included in, or enclosed with, the notice of the meeting of shareholders called to act upon the plan of conversion a copy or a summary of the plan and a copy of Subchapter D of Chapter 15 and of this subsection.

4. The plan shall not impose any additional liability upon any existing patron of the business of the corporation, whether or not that person becomes a member of the corporation pursuant to the plan, unless the patron expressly assumes such liability.

Sec. 2105. Termination of nonstock corporation status.

(a) General rule.--A nonstock corporation may terminate its status as such and cease to be subject to this chapter by:

1. Adopting a plan of conversion providing for the issue of appropriate shares to its members and adjusting its affairs so as to comply with the requirements of this subpart applicable to business corporations that are not nonstock corporations.

2. Amending its articles to delete therefrom the additional provisions required or permitted by sections 2102(a)(1) (relating to formation of nonstock corporations) and 2103 (relating to contents of articles and other documents of nonstock corporations) to be stated in the articles of a nonstock corporation. The plan of conversion (which plan shall include the amendment of the articles required by this section) shall be adopted in accordance with Subchapter B of

Chapter 19 (relating to amendment of articles) except that:

i. The members of every class shall be entitled to vote on the plan regardless of any limitations stated in the articles or bylaws, or in a document evidencing membership, on the voting rights of any class.

ii. The plan must be approved by a majority of the votes cast by the members of each class.

(b) Increased vote requirements.--The bylaws of a nonstock corporation adopted by the members may provide that on any amendment to terminate its status as a nonstock corporation, a vote greater than that specified in subsection (a) shall be required. If the bylaws contain such a provision, that provision shall not be amended, repealed or modified by any vote less than that required to terminate the status of the corporation as a nonstock corporation.

(c) Mutual insurance companies.--With respect to the termination of the status of a mutual insurance company as a nonstock corporation, see section 103 (relating to subordination of title to regulatory laws) and the act of December 10, 1970 (P.L. 884, No. 279), referred to as the Mutual Insurance Company Conversion Law.

Subchapter B. Powers, Duties And Safeguards

Sec. 2121. Corporate name of nonstock corporations.

(a) General rule.--The corporate name of a nonstock corporation may contain the word "mutual."

Sec. 2122. Classes of membership.

The bylaws of a nonstock corporation adopted by the members may vest in the board of directors the power to establish classes of membership and to fix the several rights and liabilities thereof.

Sec. 2123. Evidence of membership; liability of members.

(a) General rule.--Every member of record of a nonstock corporation shall be entitled to a written document evidencing his membership in the corporation. The document shall state:

1. That the corporation is a nonstock corporation incorporated under the laws of this Commonwealth, unless the name of the corporation contains the word "mutual."

2. The name of the person to whom issued.

3. The class of membership, if any, held by the member.

(b) Notice of variation in rights.--If the membership of the corporation is divided into classes, the document shall set forth (or shall state that the corporation will furnish to any member, upon request and without charge) a full or summary statement of the special rights and without charge) a full or summary statement of the special rights and liabilities of membership between classes. If a membership is not fully paid or if the member is otherwise liable to assessment, the document evidencing the membership shall so state.

(c) Liability.--A subscriber to the minimum guaranteed capital of or member of a nonstock corporation shall not be under any liability to the corporation or any creditor thereof other than the obligations of complying with the terms of the subscription to the minimum guaranteed capital, if any, and with the terms of the document evidencing his membership. Otherwise, the members of a nonstock corporation shall not be personally liable for the debts, liabilities, or obligations of the corporation.

(d) Dissenters rights.--The document evidencing membership shall constitute a share certificate for the purposes of Subchapter D of Chapter 15 (relating to dissenters rights).

Sec. 2124. Voting rights of members.

Except as otherwise provided in a bylaw adopted by the members or in a written document evidencing membership, every member of record of a nonstock corporation shall have the right, at every meeting of members, to one vote.

Sec. 2125. Inapplicability of certain provisions to nonstock corporations.

(a) Share structure.--The provisions of Subchapter B of Chapter 15 (relating to shares and other securities) shall not be applicable to a nonstock corporation. A nonstock corporation shall not create or issue shares.

(b) Corporate finance.--A patronage rebate or dividend that is, or is equivalent to, a reduction in the charge made by a nonstock corporation to a member for goods or services shall not constitute a dividend or distribution within the meaning of section 1551 (relating to distributions to shareholders).

Sec. 2126. Dissolution of nonstock corporations.

If at the time of dissolution of a nonstock corporation the articles, bylaws and documents evidencing membership fail to define the respective rights and preferences of the members upon dissolution, the surplus of cash or property remaining after discharging all liabilities of the corporation shall be paid to or distributed among the members according to such a plan of distribution as the members may adopt. The plan shall be adopted in accordance with Subchapter F of Chapter 19 (relating to voluntary dissolution and winding up) except that:

1. The members of every class shall be entitled to vote on the plan regardless of any limitations stated in the articles or bylaws, or in a document evidencing membership, on the voting rights of any class.

2. The plan must be approved by a majority of the votes cast by the members of each class.

CHAPTER 29. PROFESSIONAL CORPORATIONS.

Subchapter A. Preliminary Provisions

Sec. 2901. Application and effect of chapter.

(a) General rule.-This chapter shall be applicable to a business corporation, other than a management corporation, that:

1. on the effective date of this chapter was subject to the act of July 9, 1970 (P.L. 461, No. 160), known as the Professional Corporation Law; or

2. elects to become a professional corporation in the manner provided by this chapter.

(b) Application to business corporations generally.-The existence of a provision of this chapter shall not of itself create any implication that a contrary or different rule of law is or would be applicable to a business corporation that is not a professional corporation, and this chapter shall not affect any statute or rule of law that is or would be applicable to a business corporation that is not a professional corporation. This chapter shall not alter or affect any right or privilege existing under any statute or general rule heretofore or hereafter enacted by the General Assembly or (with respect to attorneys at law), prescribed by the Supreme Court of Pennsylvania:

1. not prohibiting; or

2. in terms permitting;

performance of professional services in corporate form by a corporation that is not a professional corporation.

(c) Laws applicable to professional corporations.-Except as otherwise provided in this chapter, this subpart shall be generally applicable to all professional corporations. The specific provisions of this chapter shall control over the general provisions of this subpart. Except as otherwise provided in this article, a professional corporation may be simultaneously subject to this chapter and one or more other chapters of this article.

Sec. 2903. Formation of professional corporations.

(a) General rule.-A professional corporation shall be formed in accordance with Article B (relating to domestic business corporations generally) except that its articles shall contain a heading stating the name of the corporation and that it is a professional corporation.

(b) Legislative intent.-It is the intent of the General Assembly to authorize by this chapter licensed persons to render professional services by means of a professional corporation in all cases.

(c) Single-purpose corporations.-Except as provided in subsection (d), a professional corporation may be incorporated only for the purpose of rendering one specific kind of professional service.

(d) Multiple-purpose corporations.-

1. A professional corporation may be incorporated to render two or more specific kinds of professional services to the extent that:

 i. the several shareholders of the professional corporation, if organized as a partnership, could conduct a combined practice of such specific kinds of professional services; or

 ii. the court, department, board, commission or other government unit regulating each professional involved in the professional corporation has by rule or regulation applicable to professional corporations expressly authorized the combined practice of the profession with each other profession involved in the corporation.

Except as otherwise provided by statute, the government unit may promulgate regulations authorizing combined practice to the extent consistent with the public interest or required by the public health or welfare.

2. The provisions of paragraph (1) shall not create any vested rights. If by reason of a change in law, rule or regulation the right to practice professions in any particular combination is terminated, all existing professional corporations rendering a combination of professional services shall promptly reduce the specific kinds of professional services rendered by the corporation or shall otherwise reconstitute them-

selves so as to comply with the currently applicable restrictions applicable to all professions involved.

Sec. 2904. Election of an existing business corporation to become a professional corporation.
(a) General rule.-A business corporation may become a professional corporation under this chapter by filing articles of amendment which shall contain, in addition to the requirements of section 1915 (relating to articles of amendment):
1. A heading stating the name of the corporation and that it is a professional corporation.
2. A statement that it elects to become a professional corporation.
3. Such other changes, if any, that may be desired in the articles, including any changes necessary to conform to section 2903(c) and (d) (relating to formation of professional corporations).
(b) Procedure.-The amendment shall be adopted in accordance with the requirements of Subchapter B of Chapter 19 (relating to amendment of articles) except that the amendment must be approved by unanimous consent of all shareholders of the corporation regardless of any limitations on voting rights stated in the articles or bylaws.

Sec. 2905. Election of professional associations to become professional corporations.
(a) General rule.-This chapter applies to every professional association subject to Chapter 93 (relating to professional associations) that elects to accept the provisions of this chapter in the manner set forth in subsection (b).
(b) Procedure for election.-A professional association may elect to accept this chapter by filing in the Department of State a statement of election of professional corporation status which shall be executed by all of the associates of the professional association and shall set forth:
1. The name of the professional association and, subject to section 109 (relating to name of commercial registered office provider in lieu of registered address), the address, including street and number, if any, of its proposed registered office.
2. The name of the county in the office of the prothonotary of which the initial articles of association of the association were filed.
3. A statement that the associates of the professional association have elected at accept the provisions of

this chapter for the government and regulation of the affairs of the association.
(c) Date of incorporation.-This chapter shall become applicable to the professional association, and it shall be deemed incorporated, on the date the statement of election is filed in the department.

Sec. 2906. Termination of professional corporation status.
A professional corporation may terminate its status as such and cease to be subject to this chapter by amending its articles to delete therefrom the additional provisions required by section 2903(a) (relating to formation of professional corporations). The amendment shall be adopted in accordance with Subchapter B of Chapter 19 (relating to amendment of articles).
Subchapter B. Powers, Duties and Safeguards

Sec. 2921. Corporate name.
(a) General rule.-A professional corporation may adopt any name that is not prohibited by law or the ethics of the profession in which the corporation is engaged or by a rule or regulation of the court, department, board, commission or other government unit regulating the profession.
(b) Additional names permitted.-The provisions of section 1303(a) (relating to corporate name) shall not prohibit the use of a name of a professional corporation if the name contains and is restricted to the name or the last name of one or more of the present, prospective or former shareholders or of individual name or names appeared in the name of the predecessor. The name may also contain:
1. the word "and" or any symbol or substitute therefor;
2. the word "associates";
3. the term "P.C."; or
4. any or all of the words or terms in paragraphs (1), (2) and (3).

Sec. 2922. Stated purposes.
(a) General rule.-A professional corporation shall not engage in any business other than the rendering of the professional service or services for which it was specifically incorporated except that a professional corporation may own real and personal property necessary for, or appropriate or desirable in, the fulfillment or rendering of its specific professional service or services and it may invest its funds in real

estate, mortgages, stocks, bonds or any other type of investment.

(b) Additional powers.-A professional corporation may be a partner in or a shareholder of a partnership or corporation engaged in the business of rendering the professional service or services for which the professional corporation was incorporated.

Sec. 2924. Rendering professional services.

(a) General rule.-A professional corporation may lawfully render professional services only through officers, employees or agents who are licensed persons. The corporation may employ persons not so licensed but those persons shall not render any professional services rendered or to be rendered by it.

(b) Supporting staff.-This section shall not be interpreted to preclude the use of clerks, secretaries, nurses, administrators, bookkeepers, technicians and other assistants or paraprofessionals who are not usually and ordinarily considered by law, custom and practice to be rendering the professional service or services for which the professional corporation was incorporated nor to preclude the use of any other person who performs all his employment under the direct supervision and control of a licensed person. A person shall not, under the guise of employment, render professional services unless duly licensed or admitted to practice as required by law.

(c) Charges.-Notwithstanding any other provision of law, a professional corporation may charge for the professional services of its officers, employees and agents, may collect those charges and may compensate those who render the professional services.

APPENDIX B
BLANK FORMS

The following forms may be photocopied or removed from this book and used immediately. They are also available online from either the Pennsylvania Department of State, Corporations Bureau at **www.dos.state.pa.us/corps** or from the Internal Revenue Service at **www.irs.gov**.

Table of Forms

**PENNSYLVANIA DEPARTMENT OF STATE
CORPORATION BUREAU**

____ Consent to Appropriation of Name
(19 Pa.Code § 17.2)
____ Consent to Use of Similar Name
(19 Pa.Code § 17.3)

Pursuant to 19 Pa. Code § 17.2 (relating to appropriation of the name of a senior corporation) and § 17.3 (relating to use of a similar name) the undersigned association, desiring to consent to the appropriation/use of similar name of its name by another association, hereby certifies that:

1. The name of the association executing this Consent of Name is:

2. The (a) address of this corporation's current registered office in this Commonwealth or (b) name of its commercial registered office provider and the county of venue is (the Department is hereby authorized to correct the following information to conform to the records of the Department):
(a) Number and Street   City   State   Zip   County

(b) Name of Commercial Registered Office Provider   County
c/o

3. The date of its incorporation or other organization is:

4. The statute under which it was incorporated or otherwise organized is:

5. The association(s) entitled to the benefit of this Consent of Name is(are):

6. *If Consent to Appropriation of Name, the association is about to (check one)*:

____ Change its name ____ Cease to do business ____ Withdrawal from doing business in PA ____ Being wound up

7. *If Consent to Use of Similar Name, check box*:
____ Indicates that the association executing this Consent to Use of Similar Name is the parent or prime affiliate of a group of associations using the same name with geographic or other designations, and that such association is authorized to and does hereby act on behalf of all such affiliated associations, including the following (see 19 Pa. Code § 17.3(c)(6)):

IN TESTIMONY WHEREOF, the undersigned association has caused this consent to be signed by a duly authorized officer thereof this
_____day of _____, _____.

_____
Signature
_____
Title

DSCB:17.2.3

Department of State
Corporation Bureau
P.O. Box 8722
Harrisburg, PA 17105-8722
(717) 787-1057
web site: www.dos.state.pa.us/corp.htm

Instructions for Completion of Form:

A. This form will be deemed to be incorporated by reference into the filing to which it relates, e.g., articles of incorporation, articles of amendment effecting a change of name, articles of merger effecting a change of name, articles of division, application for a certificate of authority, application for an amended certificate of authority, certificate of limited partnership, amended certificate of limited partnership effecting a change of name, documents merging a partnership or other association effecting a change of name, instrument with respect to a business trust, amended instrument with respect to a business trust effecting a change of name, etc. Therefore an executed copy (which may be a photocopy) of this form should be attached to each copy of the filing to which it relates which is submitted to the Department, and no separate docketing statement should be submitted with respect to this form.

B. Under 15 Pa.C.S. § 135(c) (relating to addresses) an actual street or rural route box number must be used as an address, and the Department of State is required to refuse to receive or file any document that sets forth only a post office box address.

PENNSYLVANIA DEPARTMENT OF STATE
CORPORATION BUREAU

Entity Number

Application for Registration of Fictitious Name
54 Pa.C.S. § 311

Name _____

Address _____

City _____ State _____ Zip Code _____

Document will be returned to the name and address you enter to the left.
⇐

Fee: $52

Filed in the Department of State on _____

_____
Secretary of the Commonwealth

In compliance with the requirements of 54 Pa.C.S. § 311 (relating to registration), the undersigned entity(ies) desiring to register a fictitious name under 54 Pa.C.S. Ch. 3 (relating to fictitious names), hereby state(s) that:

1. The fictitious name is:

_____

2. A brief statement of the character or nature of the business or other activity to be carried on under or through the fictitious name is:

_____

3. The address, including number and street, if any, of the principal place of business (P.O. Box alone is **not** acceptable):

_____
Number and street   City   State   Zip   County

4. The name and address, including number and street, if any, of each individual interested in the business is:
Name   Number and Street   City   State   Zip

_____

_____

_____

_____

5. Each entity, other than an individual, interested in such business is (are):

_____
Name   Form of Organization   Organizing Jurisdiction

_____
Principal Office Address

_____
PA Registered Office, if any

_____
Name   Form of Organization   Organizing Jurisdiction

_____
Principal Office Address

_____
PA Registered Office, if any

6. The applicant is familiar with the provisions of 54 Pa.C.S. § 332 (relating to effect of registration) and understands that filing under the Fictitious Names Act does not create any exclusive or other right in the fictitious name.

7. Optional): The name(s) of the agent(s), if any, any one of whom is authorized to execute amendments to, withdrawals from or cancellation of this registration in behalf of all then existing parties to the registration, is (are):

_____

IN TESTIMONY WHEREOF, the undersigned have caused this Application for Registration of Fictitious Name to be executed this

_____ day of _____,_____.

_____   _____
Individual Signature   Individual Signature

_____   _____
Individual Signature   Individual Signature

_____   _____
Entity Name   Entity Name

_____   _____
Signature   Signature

_____   _____
Title   Title

Department of State
Corporation Bureau
P.O. Box 8722
Harrisburg, PA 17105-8722
(717) 787-1057
Web site: www.dos.state.pa.us/corp.htm

Instructions for Completion of Form:

A. Typewritten is preferred. If not, the form shall be completed in black or blue-black ink in order to permit reproduction. The filing fee for this form is $52 made payable to the Department of State.

B. Under 15 Pa.C.S. § 135(c) (relating to addresses) an actual street or rural route box number must be used as an address, and the Department of State is required to refuse to receive or file any document that sets forth only a post office box address.

C. The following, in addition to the filing fee, shall accompany this form:

   (1) Any necessary copies of form DSCB:17.2.3 (Consent to Appropriation or Use of Similar Name).

   (2) An necessary governmental approvals.

D. For general instructions relating to fictitious name registration see 19 Pa. Code Subch. 17C (relating to fictitious names). These instructions relate to such matters as voluntary and mandatory registration, general restrictions on name availability, use of corporate designators, agent for effecting amendments, etc., execution, official advertising when an individual is a party to the registration, and effect of registration and non-registration.

E. The name of a commercial registered office provider may not be used in Paragraph 3 in lieu of an address.

F. Insert in Paragraph 5 for each entity which is not an individual the following information: (i) the name of the entity and a statement of its form of organization, e.g., corporation, general partnership, limited partnership, business trust, (ii) the name of the jurisdiction under the laws of which it is organized, (iii) the address, including street and number, if any, of its principal office under the laws of its domiciliary jurisdiction and (iv) the address, including street and number, if any, of its registered office, if any, in this Commonwealth. If any of the entities has an association which has designated the name of a commercial registered office provider in lieu of a registered office address as permitted by 15 Pa.C.S. § 109, the name of the provider and the venue county should be inserted in the last column.

G. Every individual whose name appears in Paragraph 4 of the form **must sign** the form exactly as the name is set forth in Paragraph 4. The name of every other entity listed in Paragraph 5 shall be signed on its behalf by an officer, trustee or other authorized person. See 19 Pa. Code § 13.8(b) (relating to execution), which permits execution pursuant to power of attorney. A copy of the underlying power of attorney or other authorization should not be submitted to, and will not be received by or filed in, the Department.

H. If an individual is a party to the registration, the parties are required by 54 Pa.C.S. § 311(g) to advertise their intention to file or the filing of an application for registration of fictitious name. Proofs of publication of such advertising should not be submitted to the Department, and will not be received by or filed in the Department, but should be kept with the permanent records of the business.

DSCB: 54-311

I. This form and all accompanying documents shall be mailed to the address stated above.

J. To receive confirmation of the file date prior to receiving the microfilmed original, send either a self-addressed, stamped postcard with the filing information noted or a self-addressed, stamped envelope with a copy of the filing document.

PENNSYLVANIA DEPARTMENT OF STATE
CORPORATION BUREAU

Articles of Incorporation-For Profit
(15 Pa.C.S.)

Entity Number	____ Business-stock (§ 1306)	____ Management (§ 2703)
	____ Business-nonstock (§ 2102)	____ Professional (§ 2903)
	____ Business-statutory close (§ 2303)	____ Insurance (§ 3101)
	____ Cooperative (§ 7102)	

Name

Address

City   State   Zip Code

Document will be returned to the name and address you enter to the left.
⇐

Fee: $100

Filed in the Department of State on _____

Secretary of the Commonwealth

In compliance with the requirements of the applicable provisions (relating to corporations and unincorporated associations), the undersigned, desiring to incorporate a corporation for profit, hereby states that:

1. The name of the corporation *(corporate designator required, i.e., "corporation"," incorporated", "limited" "company" or any abbreviation. "Professional corporation" or "P.C")*:

2. The (a) address of this corporation's current registered office in this Commonwealth *(post office box, alone, is not acceptable)* or (b) name of its commercial registered office provider and the county of venue is:

(a) Number and Street   City   State   Zip   County

(b) Name of Commercial Registered Office Provider   County

c/o:

3. The corporation is incorporated under the provisions of the Business Corporation Law of 1988.

4. The aggregate number of shares authorized:

DSCB:15-1306,2102/2303/2702/2903/3101/7102A-2

5. The name and address, including number and street, if any, of each incorporator *(all incorporators must sign below)*:

Name   Address

_____

_____

6. The specified effective date, if any:_____.
                          month/day/year   hour, if any

7. Additional provisions of the articles, if any, attach an 8½ by 11 sheet.

8. *Statutory close corporation only*: Neither the corporation nor any shareholder shall make an offering of any of its shares of any class that would constitute a "public offering" within the meaning of the Securities Act of 1933 (15 U.S.C. 77a et seq.)

9. *Cooperative corporations only: Complete and strike out inapplicable term:*

The common bond of membership among its members/shareholders is:_____.

IN TESTIMONY WHEREOF, the incorporator(s) has/have signed these Articles of Incorporation this

_____ day of _____,_____.

_____
                    Signature

_____
                    Signature

DSCB:15-1306/2102/2303/2702/2903/3101/7102A-3

Department of State
Corporation Bureau
P.O. Box 8722
Harrisburg, PA 17105-8722
(717) 787-1057
Web site: www.dos.state.pa.us/corp.htm

Instructions for Completion of Form:

A. Typewritten is preferred. If not, the form shall be completed in black or blue-black ink in order to permit reproduction. The filing fee for this form is $100 made payable to the Department of State.

B. Under 15 Pa.C.S. § 135(c) (relating to addresses) an actual street or rural route box number must be used as an address, and the Department of State is required to refuse to receive or file any document that sets forth only a post office box address.

C. The following, in addition to the filing fee, shall accompany this form:

   (1) One copy of a completed form DSCB:15-134A (Docketing Statement).
   (2) Any necessary copies of form DSCB:17.2.3 (Consent to Appropriation or Use of Similar Name).
   (3) Any necessary governmental approvals.

D. For general instructions relating to the incorporation of business corporations see 19 Pa. Code Ch. 23 (relating to business corporations generally). These instructions relate to such matters as corporate name, stated purposes, term of existence, nonstock status, authorized share structure and related authority of the board of directors, inclusion of names of first directors in the Articles of Incorporation, optional provisions on cumulative voting for election of directors, etc.

E. For required provisions in the Articles of a management corporation, see 15 Pa.C.S. § 2703 (relating to additional contents of articles of management corporations).

F. For restrictions on the stated purposes of professional corporations, see 15 Pa.C.S. § 2903 (relating to formation of professional corporations).

G. Articles for a nonprofit cooperative corporation should be filed on Form DSCB:15-5306/7102B (Articles of Incorporation Nonprofit).

H. One or more corporations or natural persons of full age may incorporate a business corporation.

I. 15 Pa.C.S. § 1307 (relating to advertisement) requires that the incorporators shall advertise their intention to file or the corporation shall advertise the filing of articles of incorporation. Proofs of publication of such advertising should not be submitted to, and will not be received by or filed in, the Department, but should be filed with the minutes of the corporation.

J. This form and all accompanying documents shall be mailed to the address stated above.

K. To receive confirmation of the file date prior to receiving the microfilmed original, send either a self-addressed, stamped postcard with the filing information noted or a self-addressed, stamped envelope with a copy of the filing document.

Docketing Statement DSCB:15-134A (Rev 2001)
Departments of State and Revenue

One (1) copy required

BUREAU USE ONLY:
Dept. of State Entity # _____
Dept. of Rev. Box # _____
Filing Period _____ Date 3 4 5 _____
SIC/NAICS _____ Report Code _____

Check proper box:

Pennsylvania Entities

____ business stock
____ business non-stock
____ professional
____ nonprofit stock
____ nonprofit non-stock
____ statutory close
____ management
____ cooperative
____ insurance
____ limited liability company
____ restricted professional
   limited liability company
____ business trust

Foreign Entities
State/Country _____ Date_____

____ business
____ nonprofit
____ limited liability company
____ restricted professional
   limited liability company
____ business trust

Other

____ domestication
____ division
____ consolidation

1. Entity Name:
   _____

2. Individual name and mailing address responsible for initial tax reports:
   _____
   Name   Number and street   City   State   Zip

3. Description of business activity:
   _____

4. Specified effective date, if any:
   _____
   month/day/year   hour, if any

5. EIN (Employee Identification Number), if any:
   _____

6. Fiscal Year End:
   _____

7. Fictitious Name (only if foreign corporation is transacting business in PA under a fictitious name):
   _____

Form **2553**
(Rev. December 2002)

Department of the Treasury
Internal Revenue Service

Election by a Small Business Corporation

(Under section 1362 of the Internal Revenue Code)

▶ See Parts II and III on back and the separate instructions.
▶ **The corporation may either send or fax this form to the IRS. See page 2 of the instructions.**

OMB No. 1545-0146

Notes: 1. *Do not file Form 1120S,* U.S. Income Tax Return for an S Corporation, for any tax year before the year the election takes effect.
2. *This election to be an S corporation can be accepted only if all the tests are met under **Who May Elect** on page 1 of the instructions; all shareholders have signed the consent statement; and the exact name and address of the corporation and other required form information are provided.*
3. *If the corporation was in existence before the effective date of this election, see **Taxes an S Corporation May Owe** on page 1 of the instructions.*

Part I	Election Information

Please Type or Print

Name of corporation (see instructions)	**A** Employer identification number
Number, street, and room or suite no. (If a P.O. box, see instructions.)	**B** Date incorporated
City or town, state, and ZIP code	**C** State of incorporation

D Check the applicable box(es) if the corporation, after applying for the EIN shown in **A** above, changed its name ☐ or address ☐

E Election is to be effective for tax year beginning (month, day, year) . . . . ▶   /   /

F Name and title of officer or legal representative who the IRS may call for more information	**G** Telephone number of officer or legal representative ( )

H If this election takes effect for the first tax year the corporation exists, enter month, day, and year of the **earliest** of the following: (1) date the corporation first had shareholders, (2) date the corporation first had assets, or (3) date the corporation began doing business . . . . ▶   /   /

I Selected tax year: Annual return will be filed for tax year ending (month and day) ▶ ------------------------------------

If the tax year ends on any date other than December 31, except for a 52–53-week tax year ending with reference to the month of December, you **must** complete Part II on the back. If the date you enter is the ending date of a 52–53-week tax year, write "52–53-week year" to the right of the date.

J Name and address of each shareholder; shareholder's spouse having a community property interest in the corporation's stock; and each tenant in common, joint tenant, and tenant by the entirety. (A husband and wife (and their estates) are counted as one shareholder in determining the number of shareholders without regard to the manner in which the stock is owned.)	**K** Shareholders' Consent Statement. Under penalties of perjury, we declare that we consent to the election of the above-named corporation to be an S corporation under section 1362(a) and that we have examined this consent statement, including accompanying schedules and statements, and to the best of our knowledge and belief, it is true, correct, and complete. We understand our consent is binding and may not be withdrawn after the corporation has made a valid election. (Shareholders sign and date below.)		**L** Stock owned		**M** Social security number or employer identification number (see instructions)	**N** Share- holder's tax year ends (month and day)
	Signature	Date	Number of shares	Dates acquired		

Under penalties of perjury, I declare that I have examined this election, including accompanying schedules and statements, and to the best of my knowledge and belief, it is true, correct, and complete.

Signature of officer ▶   Title ▶   Date ▶

For Paperwork Reduction Act Notice, see page 4 of the instructions.   Cat. No. 18629R   Form **2553** (Rev. 12-2002)

Part II   Selection of Fiscal Tax Year (All corporations using this part must complete item O and item P, Q, or R.)

O Check the applicable box to indicate whether the corporation is:

1. ☐ A new corporation adopting the tax year entered in item I, Part I.

2. ☐ An existing corporation retaining the tax year entered in item I, Part I.

3. ☐ An existing corporation changing to the tax year entered in item I, Part I.

P Complete item P if the corporation is using the automatic approval provisions of Rev. Proc. 2002-38, 2002-22 I.R.B. 1037, to request **(1)** a natural business year (as defined in section 5.05 of Rev. Proc. 2002-38) or **(2)** a year that satisfies the ownership tax year test (as defined in section 5.06 of Rev. Proc. 2002-38). Check the applicable box below to indicate the representation statement the corporation is making.

1. Natural Business Year ▶ ☐ I represent that the corporation is adopting, retaining, or changing to a tax year that qualifies as its natural business year as defined in section 5.05 of Rev. Proc. 2002-38 and has attached a statement verifying that it satisfies the 25% gross receipts test (see instructions for content of statement). I also represent that the corporation is not precluded by section 4.02 of Rev. Proc. 2002-38 from obtaining automatic approval of such adoption, retention, or change in tax year.

2. Ownership Tax Year ▶ ☐ I represent that shareholders (as described in section 5.06 of Rev. Proc. 2002-38) holding more than half of the shares of the stock (as of the first day of the tax year to which the request relates) of the corporation have the same tax year or are concurrently changing to the tax year that the corporation adopts, retains, or changes to per item I, Part I, and that such tax year satisfies the requirement of section 4.01(3) of Rev. Proc. 2002-38. I also represent that the corporation is not precluded by section 4.02 of Rev. Proc. 2002-38 from obtaining automatic approval of such adoption, retention, or change in tax year.

Note: *If you do not use item P and the corporation wants a fiscal tax year, complete either item Q or R below. Item Q is used to request a fiscal tax year based on a business purpose and to make a back-up section 444 election. Item R is used to make a regular section 444 election.*

Q Business Purpose—To request a fiscal tax year based on a business purpose, you must check box Q1. See instructions for details including payment of a user fee. You may also check box Q2 and/or box Q3.

1. Check here ▶ ☐ if the fiscal year entered in item I, Part I, is requested under the prior approval provisions of Rev. Proc. 2002-39, 2002-22 I.R.B. 1046. Attach to Form 2553 a statement describing the relevant facts and circumstances and, if applicable, the gross receipts from sales and services necessary to establish a business purpose. See the instructions for details regarding the gross receipts from sales and services. If the IRS proposes to disapprove the requested fiscal year, do you want a conference with the IRS National Office?
☐ Yes   ☐ No

2. Check here ▶ ☐ to show that the corporation intends to make a back-up section 444 election in the event the corporation's business purpose request is not approved by the IRS. (See instructions for more information.)

3. Check here ▶ ☐ to show that the corporation agrees to adopt or change to a tax year ending December 31 if necessary for the IRS to accept this election for S corporation status in the event (1) the corporation's business purpose request is not approved and the corporation makes a back-up section 444 election, but is ultimately not qualified to make a section 444 election, or (2) the corporation's business purpose request is not approved and the corporation did not make a back-up section 444 election.

R Section 444 Election—To make a section 444 election, you must check box R1 and you may also check box R2.

1. Check here ▶ ☐ to show the corporation will make, if qualified, a section 444 election to have the fiscal tax year shown in item I, Part I. To make the election, you must complete **Form 8716,** Election To Have a Tax Year Other Than a Required Tax Year, and either attach it to Form 2553 or file it separately.

2. Check here ▶ ☐ to show that the corporation agrees to adopt or change to a tax year ending December 31 if necessary for the IRS to accept this election for S corporation status in the event the corporation is ultimately not qualified to make a section 444 election.

Part III   Qualified Subchapter S Trust (QSST) Election Under Section 1361(d)(2)*

Income beneficiary's name and address	Social security number
Trust's name and address	Employer identification number

Date on which stock of the corporation was transferred to the trust (month, day, year) . . . .▶   /   /

In order for the trust named above to be a QSST and thus a qualifying shareholder of the S corporation for which this Form 2553 is filed, I hereby make the election under section 1361(d)(2). Under penalties of perjury, I certify that the trust meets the definitional requirements of section 1361(d)(3) and that all other information provided in Part III is true, correct, and complete.

_____   _____
Signature of income beneficiary or signature and title of legal representative or other qualified person making the election   Date

*Use Part III to make the QSST election only if stock of the corporation has been transferred to the trust on or before the date on which the corporation makes its election to be an S corporation. The QSST election must be made and filed separately if stock of the corporation is transferred to the trust after the date on which the corporation makes the S election.

Instructions for Form 2553

Department of the Treasury
Internal Revenue Service

(Rev. December 2002)

Election by a Small Business Corporation

Section references are to the Internal Revenue Code unless otherwise noted.

General Instructions

Purpose

To elect to be an S corporation, a corporation must file Form 2553. The election permits the income of the S corporation to be taxed to the shareholders of the corporation rather than to the corporation itself, except as noted below under **Taxes an S Corporation May Owe.**

Who May Elect

A corporation may elect to be an S corporation only if it meets all of the following tests:

1. It is a domestic corporation.

Note: *A limited liability company (LLC)* **must** *file* **Form 8832**, *Entity Classification Election, to elect to be treated as an association taxable as a corporation in order to elect to be an S corporation.*

2. It has no more than 75 shareholders. A husband and wife (and their estates) are treated as one shareholder for this requirement. All other persons are treated as separate shareholders.

3. Its only shareholders are individuals, estates, exempt organizations described in section 401(a) or 501(c)(3), or certain trusts described in section 1361(c)(2)(A). See the instructions for Part III regarding qualified subchapter S trusts (QSSTs).

A trustee of a trust wanting to make an election under section 1361(e)(3) to be an electing small business trust (ESBT) should see Notice 97-12, 1997-1 C.B. 385. However, in general, for tax years beginning after May 13, 2002, Notice 97-12 is superseded by Regulations section 1.1361-1(c)(1). Also see Rev. Proc. 98-23, 1998-1 C.B. 662, for guidance on how to convert a QSST to an ESBT. However, in general, for tax years beginning after May 13, 2002, Rev. Proc. 98-23 is superseded by Regulations section 1.1361-1(j)(12). If there was an inadvertent failure to timely file an ESBT election, see the relief provisions under Rev. Proc. 98-55, 1998-2 C.B. 643.

4. It has no nonresident alien shareholders.

5. It has only one class of stock (disregarding differences in voting rights). Generally, a corporation is treated as having only one class of stock if all outstanding shares of the corporation's stock confer identical rights to distribution and liquidation proceeds. See Regulations section 1.1361-1(l) for details.

6. It is not one of the following ineligible corporations:

a. A bank or thrift institution that uses the reserve method of accounting for bad debts under section 585,

b. An insurance company subject to tax under the rules of subchapter L of the Code,

c. A corporation that has elected to be treated as a possessions corporation under section 936, or

d. A domestic international sales corporation (DISC) or former DISC.

7. It has a permitted tax year as required by section 1378 or makes a section 444 election to have a tax year other than a permitted tax year. Section 1378 defines a permitted tax year as a tax year ending December 31, or any other tax year for which the corporation establishes a business purpose to the satisfaction of the IRS. See Part II for details on requesting a fiscal tax year based on a business purpose or on making a section 444 election.

8. Each shareholder consents as explained in the instructions for column K.

See sections 1361, 1362, and 1378 for additional information on the above tests.

A parent S corporation can elect to treat an eligible wholly-owned subsidiary as a qualified subchapter S subsidiary (QSub). If the election is made, the assets, liabilities, and items of income, deduction, and credit of the QSub are treated as those of the parent. To make the election, get **Form 8869,** Qualified Subchapter S Subsidiary Election. If the QSub election was not timely filed, the corporation may be entitled to relief under Rev. Proc. 98-55.

Taxes an S Corporation May Owe

An S corporation may owe income tax in the following instances:

1. If, at the end of any tax year, the corporation had accumulated earnings and profits, and its passive investment income under section 1362(d)(3) is more than 25% of its gross receipts, the corporation may owe tax on its excess net passive income.

2. A corporation with net recognized built-in gain (as defined in section 1374(d)(2)) may owe tax on its built-in gains.

3. A corporation that claimed investment credit before its first year as an S corporation will be liable for any investment credit recapture tax.

4. A corporation that used the LIFO inventory method for the year immediately preceding its first year as an S corporation may owe an additional tax due to LIFO recapture. The tax is paid in four equal installments, the first of which must be paid by the due date (not including extensions) of the corporation's income tax return for its last tax year as a C corporation.

For more details on these taxes, see the Instructions for Form 1120S.

Where To File

Send the original election (no photocopies) or fax it to the Internal Revenue Service Center listed below. If the corporation files this election by fax, keep the original Form 2553 with the corporation's permanent records.

If the corporation's principal business, office, or agency is located in ▼	Use the following Internal Revenue Service Center address or fax number ▼
Connecticut, Delaware, District of Columbia, Illinois, Indiana, Kentucky, Maine, Maryland, Massachusetts, Michigan, New Hampshire, New Jersey, New York, North Carolina, Ohio, Pennsylvania, Rhode Island, South Carolina, Vermont, Virginia, West Virginia, Wisconsin	Cincinnati, OH 45999 (859) 669-5748
Alabama, Alaska, Arizona, Arkansas, California, Colorado, Florida, Georgia, Hawaii, Idaho, Iowa, Kansas, Louisiana, Minnesota, Mississippi, Missouri, Montana, Nebraska, Nevada, New Mexico, North Dakota, Oklahoma, Oregon, South Dakota, Tennessee, Texas, Utah, Washington, Wyoming	Ogden, UT 84201 (801) 620-7116

When To Make the Election

Complete and file Form 2553 **(a)** at any time before the 16th day of the 3rd month of the tax year, if filed during the tax year the election is to take effect, or **(b)** at any time during the preceding tax year. An election made no later than 2 months and 15 days after the beginning of a tax year that is less than 2½ months long is treated as timely made for that tax year. **An election made after the 15th day of the 3rd month but before the end of the tax year is effective for the next year.** For example, if a calendar tax year corporation makes the election in April 2002, it is effective for the corporation's 2003 calendar tax year.

However, an election made after the due date will be accepted as timely filed if the corporation can show that the failure to file on time was due to reasonable cause. To request relief for a late election, the corporation generally must request a private letter ruling and pay a user fee in accordance with Rev. Proc. 2002-1, 2002-1 I.R.B. 1 (or its successor). But if the election is filed within 12 months of its due date and the original due date for filing the corporation's initial Form 1120S has not passed, the ruling and user fee requirements do not apply. To

request relief in this case, write "FILED PURSUANT TO REV. PROC. 98-55" at the top of page 1 of Form 2553, attach a statement explaining the reason for failing to file the election on time, and file Form 2553 as otherwise instructed. See Rev. Proc. 98-55 for more details.

See Regulations section 1.1362-6(b)(3)(iii) for how to obtain relief for an inadvertent invalid election if the corporation filed a timely election, but one or more shareholders did not file a timely consent.

Acceptance or Nonacceptance of Election

The service center will notify the corporation if its election is accepted and when it will take effect. The corporation will also be notified if its election is not accepted. The corporation should generally receive a determination on its election within 60 days after it has filed Form 2553. If box Q1 in Part II is checked on page 2, the corporation will receive a ruling letter from the IRS in Washington, DC, that either approves or denies the selected tax year. When box Q1 is checked, it will generally take an additional 90 days for the Form 2553 to be accepted.

Care should be exercised to ensure that the IRS receives the election. If the corporation is not notified of acceptance or nonacceptance of its election within 3 months of the date of filing (date mailed), or within 6 months if box Q1 is checked, take follow-up action by corresponding with the service center where the corporation filed the election.

If the IRS questions whether Form 2553 was filed, an acceptable proof of filing is **(a)** certified or registered mail receipt (timely postmarked) from the U.S. Postal Service, or its equivalent from a designated private delivery service (see Notice 2002-62, 2002-39 I.R.B. 574 (or its successor)); **(b)** Form 2553 with accepted stamp; **(c)** Form 2553 with stamped IRS received date; or **(d)** IRS letter stating that Form 2553 has been accepted.

 *Do not file Form 1120S for any tax year before the year the election takes effect. If the corporation is now required to file **Form 1120**, U.S. Corporation Income Tax Return, or any other applicable tax return, continue filing it until the election takes effect.*

End of Election

Once the election is made, it stays in effect until it is terminated. If the election is terminated in a tax year beginning after 1996, IRS consent is generally required for another election by the corporation (or a successor corporation) on Form 2553 for any tax year before the 5th tax year after the first tax year in which the termination took effect. See Regulations section 1.1362-5 for details.

Specific Instructions

Part I (*All corporations must complete.*)

Name and Address of Corporation

Enter the true corporate name as stated in the corporate charter or other legal document creating it. If the corporation's mailing address is the same as someone else's, such as a shareholder's, enter "c/o" and this person's name following the name of the corporation. Include the suite, room, or other unit number after the street address. If the Post Office does not deliver to the street address and the corporation has a P.O. box, show the box number instead of the street address. If the corporation changed its name or address after applying for its employer identification number, be sure to check the box in item D of Part I.

Item A. Employer Identification Number (EIN)

If the corporation has applied for an EIN but has not received it, enter "applied for." If the corporation does not have an EIN, it should apply for one on **Form SS-4,** Application for Employer Identification Number. You can order Form SS-4 by calling 1-800-TAX-FORM (1-800-829-3676) or by accessing the IRS Web Site **www.irs.gov**.

Item E. Effective Date of Election

Enter the beginning effective date (month, day, year) of the tax year requested for the S corporation. Generally, this will be the beginning date of the tax year for which the ending effective date is required to be shown in item I, Part I. For a new corporation (first year the corporation exists) it will generally be the date required to be shown in item H, Part I. The tax year of a new corporation starts on the date that it has shareholders, acquires assets, or begins doing business, whichever happens first. If the effective date for item E for a newly formed corporation is later than the date in item H, the corporation should file Form 1120 or Form 1120-A for the tax period between these dates.

Column K. Shareholders' Consent Statement

Each shareholder who owns (or is deemed to own) stock at the time the election is made must consent to the election. If the election is made during the corporation's tax year for which it first takes effect, any person who held stock at any time during the part of that year that occurs before the election is made, must consent to the election, even though the person may have sold or transferred his or her stock before the election is made.

An election made during the first 2½ months of the tax year is effective for the following tax year if any person who held stock in the corporation during the part of the tax year before the election was made, and who did not hold stock at the time the election was made, did not consent to the election.

Note: *Once the election is made, a new shareholder is not required to consent to the election; a new Form 2553 will not be required.*

Each shareholder consents by signing and dating in column K or signing and dating a separate consent statement described below. The following special rules apply in determining who must sign the consent statement.
- If a husband and wife have a community interest in the stock or in the income from it, both must consent.
- Each tenant in common, joint tenant, and tenant by the entirety must consent.
- A minor's consent is made by the minor, legal representative of the minor, or a natural or adoptive parent of the minor if no legal representative has been appointed.
- The consent of an estate is made by the executor or administrator.
- The consent of an electing small business trust is made by the trustee.
- If the stock is owned by a trust (other than an electing small business trust), the deemed owner of the trust must consent. See section 1361(c)(2) for details regarding trusts that are permitted to be shareholders and rules for determining who is the deemed owner.

Continuation sheet or separate consent statement. If you need a continuation sheet or use a separate consent statement, attach it to Form 2553. The separate consent statement must contain the name, address, and EIN of the corporation and the shareholder information requested in columns J through N of Part I. If you want, you may combine all the shareholders' consents in one statement.

Column L

Enter the number of shares of stock each shareholder owns and the dates the stock was acquired. If the election is made during the corporation's tax year for which it first takes effect, do not list the shares of stock for those shareholders who sold or transferred all of their stock before the election was made. However, these shareholders must still consent to the election for it to be effective for the tax year.

Column M

Enter the social security number of each shareholder who is an individual. Enter the EIN of each shareholder that is an estate, a qualified trust, or an exempt organization.

Column N

Enter the month and day that each shareholder's tax year ends. If a shareholder is changing his or her tax year, enter the tax year the shareholder is changing to, and attach an explanation indicating the present tax year and the basis for the change (e.g., automatic revenue procedure or letter ruling request).

Signature

Form 2553 must be signed by the president, treasurer, assistant treasurer, chief accounting officer, or other corporate officer (such as tax officer) authorized to sign.

Part II

Complete Part II if you selected a tax year ending on any date other than December 31 (other than a 52-53-week tax year ending with reference to the month of December).

Note: *In certain circumstances the corporation may not obtain automatic approval of a fiscal year under the natural business year (Box P1) or ownership tax year (Box P2) provisions if it is under examination, before an area office, or before a federal court with respect to any income tax issue and the annual accounting period is under consideration. For details, see section 4.02 of Rev. Proc. 2002-38, 2002-22 I.R.B. 1037.*

Box P1

Attach a statement showing separately for each month the amount of gross receipts for the most recent 47 months. A corporation that does not have a 47-month period of gross receipts cannot automatically establish a natural business year.

Box Q1

For examples of an acceptable business purpose for requesting a fiscal tax year, see section 5.02 of Rev. Proc. 2002-39, 2002-22 I.R.B. 1046, and Rev. Rul. 87-57, 1987-2 C.B. 117.

Attach a statement showing the relevant facts and circumstances to establish a business purpose for the requested fiscal year. For details on what is sufficient to establish a business purpose, see section 5.02 of Rev. Proc. 2002-39.

If your business purpose is based on one of the natural business year tests provided in section 5.03 of Rev. Proc. 2002-39, identify if you are using the 25% gross receipts, annual business cycle, or seasonal business test. For the 25% gross receipts test, provide a schedule showing the amount of gross receipts for each month for the most recent 47 months. For either the annual business cycle or seasonal business test, provide the gross receipts from sales and services (and inventory costs, if applicable) for each month of the short period, if any, and the three immediately preceding tax years. If the corporation has been in existence for less than three tax years, submit figures for the period of existence.

If you check box Q1, you will be charged a user fee of up to $600 (subject to change—see Rev. Proc. 2002-1 or its successor). Do not pay the fee when filing Form 2553. The service center will send Form 2553 to the IRS in Washington, DC, who, in turn, will notify the corporation that the fee is due.

Box Q2

If the corporation makes a back-up section 444 election for which it is qualified, then the election will take effect in the event the business purpose request is not approved. In some cases, the tax year requested under the back-up section 444 election may be different than the tax year requested under business purpose. See **Form 8716, Election To Have a Tax Year Other Than a Required Tax Year,** for details on making a back-up section 444 election.

Boxes Q2 and R2

If the corporation is not qualified to make the section 444 election after making the item Q2 back-up section 444 election or indicating its intention to make the election in item R1, and therefore it later files a calendar year return, it should write "Section 444 Election Not Made" in the top left corner of the first calendar year Form 1120S it files.

Part III

Certain qualified subchapter S trusts (QSSTs) may make the QSST election required by section 1361(d)(2) in Part III. Part III may be used to make the QSST election only if corporate stock has been transferred to the trust on or before the date on which the corporation makes its election to be an S corporation. However, a statement can be used instead of Part III to make the election. If there was an inadvertent failure to timely file a QSST election, see the relief provisions under Rev. Proc. 98-55.

Note: *Use Part III only if you make the election in Part I (i.e., Form 2553 cannot be filed with only Part III completed).*

The deemed owner of the QSST must also consent to the S corporation election in column K, page 1, of Form 2553. See section 1361(c)(2).

PENNSYLVANIA DEPARTMENT OF STATE
CORPORATION BUREAU

Application for Certificate of Authority
(15 Pa.C.S.)

Entity Number

_____ Foreign Business Corporation (§ 4124)
_____ Foreign Nonprofit Corporation (§ 6124)

Name

Address

City   State   Zip Code

Document will be returned to the name and address you enter to the left.
⇐

Fee: $180

Filed in the Department of State on _____

Secretary of the Commonwealth

In compliance with the requirements of the applicable provisions of 15 Pa.C.S. (relating to corporations and unincorporated associations), the undersigned, hereby states that:

1. The name of the corporation is:

2. *Complete only when the corporation must adopt a corporate designator for use in Pennsylvania.*
   The name which the corporation adopts for use in this Commonwealth is:

3. *If the name set forth in paragraph 1 or 2 is not available for use in this Commonwealth, complete the following:*
   The fictitious name which the corporation adopts for use in transacting business in this Commonwealth is:

   The corporation shall do business in Pennsylvania only under such fictitious name pursuant to the attached resolution of the board of directors under the applicable provisions of 15 Pa.C.S. (relating to corporations and unincorporated associations) and the attached form DSCB:54-311 (Application for Registration of Fictitious Name).

4. The name of the jurisdiction under the laws of which the corporation is incorporated is:

5. The address of its principal office under the laws of the jurisdiction in which it is incorporated is:

   Number and street   City   State   Zip

DSCB:15-4124/6124-2

6. The (a) address of this corporation's proposed registered office in this Commonwealth or (b) name of its commercial registered office provider and the county of venue is:

   (a) Number and street   City   State   Zip   County

   (b) Name of Commercial Registered Office Provider   County

c/o:

7. *Check one of the following*:

____ *Business Corporation*: The corporation is a corporation incorporated for a purpose or purposes involving pecuniary profit, incidental or otherwise.

____ *Nonprofit Corporation*: The corporation is a corporation incorporated for a purpose or purposes not involving pecuniary profit, incidental or otherwise.

IN TESTIMONY WHEREOF, the undersigned corporation has caused this Application for Certificate of Authority to be signed by a duly authorized officer thereof this

_____ day of _____,

_____.

_____
Name of Corporation

_____
Signature

_____
Title

DSCB: 15-4124/6124

Department of State
Corporation Bureau
P.O. Box 8722
Harrisburg, PA 17105-8722
(717) 787-1057
Web site: www.dos.state.pa.us/corp.htm

Instructions for Completion of Form:

A. Typewritten is preferred. If not, the form shall be completed in black or blue-black ink in order to permit reproduction. The filing fee for this form is $180 made payable to the Department of State.

B. Under 15 Pa.C.S. § 135(c) (relating to addresses) an actual street or rural route box number must be used as an address, and the Department of State is required to refuse to receive or file any document that sets forth only a post office box address.

C. The following, in addition to the filing fee, shall accompany this form:
    (1) One copy of a completed form DSCB:15-134A (Docketing Statement).
    (2) Any necessary copies of form DSCB:17.2.3 (Consent to Appropriation or Use of Similar Name). If Letter of Consent cannot be obtained, the applicant may file in the Department a resolution of its board of directors adopting a fictitious name for use in transacting business in the Commonwealth of Pennsylvania which fictitious name is distinguishable upon the record to the name of any conflicting profit or nonprofit corporation or other association and that is otherwise available for use by a domestic business or nonprofit corporation. See 15 Pa.C.S. §§ 4123(b)(1)(i) and 6123(b)(1)(i). An additional filing fee of $52 shall accompany form DSCB:54-311
    (Application for Registration of Fictitious Name).
    (3) Any necessary governmental approvals. If required governmental approvals for the use of the name cannot be obtained, the applicant may file in the Department a resolution of its board of directors adopting a fictitious name that is otherwise available for use by a domestic business or nonprofit corporation. See 15 Pa.C.S. §§ 4123(b)(2) and 6123(b)(2).

D. Where the name of the corporation does not comply with 19 Pa. Code § 23.3 (relating to business corporation names) or with 19 Pa. Code § 41.3 (relating to nonprofit corporation names) the corporation must adopt a corporate designator (corporation, incorporated, limited, etc. or abbreviation) for use in Pennsylvania and set forth the resulting name in Paragraph 2. Otherwise Paragraph 2 should remain blank. See also 19 Pa. Code § 17.41 (relating to foreign association names).

E. The corporation is required by 15 Pa.C.S. § 4124(b) or by 15 Pa.C.S. § 6124(b) (relating to advertisement) to advertise its intention to apply or its application for a Certificate of Authority. Proofs of publication of such advertising should not be submitted to, and will not be received by or filed in, the Department, but should be filed with the minutes of the corporation.

F. This form and all accompanying documents shall be mailed to the address stated above.
    Under 15 Pa.C.S. § 4125 or under 15 Pa.C.S. § 6125 upon the filing of this form the applicant corporation shall be deemed to hold a Certificate of Authority, and no actual certificate will be issued to the applicant by the Department.

G. To receive confirmation of the file date prior to receiving the microfilmed original, send either a self-addressed, stamped postcard with the filing information noted or a self-addressed, stamped envelope with a copy of the filing document.

PENNSYLVANIA DEPARTMENT OF STATE
CORPORATION BUREAU

Application for Amended Certificate of Authority
Foreign Corporation
(15 Pa.C.S.)

_____ Foreign Business Corporation (§ 4126)
_____ Foreign Nonprofit Corporation (§ 6126)

Entity Number

Name _____

Address _____

City _____ State _____ Zip Code _____

Document will be returned to the name and address you enter to the left.
⇐

Fee: $180

Filed in the Department of State on _____

_____
Secretary of the Commonwealth

In compliance with the requirements of the applicable provisions of 15 Pa.C.S. (relating to corporations and unincorporated associations), the undersigned foreign corporation, desiring to receive an amended certificate of authority, hereby states that:

1. The name under which the corporation currently holds a certificate of authority to do business within the Commonwealth of Pennsylvania is:

   _____

2. The name of the jurisdiction under the laws of which the corporation is incorporated is:

3. The address of its principal office under the laws of the jurisdiction in which it is incorporated is:

   _____
   Number and Street   City   State   Zip

4. The (a) address of this corporation's registered office in this Commonwealth or (b) name of its commercial registered office provider and the county of venue is:

   (a) Number and Street   City   State   Zip   County

   _____

   (b) Name of Commercial Registered Office Provider   County
   c/o:

   _____

   Check if applicable:

   _____ The foregoing reflects a change in Pennsylvania registered office.

DSCB:15-4126/6126-2

5. The corporation desires that its certificate of authority be amended to change the name under which it is authorized to transact business in the Commonwealth of Pennsylvania to:

_____

6. *If the name set forth in Paragraph 5 is not available for use in this Commonwealth, complete the following:*

The fictitious name which the corporation adopts for use in transacting business in this Commonwealth is:

_____

The corporation shall do business in Pennsylvania only under such fictitious name pursuant to the attached resolution of the board of directors under the applicable provisions of 15 Pa.C.S. (relating to corporations and unincorporated associations) and the attached form DSCB:54-311 (Application for Registration of Fictitious Name).

7. *Check one of the following*:

____ The change of name reflects a change effected in the jurisdiction of incorporation

____ Documents complying with the applicable provisions of 15 Pa.C.S. § 4123(b) or 6123(b) (relating to exception; name) accompany this application.

IN TESTIMONY WHEREOF, the undersigned corporation has caused this Application for an Amended Certificate of Authority to be signed by a duly authorized officer thereof this

_____ day of _____,

_____.

_____
Name of Corporation

_____
Signature

_____
Title

DSCB: 15-4126/6126

Department of State
Corporation Bureau
P.O. Box 8722
Harrisburg, PA 17105-8722
(717) 787-1057
Web site: www.dos.state.pa.us/corp.htm

Instructions for Completion of Form:

A. Typewritten is preferred. If not, the form shall be completed in black or blue-black ink in order to permit reproduction. The filing fee for this form is $180 made payable to the Department of State.

B. Under 15 Pa.C.S. § 135(c) (relating to addresses) an actual street or rural route box number must be used as an address, and the Department of State is required to refuse to receive or file any document that sets forth only a post office box address.

C. The following, in addition to the filing fee, shall accompany this form:

   (1) Two copies of a completed form DSCB:15-134B (Docketing Statement-Changes).

   (2) Any necessary copies of form DSCB:17.2.3 (Consent to Appropriation or Use of Similar Name). If Letter of Consent cannot be obtained, the applicant may file in the Department a resolution of its board of directors adopting a fictitious name for use in transacting business in the Commonwealth of Pennsylvania which fictitious name is distinguishable upon the record to the name of any conflicting profit or nonprofit corporation or other association and that is otherwise available for use by a domestic business or nonprofit corporation. See 15 Pa.C.S. §§ 4123(b)(1)(i) and 6123(b)(1)(i). An additional filing fee of $52 shall accompany form DSCB:54-311 (Application for Registration of Fictitious Name).

   (3) Any necessary governmental approvals. If required governmental approvals for the use of the name cannot be obtained, the applicant may file in the Department a resolution of its board of directors adopting a fictitious name that is otherwise available for use by a domestic business or nonprofit corporation. See 15 Pa.C.S. §§ 4123(b)(2) and 6123(b)(2).

D. Where the name of the corporation does not comply with 19 Pa. Code § 23.3 (relating to business corporation names) or with 19 Pa. Code § 41.3 (relating to nonprofit corporation names) the corporation must adopt a corporate designator for use in Pennsylvania and set forth the resulting name in Paragraph 5. See also 19 Pa. Code § 17.41 (relating to foreign association names).

E. This form and all accompanying documents shall be mailed to the address stated above.

   Under 15 Pa.C.S. §§ 4126(b) or 6126(b) upon the filing of this form the applicant corporation shall be deemed to hold an amended certificate of authority, and no actual amended certificate will be issued to the applicant by the Department.

F. To receive confirmation of the file date prior to receiving the microfilmed original, send either a self-addressed, stamped postcard with the filing information noted or a self-addressed, stamped envelope with a copy of the filing document.

PENNSYLVANIA DEPARTMENT OF STATE
CORPORATION BUREAU

Application for Termination of Authority
Foreign Corporation
(15 Pa.C.S.)
_____ Business Corporation (§ 4129)
_____ Nonprofit Corporation (§ 6129)

Entity Number

Name

Address

City   State   Zip Code

Document will be returned to the name and address you enter to the left.
⇐

Fee: $52

Filed in the Department of State on _____

_____
Secretary of the Commonwealth

In compliance with the requirements of the applicable provisions of 15 Pa.C.S. (relating to corporations and unincorporated associations), the undersigned qualified foreign corporation, desiring to withdraw from doing business in this Commonwealth, hereby states that:

1. The name of the corporation is:

2. The (a) address of this corporation's current registered office in this Commonwealth or (b) name of its commercial registered office provider and the county of venue is (the Department is hereby authorized to correct the following information to conform to the records of the Department):

   (a) Number and Street   City   State   Zip   County

   (b) Name of Commercial Registered Office Provider   County
   c/o:

3. The name of the jurisdiction under the laws of which the corporation is incorporated is:

4. The date the corporation received a Certificate of Authority to do business in this Commonwealth:

5. The corporation herewith surrenders its Certificate of Authority to do business in this Commonwealth.

DSCB:15-4129/6129-2

6. Notice of its intention to withdraw from doing business in this Commonwealth was mailed by certified or registered mail to each municipal corporation in which the registered office or principal place of business of the corporation in this Commonwealth is located and official publication required by 15 Pa.C.S. § 4129(b) or 6129(b) has been effected.

7. Process in any action or proceeding upon any liability incurred before the filing hereof may be sent to the following:

Number and Street	City	State	Zip	County

IN TESTIMONY WHEREOF, the undersigned corporation has caused this Application for Termination of Authority to be signed by a duly authorized officer thereof this

_____ day of _____,

_____.

_____
Name of Corporation

_____
Signature

_____
Title

DSCB: 15-4129/6129

Department of State
Corporation Bureau
P.O. Box 8722
Harrisburg, PA 17105-8722
(717) 787-1057
Web site: www.dos.state.pa.us/corp.htm

Instructions for Completion of Form:

A. Typewritten is preferred. If not, the form shall be completed in black or blue-black ink in order to permit reproduction. The filing fee for this form is $52 made payable to the Department of State.

B. Under 15 Pa.C.S. § 135(c) (relating to addresses) an actual street or rural route box number must be used as an address, and the Department of State is required to refuse to receive or file any document that sets forth only a post office box address.

C. The following, in addition to the filing fee, shall accompany this form:

   (1) Tax clearance certificates from the Department of Revenue and from the Bureau of Employment Security of the Department of Labor and Industry evidencing payment of all taxes and charges payable to the Commonwealth.

   (2) Any necessary governmental approvals.

   It is not necessary to submit to the Department the original or an amended certificate of authority for cancellation.

D. The corporation is required by 15 Pa.C.S. § 4129(b) or 6129(b) (relating to advertisement) to advertise its intention to withdraw or its withdrawal from doing business in Pennsylvania. Proofs of publication of such advertising should not be submitted to, and will not be received by or fled in the Department, but should be filed with the minutes of the corporation.

E. This form and all accompanying documents shall be mailed to the address stated above.

F. To receive confirmation of the file date prior to receiving the microfilmed original, send either a self-addressed, stamped postcard with the filing information noted or a self-addressed, stamped envelope with a copy of the filing document.

PENNSYLVANIA DEPARTMENT OF STATE
CORPORATION BUREAU

Entity Number

Statement of Election of
Professional Corporation Status
(15 Pa.C.S. § 2905)

Name

Address

City   State   Zip Code

Document will be returned to the name and address you enter to the left.
⇐

Fee: $100

Filed in the Department of State on _____

Secretary of the Commonwealth

       In compliance with the requirements of 15 Pa.C.S. § 2905 (relating to election of professional associations to become professional corporations), the undersigned, constituting all of the associates of a professional association, desiring to elect professional corporation status, hereby states that:

1. The name of the association is:

2. The (a) address of this corporation's current registered office in this Commonwealth or (b) name of its commercial registered office provider and the county of venue is (the Department is hereby authorized to correct the following information to conform to the records of the Department):
(a) Number and Street   City   State   Zip   County

    (b) Name of Commercial Registered Office Provider   County
c/o:

3. The initial Articles of Association of the association were filed in the Office of the Prothonotary of _____ County, Pennsylvania.

DSCB:15-2905-2

4. The associates of the professional association have elected to accept the provisions of 15 Pa.C.S. Ch. 29 (relating to professional corporations) for the government and regulation of the affairs of the association.

IN TESTIMONY WHEREOF, the undersigned constituting all of the associates of the professional association, have executed this Statement of Election of Professional Corporation Status this

_____ day of _____,_____.

_____(Seal)   _____(Seal)

_____(Seal)   _____(Seal)

_____(Seal)   _____(Seal)

_____(Seal)   _____(Seal)

_____(Seal)   _____(Seal)

_____(Seal)   _____(Seal)

Department of State
Corporation Bureau
P.O. Box 8722
Harrisburg, PA 17105-8722
(717) 787-1057
web site: www.dos.state.pa.us/corp.htm

Instructions for Completion of Form:

A. Typewritten is preferred. If not, the form shall be completed in black or blue-black ink in order to permit reproduction. The filing fee for this form is $100 made payable to the Department of State.

B. Under 15 Pa.C.S. § 135(c) (relating to addresses) an actual street or rural route box number must be used as an address, and the Department of State is required to refuse to receive or file any document that sets forth only a post office box address.

C. The following, in addition to the filing fee, shall accompany this form:

(1) One copy of a completed form DSCB:134A (Docketing Statement).

(2) One copy of a completed form DSCB:15-1311/5311/9305 (Statement of Summary of Record) and form DSCB:15-1915/5915 (Articles of Amendment-Domestic Corporation), restating the Articles to set forth all of the information required to be set forth in restated articles of a professional corporation. See 15 Pa.C.S. § 1311(a)(6).

D. For general instructions relating to the incorporation of professional corporations see 19 Pa. Code Ch. 33 (relating to professional corporations). These instructions relate to incorporators, corporate name and stated purposes. For specific information relating to professional corporation names see 19 Pa. Code § 17.9 (relating to professional names). For general instructions relating to the incorporation of business corporations see 19 Pa. Code Ch. 23 (relating to business corporations generally). These instructions relate to such matters as corporate name, stated purposes, term of existence, nonstock status, authorized share structure and related authority of the board of directors, inclusion of names of first directors in the Articles of Incorporation, optional provisions on cumulative voting for election of directors, etc.

E. This form and all accompanying documents shall be mailed to the address stated above.

F. To receive confirmation of the file date prior to receiving the microfilmed original, send either a self-addressed, stamped postcard with the filing information noted or a self-addressed, stamped envelope with a copy of the filing document.

Application for Employer Identification Number

(For use by employers, corporations, partnerships, trusts, estates, churches, government agencies, Indian tribal entities, certain individuals, and others.)

· See separate instructions for each line. · Keep a copy for your records.

EIN

OMB No. 1545-0003

Type or print clearly.

1 Legal name of entity (or individual) for whom the EIN is being requested

2 Trade name of business (if different from name on line 1)

3 Executor, trustee, "care of" name

4a Mailing address (room, apt., suite no. and street, or P.O. box)

5a Street address (if different) (Do not enter a P.O. box.)

4b City, state, and ZIP code

5b City, state, and ZIP code

6 County and state where principal business is located

7a Name of principal officer, general partner, grantor, owner, or trustor

7b SSN, ITIN, or EIN

8a **Type of entity** (check only one box)

☐ Sole proprietor (SSN) _____

☐ Partnership

☐ Corporation (enter form number to be filed) · _____

☐ Personal service corp.

☐ Church or church-controlled organization

☐ Other nonprofit organization (specify) · _____

☐ Other (specify) ·

☐ Estate (SSN of decedent) _____

☐ Plan administrator (SSN) _____

☐ Trust (SSN of grantor) _____

☐ National Guard ☐ State/local government

☐ Farmers' cooperative ☐ Federal government/military

☐ REMIC ☐ Indian tribal governments/enterprises

Group Exemption Number (GEN) · _____

8b If a corporation, name the state or foreign country (if applicable) where incorporated

State

Foreign country

9 **Reason for applying** (check only one box)

☐ Started new business (specify type) · _____

☐ Hired employees (Check the box and see line 12.)

☐ Compliance with IRS withholding regulations

☐ Other (specify) ·

☐ Banking purpose (specify purpose) · _____

☐ Changed type of organization (specify new type) · _____

☐ Purchased going business

☐ Created a trust (specify type) · _____

☐ Created a pension plan (specify type) · _____

10 Date business started or acquired (month, day, year)

11 Closing month of accounting year

12 First date wages or annuities were paid or will be paid (month, day, year). **Note:** *If applicant is a withholding agent, enter date income will first be paid to nonresident alien. (month, day, year)* . . . . ·

13 Highest number of employees expected in the next 12 months. **Note:** *If the applicant does not expect to have any employees during the period, enter "-0-."* . . . . ·

Agricultural	Household	Other

14 Check **one** box that best describes the principal activity of your business.

☐ Construction ☐ Rental & leasing ☐ Transportation & warehousing

☐ Real estate ☐ Manufacturing ☐ Finance & insurance

☐ Health care & social assistance ☐ Wholesale–agent/broker

☐ Accommodation & food service ☐ Wholesale–other ☐ Retail

☐ Other (specify)

15 Indicate principal line of merchandise sold; specific construction work done; products produced; or services provided.

16a Has the applicant ever applied for an employer identification number for this or any other business? . . . . . ☐ **Yes** ☐ **No**

Note: *If "Yes," please complete lines 16b and 16c.*

16b If you checked "Yes" on line 16a, give applicant's legal name and trade name shown on prior application if different from line 1 or 2 above.

Legal name ·

Trade name ·

16c Approximate date when, and city and state where, the application was filed. Enter previous employer identification number if known.

Approximate date when filed (mo., day, year)

City and state where filed

Previous EIN

Third Party Designee	Complete this section **only** if you want to authorize the named individual to receive the entity's EIN and answer questions about the completion of this form.	
	Designee's name	Designee's telephone number (include area code) ( )
	Address and ZIP code	Designee's fax number (include area code) ( )

Under penalties of perjury, I declare that I have examined this application, and to the best of my knowledge and belief, it is true, correct, and complete.

Applicant's telephone number (include area code) ( )

Name and title (type or print clearly) ·

Signature ·

Date ·

Applicant's fax number (include area code) ( )

For Privacy Act and Paperwork Reduction Act Notice, see separate instructions.

Cat. No. 16055N

Form **SS-4** (Rev. 12-2001)

Do I Need an EIN?

File Form SS-4 if the applicant entity does not already have an EIN but is required to show an EIN on any return, statement, or other document.[1] **See also the separate instructions for each line on Form SS-4.**

IF the applicant...	AND...	THEN...
Started a new business	Does not currently have (nor expect to have) employees	Complete lines 1, 2, 4a-6, 8a, and 9-16c.
Hired (or will hire) employees, including household employees	Does not already have an EIN	Complete lines 1, 2, 4a-6, 7a-b (if applicable), 8a, 8b (if applicable), and 9-16c.
Opened a bank account	Needs an EIN for banking purposes only	Complete lines 1-5b, 7a-b (if applicable), 8a, 9, and 16a-c.
Changed type of organization	Either the legal character of the organization or its ownership changed (e.g., you incorporate a sole proprietorship or form a partnership)[2]	Complete lines 1-16c (as applicable).
Purchased a going business[3]	Does not already have an EIN	Complete lines 1-16c (as applicable).
Created a trust	The trust is other than a grantor trust or an IRA trust[4]	Complete lines 1-16c (as applicable).
Created a pension plan as a plan administrator[5]	Needs an EIN for reporting purposes	Complete lines 1, 2, 4a-6, 8a, 9, and 16a-c.
Is a foreign person needing an EIN to comply with IRS withholding regulations	Needs an EIN to complete a Form W-8 (other than Form W-8ECI), avoid withholding on portfolio assets, or claim tax treaty benefits[6]	Complete lines 1-5b, 7a-b (SSN or ITIN optional), 8a-9, and 16a-c.
Is administering an estate	Needs an EIN to report estate income on Form 1041	Complete lines 1, 3, 4a-b, 8a, 9, and 16a-c.
Is a withholding agent for taxes on non-wage income paid to an alien (i.e., individual, corporation, or partnership, etc.)	Is an agent, broker, fiduciary, manager, tenant, or spouse who is required to file **Form 1042,** Annual Withholding Tax Return for U.S. Source Income of Foreign Persons	Complete lines 1, 2, 3 (if applicable), 4a-5b, 7a-b (if applicable), 8a, 9, and 16a-c.
Is a state or local agency	Serves as a tax reporting agent for public assistance recipients under Rev. Proc. 80-4, 1980-1 C.B. 581[7]	Complete lines 1, 2, 4a-5b, 8a, 9, and 16a-c.
Is a single-member LLC	Needs an EIN to file **Form 8832,** Classification Election, for filing employment tax returns, **or** for state reporting purposes[8]	Complete lines 1-16c (as applicable).
Is an S corporation	Needs an EIN to file **Form 2553,** Election by a Small Business Corporation[9]	Complete lines 1-16c (as applicable).

[1] For example, a sole proprietorship or self-employed farmer who establishes a qualified retirement plan, or is required to file excise, employment, alcohol, tobacco, or firearms returns, must have an EIN. **A partnership, corporation, REMIC (real estate mortgage investment conduit), nonprofit organization (church, club, etc.), or farmers' cooperative must use an EIN for any tax-related purpose even if the entity does not have employees.**

[2] However, **do not** apply for a new EIN if the existing entity only **(a)** changed its business name, **(b)** elected on Form 8832 to change the way it is taxed (or is covered by the default rules), or **(c)** terminated its partnership status because at least 50% of the total interests in partnership capital and profits were sold or exchanged within a 12-month period. (The EIN of the terminated partnership should continue to be used. See Regulations section 301.6109-1(d)(2)(iii).)

[3] Do not use the EIN of the prior business unless you became the "owner" of a corporation by acquiring its stock.

[4] However, IRA trusts that are required to file **Form 990-T,** Exempt Organization Business Income Tax Return, must have an EIN.

[5] A plan administrator is the person or group of persons specified as the administrator by the instrument under which the plan is operated.

[6] Entities applying to be a Qualified Intermediary (QI) need a QI-EIN even if they already have an EIN. **See Rev. Proc. 2000-12.**

[7] See also *Household employer* on page 4. **(Note:** State or local agencies may need an EIN for other reasons, e.g., hired employees.)

[8] Most LLCs **do not** need to file Form 8832. See **Limited liability company (LLC)** on page 4 for details on completing Form SS-4 for an LLC.

[9] An existing corporation that is electing or revoking S corporation status should use its previously-assigned EIN.

✸

Instructions for Form SS-4

Department of the Treasury
Internal Revenue Service

(Rev. December 2001)

Application for Employer Identification Number

Section references are to the Internal Revenue Code unless otherwise noted.

General Instructions

Use these instructions to complete **Form SS-4,** Application for Employer Identification Number. Also see **Do I Need an EIN?** on page 2 of Form SS-4.

Purpose of Form

Use Form SS-4 to apply for an employer identification number (EIN). An EIN is a nine-digit number (for example, 12-3456789) assigned to sole proprietors, corporations, partnerships, estates, trusts, and other entities for tax filing and reporting purposes. The information you provide on this form will establish your business tax account.

 *An EIN is for use in connection with your business activities only. Do **not** use your EIN in place of your social security number (SSN).*

File only one Form SS-4. Generally, a sole proprietor should file only one Form SS-4 and needs only one EIN, regardless of the number of businesses operated as a sole proprietorship or trade names under which a business operates. However, if the proprietorship incorporates or enters into a partnership, a new EIN is required. Also, each corporation in an affiliated group must have its own EIN.

EIN applied for, but not received. If you do not have an EIN by the time a **return** is due, write "Applied For" and the date you applied in the space shown for the number. **Do not** show your social security number (SSN) as an EIN on returns.

If you do not have an EIN by the time a **tax deposit** is due, send your payment to the Internal Revenue Service Center for your filing area as shown in the instructions for the form that you are are filing. Make your check or money order payable to the **"United States Treasury"** and show your name (as shown on Form SS-4), address, type of tax, period covered, and date you applied for an EIN.

Related Forms and Publications

The following **forms** and **instructions** may be useful to filers of Form SS-4:
- **Form 990-T,** Exempt Organization Business Income Tax Return
- **Instructions for Form 990-T**
- **Schedule C (Form 1040),** Profit or Loss From Business
- **Schedule F (Form 1040),** Profit or Loss From Farming
- **Instructions for Form 1041 and Schedules A, B, D, G, I, J, and K-1,** U.S. Income Tax Return for Estates and Trusts

- **Form 1042,** Annual Withholding Tax Return for U.S. Source Income of Foreign Persons
- **Instructions for Form 1065,** U.S. Return of Partnership Income
- **Instructions for Form 1066,** U.S. Real Estate Mortgage Investment Conduit (REMIC) Income Tax Return
- **Instructions for Forms 1120 and 1120-A**
- **Form 2553,** Election by a Small Business Corporation
- **Form 2848,** Power of Attorney and Declaration of Representative
- **Form 8821,** Tax Information Authorization
- **Form 8832,** Entity Classification Election
  For more **information** about filing Form SS-4 and related issues, see:
- **Circular A,** Agricultural Employer's Tax Guide (Pub. 51)
- **Circular E,** Employer's Tax Guide (Pub. 15)
- **Pub. 538,** Accounting Periods and Methods
- **Pub. 542,** Corporations
- **Pub. 557,** Exempt Status for Your Organization
- **Pub. 583,** Starting a Business and Keeping Records
- **Pub. 966,** EFTPS: Now a Full Range of Electronic Choices to Pay All Your Federal Taxes
- **Pub. 1635,** Understanding Your EIN
- **Package 1023,** Application for Recognition of Exemption
- **Package 1024,** Application for Recognition of Exemption Under Section 501(a)

How To Get Forms and Publications

Phone. You can order forms, instructions, and publications by phone 24 hours a day, 7 days a week. Just call 1-800-TAX-FORM (1-800-829-3676). You should receive your order or notification of its status within 10 workdays.

Personal computer. With your personal computer and modem, you can get the forms and information you need using the IRS Web Site at **www.irs.gov** or File Transfer Protocol at **ftp.irs.gov.**

CD-ROM. For small businesses, return preparers, or others who may frequently need tax forms or publications, a CD-ROM containing over 2,000 tax products (including many prior year forms) can be purchased from the National Technical Information Service (NTIS).

To order **Pub. 1796,** Federal Tax Products on CD-ROM, call **1-877-CDFORMS** (1-877-233-6767) toll free or connect to **www.irs.gov/cdorders.**

Tax Help for Your Business

IRS-sponsored Small Business Workshops provide information about your Federal and state tax obligations. For information about workshops in your area, call 1-800-829-1040 and ask for your Taxpayer Education Coordinator.

How To Apply

You can apply for an EIN by telephone, fax, or mail depending on how soon you need to use the EIN.

Application by Tele-TIN. Under the Tele-TIN program, you can receive your EIN by telephone and use it immediately to file a return or make a payment. To receive an EIN by telephone, IRS suggests that you complete Form SS-4 so that you will have all relevant information available. Then call the Tele-TIN number at 1-866-816-2065. (International applicants must call 215-516-6999.) Tele-TIN hours of operation are 7:30 a.m. to 5:30 p.m. The person making the call must be authorized to sign the form or be an authorized designee. See **Signature** and **Third Party Designee** on page 6. Also see the **TIP** below.

An IRS representative will use the information from the Form SS-4 to establish your account and assign you an EIN. Write the number you are given on the upper right corner of the form and sign and date it. Keep this copy for your records.

If requested by an IRS representative, mail or fax (facsimile) the signed Form SS-4 (including any Third Party Designee authorization) **within 24 hours** to the Tele-TIN Unit at the service center address provided by the IRS representative.

TIP *Taxpayer representatives can use Tele-TIN to apply for an EIN on behalf of their client and request that the EIN be faxed to their **client** on the same day. (**Note:** By utilizing this procedure, you are authorizing the IRS to fax the EIN without a cover sheet.)*

Application by Fax-TIN. Under the Fax-TIN program, you can receive your EIN by fax within 4 business days. Complete and fax Form SS-4 to the IRS using the Fax-TIN number listed below for your state. A long-distance charge to callers outside of the local calling area will apply. Fax-TIN numbers can only be used to apply for an EIN. **The numbers may change without notice.** Fax-TIN is available 24 hours a day, 7 days a week.

Be sure to provide your fax number so that IRS can fax the EIN back to you. (**Note:** By utilizing this procedure, you are authorizing the IRS to fax the EIN without a cover sheet.)

Do not call Tele-TIN for the same entity because duplicate EINs may be issued. See **Third Party Designee** on page 6.

Application by mail. Complete Form SS-4 at least 4 to 5 weeks before you will need an EIN. Sign and date the application and mail it to the service center address for your state. You will receive your EIN in the mail in approximately 4 weeks. See also **Third Party Designee** on page 6.

Call 1-800-829-1040 to verify a number or to ask about the status of an application by mail.

If your principal business, office or agency, or legal residence in the case of an individual, is located in:	Call the Tele-TIN or Fax-TIN number shown or file with the "Internal Revenue Service Center" at:
Connecticut, Delaware, District of Columbia, Florida, Georgia, Maine, Maryland, Massachusetts, New Hampshire, New Jersey, New York, North Carolina, Ohio, Pennsylvania, Rhode Island, South Carolina, Vermont, Virginia, West Virginia	Attn: EIN Operation Holtsville, NY 00501 Tele-TIN 866-816-2065 Fax-TIN 631-447-8960
Illinois, Indiana, Kentucky, Michigan	Attn: EIN Operation Cincinnati, OH 45999 Tele-TIN 866-816-2065 Fax-TIN 859-669-5760
Alabama, Alaska, Arizona, Arkansas, California, Colorado, Hawaii, Idaho, Iowa, Kansas, Louisiana, Minnesota, Mississippi, Missouri, Montana, Nebraska, Nevada, New Mexico, North Dakota, Oklahoma, Oregon, Puerto Rico, South Dakota, Tennessee, Texas, Utah, Washington, Wisconsin, Wyoming	Attn: EIN Operation Philadelphia, PA 19255 Tele-TIN 866-816-2065 Fax-TIN 215-516-3990
If you have no legal residence, principal place of business, or principal office or agency in any state:	Attn: EIN Operation Philadelphia, PA 19255 Tele-TIN 215-516-6999 Fax-TIN 215-516-3990

Specific Instructions

Print or type all entries on Form SS-4. Follow the instructions for each line to expedite processing and to avoid unnecessary IRS requests for additional information. Enter "N/A" (nonapplicable) on the lines that do not apply.

Line 1—Legal name of entity (or individual) for whom the EIN is being requested. Enter the legal name of the entity (or individual) applying for the EIN exactly as it appears on the social security card, charter, or other applicable legal document.

Individuals. Enter your first name, middle initial, and last name. If you are a sole proprietor, enter your individual name, not your business name. Enter your business name on line 2. Do not use abbreviations or nicknames on line 1.

Trusts. Enter the name of the trust.

Estate of a decedent. Enter the name of the estate.

Partnerships. Enter the legal name of the partnership as it appears in the partnership agreement.

Corporations. Enter the corporate name as it appears in the corporation charter or other legal document creating it.

Plan administrators. Enter the name of the plan administrator. A plan administrator who already has an EIN should use that number.

Line 2—Trade name of business. Enter the trade name of the business if different from the legal name. The trade name is the "doing business as " (DBA) name.

 *Use the full legal name shown on line 1 on all tax returns filed for the entity. (However, if you enter a trade name on line 2 and choose to use the trade name instead of the legal name, enter the trade name on **all returns** you file.) To prevent processing delays and errors, **always** use the legal name only (or the trade name only) on **all** tax returns.*

Line 3—Executor, trustee, "care of" name. Trusts enter the name of the trustee. Estates enter the name of the executor, administrator, or other fiduciary. If the entity applying has a designated person to receive tax information, enter that person's name as the "care of" person. Enter the individual's first name, middle initial, and last name.

Lines 4a-b—Mailing address. Enter the mailing address for the entity's correspondence. If line 3 is completed, enter the address for the executor, trustee or "care of" person. Generally, this address will be used on all tax returns.

 *File **Form 8822**, Change of Address, to report any subsequent changes to the entity's mailing address.*

Lines 5a-b—Street address. Provide the entity's physical address **only** if different from its mailing address shown in lines 4a-b. **Do not** enter a P.O. box number here.

Line 6—County and state where principal business is located. Enter the entity's primary **physical** location.

Lines 7a-b—Name of principal officer, general partner, grantor, owner, or trustor. Enter the first name, middle initial, last name, and SSN of **(a)** the principal officer if the business is a corporation, **(b)** a general partner if a partnership, **(c)** the owner of an entity that is disregarded as separate from its owner (disregarded entities owned by a corporation enter the corporation's name and EIN), or **(d)** a grantor, owner, or trustor if a trust.

If the person in question is an **alien individual** with a previously assigned individual taxpayer identification number (ITIN), enter the ITIN in the space provided and submit a copy of an official identifying document. If necessary, complete **Form W-7,** Application for IRS Individual Taxpayer Identification Number, to obtain an ITIN.

You are **required** to enter an SSN, ITIN, or EIN unless the only reason you are applying for an EIN is to make an entity classification election (see Regulations section 301.7701-1 through 301.7701-3) and you are a nonresident alien with no effectively connected income from sources within the United States.

Line 8a—Type of entity. Check the box that best describes the type of entity applying for the EIN. If you are an alien individual with an ITIN previously assigned to you, enter the ITIN in place of a requested SSN.

 This is not an election for a tax classification of an entity. See "Limited liability company (LLC)" on page 4.

Other. If not specifically mentioned, check the "Other" box, enter the type of entity and the type of return, if any, that will be filed (for example, "Common Trust Fund, Form 1065" or "Created a Pension Plan"). Do not enter "N/A." If you are an alien individual applying for an EIN, see the **Lines 7a-b** instructions above.

● **Household employer.** If you are an individual, check the "Other" box and enter "Household Employer" and your SSN. If you are a state or local agency serving as a tax reporting agent for public assistance recipients who become household employers, check the "Other" box and enter "Household Employer Agent." If you are a trust that qualifies as a household employer, you do not need a separate EIN for reporting tax information relating to household employees; use the EIN of the trust.

● **QSub.** For a qualified subchapter S subsidiary (QSub) check the "Other" box and specify "QSub."

● **Withholding agent.** If you are a withholding agent required to file Form 1042, check the "Other" box and enter "Withholding Agent."

Sole proprietor. Check this box if you file Schedule C, C-EZ, or F (Form 1040) and have a qualified plan, or are required to file excise, employment, or alcohol, tobacco, or firearms returns, or are a payer of gambling winnings. Enter your SSN (or ITIN) in the space provided. If you are a nonresident alien with no effectively connected income from sources within the United States, you do not need to enter an SSN or ITIN.

Corporation. This box is for any corporation **other than a personal service corporation.** If you check this box, enter the income tax form number to be filed by the entity in the space provided.

 *If you entered "1120S" after the "Corporation" checkbox, the corporation **must** file Form 2553 no later than the 15th day of the 3rd month of the tax year the election is to take effect. Until Form 2553 has been received and approved, you will be considered a Form 1120 filer. See the Instructions for Form 2553.*

Personal service corp. Check this box if the entity is a personal service corporation. An entity is a personal service corporation for a tax year only if:

● The principal activity of the entity during the testing period (prior tax year) for the tax year is the performance of personal services substantially by employee-owners, and

● The employee-owners own at least 10% of the fair market value of the outstanding stock in the entity on the last day of the testing period.

Personal services include performance of services in such fields as health, law, accounting, or consulting. For more information about personal service corporations, see the Instructions for Forms 1120 and 1120-A and Pub. 542.

Other nonprofit organization. Check this box if the nonprofit organization is other than a church or church-controlled organization and specify the type of nonprofit organization (for example, an educational organization).

 *If the organization also seeks tax-exempt status, you **must** file either Package 1023 or Package 1024. See Pub. 557 for more information.*

If the organization is covered by a group exemption letter, enter the four-digit **group exemption number (GEN).** (Do not confuse the GEN with the nine-digit EIN.) If you do not know the GEN, contact the parent organization. Get Pub. 557 for more information about group exemption numbers.

Plan administrator. If the plan administrator is an individual, enter the plan administrator's SSN in the space provided.

REMIC. Check this box if the entity has elected to be treated as a real estate mortgage investment conduit (REMIC). See the Instructions for Form 1066 for more information.

Limited liability company (LLC). An LLC is an entity organized under the laws of a state or foreign country as a limited liability company. For Federal tax purposes, an LLC may be treated as a partnership or corporation or be disregarded as an entity separate from its owner.

By **default,** a domestic LLC with only one member is **disregarded** as an entity separate from its owner and must include all of its income and expenses on the owner's tax return (e.g., **Schedule C (Form 1040)**). Also by default, a domestic LLC with two or more members is treated as a partnership. A domestic LLC may file Form 8832 to avoid either default classification and elect to be classified as an association taxable as a corporation. For more information on entity classifications (including the rules for foreign entities), see the instructions for Form 8832.

 Do not *file Form 8832 if the LLC accepts the default classifications above.* **However, if the LLC will be electing S Corporation status, it must timely file both Form 8832 and Form 2553.**

Complete Form SS-4 for LLCs as follows:
• A single-member, domestic LLC that accepts the default classification (above) does not need an EIN and generally should not file Form SS-4. Generally, the LLC should use the name and EIN of its **owner** for all Federal tax purposes. However, the reporting and payment of employment taxes for employees of the LLC may be made using the name and EIN or **either** the owner or the LLC as explained in Notice 99-6, 1999-1 C.B. 321. You can find Notice 99-6 on page 12 of Internal Revenue Bulletin 1999-3 at **www.irs.gov. (Note:** If the LLC-applicant indicates in box 13 that it has employees or expects to have employees, the owner (whether an individual or other entity) of a single-member domestic LLC will also be assigned its own EIN (if it does not

already have one) even if the LLC will be filing the employment tax returns.)
• A single-member, domestic LLC that accepts the default classification (above) and wants an EIN for filing employment tax returns (see above) or non-Federal purposes, such as a state requirement, must check the "Other" box and write "Disregarded Entity" or, when applicable, "Disregarded Entity—Sole Proprietorship" in the space provided.
• A multi-member, domestic LLC that accepts the default classification (above) must check the "Partnership" box.
• A domestic LLC that will be filing Form 8832 to elect corporate status must check the "Corporation" box and write in "Single-Member" or "Multi-Member" immediately below the "form number" entry line.

Line 9—Reason for applying. Check only **one** box. Do not enter "N/A."

Started new business. Check this box if you are starting a new business that requires an EIN. If you check this box, enter the type of business being started. **Do not** apply if you already have an EIN and are only adding another place of business.

Hired employees. Check this box if the existing business is requesting an EIN because it has hired or is hiring employees and is therefore required to file employment tax returns. **Do not** apply if you already have an EIN and are only hiring employees. For information on employment taxes (e.g., for family members), see Circular E.

 You may be required to make electronic deposits of all depository taxes (such as employment tax, excise tax, and corporate income tax) using the Electronic Federal Tax Payment System (EFTPS). See section 11, Depositing Taxes, of Circular E and Pub. 966.

Created a pension plan. Check this box if you have created a pension plan and need an EIN for reporting purposes. Also, enter the type of plan in the space provided.

 Check this box if you are applying for a trust EIN when a new pension plan is established. In addition, check the "Other" box in line 8a and write "Created a Pension Plan" in the space provided.

Banking purpose. Check this box if you are requesting an EIN for banking purposes only, and enter the banking purpose (for example, a bowling league for depositing dues or an investment club for dividend and interest reporting).

Changed type of organization. Check this box if the business is changing its type of organization for example, the business was a sole proprietorship and has been incorporated or has become a partnership. If you check this box, specify in the space provided (including available space immediately below) the type of change made. For example, "From Sole Proprietorship to Partnership."

Purchased going business. Check this box if you purchased an existing business. **Do not** use the former owner's EIN unless you became the "owner" of a corporation by acquiring its stock.

Created a trust. Check this box if you created a trust, and enter the type of trust created. For example, indicate if the trust is a nonexempt charitable trust or a split-interest trust.

Exception. Do **not** file this form for certain grantor-type trusts. The trustee does not need an EIN for the trust if the trustee furnishes the name and TIN of the grantor/owner and the address of the trust to all payors. See the Instructions for Form 1041 for more information.

 Do not check this box if you are applying for a trust EIN when a new pension plan is established. Check "Created a pension plan."

Other. Check this box if you are requesting an EIN for any other reason; and enter the reason. For example, a newly-formed state government entity should enter "Newly-Formed State Government Entity" in the space provided.

Line 10—Date business started or acquired. If you are starting a new business, enter the starting date of the business. If the business you acquired is already operating, enter the date you acquired the business. Trusts should enter the date the trust was legally created. Estates should enter the date of death of the decedent whose name appears on line 1 or the date when the estate was legally funded.

Line 11—Closing month of accounting year. Enter the last month of your accounting year or tax year. An accounting or tax year is usually 12 consecutive months, either a calendar year or a fiscal year (including a period of 52 or 53 weeks). A calendar year is 12 consecutive months ending on December 31. A fiscal year is either 12 consecutive months ending on the last day of any month other than December or a 52-53 week year. For more information on accounting periods, see Pub. 538.

Individuals. Your tax year generally will be a calendar year.

Partnerships. Partnerships must adopt one of the following tax years:
- The tax year of the majority of its partners,
- The tax year common to all of its principal partners,
- The tax year that results in the least aggregate deferral of income, or
- In certain cases, some other tax year.
  See the Instructions for Form 1065 for more information.

REMICs. REMICs must have a calendar year as their tax year.

Personal service corporations. A personal service corporation generally must adopt a calendar year unless:
- It can establish a business purpose for having a different tax year, or
- It elects under section 444 to have a tax year other than a calendar year.

Trusts. Generally, a trust must adopt a calendar year except for the following:
- Tax-exempt trusts,
- Charitable trusts, and
- Grantor-owned trusts.

Line 12—First date wages or annuities were paid or will be paid. If the business has or will have employees, enter the date on which the business began or will begin to pay wages. If the business does not plan to have employees, enter "N/A."

Withholding agent. Enter the date you began or will begin to pay income (including annuities) to a nonresident alien. This also applies to individuals who are required to file Form 1042 to report alimony paid to a nonresident alien.

Line 13—Highest number of employees expected in the next 12 months. Complete each box by entering the number (including zero ("-0-")) of "Agricultural," "Household," or "Other" employees expected by the applicant in the next 12 months. For a definition of agricultural labor (farmwork), see Circular A.

Lines 14 and 15. Check the **one** box in line 14 that best describes the principal activity of the applicant's business. Check the "Other" box (and specify the applicant's principal activity) if none of the listed boxes applies.

Use line 15 to describe the applicant's principal line of business in more detail. For example, if you checked the "Construction" box in line 14, enter additional detail such as "General contractor for residential buildings" in line 15.

 Do not complete lines 14 and 15 if you entered zero "(-0-)" in line 13.

Construction. Check this box if the applicant is engaged in erecting buildings or other structures, (e.g., streets, highways, bridges, tunnels). The term "Construction" also includes special trade contractors, (e.g., plumbing, HVAC, electrical, carpentry, concrete, excavation, etc. contractors).

Real estate. Check this box if the applicant is engaged in renting or leasing real estate to others; managing, selling, buying or renting real estate for others; or providing related real estate services (e.g., appraisal services).

Rental and leasing. Check this box if the applicant is engaged in providing tangible goods such as autos, computers, consumer goods, or industrial machinery and equipment to customers in return for a periodic rental or lease payment.

Manufacturing. Check this box if the applicant is engaged in the mechanical, physical, or chemical transformation of materials, substances, or components into new products. The assembling of component parts of manufactured products is also considered to be manufacturing.

Transportation & warehousing. Check this box if the applicant provides transportation of passengers or cargo; warehousing or storage of goods; scenic or sight-seeing transportation; or support activities related to these modes of transportation.

Finance & insurance. Check this box if the applicant is engaged in transactions involving the creation, liquidation, or change of ownership of financial assets and/or facilitating such financial transactions;

underwriting annuities/insurance policies; facilitating such underwriting by selling insurance policies; or by providing other insurance or employee-benefit related services.

Health care and social assistance. Check this box if the applicant is engaged in providing physical, medical, or psychiatric care using licensed health care professionals or providing social assistance activities such as youth centers, adoption agencies, individual/family services, temporary shelters, etc.

Accommodation & food services. Check this box if the applicant is engaged in providing customers with lodging, meal preparation, snacks, or beverages for immediate consumption.

Wholesale–agent/broker. Check this box if the applicant is engaged in arranging for the purchase or sale of goods owned by others or purchasing goods on a commission basis for goods traded in the wholesale market, usually between businesses.

Wholesale–other. Check this box if the applicant is engaged in selling goods in the wholesale market generally to other businesses for resale on their own account.

Retail. Check this box if the applicant is engaged in selling merchandise to the general public from a fixed store; by direct, mail-order, or electronic sales; or by using vending machines.

Other. Check this box if the applicant is engaged in an activity not described above. Describe the applicant's principal business activity in the space provided.

Lines 16a-c. Check the applicable box in line 16a to indicate whether or not the entity (or individual) applying for an EIN was issued one previously. Complete lines 16b and 16c **only** if the "Yes" box in line 16a is checked. If the applicant previously applied for **more than one** EIN, write "See Attached" in the empty space in line 16a and attach a separate sheet providing the line 16b and 16c information for each EIN previously requested.

Third Party Designee. Complete this section **only** if you want to authorize the named individual to receive the entity's EIN and answer questions about the completion of Form SS-4. The designee's authority terminates at the time the EIN is assigned and released to the designee. **You must complete the signature area for the authorization to be valid.**

Signature. When required, the application must be signed by **(a)** the individual, if the applicant is an individual, **(b)** the president, vice president, or other principal officer, if the applicant is a corporation, **(c)** a responsible and duly authorized member or officer having knowledge of its affairs, if the applicant is a partnership, government entity, or other unincorporated organization, or **(d)** the fiduciary, if the applicant is a trust or an estate. Foreign applicants may have any duly-authorized person, (e.g., division manager), sign Form SS-4.

Privacy Act and Paperwork Reduction Act Notice. We ask for the information on this form to carry out the Internal Revenue laws of the United States. We need it to comply with section 6109 and the regulations thereunder which generally require the inclusion of an employer identification number (EIN) on certain returns, statements, or other documents filed with the Internal Revenue Service. If your entity is required to obtain an EIN, you are required to provide all of the information requested on this form. Information on this form may be used to determine which Federal tax returns you are required to file and to provide you with related forms and publications.

We disclose this form to the Social Security Administration for their use in determining compliance with applicable laws. We may give this information to the Department of Justice for use in civil and criminal litigation, and to the cities, states, and the District of Columbia for use in administering their tax laws. We may also disclose this information to Federal, state, or local agencies that investigate or respond to acts or threats of terrorism or participate in intelligence or counterintelligence activities concerning terrorism.

We will be unable to issue an EIN to you unless you provide all of the requested information which applies to your entity. Providing false information could subject you to penalties.

You are not required to provide the information requested on a form that is subject to the Paperwork Reduction Act unless the form displays a valid OMB control number. Books or records relating to a form or its instructions must be retained as long as their contents may become material in the administration of any Internal Revenue law. Generally, tax returns and return information are confidential, as required by section 6103.

The time needed to complete and file this form will vary depending on individual circumstances. The estimated average time is:

Recordkeeping	6 min.
Learning about the law or the form	22 min.
Preparing the form	46 min.
Copying, assembling, and sending the form to the IRS	20 min.

If you have comments concerning the accuracy of these time estimates or suggestions for making this form simpler, we would be happy to hear from you. You can write to the Tax Forms Committee, Western Area Distribution Center, Rancho Cordova, CA 95743-0001. **Do not** send the form to this address. Instead, see **How To Apply** on page 2.

PENNSYLVANIA DEPARTMENT OF STATE
CORPORATION BUREAU

Articles of Amendment-Domestic Corporation
(15 Pa.C.S.)

_____ Business Corporation (§ 1915)
_____ Nonprofit Corporation (§ 5915)

Entity Number

Name

Address

City   State   Zip Code

Document will be returned to the name and address you enter to the left.
⇐

Fee: $52

Filed in the Department of State on _____

_____
Secretary of the Commonwealth

In compliance with the requirements of the applicable provisions (relating to articles of amendment), the undersigned, desiring to amend its articles, hereby states that:

1. The name of the corporation is:

2. The (a) address of this corporation's current registered office in this Commonwealth or (b) name of its commercial registered office provider and the county of venue is (the Department is hereby authorized to correct the following information to conform to the records of the Department):
   (a) Number and Street   City   State   Zip   County

   (b) Name of Commercial Registered Office Provider   County
c/o

3. The statute by or under which it was incorporated:

4. The date of its incorporation:

5. *Check, and if appropriate complete, one of the following*:

_____ The amendment shall be effective upon filing these Articles of Amendment in the Department of State.

_____ The amendment shall be effective on: _____ at _____
                                              Date   Hour

DSCB:15-1915/5915–2

6. *Check one of the following*:

____ The amendment was adopted by the shareholders or members pursuant to 15 Pa.C.S. § 1914(a) and (b) or § 5914(a).

____ The amendment was adopted by the board of directors pursuant to 15 Pa. C.S. § 1914(c) or § 5914(b).

7. *Check, and if appropriate, complete one of the following:*

____ The amendment adopted by the corporation, set forth in full, is as follows

_____

_____

____ The amendment adopted by the corporation is set forth in full in Exhibit A attached hereto and made a part hereof.

8. *Check if the amendment restates the Articles:*

____ The restated Articles of Incorporation supersede the original articles and all amendments thereto.

IN TESTIMONY WHEREOF, the undersigned corporation has caused these Articles of Amendment to be signed by a duly authorized officer thereof this

_____ day of _____,

_____.

_____
Name of Corporation

_____
Signature

_____
Title

Department of State
Corporation Bureau
P.O. Box 8722
Harrisburg, PA 17105-8722
(717) 787-1057
web site: www.dos.state.pa.us/corp.htm

Instructions for Completion of Form:

A. Typewritten is preferred. If not, the form shall be completed in black or blue-black ink in order to permit reproduction. The filing fee for this form is $52 made payable to the Department of State.

B. Under 15 Pa.C.S. § 135(c) (relating to addresses) an actual street or rural route box number must be used as an address, and the Department of State is required to refuse to receive or file any document that sets forth only a post office box address.

C. The following, in addition to the filing fee, shall accompany this form:

  (1) Two copies of a completed form DSCB:15-134B (Docketing Statement-Changes).

  (2) Any necessary copies of form DSCB:17.2.3 (Consent to Appropriation or Use of Similar Name) shall accompany Articles of Amendment effecting a change of name and the change in name shall contain a statement of the complete new name.

  (3) Any necessary governmental approvals.

D. *Nonprofit Corporations:* If the action was authorized by a body other than the board of directors Paragraph 6 should be modified accordingly.

E. This form and all accompanying documents shall be mailed to the above stated address.

F. To receive confirmation of the file date prior to receiving the microfilmed original, send either a self-addressed, stamped postcard with the filing information noted or a self-addressed, stamped envelope with a copy of the filing document.

Docketing Statement (Changes)
DSCB:15-134B

<table>
<tr><td colspan="2">BUREAU USE ONLY:</td></tr>
<tr><td>☐ Revenue</td><td>☐ Labor & Industry</td></tr>
<tr><td colspan="2">☐ Other _____</td></tr>
<tr><td colspan="2">File Code_____ Filed Date _____</td></tr>
</table>

Part I. Complete for each filing:

Current name of entity or registrant *(survivor or new entity if merger or consolidation):*

Entity number, if known: _____   Incorporation/qualification date in PA: _____

State of Inc: _____   Federal EIN: _____   Specified effective date, if any: _____

Part II. Check proper box:

____ Amendment (complete Section A)   ____ Merger, Consolidation or Division (complete Section B,C or D)

____ Consolidation (complete Section C)   ____ Division (complete Section D)

____ Conversion (complete Section A & E)   ____ Correction (complete Section A)

____ Termination (complete Section H)   ____ Revival (complete Section G)

____ Dissolution before Commencement of Business (complete Section F)

____ **Section A** – *Check box(es) which pertain to changes:*
     ___ Name:

___ Registered Office: Number & street/RD number & box number City   State   Zip   County

___ Purpose:

___ Stock (aggregate number of share authorized):_____   ___ Effective date:_____.

___ Term of Existence:_____   ___ Other:_____.

____ **Section B** – **Merger** *Complete Section A if any changes to surviving entity:*
     Merging Entities are: *(attach sheet for additional merging entities)*

Name: Entity #, if known:

Effective date: Inc./qual. date in PA.   State of Inc.

Name: Entity #, if known:

Effective date: Inc./qual. date in PA.   State of Inc.

____ **Section C - Consolidation**

Consolidating Entities are: *(attach sheet for additional consolidating entities)*
Name:

_____

Entity #, if known: Inc./qual. date in PA.   State of Inc.

_____

Name:

_____

Entity #, if known: Inc./qual. date in PA.   State of Inc.

_____

____ **Section D – Division**

Forming new entity(s) named below: (attached sheet for additional entities)

Name: Entity Number:

_____

Name: Entity Number:

_____

Check one: ____ Entity named in Part I survives. (any changes, complete Section A)

              ____ Entity named in Part I does not survive.

____ **Section E – Conversion** *(complete Section A)*

Check one: ____ Converted from nonprofit to profit   ____ Converted from profit to nonprofit

____ **Section F – Dissolved by Shareholders or Incorporators Before Commencement of Business**

____ **Section G – Statement of Revival** *(complete Section A for any changes to revived entity)*

     Entity named in Part I hereby revives its charter or articles which were forfeited by Proclamation or expired.

____ **Section H – Statement of Termination** *(attach sheet for additional entities involved)*

_____ filed in the Department of State on _____is/are hereby terminated.
(type of filing made)   month/date/year   hour, if any

     If merger, consolidation or division, list all entities involved, other than that listed in Part I:
Name: Entity number:

_____

Name: Entity number:

_____

PENNSYLVANIA DEPARTMENT OF STATE
CORPORATION BUREAU

Articles/Certificate of Merger
(15 Pa.C.S.)

____ Domestic Business Corporation (§ 1926)
____ Domestic Nonprofit Corporation (§ 5926)
____ Limited Partnership (§ 8547)

Entity Number

Name

Address

City   State   Zip Code

Document will be returned to the name and address you enter to the left.
⇐

Fee: $108 plus $28 additional for each Party in additional to two

Filed in the Department of State on _____

Secretary of the Commonwealth

In compliance with the requirements of the applicable provisions (relating to articles of merger or consolidation), the undersigned, desiring to effect a merger, hereby state that:

1. The name of the corporation/limited partnership surviving the merger is:

2. *Check and complete one of the following:*
____ The surviving corporation/limited partnership is a domestic business/nonprofit corporation/limited partnership and the (a) address of its current registered office in this Commonwealth or (b) name of its commercial registered office provider and the county of venue is (the Department is hereby authorized to correct the following information to conform to the records of the Department):

(a) Number and Street   City   State   Zip   County

(b) Name of Commercial Registered Office Provider   County
c/o

____ The surviving corporation/limited partnership is a qualified foreign business/nonprofit corporation /limited partnership incorporated/formed under the laws of _____ and the (a) address of its current registered office in this Commonwealth or (b) name of its commercial registered office provider and the county of venue is (the Department is hereby authorized to correct the following information to conform to the records of the Department):

(a) Number and Street   City   State   Zip   County

(b) Name of Commercial Registered Office Provider   County
c/o

____ The surviving corporation/limited partnership is a nonqualified foreign business/nonprofit corporation/limited partnership incorporated/formed under the laws of_____ and the address of its principal office under the laws of such domiciliary jurisdiction is:

Number and Street   City   State   Zip

DSCB:15-1926/5926/8547–2

3. The name and the address of the registered office in this Commonwealth or name of its commercial registered office provider and the county of venue of each other domestic business/nonprofit corporation/limited partnership and qualified foreign business/nonprofit corporation/limited partnership which is a party to the plan of merger are as follows:

Name	Registered Office Address	Commercial Registered Office Provider	County

4. *Check, and if appropriate complete, one of the following:*

____ The plan of merger shall be effective upon filing these Articles/Certificate of Merger in the Department of State.

____ The plan of merger shall be effective on: _____ at_____ .
　　　　　　　　　　　　　　　　　　　　　　　Date　　　　　　　　　Hour

5. The manner in which the plan of merger was adopted by each domestic corporation/limited partnership is as follows:

Name	Manner of Adoption

6. *Strike out this paragraph if no foreign corporation/limited partnership is a party to the merger.*
The plan was authorized, adopted or approved, as the case may be, by the foreign business/nonprofit corporation/limited partnership (or each of the foreign business/nonprofit corporations/limited partnerships) party to the plan in accordance with the laws of the jurisdiction in which it is incorporated/organized.

7. *Check, and if appropriate complete, one of the following:*

____ The plan of merger is set forth in full in Exhibit A attached hereto and made a part hereof.

____ Pursuant to 15 Pa.C.S. § 1901/§ 8547(b) (relating to omission of certain provisions from filed plans) the provisions, if any, of the plan of merger that amend or constitute the operative provisions of the Articles of Incorporation/Certificate of Limited Partnership of the surviving corporation/limited partnership as in effect subsequent to the effective date of the plan are set forth in full in Exhibit A attached hereto and made a party hereof. The full text of the plan of merger is on file at the principal place of business of the surviving corporation/limited partnership, the address of which is.

Number and street	City	State	Zip	County

162 ◆

DSCB: 15-1926/5926/8547-3

IN TESTIMONY WHEREOF, the undersigned corporation/limited partnership has caused these Articles/Certificate of Merger to be signed by a duly authorized officer thereof this

_____ day of _____,

_____.

_____
Name of Corporation/Limited Partnership

_____
Signature

_____
Title

_____
Name of Corporation/Limited Partnership

_____
Signature

_____
Title

DSCB: 15-1926/5926/8547

Department of State
Corporation Bureau
P.O. Box 8722
Harrisburg, PA 17105-8722
(717) 787-1057
web site: www.dos.state.pa.us/corp.htm

Instructions for Completion of Form:

A. Typewritten is preferred. If not, the form shall be completed in black or blue-black ink in order to permit reproduction. The filing fee for this form is $108 plus $28 additional for each party in addition to two, made payable to the Department of State.

B. Under 15 Pa.C.S. § 135(c) (relating to addresses) an actual street or rural route box number must be used as an address, and the Department of State is required to refuse to receive or file any document that sets forth only a post office box address.

C. The following, in addition to the filing fee, shall accompany this form:

    (1) Two copies of a completed form DSCB:15-134B (Docketing Statement-Changes).

    (2) One copy of a completed from DSCB:15-134A (Docketing Statement), with respect to the new corporation resulting from a consolidation, unless the new corporation is a nonqualified foreign corporation.

    (3) Any necessary copies of form DSCB:17.2.3 (Consent to Appropriation or Use of Similar Name) shall accompany Articles of Merger effecting a change of name, and the change in name shall contain a statement of the complete new name.

    (4) Any necessary governmental approvals.

D. If a new corporation/limited partnership results from the transaction the form should be rewritten as Articles/Certificate of Consolidation and modified accordingly. *For Limited Partnerships*-Similarly, if a general partnership, corporation, business trust or other association is a party to the plan pursuant to 15 Pa.C.S. § 8545 (c) (relating to business trusts and other associations)this form should be modified accordingly.

E. A foreign business/nonprofit corporation/limited partnership may be a party to a merger notwithstanding the fact that it has not been authorized to do business in Pennsylvania. However, if the surviving corporation/limited partnership is a foreign corporation /limited partnership which is not the holder of a Certificate of Authority under the Business/Nonprofit Corporation Law or is not authorized to do business in Pennsylvania under the Pennsylvania Revised Uniform Limited Partnership Act on the effective date of the merger, there must be submitted with this form tax clearance certificates from the Department of Revenue and the Bureau of Employment Security of the Department of Labor and Industry with respect to each domestic corporation/limited partnership and qualified foreign corporation/limited partnership evidencing the payment of all taxes and charges payable to the Commonwealth.

F. If the name of a commercial registered office provider is used in Paragraph 3, it must be preceded by "**c/o**". See 15 Pa.C.S. § 109 (relating to name of commercial registered office provider in lieu of registered address).

G. The effective date in Paragraph 4 may not be prior to the filing date, but the plan of merger may state a prior effective date "for accounting purposes only."

H. One of the following statements or the equivalent should be used in the second column of Paragraph 5 to set forth the manner of adoption.

    For Articles of Merger (Corporations)
    "Adopted by action of the shareholders (or members) pursuant to 15 Pa.C.S. § 1905" or "Adopted by action of the members (or shareholders) pursuant to 15 Pa.C.S. § 5905."

DSCB:15-1926/5926/8547

"Adopted by the directors and shareholders (or members) pursuant to 15 Pa.C.S. § 1924(a)" or "Adopted by the directors and members (or shareholders) pursuant to 15 Pa.C.S. § 5924(a)".

"Adopted by action of the board of directors of the corporation pursuant to 15 Pa.C.S. § 1924(b)(2)" or "Adopted by action of the board of directors of the corporation pursuant to 15 Pa.C.S. § 5924(b)". (*If the action was authorized by a body other than the board of directors this statement should be modified accordingly*).

"Adopted by action of the board of directors of the parent corporation pursuant to 15 Pa.C.S. § 1924(b)(3)."

For Certificate of Merger-(Limited Partnerships)
"Adopted by the partners pursuant to 15 Pa.C.S. § 8546(f)."

"Adopted by the general partners pursuant to 15 Pa.C.S. § 8546(g)."

I. *For Business Corporation Only:* If partnership, business trust or other non-corporate association is a party to the plan under 15 Pa.C.S. §1921(c) (relating to business trusts, partnerships and other associations) appropriate changes should be made in the form.

J. *For Business Corporations Only:* If the second option in Paragraph 7 is checked, the surviving corporation is required by 15 Pa.C.S. § 1901(relating to omission of certain provisions from filed plans) to furnish a copy of the full text of the plan, on request and without cost, to any shareholder and, unless the surviving corporation is a closely-held corporation as defined in 15 Pa.C.S. § 1103 (relating to definitions), on request and at cost to any other person.

K. *For Nonprofit Corporations Only:* If the second option in Paragraph 7 is checked, the surviving corporation is required by 15 Pa.C.S. § 5901 (relating to omission of certain provisions from filed plans) to furnish a copy of the full text of the plan, on request and without cost, to any person.

L. *For Limited Partnerships Only:* If the second option in Paragraph 7 is checked, the surviving limited partnership is required by 15 Pa.C.S. § 8547(b) (relating to omission of certain provisions of plan of merger or consolidation) to furnish a copy of the full text of the plan, on request and without cost, to any partner of the limited partnership that was a party to the plan and, unless all parties to the plan had fewer than 30 partners each, on request and at cost to any other person.

M. Where more than two corporations/limited partnerships are parties to the merger appropriate additional corporate signatures should be added. All parties to the merger shall execute the Articles of Merger, including a nonqualified foreign business/nonprofit corporation/limited partnership which is not the surviving corporation/limited partnership and which is not otherwise mentioned in the body of the Articles/Certificate of Merger and with respect to which no docketing statement is submitted, except where the parent corporation (*Business Corporations Only*) is the sole signatory under 15 Pa.C.S. § 1924(b)(3)).

N. This form and all accompanying documents shall be mailed to the address stated above.

O. To receive confirmation of the file date prior to receiving the microfilmed original, send either a self-addressed, stamped postcard with the filing information noted or a self-addressed, stamped envelope with a copy of the filing document.

PENNSYLVANIA DEPARTMENT OF STATE
CORPORATION BUREAU

Articles of Exchange
Domestic Business Corporation
(15 Pa.C.S. §1931)

Entity Number

Name	**Document will be returned to the name and address you enter to the left.**
Address	⇐
City State Zip Code	

Fee: $52

Filed in the Department of State on_____

_____
Secretary of the Commonwealth

In compliance with the requirements of 15 Pa.C.S. § 1931(e) (relating to articles of exchange), the undersigned business corporation, desiring to effect an exchange, hereby states that:

1. The name of the exchanging corporation is:

_____

2. The (a) address of its initial registered office in this Commonwealth or (b) name of its commercial registered office provider and the county of venue is (the Department is hereby authorized to correct the following information to conform to the records of the Department):

   (a) Number and street   City   State   Zip   County

_____

   (b) Name of Commercial Registered Office Provider   County
   c/o
_____

3. *Check and if appropriate complete, one of the following:*

_____ The plan of exchange shall be effective upon filing these Articles of Exchange in the Department of State.

_____ The plan of exchange shall be effective on: _____ at_____.
                                                          Date   Hour

DSCB:15-1931-2

4. *Check one of the following:*

____ The plan of exchange was adopted by act of the shareholders (or members) pursuant to 15 Pa.C.S. § 1905.

____ The plan of exchange was adopted by the directors and shareholders (or members) pursuant to 15 Pa.C.S. §§ 1924(a) and 1931(c).

5. *Check, and if appropriate complete, one of the following:*

____ The plan of exchange is set forth in full in Exhibit A attached hereto and made a part hereof.

____ Pursuant to 15 Pa.C.S. § 1901 (relating to omission of certain provisions from filed plans) the provisions, if any, of the plan of exchange that amend or constitute the operative Articles of Incorporation of the exchanging corporation as in effect subsequent to the effective date of the plan is set forth in full in Exhibit A attached hereto and made a part hereof. The full text of the plan of exchange is on file at the principal place of business of the exchanging corporation, the address of which is:

Number and street	City	State	Zip	County

IN TESTIMONY WHEREOF, the undersigned corporation has caused these Articles of exchange to be signed by a duly authorized officer thereof this

_____ day of _____,

_____ .

_____
Name of Corporation

_____
Signature

_____
Title

Department of State
Corporation Bureau
P.O. Box 8722
Harrisburg, PA 17105-8722
(717) 787-1057
Web site: www.dos.state.pa.us/corp.htm

Instructions for Completion of Form:

A. Typewritten is preferred. If not, the form shall be completed in black or blue-black ink in order to permit reproduction. The filing fee for this form is $52 made payable to the Department of State.

B. Under 15 Pa.C.S. § 135(c) (relating to addresses) an actual street or rural route box number must be used as an address, and the Department of State is required to refuse to receive or file any document that sets forth only a post office box address.

C. The following, in addition to the filing fee, shall accompany this form:

   (1) Any necessary copies of form DSCB:17.2.3 (Consent to Appropriation or Use of Similar Name) shall accompany Articles of Exchange effecting a change of name, and the change in name shall contain a statement of the complete new name.

   (2) Any necessary governmental approvals.

D. The effective date in Paragraph 3 may not be prior to the filing date, but the plan of exchange may state a prior effective date "for accounting purposes only."

E. If the second option in Paragraph 5 is checked, the exchanging corporation is required by 15 Pa.C.S. § 1901 (relating to omission of certain provisions from filed plans) to furnish a copy of the full text of the plan, on request and without cost, to any shareholder and, unless the exchanging corporation is a closely-held corporation as defined in 15 Pa.C.S. § 1103 (relating to definitions), on request and at cost to any other person.

F. This form and all accompanying documents shall be mailed to the address stated above.

G. To receive confirmation of the file date prior to receiving the microfilmed original, send either a self-addressed, stamped postcard with the filing information noted or a self-addressed, stamped envelope with a copy of the filing document.

PENNSYLVANIA DEPARTMENT OF STATE
CORPORATION BUREAU

Articles/Certificate of Division
(15 Pa.C.S.)

Entity Number	

____ Business Corporation (§ 1954)
____ Non-Profit Corporation (§ 5954)
____ Limited Partnership (§ 8579)
____ Limited Liability Company (§ 8964)

Name

Address

City   State   Zip Code

Document will be returned to the name and address you enter to the left.
⇐

Fee: $152 plus $100 for each additional
Entity in excess of one

Filed in the Department of State on _____

_____
Secretary of the Commonwealth

In compliance with the requirements of the applicable provisions (relating to articles/certificate of division), the undersigned desiring to effect a division, hereby states that:

1. The name of the dividing corporation/limited partnership/limited liability company is:

2. *Check and complete one of the following:*
____ The dividing corporation/limited partnership/limited liability company is a domestic business/nonprofit corporation /limited partnership/limited liability company and the (a) address of its current registered office in this Commonwealth or (b) name of its commercial registered office provider and the county of venue is (the Department is hereby authorized to correct the following information to conform to the records of the Department):

(a) Number and Street   City   State   Zip   County

(b) Name of Commercial Registered Office Provider   County
c/o

____ The dividing corporation/limited partnership/limited liability company is a qualified foreign business/nonprofit corporation/limited partnership/limited liability company incorporated/organized under the laws of _____ and the (a) address of its current registered office in this Commonwealth or (b) name of its commercial registered office provider and the county of venue is (the Department is hereby authorized to correct the following information to conform to the records of the Department):

(a) Number and Street   City   State   Zip   County

(b) Name of Commercial Registered Office Provider   County
c/o

____ The dividing corporation/limited partnership/limited liability company is a nonqualified foreign business/nonprofit corporation/limited partnership/limited liability company incorporated/organized under the laws of _____ and the address of its principal office under the laws of such domiciliary jurisdiction is:

Number and Street   City   State   Zip

DSCB:15-1954/5954/8579/8964–2

3. The statute by or under which it was incorporated/organized is:

4. The date of its incorporation/organization is:

5. *Check one of the following:*

___ The dividing corporation/limited partnership/limited liability company will survive the division.

___ The dividing corporation/limited partnership/limited liability company will not survive the division.

6. The name and the address of the registered office in this Commonwealth or name of its commercial registered office provider and the county of venue of each domestic business/nonprofit corporation/limited partnership/limited liability company and qualified foreign business/nonprofit corporation/limited partnership/limited liability company resulting from the division are as follows:

Name	Registered Office Address/Commercial Registered Office Provider	County

7. *Check, and if appropriate complete, one of the following:*

___ The plan of division shall be effective upon filing these Articles/Certificate of Division in the Department of State.

___ The plan of division shall be effective on: _____ at_____.
                                                            Date   Hour

Certificate of Division-Limited Partnership/Limited Liability Company: Complete paragraphs 8 and 9

8. The manner in which the plan of division was adopted is as follows:

9. The plan of division is set forth in full in Exhibit A attached hereto and made a part hereof.

170 ◆

DSCB: 15-1954/5954-3

Articles of Division-Business and Nonprofit Corporations: complete paragraphs 10 and 11

10. *Check one of the following:*

____The dividing corporation is a domestic business/nonprofit corporation and the plan of division was adopted by action of the shareholders (or member) pursuant to 15 Pa.C.S. § 1905 or adopted by action of the members (or shareholders) pursuant to 15 Pa.C.S. § 5905.

____The dividing corporation is a domestic business/nonprofit corporation and the plan of division was adopted by action of the directors and shareholders (or members) pursuant to 15 Pa.C.S. §§ 1924(a) and 1952 or adopted by action of the members (or shareholders) pursuant to 15 Pa.C.S. §§ 5924(a) and 5952(c) and (d).

____The dividing corporation is a domestic business/nonprofit corporation and the plan of division was adopted by action of the board of directors pursuant to 15 Pa.C.S. § 1953 or §§ 5924(b) and 5952(c) and (d).

11. *Check, and if appropriate complete, one of the following:*

____The plan of division is set forth in full in Exhibit A attached hereto and made a part hereof.

____Pursuant to 15 Pa.C.S. § 1901/5901 (relating to omission of certain provisions from filed plans) the provisions, if any, of the plan of division that amends or constitutes the operative provisions of the Articles of Incorporation of the resulting corporations as in effect subsequent to the effective date of the plan are set forth in full in Exhibit A attached hereto and made a party hereof. The full text of the plan of division is on file at the principal place of business of the resulting corporation, the name and address of which is.

Name of Resulting Corporation	Number and street	City	State	Zip	County

IN TESTIMONY WHEREOF, the undersigned has caused these Articles/Certificate of Division to be signed by a duly authorized officer/general partner/member or manager thereof this

_____ day of _____,

_____.

_____
Name of Corporation/Limited Partnership/Limited Liability Company

_____
Signature

_____
Title

DSCB: 15-1954/5954

**Department of State
Corporation Bureau
P.O. Box 8722
Harrisburg, PA 17105-8722
(717) 787-1057
web site: www.dos.state.pa.us/corp.htm**

Instructions for Completion of Form:

A. Typewritten is preferred. If not, the form shall be completed in black or blue-black ink in order to permit reproduction. The filing fee for this form is $152 plus $100 additional for each new corporation/limited partnership/limited liability company in excess of one resulting from the division, made payable to the Department of State.

B. Under 15 Pa.C.S. 135(c) (relating to addresses) an actual street or rural route box number must be used as an address, and the Department of State is required to refuse to receive or file any document that sets forth only a post office box address.

C. The following, in addition to the filing fee, shall accompany this form:

   (1) Two copies of a completed form DSCB:15-134B (Docketing Statement-Changes).

   (2) *Business/Nonprofit Corporation Only:* One copy of a separate completed form DSCB:15-134A (Docketing Statement), with respect to each new corporation resulting from the division, unless the new corporation is a nonqualified foreign corporation.

   (3) Any necessary copies of form DSCB:17.2.3 (Consent to Appropriation or Use of Similar Name). A change in name of a surviving corporation/limited partnership/limited liability company shall contain a statement of the complete new name.

   (4) Any necessary governmental approvals.

   (5) Tax clearance certificates are required from the Department of Revenue and the Bureau of Employment security of the Department of Labor and Industry as described in Instruction G.

D. The second alternate of Paragraph 5 is not applicable unless at least two new corporations/limited partnerships/limited liability companies result from the division.

E. A completed form DSCB:15-1306/2102/2303/2702/2903/3101/7102A (Articles of Incorporation-For Profit)/DSCB:15-5306 (Articles of Incorporation-Nonprofit)/DSCB:15-8511 (Certificate of Limited Partnership)/DSCB:15-8913 (Certificate of Organization) should be attached to the plan of division with respect to each new domestic business/nonprofit corporation/limited partnership/limited liability company resulting from the division. It is not necessary to execute such articles of Incorporation/Certificate of Limited Partnership/Certificate of Organization and an additional fee or fees relating the form should not be tendered.

F. A foreign business/nonprofit corporation/limited partnership/limited liability company may effect a division resulting in one or more new domestic business/nonprofit corporations/limited partnerships/limited liability companies notwithstanding the fact that such foreign business/nonprofit corporation/limited partnership/limited liability company has not received a certificate of authority/application for registration to do business in Pennsylvania.

G. If the dividing corporation/limited partnership/limited liability company will not survive the division and is a domestic business/nonprofit corporation/limited partnership/limited liability company or a qualified foreign business/nonprofit corporation/limited partnership/limited liability company and if none of the new corporations/limited partnerships/limited

liability companies resulting from the division will be either a domestic business/nonprofit corporation/limited
DSCB:15-1954/5954

partnership/limited liability company or a qualified foreign business/nonprofit corporation/limited partnership/limited liability company there must be submitted with this form tax clearance certificates from the Department of Revenue and the Bureau of Employment Security of the Department of Labor and Industry with respect to each domestic business/nonprofit corporation/limited partnership/limited liability company and qualified foreign business/nonprofit corporation/limited partnership/limited liability company evidencing payment of all taxes and charges payable to the Commonwealth.

H. If the name of a commercial registered office provider is used in Paragraph 6 it must be preceded by a "c/o". See 15 Pa.C.S. § 109 (relating to name of commercial registered office provider in lieu of registered address).

I. The effective date in Paragraph 7 may not be prior to the filing date, but the plan of division may state a prior effective date "for accounting purposes only."

J. *Business Corporation Only:* If the dividing corporation is a foreign business corporation the following statement should be substituted in Paragraph 8: "The plan was authorized, adopted or approved, as the case may be, by the dividing foreign business corporation in accordance with the laws of the jurisdiction in which it is incorporated."

K. *Business Corporation Only:* If the second option in Paragraph 9 is checked, the named resulting corporation is required by 15 Pa.C.S. § 1901 (relating to omission of certain provisions from filed plans) to furnish a copy of the full text of the plan, on request and without cost, to any shareholder of any corporation that was a party to the plan and, unless all parties are closely-held corporations as defined in 15 Pa.C.S. 1103 (relating to definitions), on request and at cost to any other person.

L. *Nonprofit Corporation Only:* If the action was authorized by a body other than the board of directors or the members Paragraph 8 should be modified accordingly. If the dividing corporation is a foreign nonprofit corporation the following statement should be substituted in Paragraph 8: "The plan was authorized, adopted or approved, as the case may be, by the dividing foreign nonprofit corporation in accordance with the laws of the jurisdiction in which it is incorporated."

M. *Nonprofit Corporation Only:* If the second option in Paragraph 9 is checked, the named resulting corporation is required by 15 Pa.C.S. § 5901(relating to omission of certain provisions from filed plans) to furnish a copy of the full text of the plan, on request and without cost, to any person.

N. *Limited Partnership/Limited Liability Company:* If the dividing limited partnership/limited liability company is a foreign limited partnership/limited liability company the following statement should be substituted in Paragraph 8: "The plan was authorized, adopted or approved, as the case may be, by the dividing foreign limited partnership/limited liability company in accordance with the laws of the jurisdiction in which it is organized.

O. This form and all accompanying documents shall be mailed to the address stated above.

P. To receive confirmation of the file date prior to receiving the microfilmed original, send either a self-addressed, stamped postcard with the filing information noted or a self-addressed, stamped envelope with a copy of the filing document.

PENNSYLVANIA DEPARTMENT OF STATE
CORPORATION BUREAU

Entity Number

Articles of Dissolution-Domestic
(15 Pa.C.S.)
_____ Business Corporation (§ 1977)
_____ Nonprofit Corporation (§ 5977)

Name _____

Address _____

City _____ State _____ Zip Code _____

Document will be returned to the name and address you enter to the left.
⇐

Fee: $52

Filed in the Department of State on _____

_____
Secretary of the Commonwealth

In compliance with the requirements of the applicable provisions (relating to articles of dissolution), the undersigned corporation, desiring to dissolve, hereby states that:

1. The name of the corporation is:

2. The (a) address of this corporation's current registered office in this Commonwealth or (b) name of its commercial registered office provider and the county of venue is (the Department is hereby authorized to correct the following information to conform to the records of the Department):

   (a) Number and Street   City   State   Zip   County

   (b) Name of Commercial Registered Office Provider   County
   c/o

3. The statute by or under which it was incorporated:

4. The date of its incorporation:

DSCB:15-1977/5977–2

5. The names and addresses, including number and street, of its directors are:

_____

_____

_____

6. The names and addresses, including number and street, and official titles of its officers are:

_____

_____

_____

7. *Check one of the following:*

____ The proposal to dissolve voluntarily was adopted by the shareholders or members pursuant to 15 Pa.C.S. § 1905 or § 5905.

____ The proposal to dissolve voluntarily was adopted by the directors and shareholders (or members) pursuant to 15 Pa.C.S. § 1974(a) or directors and member (or shareholders) pursuant to 15 Pa.C.S. § 5974(b).

____ *Option for Nonprofit Corporation Only:* The proposal to dissolve voluntarily was adopted by the board of directors pursuant to 15 Pa.C.S. § 5974(b).

8. *Check one of the following:*

____ All liabilities of the corporation have been discharged.

____ Adequate provision has been made for the discharge of the liabilities of the corporation.

____ The assets of the corporation are not sufficient to satisfy and discharge its liabilities, and all the assets of the corporation have been fairly and equitably applied, as far as they will go, to the payment of such liabilities.

9. *Check one of the following:*

____ All remaining assets of the corporation, if any, have been distributed as provided in the Business or Nonprofit Corporation Law of 1988.

____ The corporation has elected to proceed under 15 Pa.C.S. Subch. 19H or 59H (relating to post dissolution claims) and any remaining assets of the corporation will be distributed as provided in that subchapter.

10. *Check one of the following:*

____There are no actions or proceedings pending against the corporation in any court.

____Adequate provision has been made for the satisfaction of any judgment or decree that may be obtained against the corporation in each action or proceeding pending against the corporation.

DSCB:15-1977/5977-3

> 11. Notice of the winding-up proceedings of the corporation was mailed by certified or registered mail to each known creditor and claimant of the corporation and to each municipal corporation in which the corporation's registered office or principal place of business in this Commonwealth is located.

IN TESTIMONY WHEREOF, the undersigned corporation has caused these Articles of Dissolution to be signed by a duly authorized officer thereof this

_____ day of _____,_____.

_____
Name of Corporation

_____
Signature

_____
Title

176 ◆

Department of State
Corporation Bureau
P.O. Box 8722
Harrisburg, PA 17105-8722
(717) 787-1057
web site: www.dos.state.pa.us/corp.htm

Instructions for Completion of Form:

A. Typewritten is preferred. If not, the form shall be completed in black or blue-black ink in order to permit reproduction. The filing fee for this form is $52 made payable to the Department of State.

B. Under 15 Pa.C.S. § 135(c) (relating to addresses) an actual street or rural route box number must be used as an address, and the Department of State is required to refuse to receive or file any document that sets forth only a post office box address.

C. The second option in Paragraph 8 should be checked by a corporation that elects to proceed under 15 Pa.C.S. Subch. 19H or 59H (relating to post dissolution claims).

D. The following, in addition to the filing fee, shall accompany this form:

   (1) Tax clearance certificates from the Department of Revenue and from the Bureau of Employment Security of the Department of Labor and Industry evidencing payment of all taxes and charges payable to the Commonwealth.
   (2) Any necessary governmental approvals.

E. The corporation is required by 15 Pa.C.S. § 1975(b) or § 5975(b) (relating to notice to creditors and taxing authorities) to publish notice of the winding-up proceedings one time in the legal journal and newspaper of general circulation published in the county of its registered office, or in two newspapers of general circulation if no legal journal exists in such county, or in one newspaper of general circulation if that is the only one published in the county. Proofs of such publication should be kept with the corporate records of the corporation, and should not be submitted to, and will not be received by or filed in, the Department.

F. This form and all accompanying documents shall be mailed to the above stated address.

G. To receive confirmation of the file date prior to receiving the microfilmed original, send either a self-addressed, stamped postcard with the filing information noted or a self-addressed, stamped envelope with a copy of the filing document.

Form **966**

(Rev. June 2001)

Department of the Treasury
Internal Revenue Service

Corporate Dissolution or Liquidation

(Required under section 6043(a) of the Internal Revenue Code)

OMB No. 1545-0041

Please type or print

Name of corporation	**Employer identification number**
Number, street, and room or suite no. (If a P.O. box number, see instructions below.)	Check type of return
City or town, state, and ZIP code	☐ 1120 ☐ 1120-L ☐ 1120-IC-DISC ☐ 1120S ☐ Other ▶

1 Date incorporated	**2** Place incorporated	**3** Type of liquidation ☐ Complete ☐ Partial	**4** Date resolution or plan of complete or partial liquidation was adopted
5 Service Center where corporation filed its immediately preceding tax return	**6** Last month, day, and year of immediately preceding tax year	**7a** Last month, day, and year of final tax year	**7b** Was corporation's final tax return filed as part of a consolidated income tax return? If "Yes," complete 7c, 7d, and 7e. ☐ Yes ☐ No
7c Name of common parent		**7d** Employer identification number of common parent	**7e** Service Center where consolidated return was filed

	Common	Preferred
8 Total number of shares outstanding at time of adoption of plan of liquidation		
9 Date(s) of any amendments to plan of dissolution		
10 Section of the Code under which the corporation is to be dissolved or liquidated . . .		
11 If this return concerns an amendment or supplement to a resolution or plan, enter the date the previous Form 966 was filed		

Attach a certified copy of the resolution or plan and all amendments or supplements not previously filed.

Under penalties of perjury, I declare that I have examined this return, including accompanying schedules and statements, and to the best of my knowledge and belief, it is true, correct, and complete.

▶

Signature of officer	Title	Date

Instructions

Who must file. A corporation must file Form 966 if it adopts a resolution or plan to dissolve the corporation or liquidate any of its stock. Exempt organizations and qualified subchapter S subsidiaries are not required to file Form 966. These organizations should see the instructions for **Form 990,** Return of Organization Exempt from Income Tax or **Form 990-PF,** Return of Private Foundation or Section 4947(a)(1) Nonexempt Charitable Trust Treated as a Private Foundation and **Form 8869,** Qualified Subchapter S Subsidiary Election, respectively.

Caution: Do not file Form 966 for a deemed liquidation (such as a section 338 election or an election to be treated as a disregarded entity under Regulations section 301.7701-3).

When and where to file. File Form 966 within 30 days after the resolution or plan is adopted to dissolve the corporation or liquidate any of its stock. If the resolution or plan is amended or supplemented after Form 966 is filed, file another Form 966 within 30 days after the amendment or supplement is adopted. The additional form will be sufficient if the date the earlier form was filed is entered on line 11 and a certified copy of the amendment or supplement is attached. Include all information required by Form 966 that was not given in the earlier form.

File Form 966 with the Internal Revenue Service Center where the corporation is required to file its income tax return.

Distribution of property. A corporation must recognize gain or loss on the distribution of its assets in the complete liquidation of its stock. For purposes of determining gain or loss, the distributed assets are valued at fair market value. Exceptions to this rule apply to a liquidation of a subsidiary and to a distribution that is made according to a plan of reorganization.

Address. Include the suite, room, or other unit number after the street address. If mail is not delivered to the street address and the corporation has a P.O. box, enter the box number instead of the street address.

Signature. The return must be signed and dated by the president, vice president, treasurer, assistant treasurer, chief accounting officer, or any other corporate officer (such as tax officer) authorized to sign. A receiver, trustee, or assignee must sign and date any return required to be filed on behalf of a corporation.

Paperwork Reduction Act Notice. We ask for the information on this form to carry out the Internal Revenue laws of the United States. You are required to give us the information. We need it to ensure that you are complying with these laws and to allow us to figure and collect the right amount of tax.

You are not required to provide the information requested by a form or its instructions that is subject to the Paperwork Work Reduction Act unless the form displays a valid OMB control number. Books and records relating to a form or its instructions must be retained as long as their content may become material in the administration of any Internal Revenue law. Generally, tax returns and return information are confidential, as required by section 6103.

The time needed to complete and file this form will vary depending on individual circumstances. The estimated average time is:

Recordkeeping . . . . 5 hr., 1 min.

Learning about the law or the form . . . . 24 min.

Preparing and sending the form to the IRS . . . . . 29 min.

If you have comments concerning the accuracy of these time estimates or suggestions for making this form simpler, we would be happy to hear from you. You can write to the Tax Forms Committee, Western Area Distribution Center, Rancho Cordova, CA 95743-0001. **Do not** send the tax form to this office. Instead, see **When and where to file** on this page.

INDEX

This book is a project of Eat for Health. This organization is dedicated to promoting nutritional solutions to the problems of obesity, cardiovascular disease and type 2 diabetes.

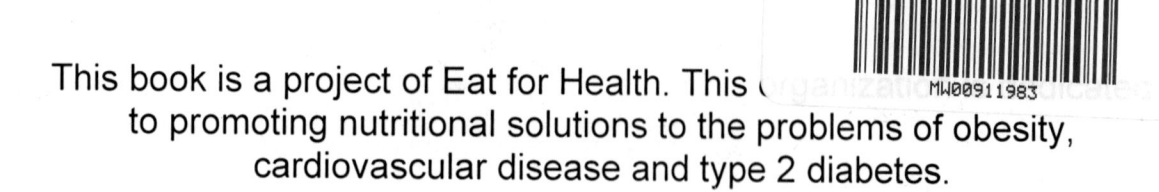

Dr. Arnold Slyper is a practicing Pediatric Endocrinologist at Lehigh Valley Hospital in Allentown, Pennsylvania and a Professor of Pediatrics.

Published by Eat for Health

Cover design by www.betterlivingthroughebooks.com

This book is dedicated to my dear wife Judy, who taught me that healthy food does not have to be bland and tasteless. To the contrary, healthy meal planning is an adventure in the discovery of new and delicious tastes.

She watches over the ways of her household,
and never eats the bread of idleness.
Her children rise and call her happy; her husband also praises her:
"Many women have excelled, but you surpass them all."
(Proverbs 31)

<u>CONTENTS</u>

Chapter 1

Why Changing Carbohydrate is so Important

Let me tell you one of the fundamental principles of nutrition science.

If your diet disagrees with you – change it.

The amount of obesity in this country has risen to astronomical proportions. Clearly, millions of people are being harmed by their diet.

Given this situation, one might think that the overweight of this country would be clamoring to change what they eat.

Now overweight individuals certainly do make changes in their diets – a bit less fat here and a few less calories there - but these are minor changes.

There is only one way to change one's diet in a significant way and that is to change its main constituent, carbohydrate.

So let me tell you the first important message of this book:

- **It's not dietary fat or even calories that is the driving force behind much of the obesity in this country, but eating the wrong type of carbohydrate.**[1]

Let me introduce myself. I'm a pediatric endocrinologist. A pediatric endocrinologist is a specialist in hormonal and metabolic problems affecting children and adolescents. I spend most of my working day seeing patients and in my "spare time" I research into pediatric cardiovascular disease. I also have a long-standing interest in nutrition.

As a pediatric endocrinologist, I see every day the victims from this country's obesity epidemic – adolescents and even children with diabetes who require tablets and sometimes even insulin injections to control their blood sugars, young people whose school progress is devastated by nighttime obstructive airway problems, children with early liver disease that may eventually progress to liver failure, and young ladies whose beauty has become marred by unsightly facial and body hair as a result of polycystic ovary syndrome. And I do my best to help them.

Some years ago I realized I had a problem with the accepted wisdom that obesity is solely due to individuals with a genetic predisposition to being overweight eating too much and exercising too little. It just didn't seem to fit the patients I was seeing. For starters, many of the heavy children I was looking after weren't overeating. Their portion sizes were no bigger and were sometimes even smaller than those of their siblings and other kids their age. Nor were all of these patients physically inactive. Many were heavily involved in sports and other outdoor activities. A calories-in calories-out type of model just didn't seem to reflect these children's weight problem.

Moreover, as the obesity epidemic raged, like other pediatricians and pediatric endocrinologists in this country, I began seeing a new phenomenon – numerous children with insatiable appetites. These were kids who never seemed satisfied with the meal they had just eaten and were always asking for seconds. No sooner had they finished one meal or snack and

they were asking for the next. I certainly saw children like this 10 or 15 years ago, but never in the numbers I was seeing now.

Excess calories would certainly explain the weight gain these kids were experiencing, but what was causing their non-stop eating? I for one found it difficult to believe this was all a simple "behavioral problem" that could be turned off at will with a few behavioral tricks. It seemed extremely physiological to me. It was almost as if their diets were making them hungrier.

As a result of my questioning, reading a lot of scientific papers and writing nutrition reviews, I began to explore new ideas as to how our obesity epidemic might have come about and how best to treat it.

Challenging current obesity treatment

The more I looked at the nutritional mess this country had gotten into, the more I was struck with some radical ideas. Was it possible, I wondered, that the obesity epidemic in this country was due primarily to people eating the wrong type of food rather than excess food? And was it possible that fat was not the main culprit in this story but "bad carbohydrate?" And could it be that eating less fat not only didn't help people control their weight but was making matters worse?[1]

It was in the 1970's that the nutritional experts in this country came up with a wonderful plan for preventing coronary heart disease. Fat, particularly saturated fat, raises blood cholesterol levels. Therefore, they argued, if everyone would eat a bit less fat, particularly saturated fat, the population's cholesterol levels would come down and so would the amount of cardiovascular disease. Furthermore, since fat contains twice as many calories as the same weight of carbohydrate or protein, restricting fat would be a great way for preventing everyone from becoming too heavy.

The nutritional experts forgot one thing. When people cut back on fat, they also cut back on calories. If those lost calories would have been replaced by healthy veggies and whole grains, the health benefits could have been enormous and our obesity epidemic might well have been avoided. But it didn't happen like this. A low-fat "good carb" diet happens to be quite a difficult diet to keep to. Remove the creaminess and sweetness from food and what's left behind is often not very appetizing. Thus, more and more people began eating so-called "healthy diets" that were low in fat but high in "bad carbohydrate."

The food industry was also an important player in this story. People wanted low-fat foods and this is what the food industry provided. Fat was removed from foods and in order to keep the food tasty was replaced with sugar, high-fructose corn syrup, highly refined starches and salt. Was it possible, I wondered, that these changes were making people fat?

Good carbs and bad carbs - understanding the glycemic index system

So why might too much sugar and highly-refined carbohydrate lead to weight gain and so many other health problems? The answer has a lot to do with the important concept of glycemic index.

Let me explain. Carbohydrates are made up of sugar units (or molecules) attached to one another. *Simple carbohydrates* are (as their name implies) pretty simple and consist of just one or two sugar units. *Complex carbohydrates,* and this includes starches such as bread, cake, potatoes and spaghetti, are made up of long chains of sugar molecules, primarily glucose. With respect to simple carbohydrates, the gut absorbs the sugar units very readily and this leads to a rapid rise in blood glucose. However, for complex carbohydrates, glucose absorption depends very much on how the starch is composed.

Consider the two starches white bread and Italian pasta. Both are made from wheat and both consist of long chains of glucose molecules. But the similarities end there, since what happens to them in the gut is very different. The starch in white bread is broken down very rapidly and large amounts of glucose enter quickly into the blood stream. White bread is therefore called a *high-glycemic carbohydrate* (see the following figure). Italian pasta, on the other hand, is made from semolina. Semolina is a milled flour in which the grain particles are larger and coarser than in regular white flour. Pasta is also made from Durum wheat, which is the hardest form of wheat. Because of these two factors, starch granules get trapped in the dough and are broken down slowly in the small intestine. This leads to a smaller and more prolonged glucose rise in the blood. Pasta is therefore considered to be a *low-glycemic carbohydrate.*

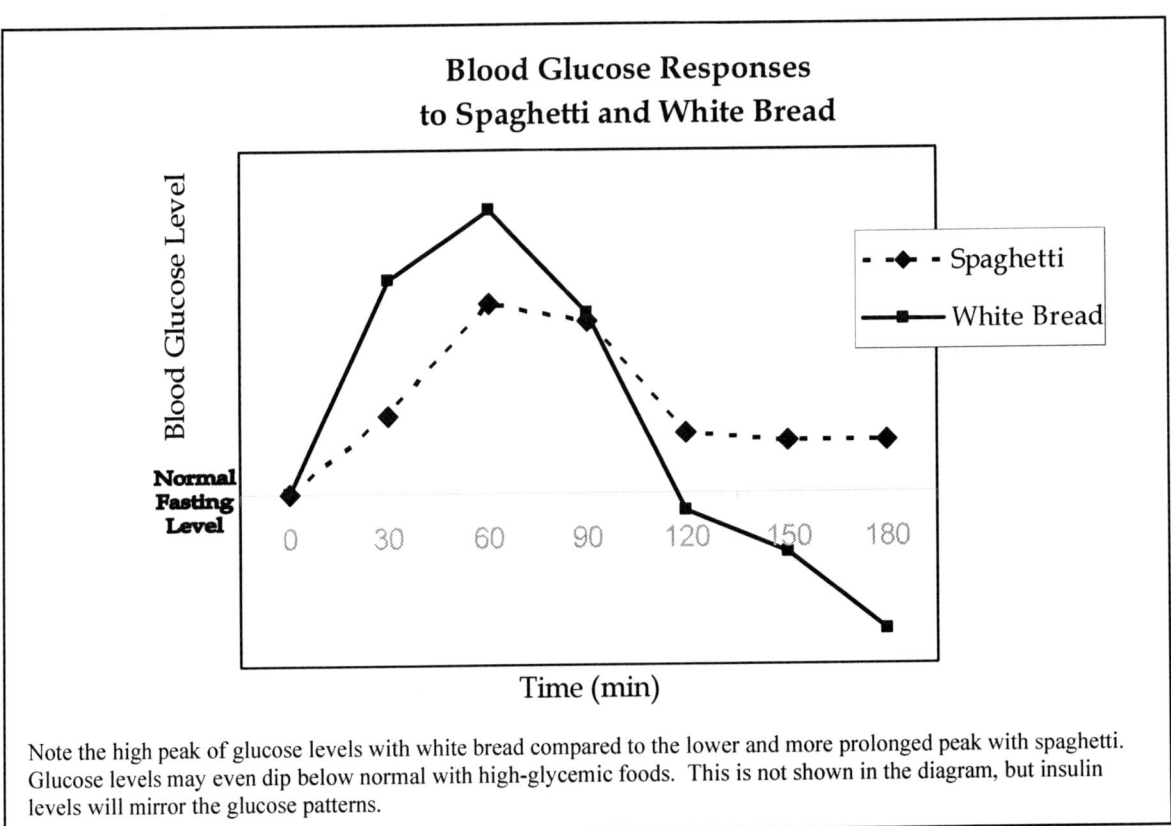

Note the high peak of glucose levels with white bread compared to the lower and more prolonged peak with spaghetti. Glucose levels may even dip below normal with high-glycemic foods. This is not shown in the diagram, but insulin levels will mirror the glucose patterns.

This brings us to the important role of insulin. Whenever one eats a carbohydrate load, specialized cells within the pancreas called islet cells pour out insulin. This hormone allows the body to use the glucose that's just been released into the blood stream. The problem with consuming a lot of high-glycemic foods is that this leads to continually high glucose and insulin levels in the blood and ever more demands on the insulin-producing cells in the pancreas. Many

nutritional experts suspect that these high insulin levels are a set-up for obesity.[2] They may also lead to "insulin resistance" as the body tries to protect itself from the high insulin levels.

[It is the nature of a book like this that somewhat complicated concepts are painted in broad strokes. If you interested in more scientific detail, are skeptical about what you are reading, or are in the health field [or all three], you should definitely read the section References for the Scientifically Bold at the back of this book].

The consequences of high insulin levels

Insulin resistance and high insulin levels can lead to a host of health problems, including a high blood pressure, blood lipid abnormalities and blood sugar problems. These abnormalities frequently cluster together (since they have the same cause) and this combination of abnormalities is often called the "metabolic syndrome". Current estimates are that more than 30% of the U.S. population has this syndrome.

A very common sign of insulin resistance, especially in children, is a condition called *acanthosis nigricans*. This is a dirty-looking pigmentation found most often in the armpits and around the back and front of the lower neck. The more extensive and darker the pigmentation, the more severe is the insulin resistance. If you see this type of pigmentation in your child, you can be sure that he or she has substantial insulin resistance. However, absence of this pigmentation does not necessarily mean that your child is free of insulin resistance. About 50% of children with insulin resistance have no signs of acanthosis nigricans. Moreover, not everyone with insulin resistance is obese, and insulin resistance may be a lot more common than suspected.[3]

One of the most serious long-term complications of insulin resistance and the metabolic syndrome is vascular disease: heart attacks, peripheral vascular disease and strokes. Other serious problems include fat accumulation in the liver and obstructive sleep problems. In female adolescents and women of child-bearing age, high insulin levels can lead to a hormone imbalance in the ovaries and a condition known as polycystic ovary syndrome. This is associated with obesity, the development of excessive body hair, and irregular and even absent periods.

Working towards a solution

Please follow along with the following logic: Most people with obesity have high insulin levels. High insulin levels contribute to obesity. High-glycemic foods lead to high insulin levels, whereas low-glycemic food leads to lower insulin levels. Therefore, the first step in treating obesity is to bring insulin levels down by reducing on high-glycemic carbohydrate and eating low-glycemic carbohydrate instead.

Portion control and low-calorie diets are useful over the short term, but if high-glycemic foods are not removed from one's diet it is going to be very difficult to achieve long-lasting weight control and weight reduction.

So which carbohydrates are the high-glycemic ones that need to be reduced or eliminated? The bad guys are high sugar-containing foods and highly refined carbohydrate such as soda, candies, crackers, pretzels and many breakfast cereals. "White starches" such as white bread, potato and white rice are also high-glycemic. Instead of these foods, you should be

choosing low-glycemic carbohydrates such as whole grains, pasta, vegetables, fruit, beans, seeds and nuts.

As a physician with an interest in nutrition, I've spent a lot of time trying to figure out how to make low-glycemic and unrefined carbohydrate more enticing to American families. Let's face it, "eating low-glycemic" doesn't have a particularly appealing ring about it. The reality is that whole grains and vegetables are not particularly high on the shopping list of most American families, if they get there at all.

It turned out that the answer to my (and your) problem was literally jumping out of the cookbooks.

For centuries, Mediterranean people have been cooking appetizing dishes made from vegetables, fruit and whole grains (or they were until they started eating like Americans).

Mediterranean people also learned to put foods together in combinations - grains together with vegetables, meat and fowl together with grains and/or vegetables - and they created mouth-watering dishes from otherwise very ordinary ingredients.

Of course, Mediterranean countries are not the only places in the world that figured out how to put foods together in tasty combinations. Many other countries use the same type of cooking, which is why I call this "Mediterranean-*style*" meal planning.

Mediterranean-style meal planning is all about:

- **Eating lots of vegetables**

- **Using whole grains and low-glycemic starches**

- **Eating a moderate amount of healthful fat such as olive oil and canola oil**

- **Limiting red meat and eating more fish and fowl**

- **Eating fruit, nuts and seeds**

One of the first studies to show the health benefits of a Mediterranean diet was the Lyon Diet Heart Study carried out in Lyon, France. Researchers wanted to know whether a "Mediterranean diet" was any better than a moderately low-fat diet in preventing heart disease. The people chosen to participate in this study were individuals who had already suffered a heart attack and who were therefore very much at risk for future cardiovascular problems.

The results were amazing. For subjects on the Mediterranean diet, cardiovascular events were reduced by 30% over 4 years and death by an incredible 70% compared to the low-fat diet.[4] In most other cardiovascular studies, the protective effects of an intervention, whether it be a drug or a diet, are usually rather modest and take years to show up. Not so in this study. Within 28 months, subjects on this diet were already showing less cardiovascular problems, indicating that this diet was having an extremely rapid effect.

Since this paper was published, more and more scientific literature has appeared showing that people who "eat Mediterranean" develop less cardiovascular disease, less obesity, and less cancer.[5]

So, change your carbohydrates and begin eating Mediterranean-style and the following health benefits will start to kick in:

- **Portion control will become more manageable and not a constant struggle against the body's physiology**

- **Blood insulin levels and features of the insulin resistance syndrome will begin improving**

- **Weight control will become more manageable**

- **Blood pressure will start to come down**

- **Blood lipids (particularly triglyceride) will improve**

- **Blood sugars will fall and your chances of developing diabetes will lessen**

- **Your risk of developing one of the most serious complications of obesity – cardiovascular disease – will be reduced**

This brings me back to those children who have non-stop eating and who never seem satisfied with the meal they have just eaten. It is very likely that this type of eating pattern is a lot more than a simple behavioral problem. There is now a lot of scientific evidence that high-glycemic food increases hunger, and it is very possible that the food these people are eating is actually making them hungrier.[6]

To explain this, I often give the example of a hamburger roll. Eat a hamburger with white bread and there's a good chance that you will soon be asking for another one. It might taste good, but it's just not very satisfying. However, if you were to place that same hamburger between two slices of heavy whole grain bread containing lots of whole grains the chances are that you will be less inclined to ask for seconds.

So, if members of your family are always hungry, they need to stop eating so much high-glycemic carbohydrate and start eating more vegetables and whole grains. The more severe their continual hunger, the more low-glycemic vegetables and whole grains they need to eat.

Fat, vegetables and antioxidants

There are two other important aspects to Mediterranean-style meal planning that I always emphasize to patients.

Firstly, Mediterranean-style meal planning does not have to be low-fat.[7]

Low-fat dieting can indeed be helpful for adults at high risk for heart disease, for

example because of their medical history, family history or blood lipids. However, for everyone else low-fat dieting is usually unnecessary and may even be counterproductive if becomes a bad-carb diet.[8]

A further problem with low-fat diets is that they often eliminate fats that have no reason to be eliminated. This is discussed in detail in chapter four (Clogging and Unclogging Arteries). Olive oil, for example, is jam-packed with health benefits, probably because of its high content of antioxidants. Canola oil contains omega-3 fat that protects against heart disease and possibly other diseases as well. Dairy fat has gotten a far worse reputation than it truly warrants. The bottom line is that for the average healthy person, there's no reason to eliminate all these fats.

- **For most people, eating the right type of fat is more important than avoiding it.**

Especially if you have gotten used to low-fat cooking, it's easy to forget how much this limits the type of food you can serve to your family. Add back healthy fats and not only will your food taste better, but you will find a wealth of fantastic new dishes to try out. With Mediterranean-style meal planning there's no reason to think twice about dressing salads with olive oil, frying or sautéing with olive or canola oil, or adding a bit of cheese to a dish. No reason either to have a guilt trip every time you sprinkle olive oil onto some vegetables before putting them in the oven.

The second point I make a big deal of is the importance of vegetables.

Eating vegetables is an essential part of Mediterranean-style meal planning for a number of reasons: most vegetables are low-glycemic, they contain antioxidants, and they have a high fiber content.

- **It's extremely difficult to successfully treat an obesity problem over the long term without increasing one's intake of vegetables.**

I've mentioned the term "antioxidants" a few times in this section, so let me explain what they are all about.

The science of antioxidants is a new, exciting and rapidly expanding field and there is still a tremendous amount we need to learn. You may have read that certain foods such as tomatoes, chocolate and green tea are particularly healthful. What is being emphasized here are the effects of the antioxidants found within these foods. Many of the chemicals that provide natural coloring to fruits and vegetables are antioxidants. There are literally several thousand of these compounds contained within the foods we eat and we are just beginning to understand their role in the prevention of cardiovascular disease, insulin resistance and perhaps even cancer.

So what exactly is an antioxidant?

Whenever one eats a meal, our blood vessel walls form noxious chemicals as a consequence of the food we have just eaten. These chemicals are called free radicals or oxidants. Fortunately, our blood vessels are able to neutralize these chemicals by making antioxidants. However, if you already have unhealthy blood vessels, for example, because you have diabetes, a high cholesterol level, or you are constantly eating a diet that's high-glycemic and/or contains a lot of unhealthy fats, these free radicals can overwhelm the blood vessel's natural defenses. This

is why additional antioxidants absorbed during a meal can be so helpful.[9] However, if you've eliminated fruit, veggies and whole grains from your diet, you've been denying your arteries this extra protection.

But what do you do if your family doesn't like vegetables? This is not an unusual scenario these days. Many kids have gotten used to vegetable-free diets and it can be extremely challenging to break this pattern.

There are two approaches I recommend. Rather than nagging your kids to eat unattractive and tasteless vegetables, make sure the vegetables you make are attractive and tasty. Secondly, sneak those vegetables into soups, protein and grain dishes, in a Mediterranean-mode, and use the protein and grains to make the vegetables taste really good.

This is where you will find the recipe section of this book very helpful. Think of it not just as a recipe section but as a do-it-yourself guide to making vegetables and grains more attractive to you and your family.

Giving up on vegetables just isn't an option.

The effect of exercise

At this stage, we need to discuss the effects of physical activity. Everyone knows that to successfully lose weight you need to exercise more to burn up all those calories. I'm constantly meeting families who are convinced that if they were just able to do a bit more exercise, body fat would melt away.

But is it true?

The more I looked at the scientific literature, the more I was surprised to learn how relatively ineffective leisure activity is in influencing body weight.[10]

Let me clarify this sentence. If you are a marathon runner or you do a lot of physical activity during your work, this will definitely help maintain your weight. Continual fidgeting also keeps a lid on excessive weight gain. But these are big calorie-loss items. For most people, a few sessions each week in the gym, on the jogging track, or on the soccer field are not going to make a lot of difference to your weight. So if you think you can exercise yourself out of your obesity with a few daily push-ups – think again!

This doesn't mean, of course, that exercise has no value. Physical activity is incredibly beneficial to health, even in small amounts. It improves the health of blood vessels, reduces high insulin levels, lowers blood sugars and makes weight control that much easier. It's just not very good at producing a lot of weight loss.

The reason for this is that leisure activity burns up only a small amount of calories relative to the total amount of energy expended by the body, and this is too little to have much influence on weight. Nevertheless, physical activity does burn up intra-abdominal fat, the fat inside one's belly. This fat loss is extremely helpful to one's metabolism, and probably accounts for the beneficial effects from even a small increase in physical activity.

This all means that increasing physical activity is a must for a weight control program, but one has to be realistic as to what it can achieve. Pounds of weight loss are not usually one of its results.

Which brings us back again to diet.

A physiological way for losing weight

Some years ago I made an observation that was to be critical to my helping overweight kids and adults. From working with diabetic children, I began realizing that carbohydrate regulation is a very effective way for influencing body weight.

Type 1 diabetics are taught and get very proficient at "counting carbs", i.e. estimating the amount of carbohydrate they are eating so they can inject themselves with the right amount of insulin. What I noticed was that I could influence the weight of my diabetic patients by decreasing or increasing the amount of carbohydrate they were eating. For example, I would negotiate with an adolescent to eliminate a mid-afternoon snack of 30 gm of carbohydrate or reduce the carbohydrate of a certain meal by 15 gm. And wonders! When they returned for their next 3-month visit, their excessive weight gain had slowed and some had even lost some. It worked the other way too. I could increase the weight of underweight diabetics by persuading them to eat more carbohydrate.

Why not, I asked myself, use the same system for overweight kids and adults? After all, the same mechanisms are at play. Whenever one reduces one's intake of carbohydrate, insulin secretion is reduced and this reduces weight-gaining tendencies. The same principle is at work when one eats low-glycemic carbohydrate, except that carbohydrate reduction has the potential to be far more potent.

It worked like a breeze!

I call this method of controlling weight "carb regulation" so as to distinguish it from low-carb dieting. There are similarities between the two, but there are also important differences. Low-carb dieting aims for rapid and extreme weight loss. It also involves a considerable increase in dietary fat or protein (depending on which diet you choose) to control the resulting hunger. By contrast, the carb regulation described in this book aims for gradual weight loss using modest carbohydrate reduction and only a small increase in dietary protein and fat. Any protein or fat added also has to be healthful.

I recall once telling a medical colleague that I intended to write a diet book that included a section on gradual weight loss using mild to moderate carbohydrate reduction. He told me to forget it. People nowadays want quick fixes - minute steaks, high-speed internet, instant potato. If it doesn't happen now, it's not worth bothering with. I told him that I thought he was mistaken. True, for themselves individuals may seek quick solutions, but when it comes to their families and loved ones, they know that the quickest way isn't always the best. And this is particularly the case when it comes to weight-loss diets.

From the scientific literature we have learnt that extreme weight loss comes at a cost. Extreme weight loss sets into motion metabolic responses that try to push body weight back to where it was previously. Nutritional experts used to call this the "set point". The set point is the weight the body would like to be at if only you would stop starving it!

What happens is that during weight loss the calories required by the body *fall* to a point *lower* than before dieting. This is why so many people who use low-carb dieting regain the weight they have lost once their initial enthusiasm has waned, since they now need to eat even less food than they did before dieting in order to stop gaining weight again. However, with gradual and sustained weight loss achieved by *carbohydrate regulation* it may be possible to avoid these wild swings in body weight.

There are two other important aspects to this weight-loss plan you need to know about.

Firstly, because Mediterranean-style meal planning and carb-regulated dieting are aiming for the same thing – to reduce weight-gaining tendencies by lowering insulin secretion – it's important that most of the carbohydrate you do eat remains low-glycemic. In this way, the carbohydrate you eat will be helping you along. With low-glycemic carbohydrate you will also feel less hungry. This will become particularly important when you reach the phase of weight maintenance.

Secondly, this program doesn't count the carbohydrates from vegetables and fruit.

Now don't misunderstand me. Vegetables and fruit do contain carbohydrate and diabetics on insulin do count the carbs from vegetables and fruit when estimating their insulin requirements, just as they do for starches. Nevertheless, it works well in this diet plan for the following reasons:

- **In general, the amount of carbohydrate in vegetables and fruit in terms of portion size is less than it is for starches, since so much of their content is water.**

- **It's much easier to count only starches without having to consider every carbohydrate you put into your mouth.**

- **This advice pushes you in the direction of eating more vegetables and fruit and away from weight gain-inducing starches.**

There are several ways for using the "carb regulation" described in this book. Many people will aim for substantial weight loss. Others may be content to lose just a few pounds. It's worth knowing that one doesn't have to become slim in order to reduce many of the major problems associated with obesity, such as high blood sugars. A weight loss of between 5 to 10% of one's current weight is often enough to make a substantial difference. Other individuals may prefer a looser system that aims just at preventing further weight gain. For children especially this is often the most realistic goal. This is all discussed in greater detail in chapter three (Control Carbs and Lose Weight).

In conclusion

In this introductory chapter, I place the emphasis where it needs to be - not on calories, fat and exercise – but on carbohydrate. In the chapters that follow I will show you how changing the type and amount of carbohydrate you eat, as well as paying attention to the type of dietary fat you use, will enable you to control your weight, and even more important – lead towards long-term health.

Chapter 2

Go Mediterranean and Control Body Weight!

Mention the word "diet" and the first thing that usually comes to mind is deprivation. However, this chapter is not about being deprived. To the contrary, this is a new and exciting way of eating. This is why I call this way Mediterranean-style *"meal planning"* and not Mediterranean-style dieting.

At this stage, regulating food intake is not our prime focus. This comes in the following chapter. Rather, our entire focus is to *change the type of foods that you and your family will be eating.*

Note that this chapter is not about changing the diet of one particular family member, although that person may well be the impetus for change. Mediterranean-style meal planning has to be approached from a family perspective. If one family member is on a special meal plan while for everyone else it's business as usual, the chances of long-term success for that person are poor. I admit that this does mean that other family members will have to make sacrifices, but in return they are buying into a meal plan that almost guarantees long-term health benefits.

This is what "Mediterranean-style" meal planning is all about:

- **Eliminating a lot of sugar and high-glycemic carbohydrate**

- **Eating more vegetables**

- **Using low-glycemic starches and whole grains**

- **Cooking with healthful fats such as olive and canola oil**

- **Eating less red meat and eating fish, fowl and vegetable protein instead**

- **Eating more fruit, nuts and seeds**

- **Mixing grains, vegetables and protein into delicious combinations of taste and color.**

Although it's at the end of the list, this last point is important. Americans and many Europeans typically place their starch, protein and the vegetable portions as separate items on their plate, and this very much limits how enticing these items can be. Mediterranean-style meal planning, on the other hand, mixes these foods, allowing for a lot more interesting and creative cooking.

This program does rely heavily on the "glycemic index" system. Nevertheless, there's no reason to get hung up on glycemic index figures, as long as you keep to the general principles outlined in this chapter. The figures quoted in these few pages are almost all you will need to remember.

Let us now take food categories one by one:

Cut back on sugar and corn syrup

This is not a sugar-free meal plan. Nevertheless, high sugar items do need to be reduced and three items in particular should be completely eliminated. This is especially important if you have a weight problem.[1]

- **Regular soda**
- **Sports drinks such as Gatorade**
- **High sugar-containing foods such as candies and fruit roll-ups.**

Stopping regular soda is a must. First, it's a source of "empty calories." Whenever one eats solid food, the body's hunger signals are turned off, but this doesn't happen with drinks such as soda. Second, drinking regular soda leads to a surge of glucose and insulin into the blood and these surges are potentially weight promoting. The same is true for sports drinks. There's no reason at all to load up on sugar before exercise, since our muscles have no need for this type of assistance.

A tip: if your family is addicted to regular soda, add a small amount of fruit juice to plain seltzer - just enough juice to give it taste. Flavored seltzer is another alternative.

Many of the fruit drinks sold in this country are high in added sugar or corn sweetener. Kool-aid is an example. Many natural juices also contain a lot of high-glycemic sugars, so that if your child has a weight problem it makes a lot of sense to limit such juices as apple juice and grape juice. Whole fruit is much healthier!

Because of their concern that excessive fruit juice can promote obesity, the American Academy of Pediatrics recommends limiting fruit juice in children and adolescents to no more than two 6-oz drinks a day. Particularly healthy fruit juices are those with a high content of the antioxidant vitamin C, such as orange juice, grapefruit juice and cranberry juice.

Sugar and high fructose corn syrup are made up of fructose and glucose. Many fruit juices are also rich in fructose. Recently, many nutritional scientists have become concerned that large amounts of dietary fructose may be even more harmful than large amounts of glucose.[2]

In moderate amounts, fructose, like glucose, is completely harmless. After all, fructose is present in such healthful foods as fruit, fruit juices and honey. However, in large amounts, fructose has some nasty metabolic effects, and in excess can lead to such problems as increased insulin resistance and high glucose and triglyceride levels.

Despite its name, high fructose corn sweetener is not pure fructose, but, like sugar, is a mixture of fructose and glucose. The corn syrup used to sweeten soft drinks contains 55% fructose and 45% glucose, while sugar contains 50% of each, so that corn syrup is not much different from sugar. The high fructose corn syrup found in breads, jams and yogurt actually contains less fructose than sugar - 42% fructose and 58% glucose.

The problem with high fructose corn sweetener is not its content, but the huge amounts that some people are eating and drinking.

Eat less of the following high-glycemic starches:

- Potatoes – eat no more than twice a week
- Potato chips (baked tortilla chips are fine)
- Cakes, cookies and donuts
- Crackers
- Snack foods such as pretzels (even the low-fat varieties)

These are all high-glycemic starches, and should be reduced or even eliminated, especially if you have a weight or high insulin problem.

Choose only healthy breads!

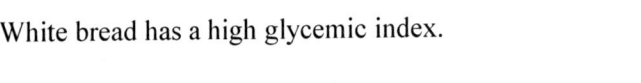

White bread has a high glycemic index.

Lower glycemic breads include:

- **Whole wheat bread**
- **Mixed grain bread**
- **Rye bread**
- **Pumpernickel bread**
- **Sourdough bread**

Unfortunately, the terminology here is confusing, since stores frequently don't distinguish whether a loaf of bread contains flour in which all components of the grain have been milled together or whether the bread contains intact grains that have not been milled at all. Both types of bread are often termed *whole grain*. However, despite the same label these two types of bread are very different.

Let me explain. Regular white flour is milled only from endosperm, which is the largest part of the grain. *Whole wheat flour,* on the other hand, is milled from the entire wheat kernel, i.e. the endosperm, germ and bran. The bran is the outer covering of the wheat kernel (see the picture below). Most of the fiber of the grain is contained within the germ and bran, so that whole wheat flour contains a lot more fiber than does white flour.

At this point, it's worth digressing for a minute to explain what fiber is. Fiber is a carbohydrate, but unlike starch is not readily broken down in the gut. Cellulose is an example of fiber. Fiber is important with respect to glycemic index, since it may influence how carbohydrate is treated in the gut and this in turn can affect the glycemic index of an entire meal.

There are two types of dietary fiber - *soluble fiber* and *insoluble fiber. Soluble fiber* is viscous (sort of jelly-like) and is found in such foods as apples, oats and legumes. Soluble fiber stays viscous even within the upper bowel and this has the effect of delaying the absorption of all other carbohydrate in the meal, resulting in the meal having a lower glycemic index. The fiber in flour, on the other hand, is *insoluble fiber* and this type of fiber has very little influence on carbohydrate absorption.

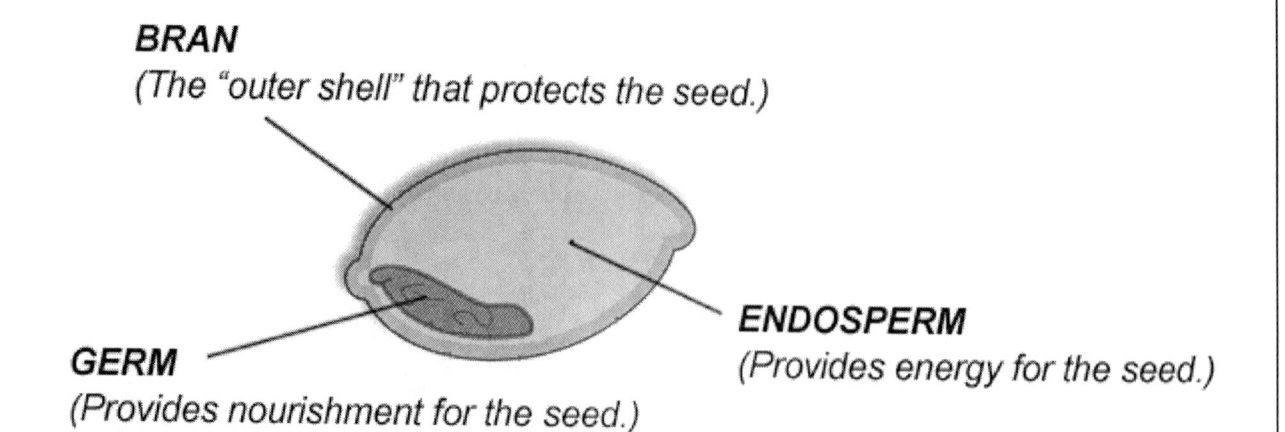

BRAN
(The "outer shell" that protects the seed.)

ENDOSPERM
(Provides energy for the seed.)

GERM
(Provides nourishment for the seed.)

This picture shows the parts of a whole grain kernel.

Thus, the glycemic index of whole wheat bread is only slightly lower than that of white bread, even though whole wheat bread contains a lot more fiber.

Despite this, there are reasons other than glycemic index to change from white to whole wheat bread. In addition to extra fiber, whole wheat flour contains important nutrients that would otherwise be removed by the milling process, such as antioxidants, trace minerals and vitamin B and vitamin E.

Nevertheless, even though whole wheat bread is a cut above white bread, it's not the optimal choice. So let's keep on looking.

Stone ground whole wheat flour is an improvement on whole wheat flour because it's less finely ground than machine ground flour and this gives it an even lower glycemic index. [3] With a bit of searching, you may be able to find whole wheat bread made from *stone ground whole wheat flour* in your grocery store.

However, even better than stone ground whole wheat bread is bread in which the kernels of grain can actually be seen within the bread. This type of bread is often sold as a *"mixed grain bread"*, since it contains a mixture of whole grains and white flour. Because of its content of white flour, it cannot be called "whole grain" (since it's not 100% whole grain). Despite containing white flour, I consider "mixed grain breads" containing a substantial amount of whole grains to be even better than whole wheat bread. [4]

In general, there's no reason to get over-focused on glycemic index values, but for foods such as bread it can be helpful. It's difficult to give figures for the glycemic index value of mixed grain breads since it very much depends on how many whole grains they contain, but it can be as low as 35 and as high as 70. (A glycemic index of over 70 is considered high-glycemic, 56-69 moderate-glycemic and less than 55 low-glycemic).

Other breads with a moderately low glycemic index are rye bread (glycemic index of 41-63), pumpernickel bread (glycemic index of 41-62) and sourdough bread (glycemic index of 54-66). Sourdough bread contains no whole grains, but its acidic nature slows its absorption from the gut. Pumpernickel bread is a type of sourdough made from a combination of rye meal and

rye flour. The rye meal is more coarsely ground than the rye flour. You may also be able to find a rye bread with intact grains, and from a glycemic index perspective this would be preferable to regular rye bread.

Experiment with low-glycemic starches, whole grains and beans!

Healthy low-glycemic starches include the following:

- **Spaghetti**
- **Pasta**
- **Corn**
- **Lentils**
- **Pearl barley**
- **Most beans**

Also consider the following whole grains:

- **Bulgur wheat**
- **Cracked wheat**
- **Whole oats**
- **Barley**
- **Quinoa**
- **Buckwheat**
- **Wheat berries**

If you are unfamiliar with some of these grains and starches you will find the recipe section entitled "Experiment with New Grains" especially helpful.

If you are the cook for the family, you should plan the introduction of these new grains carefully, since a critical and uncooperative family could put you way back with this program. Keep going - but slowly!

Pasta products are always a good standby. However, make sure that you buy Italian-style pasta made from semolina and Durum wheat. Semolina is a coarsely milled flour, while Durum wheat is a particularly hard form of wheat. These two factors account for pasta's low glycemic index. Chinese noodles and many ready-made macaroni-cheese products contain neither semolina nor Durum wheat and may therefore have quite a high glycemic index.

The difference in glycemic index between white and whole grain pasta is rather minimal. To my mind, therefore, it's not worth pushing whole grain pasta onto a reluctant family. On the other hand, whole grain pasta does contain extra fiber, minerals and antioxidants, and if your family likes the taste it should certainly be encouraged.

Cooking a pilaf is a tasty way for introducing new whole grains. A pilaf is a grain-based recipe that uses chicken soup as a base. You will find a number of excellent pilaf recipes in the recipe-section.

Be aware, however, that most bought soups, and this includes chicken soup, often contain a lot of salt, unless one buys a low-salt variety. Other foods that contain a lot of salt are soy sauce

and many tomato products such as salsa, spaghetti sauce and even canned tomatoes. This is not because these foods are naturally high in salt but because the manufacturers put the salt in. The same is true for many snack foods and pickles.

It's worth saying a few words about salt at this stage. A high salt intake is associated with an increased risk for high blood pressure, stroke and heart disease. Because of this, the American Heart Association recommends that all healthy individuals should keep their daily sodium intake below 2,400 mg. This is equivalent to a teaspoon of salt. The elderly, those with high blood pressure and African-Americans should consume even less. This advice is well worth adhering to since it can delay or even prevent a future stroke or heart attack.

On the other hand, eating more vegetables and whole grains than you did in the past is a major change, and many families may find their meals somewhat bland without added salt. How much salt one puts in one's food is an acquired taste. Because Americans eat a lot of snack food, fast foods and tomato products, the American diet is a very salty one. The average American male eats about 1¾ teaspoons of salt a day (4,160 mg of sodium) and average female about 1¼ teaspoons a day of salt (2,920 mg of sodium). However, it's not difficult to get used to less salt, provided one does it slowly. My advice therefore is to let your family first adjust to Mediterranean-style cooking with its increased grains and vegetables and only then to start reducing on salt. If you go slowly, their palates will have time to adjust and they won't even notice the change.

Eat the right type of rice!

The glycemic index of boiled white rice is between 72 to102, which makes it a high-glycemic food. Types of rice with a lower glycemic index include:

- Basmati rice (glycemic index of about 43-69)
- Brown rice (glycemic index of about 62-72)
- Long grain rice (glycemic index of about 50-69)
- Uncle Ben's rice (about 56)

Uncle Ben's rice is parboiled and this gives it a lower glycemic index.

That was a simple one!

Eat only quality breakfast cereals!

If you're accustomed to starting the day with a breakfast cereal, then eating a quality low-glycemic breakfast cereal with whole grains is important.

A few years ago, nutritional researchers in Boston carried out a revealing study.[5] Adolescent volunteers were fed three types of breakfasts and lunches – low-glycemic, intermediate-glycemic and high-glycemic. The researchers then examined how this affected their subsequent hunger and food intake. What they found was that the adolescents who ate the high-glycemic meals felt hungrier and ate significantly more food than those who had the low-glycemic meals. The intermediate-glycemic meals had an effect somewhere in between.

This study demonstrates very nicely that what you eat at mealtime has a substantial impact on how hungry you feel afterwards. Eat a high-glycemic breakfast and you will be hungry at lunch time and this will lead you to grab the closest high-glycemic food available – which of course will make you hungrier later on. In this way, a hunger cycle is perpetuated day after day.

Not having breakfast at all may be even worse than a high-glycemic breakfast. Several pediatric studies have shown that skipping breakfast on a regular basis is associated with obesity and poor school performance.[6] These are both good reasons to avoid the habit!

Unfortunately, many of the popular breakfast cereals are high-glycemic. They may have other things going for them, such as added vitamins, but all the vitamins in the world won't change a high-glycemic breakfast cereal into a low-glycemic one.

These are the glycemic index values of some popular breakfast cereals. Much of this data is for brands manufactured outside this country (since this is where the measurements were made), but American brands are probably not much different. Cereals with a high-glycemic index value are marked in italics while low-glycemic ones are in bold.

All-Bran (Kellogg's, USA) 38
Cheerios (General Mills, Canada) 74
Coco Pops (Australia) 77
Cornflakes (Kellogg's USA) 92
Crispix (Kellogg's Canada) 87
Froot Loops (Kellogg's Australia) 69
Golden Grahams (General Mills, Canada) 71
Grapenuts (Kraft, USA) 75
Life (Quaker Oats, Canada) 66
Muesli (Alpen) 55
Puffed Wheat (Quaker Oats, Canada) 67
Raisin Bran (Kellogg's, USA) 61
Rice Chex (Nabisco, Canada) 89
Rice Krispies (Kellogg's, Canada) 82
Shredded Wheat (Nabisco, Canada) 83
Total (General Mills, Canada) 76
Weetabix (Weetabix, Canada) 75

Depressingly, perhaps, you may have noticed that most or even all of your family's favorite breakfast cereals have either a high or moderately high glycemic index. This is why, incidentally, these cereals are such poor snacks for children, since despite the hype on the packet many are little different from cakes and cookies in the way they are handled by the body.

Suitable low-glycemic high-fiber cereals include the following:

- **Many Mueslis**
- **Oatmeal (made from Old Fashioned Oats)**
- **The Original Shredded Wheat spoon size**
- **Post Bran Flakes**
- **General Mills Fiber One Bran**
- **Uncle Sam Whole Flaxseed Cereal**

- **Kellog's All-Bran Original**

Hold on a minute! Don't get depressed. Whatever you do, don't give up now! We have to work this out together.

Here are some ideas:

- **Add fruit and berries to make low-glycemic cereals more appealing. This could include strawberries, blueberries or slices of apple for example.**

- **Why not make your own breakfast cereal? Turn to "Breakfast – an Essential Meal" in the recipe section for two super granola recipes and a Muesli recipe containing whole grains, seeds and nuts. These recipes can also be spruced up with fruit and berries.**

- **Try something else for breakfast besides a breakfast cereal, such as a plain yogurt with fruit, an omelet, or whole grain toast.**

Veggies forever!

Using green, red and other colored vegetables, legumes and root vegetables is an essential part of Mediterranean-style meal planning. Everyone in the family should aim for at least two veggie portions a day. As a parent, you will need to be the role model for this!

Potatoes are an exception. I agree, they look like a vegetable, feel like a vegetable and are called a vegetable - but they are also pure starch. Unlike many other vegetables, potatoes have a very high glycemic index, especially if they are baked or mashed.

I am always reminding veggie-deprived families that vegetables have to be presented in an attractive way to turn the situation around. Cooking Mediterranean-style can be especially helpful in this situation in that the vegetables are combined with meat, fowl, grains and other vegetables, thereby making extremely tasty combinations (see "Eating Mediterranean-style" in the recipe section).

Remember also that there are other ways of cooking vegetables besides boiling – roasting vegetables with olive oil in the oven, for example. For other ideas, turn to "Jazzing up Vegetables" in the recipe section.

For the confirmed veggie-hater, soups are an excellent way for starting a veggie campaign. Soups have another benefit too. Not only are they a wonderful way for introducing vegetables into your family's diet, but they also extremely filling. I didn't make this up. Scientists have confirmed it.[7]

I've noticed that few families these days begin their meal with a soup course. However, starting a meal with a soup (preferably home-made) is an excellent way for helping to control hunger, especially for the person who is always requesting seconds or who feels like snacking almost as soon as he or she has finished his or her main meal.

Fruit at least once a day!

Eating fruit is an excellent, non-fattening way to end a meal.

Here are some other suggestions for including fruit in your meal planning:

- **Make a homemade fruit-salad with fruits and nuts.**

- **Put berries and pieces of fruit on a breakfast cereal or on top of unsweetened plain yogurt.**

- **Search for exotic fruit such as mangoes, kiwis and pineapple and serve them for dessert.**

- **Try out salads containing mixtures of vegetables and fruit.**

- **The kids may appreciate a sweet apple such as a Fuji apple.**

In conclusion, Mediterranean-style meal planning is not just for overweight children and adults. This is a plan that everyone should be able to buy into – overweight or thin, with or without health problems. You may need to do a bit more cooking and food preparation than you did in the past - but it can be a life saver.

Chapter 3

Control Carbs and Lose Weight!

In most diet books, the chapter on weight loss is placed prominently at the beginning of the book. This makes a lot of sense. After all, most people read books like this one in order to lose weight.

However, this is not the case in this book, and this is because it's important you understand the concept of low-glycemic carbohydrate and Mediterranean-style meal planning *before* you start your weight-loss efforts. Ideally, you should use Mediterranean-style meal planning for at least a few weeks before you begin dieting so that you get used to this way of eating. Omit this step and there's a much greater chance that over time you will gradually regain the pounds you have shed.

In fact, you may well find that you are able to control your weight adequately just by using Mediterranean-style meal planning and adopting a sensible approach to portion control. Especially for children and young adolescents, this may be all that's needed. Let's face it, losing a substantial amount of weight means eating less food, and many people will find this difficult to do for more than a short period of time. Failing at dieting, especially if it happens time after time, is not the best of ways for buttressing self-esteem. Far better to leave off serious dieting for a few years until your child is better prepared psychologically for the effort that's going to be needed.

It's also worth appreciating that not all obesity is a risk to health. Many females, for example, carry their obesity around their hips and not inside their bellies. Unlike male pot-belly obesity, this type of female obesity is not usually associated with such long-term complications as diabetes and heart disease, and there is therefore less reason to treat it. Nevertheless, many females do carry their weight around their bellies and then, like males, become susceptible to these complications.

Parents should also be aware that every child who grows also gains weight. If this were not the case, children would get slimmer as they grew older. If you look at your obese child's growth chart you may well find that as a result of your careful parenting efforts, his or her weight has remained along the same "percentile" for many years. You should be congratulated on this, since in the absence of good dietary supervision the weight of many obese children accelerates off the chart.

Nevertheless, there are many parents who assume that as their child gets older, and particularly as he or she goes through puberty, that a slimming out will occur. It can happen. Unfortunately, the odds are against it, since most chubby children become even chubbier as they go through puberty. Unfortunately, there is no way of knowing in advance who will and who will not slim out.

One other matter to bear in mind. If you have a teenage child, especially a daughter, who is using this diet and thinning out very rapidly, you pay close attention to her weight-loss efforts. Dieting may be appropriate if she is overweight, but not if she is of normal weight. The weight-loss plan described in this chapter can be very effective, and your daughter (and sometimes even your son) could well use it to engage in unhealthy weight loss practices. If your daughter is wasting away before your eyes, she needs medical help – and quickly.

First of all, some general principles:

- **This diet program is primarily about reducing carbs.**

The focus of this chapter is on reducing carbohydrates and not on reducing fat or calories, although of course your caloric intake will fall once you begin eating less carbohydrate.

It is suggested in this book that for many overweight individuals the amount and type of carbohydrate eaten channels the body in the direction of either weight loss, maintaining the same weight, or gaining too much weight.

Eating a lot of high-glycemic carbohydrate pushes overweight individuals in the direction of weight gain. Eat no carbohydrate at all and the body goes into a weight-losing state. This may well be related to the amount of insulin made by the body.

The carb-regulated diet described in this chapter is aiming for the point at which the body is just starting to go catabolic. This point is not difficult to find. All that's needed is an accurate bathroom scale to see exactly when weight loss is starting to occur.

As you will soon appreciate as you proceed through this program, a carbohydrate-based system is a lot easier to use than one based on calories. For starters, it's much easier to look up and even remember the gram values for the carbohydrates you eat than the calorie value of every food you consume. It's also the case that most people are fairly consistent in the amount and even the type of carbohydrate they eat from day to day. It may also be more physiological than a calorie based system. [1]

- **This is a "carb-regulated" and not a low-carb diet.**

There are a number of important differences between this diet and other carbohydrate-restricted diets you may have heard about:

Firstly, the carbohydrates in this diet are only moderately restricted. By contrast, low-carb diets often plunge you into severe carbohydrate restriction at the beginning of dieting in order to obtain quick and substantial weight loss.

It sounds tempting. Lose a lot of weight quickly and then get on with life. It's also a tremendous morale booster to see that fat tissue melting away. You can do it!

Unfortunately, there's a big downside to the low-carb approach. Whenever the body experiences severe weight loss, metabolic responses are set in motion that try to push body weight back to where it was previously. In scientific terms, what happens is that during weight loss, the basal metabolic rate of the body decreases. Basal metabolic rate is the amount of energy your body uses just to keep it ticking – the lungs breathing, the heart pumping.

What this means in practice is that as you lose weight, the calories needed to keep at this new weight also decrease. Therefore, to keep your weight steady, you will now need to eat *less* calories than you did prior to dieting. This is one reason that many dieters find that over time their weight gradually creeps back to where it was previously, so that months or even a year or two later precious little has been achieved. Some people even overshoot and end up heavier than their original weight. This is the well-known "yo-yo" dieting effect.

The second big difference between this and other diets is that most other popular low-carb diets advise large increases in either dietary protein (e.g. the Zone Diet) or fat (the Atkins diet) to replace the carbs that are being restricted.

There is probably little harm in doing this over the short term. However, for most people obesity is not a short-term problem, and high fat and high protein diets are not a good prescription for long-term health.[2] And long-term health is what this book is all about!

So how does one avoid these problems?

I have a few suggestions:

- **Don't go too fast. Lose weight gradually using the carb-regulated plan outlined in this chapter and allow your body's metabolism time to adjust.**

A time frame of six months, or even a year, is quite realistic. It took time to become overweight, and it's going to take time to get rid of that excess weight.

- **Make sure that as much as possible of the carbohydrate you do eat is low-glycemic. In this way, the carbohydrate you eat will be helping you along instead of working against you. You will recall that both low-glycemic food and carbohydrate restriction have the effect of reducing blood insulin levels.**

There are additional benefits to keeping strictly to a low-glycemic diet during weight loss. A low-glycemic diet leaves you less hungry, which is obviously an important consideration when trying to lose weight. Low-glycemic carbohydrate also slightly lessens the fall in basal metabolic rate that occurs with weight loss.[3] Both these factors make it that much easier to lose weight and keep it off.

Only grains, starches, beans, nuts and high-sugar containing foods are regulated

For this diet plan, only grains, starches, beans, nuts, and foods containing a lot of sugar, either added or natural, are regulated. There is no reason to restrict vegetables, since their insulin and glucose responses are small in comparison to these other foods. Fruit also is not restricted. Although the glucose and insulin response to certain fruit is quite high, fruit usually contains so much water that its carbohydrate content in terms *of portion size* (so-called "glycemic load") is usually not that large.

The best way to regulate carbohydrate foods is to *count how much carbohydrate they contain in grams*.

This is not nearly as complicated as it sounds. Many diabetics on insulin do this every time they eat a meal in order to regulate their pre-meal insulin dose. As a result, they become very proficient at "counting carbs." Diabetics, though, (in contrast to this plan) don't ignore the carbohydrate content of vegetables and fruit, since their insulin coverage needs to be extremely precise.

Figure out your weight-loss goal in advance

This diet plan can be tailor-made to fit your weight-loss goal, so it's helpful to have an idea before you begin dieting or very soon thereafter what your goal is going to be.

For many children and adolescents, a satisfactory goal is to stop abnormal weight gain. This can often be achieved just with the Mediterranean-style meal planning described in the previous chapter and by eating a bit less carbohydrate. You may be able to manage this without formal carbohydrate counting, although if this is not working out successfully I would advise switching to more precise carbohydrate counting.

For a growing overweight person who is not yet ready for substantial weight loss, a very acceptable goal is to slow down the normal rate of weight gain so that he or she slims out over time. This type of "weight stabilization" requires less carbohydrate restriction than required for weight loss, although it is still a major commitment of effort.

For weight stabilization you should aim for just that – to keep your weight stable with no further weight gain. However, during the pubertal growth spurt, which for girls starts at the beginning of puberty and usually continues between ages 8 to 13, and which for boys starts mid-way through puberty and continues from about ages 12 to 16 years, more flexibility is appropriate, since growth is so rapid at this time. Even a weight gain of three pounds a year during this time will produce significant slimming out.

For most people, a weight loss of between 5% to 10% of body weight is often sufficient to improve many of the metabolic abnormalities that are present. Achieve this amount of weight loss and you will also feel a lot healthier and also more positive about yourself. To calculate 5% of your weight, multiply your weight by 5 and then divide this figure by 100. Reckon on losing 1 to 2 pounds a week. If things are going really well, you may wish to increase this a bit, but don't go too much above it.

- **However you are going to use this diet plan, the first step is to write down everything you eat and drink for 3 days. Next, identify all carbohydrate on your record that's not from vegetables or fruit and add up the total. Now take the average for the 3 days.**

As an aside, researchers have found that the very act of keeping track of your daily food intake can be extremely helpful for losing weight. In effect, this is food regulation by awareness – being aware of what you are eating. If you find it helpful, just continue doing it!

Calculating and allocating your carbohydrate intake

Your new carb intake should be approximately half the average figure you have just obtained from your 3-day food records.

If you need to take a shortcut, use the table on the next page. The numbers in the table represent half the amount of carbohydrate someone your age and sex usually eats. Nevertheless, it's preferable to actually calculate a carbohydrate level from your food record, since this more accurately reflects your usual intake:

	White		Black		Mexican-American	
	Men	**Women**	**Men**	**Women**	**Men**	**Women**
Age	Grams of carbohydrate					
20-29	195	122	192	127	167	116
30-39	184	116	169	116	165	116
40-49	161	112	104	103	158	110
50-59	151	101	120	104	133	102
60+	132	100	117	88	123	81

4-8 years	9–13 years boys	9–13 years girls	14–18 years boys	14–18 years girls
95 gm	125 gm	112 gm	140 gm	125 gm

For a child aiming for "weight stabilization" rather than weight loss, use ¾ of the average carbohydrate figure you obtain from your 3-day food assessment. Alternatively, if you need a short cut, use the table below:

.

4-8 years	9–13 years boys	9–13 years girls	14–18 years boys	14–18 years girls
125-140 gm	170-190 gm	170-190 gm	190-215 gm	170-190 gm

Having figured out your total carb allocation for each day, the next step is to decide how to divide up the carbohydrates.

An adolescent with a 140 gm carbohydrate allocation may well consider dividing his or her carbs as follows:

40 gm for breakfast
40 gm for lunch
20 gm for a mid-afternoon snack
40 gm for dinner

There are some theoretical advantages in chopping up your carb allocation into frequent small snacks rather than a few large meals. However, I feel that the disadvantages of doing this usually outweigh the advantages. For such a system to be effective, you will need to have healthy low-glycemic snacks readily available, and many families will find this a challenge. Plus, if everyone in the family is snacking at different times of the day, family support is lost. Most families therefore would do better to continue with the conventional three meals a day with a minimum of snacks.

Over the next few days see how this allocation fits your schedule. It's certainly permitted to "borrow" carbohydrates from one meal and add them to the next as long as your daily total remains unchanged. However, it's best to decide on one allocation scheme and to stick to it. The more "borrowing" you do each day, the greater the chance this plan will fall by the wayside.

The starchy carbohydrates you will be counting are from:

- **Bread**
- **Pasta**
- **Rice**
- **Cake**
- **Cookies**
- **Candies**
- **Other snack foods**
- **Breakfast cereals**
- **Beans**

Also, the following vegetables used as a starch dish:

- **Potato (including potato chips)**
- **Sweet potato**
- **Corn**

"Sugary" carbohydrates are counted from:

- **Milk**
- **Fruit juice**
- **Soda**
- **Yogurt**
- **Canned fruit**
- **Dried fruit**
- **Candies**
- **Chocolate**
- **Fruit rollups**
- **Granola bars**

At the end of this chapter you will find lists of the carbohydrate content of commonly eaten foods. More extensive listings can be found on the web. Just look up "carbohydrate counting" on your search engine. Most people are fairly repetitive in the carbohydrates they eat and you will find that you soon remember the carbohydrate content of the foods you eat most commonly.

For manufactured food items there is no choice but to read food labels. At the back of the food packet you will find a table with the nutritional content per "portion size". This table describes what constitutes a portion size as well as its nutritional content, and this includes grams of carbohydrate.

I rarely see this in America, but in Europe it's common practice for the mother or hostess to portion out the main part of the meal on people's plates in the kitchen. Open dishes are still available on the table, but these include only side dishes such as bread or salad. In fact, it would be quite rude to request more of the main dish from the hostess unless she specifically asks if anyone wants more. Having dishes of food on the table for everyone to help themselves to is very much an American custom. If you are the meal preparer for the home, you may well consider partially adopting this European model by counting out the carbs for everyone who needs carb regulation, while leaving out containers of vegetables, salads and fruit on the table. Your family will soon get the message!

It's a good idea to weigh yourself every two to three days to make sure your weight is heading in the right direction. Weigh yourself before rather than after eating and at a consistent time of the day. First thing in the morning before breakfast is often the most convenient.

What should you do if your weight doesn't decrease? It can happen. The dividing line between a slight catabolic state and not losing weight at all is a fine one and some individuals need more carbohydrate restriction than others in order to lose weight. The ad lib vegetables and fruit you will be eating are also a source of carbohydrate, so that your true carbohydrate intake is going to be quite a bit higher than the figure in the table.

If your weight loss is insufficient, take off 15 gm of carbohydrate from your daily allocation. If need be, continue decreasing in 15 gm carbohydrate increments every half a week until your weight is heading in the right direction.

Everything but starchy and sugary carbs are "free items"

The beauty of this diet is that it's also an ad lib diet. Few adults, much less adolescents, have the ability to voluntarily stay hungry for a long time. This is why it's important to be able to eat extra food whenever you find a meal or snack insufficiently satisfying.

Free foods can be any of the following:

Extra carbohydrate:
- **All vegetables (other than the three starches listed above)**
- **All fresh fruit (the carbohydrate content of dried fruit is counted)**

Extra protein:
- **Fish**
- **Shellfish**
- **Fowl, such as chicken and turkey**
- **Eggs**
- **Peanut butter (non-sweetened)**
- **Veggie burgers**
- **Tofu**
- **Hummus**

Extra fat:
- **Cheese**

Throughout the recipe section of this book you will find recipes labeled as "free items". These are recipes that contain only a small amount of starch and very little sugar and can therefore be eaten without any carbohydrate counting.

It goes without saying that the plan described here will only work if there are appropriate ad lib foods readily available in the house, particularly vegetables and fruit. If the only things in the pantry are cakes and cookies, then this is what will get eaten! Your job as a parent is to make sure that only appropriate choices are available.

Remember that the most important reason for losing weight is to improve your health. It's also nice to look slim, but these two reasons should complement each other and not be in

opposition. As mentioned earlier, high-fat and high-protein diets are not healthy diets. Over the short-term, it probably doesn't matter that much if you markedly increase your fat or protein intake. However, your weight problem is not going to disappear within a few months and this diet should be regarded as a long-term venture.

In general, the preference should always be for extra vegetables and fruit. However, a moderate amount of fish and fowl are fine, although be careful that you don't find yourself sliding into a high-protein diet. As will be discussed in the next chapter, keep beef, lamb, bacon, hot dogs and deli meat to a minimum, even if they are lean.

Eggs are also a free item. In fact eggs can be quite helpful within a carb-regulated diet since they are so filling.

Eggs? You may be surprised (perhaps very surprised) to learn that many scientists question whether eggs really do promote heart disease.[4] Eating a lot of eggs does raise blood cholesterol level in about 20 to 30% of people, but there's no evidence that eating eggs increases the risk for heart disease, except in diabetics. If eggs were such a potent contributor to heart disease this would have become evident from nutritional studies. Whether it's a good idea for middle-aged adults and older to add a lot of eggs to their diet is an unanswered question (and most people probably wouldn't want to take the chance), but for individuals who are not diabetic and who have neither a high cholesterol level or strong family history of heart disease, and this includes most kids, one to two eggs a day should present no risk to health.

There are a number of other simple "filling-up" techniques you could consider using. Some of these were discussed in previous chapters, but they are important enough to warrant repeating here:

- Many overweight people have gotten into the habit of rushing their eating. Try slowing down your eating so that you can savor the full flavor of the food. This habit may well be somewhat physiological (especially if you have been eating a lot of high-glycemic carbohydrate), but it can be broken. Parents and spouses should remind family members to "slow down!"

- Include a soup with a meal or snack. Clear soups with vegetables are particularly helpful in providing a feeling of fullness, but even thick soups will do the job. This was discussed in chapter 2. The vegetables in clear soups, incidentally, are regarded as "free foods" for this plan.
- Try not to miss breakfast. It sounds like a great way for losing weight, but it doesn't work. In fact, people who miss breakfast gain more weight than those who don't.

- Put berries and fruit on the bottom of your breakfast cereal bowl rather than on the top - it will lead you to eat less cereal.

- Prepare Mediterranean-style dishes that mix vegetables and grains. This way, you will eat less starch and still feel as full.

- Use "heavy" breads that are chock full of grains.

- Use an olive oil-containing Italian salad dressing rather than a low-fat one. The olive oil provides a lot of health benefits, and the oil-containing salad dressing makes the

salad that much more filling. If you can't find an olive oil dressing in the store, make a vinaigrette yourself (see recipe section).

A moderate fat intake is helpful in carb-regulated dieting

A number of scientific studies have compared weight loss on a low-fat diet versus a Mediterranean diet with a moderate fat content. This might seem contrary to everything you've been taught - but the latter always wins out.[5]

This leads again to the question of dairy fat. If you are an adult at risk for coronary disease you may want to continue with low-fat dairy since this contains less saturated fat. However, for everyone else, carb-regulation will be a lot easier if you include a moderate amount of dairy fat in your meal planning. This could be whole milk, full-fat cheese or full-fat yogurt. It's worth noting that whole milk is a satiating low-glycemic drink.

This is a family-together weight loss plan!

Children, adolescents and even spouses will need a lot of encouragement and support from their family to keep on track with this plan. There can be no greater support than having other family members also watching the type and amount of carbohydrate they're eating, especially when obesity is a family problem. In this way, weight control and weight loss become a family affair.

There's no reason that all family members – whether they be fat or thin – should not be eating the same Mediterranean-style meals. They taste good and are super-healthy. Thus, everyone in the family will be eating basically the same foods, although those needing weight stabilization or weight loss will be restricting their starchy carbohydrates.

It's that simple!

Chapter 4

Clogging and Unclogging Arteries

This chapter on fats has been saved for last. However, this doesn't mean it's less important. In fact, the information contained here is essential for Mediterranean-style meal planning and successful weight-loss.

You see, one of the major complications of obesity is cardiovascular disease. This is not an adult-only problem. We now know that obese children already show the beginnings of vessel wall disease in the form of a thickening of the inner wall of their major blood vessels. These changes are readily reversible at this age, but over time they become more adult-like. Plaque develops within the vessel wall, and this can become a threat to long-term health.

Not so long ago, nutritional experts thought they had a good understanding of the cause of cardiovascular disease. The chief villain was LDL cholesterol, the so-called "bad cholesterol". If levels were high, LDL particles got stuck in the artery wall and this led to vascular damage. There was also HDL cholesterol, the "good cholesterol," that protected against coronary disease by clearing away harmful cholesterol deposits from the arteries.

It followed from this that LDL cholesterol levels needed to be kept as close as possible to the normal range. This could be achieved by eating less cholesterol and eating less fat - since cutting back on fat lowers blood cholesterol levels. Because of this reasoning, low-fat food items began filling the grocery shelves.

It turns out, however, that there are other factors besides LDL cholesterol levels that can inflame the vessel wall and promote cardiovascular disease. These include smoking, high blood glucose levels (especially after a meal), high insulin levels, and fat particles accumulating after a high-fat meal. These all produce a biochemical stress on the vessel wall called *oxidative stress*.

Readers may be surprised to learn that reducing the total amount of fat in one's diet (as distinct from cutting back on certain fats) is not a particularly effective way for preventing heart disease. It is of some benefit to high-risk individuals – and for people at high risk for cardiovascular disease every little bit helps – but for everyone else it's not a very useful step.[1]

Furthermore, as discussed in Chapter One (Why Changing Carbohydrate is so Important), when people cut back on fat, they automatically increase their intake of carbohydrate in order to replace those lost calories. Unfortunately, these added carbohydrates are often not the best of carbohydrates. A low-fat diet frequently becomes therefore a "bad carbohydrate" diet, with too much highly refined high-glycemic starches and sugar. Just being low-fat doesn't automatically make a meal healthy!

Another problem with low-fat diets is that they frequently eliminate fats that have no reason to be eliminated. Some fats actually protect against heart disease and it's much better to leave these fats in one's diet rather than eliminate them.

It turns out that a Mediterranean-style meal plan containing a moderate amount of healthy fat as well as the right type of carbohydrate may be more protective against heart disease than the often recommended low-fat diet. It is also much better for long-term weight control.[2]

Consider the following facts from France (the French diet being more Mediterranean-like than the American diet).

Compared to the average American, the average French person in 2002 ate:

- **Four times as much butter**
- **60% more cheese**
- **Three times as much pork**
- **Slightly more fat (171 g/day versus 157 gm/day)**
- **More saturated fat**

Yet despite similar cholesterol levels the death rate from cardiovascular disease in France is about a third of that in America. The French also have less of a problem with obesity than we do.

There's only one conclusion to make from all this. Reducing on fat is not the most effective way for preventing heart disease, and there are other more important things one can do.

So which are the "healthy" fats that need to be included in your meal planning and which are the ones you should be avoiding?

To answer this question we need to understand a bit about the structure of fats and how this influences our health.

A focus on fats

Biochemically, a fat consists of a long chain of carbon atoms joined together by chemical bonds. Two important features of this chain are its length and the type of bond between the carbon atoms. When a bond is filled by a hydrogen atom we say that it's "saturated' and when there is no hydrogen atom we call it "unsaturated."

A "saturated fat" is one in which all the carbon bonds in the chain are saturated by hydrogen atoms. A "mono-unsaturated fat" is one in which all the carbon bonds are saturated except for one, and a "polyunsaturated fat" is a fat in which more than one carbon bond is unsaturated and free of hydrogen atoms.

Getting the most from olive oil

Much of the health benefits of a Mediterranean diet are thought to be due to its content of olive oil. Most of the fat (about 75%) in olive oil is mono-unsaturated fat.

Why is mono-unsaturated fat so healthful?

The truth of the matter is that scientists are still not completely sure. We know that mono-unsaturated fat has favorable effects on blood lipids. However, many health experts think that the benefits of olive oil have more to do with another constituent of olive oil called *antioxidant* and less to do with its content of mono-unsaturated fat.

Antioxidants have the effect of combating the *oxidative stress* that occurs after eating a high fat or high-glycemic meal (see Chapter One for more details about oxidative stress).

With this in mind, it's important to be aware that not all olive oil sold in the stores is rich in antioxidant. "Pure olive oil" is olive oil that has been processed, either by heat, chemicals or filtration. During this process a lot of the antioxidants are removed. "Light olive oil" is not light in fat (all olive oil contains the same amount of fat), but oil that's been filtered very finely and is therefore light in impurities. Unfortunately, antioxidants happen to be among the impurities removed. "Extra-virgin olive oil" and "virgin olive oil" are from the first press and not processed. They therefore have the highest content of antioxidant.

- **Buy extra-virgin or virgin olive oil in preference to other types of olive oil, even if they are a bit more expensive.**

Be aware when you're preparing your food that there's no health reason to be skimpy with olive oil (although there's no reason to drown the food either). Dressing salads with an olive oil-containing salad dressing, sautéing with olive oil, and baking vegetables in the oven with olive oil are all great ways for making the vegetables you eat more appetizing and at the same time adding extra antioxidants into your diet.

Avocado and nuts are another good source of both mono-unsaturated fat and antioxidant. Walnuts have a particularly high content of both. Not surprisingly, studies have shown that nuts have a protective effect against cardiovascular disease.[3]

- **Nuts (unsalted and non-sugared) make excellent snacks and are far healthier than high-glycemic snack foods such as pretzels and crackers.[4]**

Omega-3 fat – just oozing health

A polyunsaturated fat is one that contains a number of unsaturated chemical bonds within the carbon chain. Polyunsaturated fat is usually considered to be a "good fat." It is found in vegetable oils, margarine, mayonnaise, poultry and whole-grain wheat.

One particularly healthful polyunsaturated fat is called "omega-3 fat." It has this name because one of its unsaturated carbon bonds is three carbons away from one end of the carbon chain. Most other polyunsaturated fats are "omega-6 fats" with an unsaturated bond being six carbons away from the end of the chain.

Omega-3 fat has many favorable effects. It lowers blood triglyceride levels, improves vessel wall functioning, reduces inflammation and thins out the blood. That's a bundle of helpful activities.

Two important sources of omega-3 fat are fatty fish and certain plants. The Eskimos from Greenland eat a lot of fat and yet are remarkably free of cardiovascular disease. This is because a lot of the fat that they eat is from whale, seal and fish, all of which are high in omega-3 fat. Similarly, Japanese living in coastal fishing villages also have a low incidence of heart disease because of their high intake of sea food.

- **Include fish at least twice a week in your family's meal planning – and even more if you can.**

The American diet tends to be very beef-centered. As a result, many families are unfamiliar with fish and the kids are put off by its appearance and smell. It's worthwhile, therefore, to search out fish recipes that are likely to be appealing to your family. A number of excellent fish recipes are included in the recipe section of this book. This section also contains information about when to be worried about mercury and other heavy metal contamination.

Useful facts about the omega-3 fat in fish include the following:

- **Oily fish are a particularly good source of omega-3 fat, including salmon, herring, mackerel, anchovies and sardines.**
- **Tuna contains omega-3 fat, but in lesser amounts than these other fish.**

Another good source of omega-3 fat is green leafy vegetables. Certain vegetable oils such as canola, soybean and walnut oil are also excellent sources of omega-3 fat.

Omega-6 fat – healthy, but up to a point

I mentioned at the beginning of this section that polyunsaturated fat is usually regarded as being a "good fat." This is true – but up to a point. And some scientists are worried that we may have exceeded that point. These scientists suggest that an imbalance has developed in the Western diet and that we are eating far too much omega-6 at the expense of omega-3 fat.[4] Much of this omega-6 fat comes from corn oil. A problem with omega-6 fat at the level of the cell is that it crowds out omega-3 fat and prevents its use in cell membranes. It's likely that our cardiovascular systems and even our immune systems would be a lot better off if we were to include more omega-3 and monounsaturated fat into our diets instead of omega-6.

- **Cut back on corn oil for cooking.**

- **Another excellent way for increasing omega-3 fat is to use canola-based margarine and canola-based mayonnaise.**

The new villain on the block – trans fat

One of the many problems created by the low-fat campaign of the 1970's is that it gave a seal of approval to a new form of vegetable fat called trans fat for replacing saturated fat. Trans fat is made by adding extra hydrogen to the carbon bonds of vegetable oil and thereby *partially hydrogenating* the fat chain.

Food manufacturers love partially hydrogenated or trans fat – and for good reason. They are relatively cheap to make and have properties that are useful for industrial baking. Foods containing trans fat have an increased shelf life and need less refrigeration. Because of this, until recently most of the margarine and vegetable shortening in this country was made from trans fat.

It took some clever detective work by nutrition scientists to figure out that trans fats are even more harmful to health than the saturated fats they were trying to replace. Trans fat increases the risk for heart disease more than any other type of food. It adversely effects blood lipids and blood vessel function, increases insulin resistance and is strongly associated with cardiovascular disease - even in small amounts.[5]

Denmark has gone so far as to ban their use entirely. New York City has banned their use in restaurants. The use of trans fat is so widespread in this country that the U.S. government has not placed any ban on their use. However, since January 2006, food manufacturers in the U.S. have been required to list the trans fat content of their products.

As a result of consumer pressure, many food manufacturers are phasing out trans fat. Nevertheless, there are still many hold-outs.

Trans fat is found particularly in:

- **Margarine**
- **Household shortening**
- **Crackers**
- **Baked cookies and cakes**
- **Chips and snacks**
- **Deep-fried products such as fried potatoes, fish sticks and chicken nuggets**

- ***Become an intelligent reader of food labels and keep your family's intake of trans fat and "partially hydrogenated vegetable oil" to a minimum.***

Saturated fat - not so simple

We've known for years that saturated fat intake is associated with heart disease. Saturated fat is found in meat, lard, dairy foods, tropical vegetable oils such as coconut and palm kernel oil, and in coca butter. The advice from nutritional experts has therefore been to replace beef with poultry (since poultry contains more monounsaturated and polyunsaturated fat), to eat more seafood (which is rich in omega-3 fat), to eat more vegetable protein (which contains very little saturated fat), and to use lean instead of fatty meat.

- **Cut back on beef and pork and use fish, fowl and vegetable sources of protein instead.**

Dairy fat also contains a lot of saturated fat. For many years now, doctors and nutritionists have been advising everyone but very young children to lower their intake of dairy fat and to use low-fat milk and dairy products instead. This may be good advice for adults who are at high risk for cardiovascular disease but in my opinion is not the best of advice for children, adolescents and young adults.

I know this is controversial advice, so let me explain my reasoning.

Many people, including health professionals, are unaware (and probably would be surprised to discover) that the evidence linking dairy fat to cardiovascular disease is pretty well non-existent.[5] Nor is there any evidence that using low-fat dairy is helpful for weight control.[7]

These are the reasons I encourage everyone to drink a reasonable amount of milk and to use whole or 2% milk rather than 1% or skim milk:

- Milk provides the calcium needed for bone health. This is true for adults as well as children. The American Academy of Pediatrics advises all children and adolescents to drink three cups of milk a day.

- Milk contains added vitamin D. Much of the vitamin D we need is obtained from exposure to sunlight, but in winter especially this source can become limited. A large number of children have suboptimal levels of vitamin D and this is especially true for those who are overweight. Does it matter? Good evidence is coming out that it does. Low levels of vitamin D have been linked to a host of medical problems, including insulin resistance, type 2 diabetes, autoimmune disease and cancer.

- Numerous studies from across the globe have shown that adults and children who drink milk are slimmer and have less problems with insulin resistance and the metabolic syndrome than those who don't. The experts are still debating why this is so. It may be that children and adults who give up on milk are replacing it with drinks that contain sugar or high-fructose corn syrup. In large amounts these drinks are weight-inducing.

- Many people find whole milk creamier and tastier than low-fat milk. There is therefore less chance that whole milk-drinkers will give up milk for less healthy drinks such as soda, sports drinks, and sugar-containing fruit juices.

Does this mean that everyone can indulge in lots of butter and cream? After all, this could be a logical conclusion from what I have written.

The answer is – not so fast! For an adult at risk for cardiovascular disease, keeping conscientiously to a low-fat low-glycemic diet is still an excellent recommendation.

Obese children should also be careful about increasing dietary fat until they are well established on a Mediterranean-style meal plan, otherwise the added fat will just worsen their obesity.

For the average child, adolescent and young adult, however, a moderate intake of dairy fat presents no risk to health or body weight and there is no reason to discourage whole or 2% milk, high-fat cheese and full-fat yogurt.

Conclusions

Many families would benefit from having more fat in their diets, provided the fats are healthy ones. Regulating carbs in order to achieve weight loss is also difficult without adding a bit of extra fat.

However, it's important to appreciate that the advice in these chapters comes as a package. Adding more fat to a diet containing a lot of highly refined high-glycemic carbohydrate will accomplish nothing except extra weight gain and higher blood lipids.

So, first of all make the necessary changes in carbohydrate and only then consider adding more healthful fats to your family's diet.

The advice about dietary fat used to be very simple. Get rid of it. But this wasn't the most helpful of advice for kids and many adults, since there is a definite place for healthful fats in a family's meal planning.

Chapter 5

Carbohydrate Lists

"Counting the carbs" in grains and sugar-containing foods is an important skill to master when trying to control or lose weight. The following tables list commonly eaten grain and sugar-containing foods.

Beverages

Carbohydrate content

Apple juice, canned or bottled, unsweetened, 1 cup	29 gm
Beer, light, 1 can or bottle, 12 fl oz	5 gm
Beer, regular, 1 can or bottle, 12 fl oz	10 gm
Beers, non-alcoholic brews, 12 fl oz	14 gm
Chocolate syrup, 1 serving 2 tbsp	25 gm
Cocoa mix, Nestle, Carnation, No Sugar Added Hot Cocoa Mix, 1 envelope	8 gm
Cocoa mix, Nestle, Carnation Rich Chocolate Hot Cocoa Mix, 1 envelope	24 gm
Coffee, brewed from grounds, prepared with tap water, decaffeinated, 1 cup	0 gm
Coffee, brewed, espresso, restaurant-prepared, 100g	2 gm
Cola, contains caffeine, 1 can 12 fl oz	39 gm
Cola, contains caffeine, 1 bottle 16 fl oz	51 gm
Cranberry juice, unsweetened, 1 cup	28 gm
Cream soda, 1 can or bottle (12 fl oz)	47 gm
Cream soda, 1 can or bottle (16 fl oz)	63 gm
Fruit punch, frozen concentrate, prepared with water, 1 cup	29 gm
Gatorade Thirst Quencher, 8 fl oz	14 gm
Gatorade, Carbohydrate Energy, 12 fl oz	79 gm
Ginger ale, 1 can or bottle, 12 fl oz	31 gm
Grape juice, canned or bottled, unsweetened, 1 cup	37 gm
Grapefruit juice, pink, 1 cup	22 gm
Grapefruit juice, white, frozen concentrate, diluted, 1 cup	24 gm
Lemon juice, frozen, unsweetened, 1 cup	12 gm
Lemonade, frozen concentrate, pink, prepared with water, 1 cup	24 gm
Lemonade, frozen concentrate, white, prepared with water, 1 cup	33 gm
Limeade, frozen concentrate, prepared with water, 1 cup	26 gm
Orange drink, breakfast type, with juice and pulp, frozen concentrate, prepared with water, 1 cup	28 gm
Orange juice drink, drink box, 8.45 fl oz	34 gm
Orange-strawberry-banana juice, 1 cup	26 gm
Orange soda, 1 can or bottle, 12 fl oz	45 gm
Orange soda, 1 can or bottle, 16 fl oz	60 gm
Pineapple juice, canned, unsweetened, 1 cup	34 gm
Pineapple and grapefruit juice drink, canned, 1 cup	29 gm

Pineapple and orange juice drink, canned, 1 cup	28 gm
Root beer, 1 can or bottle, 12 fl oz	38 gm
Root beer, 1 can or bottle, 16 fl oz	51 gm
Snapple, Snapple Kiwi Strawberry Cocktail, ready-to-drink, 8 fl oz	29 gm
Starbucks, Coffee, 1 bottle, 9.5 fl oz	37 gm
Starbucks, Frappuccino, Caramel, 1 bottle, 9.5 fl oz	37 gm
Tea, instant, sweetened with sugar, lemon-flavored, without added ascorbic acid, powder, prepared, 1 cup	22 gm
V8 100% Vegetable Juice, 5.5 fl oz can	7 gm
Wine, dessert, dry, 1 glass, 3.5 fl oz	12 gm
Wine, dessert, sweet, 1 glass, 3.5 fl oz	14 gm

Breads and Bread-substitutes

Carbohydrate content

1 small bagel, plain/onion, 2 oz	29 gm
1 medium bagel, plain/onion, 3 oz	45 gm
1 large bagel, plain/onion, 4 oz	56 gm
Bread crumbs, plain or seasoned, 1 oz	20 gm
6"bread roll, plain, average, 2½ oz	38 gm
Challah slice, ¾ oz	17 gm
Cornbread, prepared from recipe, made with low fat (2%) milk, 1 piece	28 gm
Corn tortilla, 6", 1 oz each	15 gm
Flour tortilla, 8", 1.75 oz	26 gm
Hamburger roll, regular, 1½ oz	22 gm
Hamburger roll, large, 3 oz	40 gm
Italian bread, 1 medium slice	10 gm
Kaiser roll, small, 2 oz	35 gm
Kaiser roll, large, 3½ oz	61 gm
Mixed-grain bread (includes whole-grain, 7-grain), 1 slice, 1.3 oz	17 gm
Oat bran bread, 1 slice	12 gm
Oatmeal bread, 1 slice	13 gm
Onion roll, small, 2.4 oz size	34 gm
Pita, white, enriched,1 small slice	16 gm
Pita, white, enriched, 1 large slice	33 gm
Pita, whole-wheat, 1 small slice	15 gm
Pita, whole-wheat, 1 large slice	35 gm
Pumpernickel bread, snack-size slice	3 gm
Pumpernickel bread, 1 thin slice	9.5 gm
Pumpernickel bread, 1 regular slice	12 gm
Rice cake, regular size, 1 cake, 9 g	7.5 gm
Rye bread, 1 snack-size slice	3 gm
Rye bread, 1 thin slice	10 gm
Rye bread, 1 slice	15 gm
Sourdough, 1 medium piece	33 gm
Taco, mini size	2 gm
Taco, regular size	7 gm
Taco, large	13 gm
Wheat bread (includes wheat berry), 1 slice	12 gm
White or wheat bread, 1 thin slice, ¾ oz	10 gm
White or wheat bread, 1 sandwich slice, 1 oz	14 gm
White or wheat bread, 1 thick or large slice, 1½ oz	21 gm

Breakfast Cereals

Carbohydrate content

Alpen, 1 cup	86 gm
Cheerios Honey Nut, ¾ cup	22 gm
Corn Flakes, 1 cup	24 gm
Cream of rice, cooked with water, ¾ cup	21 gm
Cream of wheat, prepared with water, ¾ cup	24 gm
Farina, cooked with water, ¾ cup	18 gm
General Mills, Apple Cinnamon Cheerios, ¾ cup	25 gm
General Mills, Coca Puffs, ¾ cup	23 gm
General Mills, Fiber 1, ½ cup	24 gm
General Mills, Reese's Puffs, ¾ cup	22 gm
General Mills, Wheaties, ¾ cup	22 gm
Kellogg's, All Bran, original, ½ cup	23 gm
Kellogg's, Corn Flakes, original, 1 cup	24 gm
Kellogg's, Fruit Loops, original, 1 cup, 1 oz	25 gm
Kellogg's Frosted Flakes, ¾ cup	27 gm
Kellogg's Low Fat Granola with Raisins, 0.7 cup	43 gm
Kellogg's Raisin Bran, regular, 1 cup	45 gm
Kellogg's Rice Krispies, 1¼ cup	29 gm
Kellogg's Special K, 1 cup	23 gm
Oats, instant, plain, prepared with water, 1 packet	17 gm
Post Fruity pebbles, ¾ cup	24 gm
Post Grape-Nuts cereal, ½ cup	47 gm
Post Honey Bunches of Oats with Almonds Cereal, ¾ cup	24 gm
Post Raisin Bran Cereal, 1 cup	46 gm
Post The Original Shredded Wheat, 2 biscuits	38 gm
Post The Original Shredded Wheat Spoon Size, 1 cup	41 gm
Puffed wheat, 1 cup	9 gm
Puffed wheat, presweetened, ¾ cup	25 gm
Quaker, Captain Crunch, regular, ¾ cup	23 gm
Quaker, Instant Oatmeal, Regular, 1 packet, 1 oz	19 gm
Quaker, Instant Oatmeal, Maple Brown Sugar, 1 packet, 1.9 oz	33 gm
Quaker, Life, ¾ cup	26 gm
Quaker, Oatmeal Squares, Brown Sugar, ¾ cup	44 gm
Raisin Nut Bran, General Mills, 1 cup	41 gm
Total, Honey Clusters, ¾ cup	38 gm
Weetabix Whole Wheat, 1 cup	44 gm

This list is not intended to endorse any particular brand of cereal, but only to provide illustrative examples. Full details can be obtained from the cereal box.

Dairy

	Carbohydrate content
Burger King, Chocolate Shake, 12 fl oz	53 gm
Buttermilk, fluid, cultured, lowfat, 1 cup	12 gm
Cheese, Cheddar, shredded, 1 cup	1 gm
Cheese, Parmesan, grated, 1 cup	4 gm
Chocolate milk, 1 cup	26 gm
Cottage, creamed, large and small curd, 1 cup	6 gm
Cow's milk, 2% and regular, 1 cup	12 gm
Cow's milk, skim and 1%, 1 cup	11 gm
Cream, fluid, half and half	10 gm
Cream, fluid, heavy whipping, 1 cup whipped	3 gm
Ensure plus, 1 cup	50 gm
Feta cheese, 1 cup crumbled	6 gm
Milk shakes, thick chocolate, 1 container (11 oz)	55 gm
Mozzarella cheese, 1 cup	4 gm
Muenster cheese, 1 cup shredded	1 gm
Parmesan cheese, grated, 1 cup	4 gm
Sour cream, cultured, 1 cup	10 gm
Yogurt, fruit variety, nonfat, 1 container (8-oz)	43 gm
Yogurt, plain, low fat, 1 container (8-oz)	16 gm
Yogurt, plain, whole milk, 1 container (8-oz)	10 gm

Most cheese and cream contain only small amounts of carbohydrate and are usually regarded as free foods. They are shown here for comparison.

Pasta and Grains

Carbohydrate content

Barley, pearled, cooked, 1 cup	44 gm
Brown rice, long-grain, cooked, 1 cup	45 gm
Brown Rice, raw, 1 cup	143 gm
Buckwheat groats, roasted, dry, 1 cup	122 gm
Buckwheat groats, roasted, cooked, 1 cup	34 gm
Bulgur, cooked, 1 cup	34 gm
Bulgur, dry, 1 cup	106 gm
Cornmeal, self-rising, plain, enriched, white, 1 cup	86 gm
Cornstarch, 1 cup	117 gm
Couscous, cooked, 1 cup	36 gm
Couscous, dry, 1 cup	134 gm
Noodles, egg, cooked, enriched, 1 cup	40 gm
Noodles, egg, dry, enriched, 1 cup	27 gm
Macaroni, small shells, cooked, 1 cup	33 gm
Macaroni, spiral shaped, cooked, 1 cup	38 gm
Macaroni, elbow shaped, cooked, 1 cup	40 gm
Macaroni, whole-wheat, elbow shaped, cooked, 1 cup	37 gm
Macaroni, whole-wheat, elbow shaped, cooked, 1 cup	79 gm
Matzo Meal, ½ cup, 2.2 oz	48 gm
Millet, cooked, 1 cup	41 gm
Millet, raw, 1 cup	146 gm
Oat bran, cooked, 1 cup	18 gm
Oat bran, raw, 1 cup	46 gm
Oats, rolled, Old Fashioned, dry, 1 cup	54 gm
Oats, cooked, ½ cup	13 gm
Quinoa grain, 1 cup	117 gm
Rye flour, medium, 1 cup	79 gm
Semolina, 1 cup	122 gm
Spaghetti, cooked, 1 cup	40 gm
Spaghetti, dry, 16 oz	308 gm
Spaghetti, whole-wheat, cooked, 1 cup	37 gm
Spaghetti, whole-wheat, dry, 16 oz	340 gm
Tapioca, pearl, dry, 1 cup	135 gm
Wheat bran, 1 cup	37 gm
Wheat flour, white, all-purpose, enriched, bleached, 1 cup	95 gm
Wheat flour, white, all-purpose, self-rising, enriched, 1 cup	93 gm
Wheat flour, white, cake, enriched, 1 cup	107 gm
Wheat flour, whole-grain, 1 cup	87 gm
Wheat germ, 1 cup	60 gm
White rice, cooked, 1 cup	37 gm
White rice, dry, 1 cup	151 gm
Wild rice, cooked, 1 cup	35 gm
Wild rice, raw, 1 cup	120 gm

Vegetables

Carbohydrate content

Asparagus, green, cooked, from raw, 1 cup	8 gm
Beets, cooked, drained, slices, 1 cup	17 gm
Broccoli, raw, chopped, 1 cup	5 gm
Broccoli, cooked, from raw, chopped, 1 cup	8 gm
Brussels sprouts, cooked, from raw, 1 cup	14 gm
Cabbage, common varieties, shredded, raw, 1 cup	4 gm
Cabbage, red, raw, 1 cup	4 gm
Carrot juice, canned, 1 cup *	22 gm
Carrots, cooked, sliced, 1 cup	12 gm
Cauliflower, raw, 1 cup	5 gm
Cauliflower, cooked, from raw	5 gm
Celery, raw, 1 stalk	1 gm
Celery, cooked, medium stalk	2 gm
Corn, sweet, yellow, cooked, kernels on cob, 1 ear	19 gm
Corn, sweet, yellow, cooked, from frozen, 1 cup	32 gm
Corn, sweet, yellow, canned, cream style, 1 cup *	46 gm
Corn, sweet, yellow, canned, 1 cup	41 gm
Cucumber, peeled or unpeeled, sliced, 1 cup	3 gm
Garlic, raw, 1 clove	1 gm
Lettuce, iceberg, raw, 1 head	11 gm
Lettuce, romaine, shredded, 1 cup	1 gm
Mushrooms, raw, slices, 1 cup	3 gm
Onions, raw, chopped, 1 cup	14 gm
Onion rings, 2"-3"diameter, breaded, from frozen, oven heated, 10 rings *	23 gm
Peas, green, boiled, from frozen, 1 cup	23 gm
Peppers, green or red, raw, chopped, 1 cup	10 gm
Potatoes, baked, $2^1/_3$" x 4¾", with skin, 1 potato *	51 gm
Potatoes, baked, $2^1/_3$" x 4¾", flesh only, 1 potato *	34 gm
Potatoes, boiled, 2½" diameter, 1 cup *	31 gm
Potato products, french fried, from frozen, oven heated, 10 strips*	16 gm
Potato, mashed, homemade, whole milk, 1 cup *	37 gm
Potato salad, home prepared, 1 cup *	28 gm
Pumpkin, canned, 1 cup	20 gm
Sauerkraut, canned, solids and liquid, 1 cup	10 gm
Spinach, raw, chopped, 1 cup	1 gm
Spinach, cooked, from frozen, 1 cup	10 gm
Squash, summer (all varieties), cooked, 1 cup	8 gm
Sweet potato, baked, with skin *	35 gm
Sweet potato, broiled, without skin *	38 gm
Tomatoes, raw, chopped or sliced, 1 cup	8 gm
Tomatoes, stewed, canned, 1 cup	17 gm
Tomato juice, canned, 1 cup *	10 gm
Tomato sauce, canned, 1 cup	18 gm

(Vegetables marked with an asterisk contain carbohydrates that should be counted for this program)

Chapter 6

Meal suggestions

Examples of 25-40 gm carbohydrate breakfasts

("Free items" are foods that can be eaten without regard to their carbohydrate content)

Any low-glycemic breakfast cereal (serve 24 gm)
Add ½ cup of milk (6 gm)
Free item: Topping of berries and or fruit

---

1 cup of whole milk (12 gm)
8-oz of full fat plain yogurt (12 gm)
Free item: Topping of berries and/or fruit

Free item: ½ grapefruit
½ of a large whole wheat bagel (28 gm)
Free item: Serve with peanut butter, cream cheese or hard cheese

---

Free item: 2 fried eggs
2 slices of toasted multigrain or whole wheat bread (24 gm)
4 oz of grapefruit juice (17 gm)

---

1 serving of home-made granola or muesli (31-35 gm) (Breakfast – an Essential Meal, p157-159)
Add ½ cup of milk (6 gm)
Free items: Topping of berries and/or fruit

---

4 oz of orange juice (14 gm)
2 slices of toasted multigrain or whole wheat bread (24 gm)
Free item: Add peanut butter, cream cheese or hard cheese
Free item: Spanish omelet with vegetables (Breakfast – an Essential Meal, p160)

---

1 cup of a smoothie (Breakfast – an Essential Meal, p161) (34 gm)

Examples of 30-40 gm carbohydrate lunches

Good choices may be available on your child's school menu. However, bringing food from home is often a better option - you can choose the type of foods you wish your child to eat and also count out their carbohydrates content.

("Free items" are foods that can be eaten without regard to their carbohydrate content)

Sandwich-style lunches

2 slices of multigrain or whole wheat bread (24 gm)
Free item: Filling of egg salad, tuna salad (Snacking to Health! p169), or hard cheese or cream cheese together with lettuce, cucumber or tomato slices
1 cup of milk (12 gm)
Free item: 1 Fuji apple

---

1 small whole wheat pita (16 gm)
Free item: Filling of tuna salad (see: Snacking to Health! p169), or turkey roll or grilled chicken together with shredded lettuce and tomato slices
½ cup of orange juice (14 gm)
Free item: cantaloupe slices

Broiled Portabella Mushroom Sandwich with 2 slices of multigrain or whole wheat bread (Snacking to Health! p168) (28 gm)
Free item: Mediterranean Salad (see: Classy Cold Salads, p168)
¼ cup of Homemade Trailmix (18 gm) (Snacking to Health! p165)

Container lunches

2 Tuna or Salmon Patties (10-12 gm) (Encouraging Fish, p197)
Roasted Chickpeas (23 gm) (Snacking to Health! p172)
4 oz of milk (6 gm)
Free item: Fresh Garden Salad with vinaigrette (Classy Cold Salads, p128)

Spinach Orzo Salad (20 gm) (Classy Cold Salads, p142)
1 slice of multigrain or whole wheat bread with margarine or butter (12 gm)
Free item: Zucchini with Tomato (Jazzing up Vegetables, p110)
Free item: Sliced strawberries
Sopa Seca Salad (21 gm) (Classy Cold Salads, p146)

1 cup of milk (12 gm)
Free item: Roasted cauliflower (Jazzing up Vegetables, p104)
Free item: 1 or 2 plums or apricots

---

1 cup of tomato juice (10 gm)
Farfalle and Artichoke Salad (23 gm) (Snacking to Health! p174)
Free item: 1 orange

Creamy Spaghetti (29 gm) (Eating Mediterranean-style, p69)
½ cup of orange juice (13 gm)
Free item: 1 orange or banana

Eat at home lunches

Grilled cheese on multigrain or whole grain bread (15 gm)
1 cup of milk (12 gm)
Free item: Salad vegetables (e.g. tomatoes, cucumber and pepper) with home-made vinaigrette (Classy Cold Salads, p127)
Free item: Nutty Fruit Salad (Tasty Desserts! p203)

Spanish-style Fish (11 gm) (Encouraging Fish, p200)
Free item: Spanish Orange and Avocado Salad (Classy Cold Salads, p135)
2 Oatmeal Cookies (22 gm) (Tasty Desserts! p208)

---

1 corn on the cob with margarine or butter (14 gm)
Free item: 4 oz of salmon or other fish
Free item: Sautéed Green Beans (Jazzing up Vegetables, p114)
1 cup of milk (12 gm)
Free item: Fuji Apple

Free item: Easy Vegetable Soup (Satisfying Soups, p180)
Pasta Ratatouille Bake (15 gm) (Eating Mediterranean-style, p70)
Free item: Sautéed Zucchini (Jazzing up Vegetables, p111)
1 Banana Bran Muffin (22 gm) (Tasty Desserts! p205)

Baked salmon with herbs and brown rice (39 gm) (see: Encouraging Fish)
Free item: steamed asparagus
Free item: 1 Orange

Examples of 30 to 60 gm carbohydrate dinners

Zucchini-Tomato Soup (14 gm) (Satisfying Soups, p179)
Free item: Veggie burger from the store
Bulgur Pilaf with Pine Nuts (27 gm) (Experimenting with Grains, p87)
Free item: asparagus
Free item: 1 Fuji apple

Free item: Beef stew with green beans (Eating Mediterranean-style, p79)
¾ cup of cooked basmati, brown or other rice (30 gm)
Free item: Oven Roasted Vegetables (Jazzing up Vegetables, p102)
1 Apple Muffin (23 gm) (Tasty Desserts! p206)

Free item: ½ grapefruit
Free item: Grilled chicken
Pasta Ratatouille Bake (15 gm) (Eating Mediterranean-style, p70)
Free item: Winter Roasted Carrots (Jazzing up Vegetables, p100)
1 Pear Muffin (36 gm) (Tasty Desserts, p207)

Free item: Easy Vegetable Soup (Satisfying Soups, p180)
Honeyed Salmon (11 gm) (Encouraging Fish, p190)
Stuffed Zucchini with Rice (42 gm) (Eating Mediterranean-style, p78)
Free item: Steamed asparagus
Free item: Strawberries with a topping of whipped cream

Free item: Easy Vegetable Soup (Satisfying Soups, p180)
Chicken Stir Fry with Peanuts (41 gm) (Eating Mediterranean-style, p58)
Free item: Fresh Garden Salad (Classy Cold Salads, p128)
Free item: Roasted Veggie Medley (Jazzing up Vegetables, p103)
2 oatmeal cookies (16 gm) (Tasty Desserts! p208)

Chicken Couscous (48 gm) (see: Eating Mediterranean-style)
Free item: Fried Cauliflower with a Taste of Garlic (Jazzing up Vegetables, p105)
Free item: Microwaved Mushrooms (Jazzing up Vegetables, p122)
Free item: Slices of watermelon

Turkey Meatballs, Lentils and Mint (32 gm) (Eating Mediterranean-style, p61)
Bran Muffin with Raisins (28 gm) (Tasty Desserts! p204)
Free item: Nutty Fruit Salad (Tasty Desserts! p203)

Zucchini-Tomato Soup (14 gm) (Satisfying Soups, p179)
Free item: Beef Moussaka (Eating Mediterranean-style, p80)
Rice with Vegetables and Pecan (24 gm) (Experimenting with Grains, p91)
Free item: Boiled peas
Free item: Slices of mango

Red Lentil Soup (33 gm) (Satisfying Soups, p182)
Free item: Grilled chicken
Chinese Rice with Vegetables (24 gm) (Experimenting with Grains, p92)
Free item: Boiled Brussels sprouts

Pasta Primavera (22 gm) (Eating Mediterranean-style, p68)
Free item: Sautéed Green Beans (Jazzing up Vegetables, p114)
2 oatmeal cookies (22 gm) (Tasty Desserts! p208)

Chapter 7

LIST OF RECIPES

Jazzing up Vegetables

Classy Cold Salads

Breakfast – an Essential Meal

Snacking to Health!

Satisfying Soups

Encouraging Fish

Tasty Desserts!

Chapter 8

Eating Mediterranean-style

The main meal of the day in this country is typically a portion of meat, a starch dish such as potato or rice and perhaps a vegetable or salad dish on the side. However, in "Mediterranean-style" cooking, the vegetables, beans, grains and meat are often mixed together, so that each of these enhances the other.

Mediterranean-style recipes do not have to be from Mediterranean countries but they do have this characteristic. In fact, part of the fun of preparing Mediterranean-style dishes is to search through ethnic recipe books. There are a lot of treasures out there!

The recipes in this section are both Mediterranean-style and low-glycemic, so that white starches such as potato and white rice are limited. You will recall that a glycemic index of 70 or higher is considered to be high, 56-69 moderate, and less than 55 low. The glycemic index of a boiled Russet Burbank potato can be as high as 111, and that of boiled white rice is between 72 to 102. You will therefore be using a rice with a lower glycemic index such as basmati rice, long grain rice, Uncle Ben's rice (which is low-glycemic because it is parboiled), or brown rice.

Pasta of any shape or color is always a good standby. Italian-style pasta is made of semolina, which is milled flour in which the grain particles are coarser and larger than that used for white bread. It is also made from durum wheat. Because of its high protein content and gluten strength, durum wheat is the hardest wheat there is and this gives pasta a glycemic index of between 30 to 60.

It is also worthwhile working on reducing the salt content of your family's meals. Soups and tomato products are often high in salt. Many of the recipes in this book use chicken broth as a base, so look particularly for a low-salt variety.

Chicken Cantonese

■ **MARINATING** 30 minutes   ■ **COOKING** 12 minutes   ■ **SERVES** 5

OK, so Canton is nowhere near the Mediterranean. Nevertheless, this recipe illustrates well the concept of "Mediterranean-style cooking" with the vegetables enhancing the chicken and vice versa. The result is less chicken, more vegetables and a very tasty dish. Make sure that the egg noodles are made from semolina and Durum wheat.

- 1 stalk of celery, thinly biased-sliced (i.e. cut diagonally)
- 1 small green and/or red bell pepper, thinly sliced
- 5 medium mushrooms, sliced
- 1 small carrot, sliced
- 1 medium onion, chopped
- 2 cloves of garlic, minced
- $^1/_3$ cup of coarsely chopped almonds
- 6 oz of egg noodles, uncooked
- 5 teaspoons of cornstarch, divided
- 2 tablespoons of soy sauce
- 1 cup of chicken stock, preferably low sodium, divided
- 1 teaspoon of sesame oil
- 1 tablespoon of olive oil
- 2 teaspoons of grated ginger root
- 12 oz of boneless, skinless chicken breast halves, cut into thin bite-sized strips

DIRECTIONS:

1. In a medium size bowl, stir together the soy sauce, 3 teaspoons of chicken stock and 2 teaspoons of cornstarch. Stir in the chicken and let stand at room temperature for 30 minutes for the chicken to marinate.
2. Cook the egg noodles according to the packet instructions. Drain and add the sesame oil.
3. In a small bowl, stir together 1 cup of chicken stock and 3 teaspoons (1 tablespoon) of cornstarch. Set aside.
4. In a large skillet, preheat the oil over medium-high heat. Stir fry all the vegetables until soft. Remove all the vegetables from the frying pan and put aside.
5. Add the almonds to the skillet and stir fry for 2 minutes. Remove and put aside.
6. Add the un-drained chicken to the skillet, and stir fry for 4 minutes or until the chicken is tender and no pink remains.
7. Stir in the mixture of chicken stock and corn starch. Cook and stir until the mixture is thickened and bubbly.
8. Return the vegetables and almonds to the skillet, and stir all the ingredients together for about 1 minute until heated through.
9. Serve over the cooked egg noodles.

Adapted with permission from The Little Guides: Chicken, published by Fog City Press, San Francisco, CA

Nutritional information
Serving size: 1 cup. Per serving: 28 g starch carbohydrate, 35 g total carbohydrate, 357 cals, 14 g fat, 3 g saturated fat, 3 g fiber, 499 mg sodium.

Chicken Stir Fry with Peanuts

■ **MARINATING** 30 minutes   ■ **COOKING TIME** 14 minutes   ■ **SERVES** 5

For a quick and appealing dinner this dish definitely meets the grade. The peanuts provide a pleasant crunchy taste.

- 4 boneless skinless chicken breast halves (1 pound)
- 3 tablespoons of cornstarch
- 2½ tablespoons of soy sauce
- ½ teaspoon of ground ginger
- ¼ teaspoon of garlic powder
- 3 tablespoons of olive oil, divided
- $1\frac{1}{3}$ cups of uncooked basmati or other rice
- 2 cups of broccoli florets
- 3 stalks of celery, sliced into ½ inch pieces
- 2 large carrots, thinly sliced
- 1 small onion, cut into wedges
- 1 cup of chicken broth, preferably low salt
- 2 oz of roasted, unsalted peanuts

DIRECTIONS:

1. Cut the chicken into ½-inch strips and place in a resealable plastic bag. Add cornstarch and toss to coat.
2. Add the soy sauce, ginger and garlic powder to the bag and shake well.
3. Refrigerate the chicken mixture for 30 minutes.
4. Cook the white rice in twice its volume of water for 15 minutes (brown rice will need a longer cooking time).
5. In a large non-stick skillet or wok, heat 2 tablespoons of oil. Stir fry the chicken until it is no longer pink, about 3-5 minutes. Remove and keep warm.
6. Add the remaining 1 tablespoon of oil. Stir fry the broccoli, celery, carrots and onion for 4-5 minutes or until crisp tender.
7. Add the chicken broth.
8. Return the chicken to the pan and add the peanuts. Cook and stir until the mixture is thickened.
9. Serve the chicken dish over the rice.

Nutritional information
Serving size: 1 cup of cooked rice and 1 cup of chicken/vegetable combination. Per serving: 41 g grain and sugar carbohydrate, 51 g total carbohydrate, 466 cals, 16 g fat, 2 g saturated fat, 3 g fiber, 585 mg sodium.

Chicken Couscous

■ **COOKING TIME** 30 minutes ■ **SERVES** 6

This very tasty dish with its mixture of vegetables, grain, and chicken is Mediterranean-style to the core. Couscous is a form of pasta, and like pasta is often made from semolina and Durum wheat. This accounts for its low-glycemic index. Nevertheless, check the pasta's ingredients to make sure you've bought the right type.

- 12 oz of boneless, skinless chicken (breasts or thighs), cut into 1-inch cubes
- 1 cup of uncooked couscous
- 1 onion, chopped
- 1 clove garlic, minced
- 3 medium carrots, cut into 1-inch pieces
- 2 stalks of celery
- 1 medium zucchini, cut into ½ x ½ x 1-inch strips
- 2 medium tomatoes, peeled, seeded and chopped (or an 8-oz can of chopped tomatoes with juice)
- 15-oz can of garbanzo beans, rinsed and drained
- 1 tablespoon of olive oil
- 1¼ cups of chicken stock, preferably low-salt
- ¼ teaspoon of salt or to taste
- ¼ teaspoon of cumin
- ¼ teaspoon of turmeric
- ⅛ teaspoon of cayenne pepper

DIRECTIONS:

1. In a large frying pan, sauté the onion and garlic in hot oil until tender but not brown.
2. Add the chicken, carrots, celery, chicken stock, salt, cumin, turmeric, and red pepper. Bring the mixture to a boil and then reduce the heat, cover, and simmer for 20 minutes.
3. Add the zucchini, tomatoes and garbanzo beans. Cover and cook for 10 minutes more, or until the vegetables and chicken are tender.
4. In the meantime, prepare the couscous according to the packet instructions. (After the pot of water is boiled, this takes just over 10 minutes to cook)

Nutritional information
Serving size: ½ cup of cooked couscous and 1 cup of the vegetable and chicken combination. Per serving: 48 g grain and bean carbohydrate, 58 g total carbohydrate, 372 cals, 6.0 g fat, 1.3 g saturated fat, 9 g fiber, 364 mg sodium.

Adapted with permission from The Little Guides: Chicken, published by Fog City Press, San Francisco, CA

Free item!

Chicken Kabobs

■ **MARINATING** 6 to 12 hours   ■ **COOKING TIME** 6 to 12 minutes   ■ **SERVES** 4

Kids always find "doing things" with food a lot of fun, and it shouldn't be difficult to find plenty of helpers to make these kabobs. Adults soon get into the groove too! Other veggies and even fruit can be put onto the skewer. Chunks of pineapple work well for example.

- 1 lb of boneless, skinless chicken breasts, cut into 1½-inch cubes
- 1 cup of button mushrooms
- ½ of a red pepper, cut into 2 inch chunks
- ½ of a yellow pepper, cut into 2 inch chunks
- 1 cup of cherry tomatoes
- 1 cup of baby onions

Marinade:
- 2 tablespoons of olive oil
- 2 tablespoons of soy sauce (lower sodium)
- 2 tablespoons of lemon juice
- 2 tablespoons of fresh parsley, chopped
- ½ teaspoon of salt or to taste
- ⅛ teaspoon of pepper

DIRECTIONS:

1. Mix the marinade mixture in a bowl and marinate the chicken and mushrooms for 6 to 12 hours.
2. If you are using wooden skewers (which are suitable for broiling only), soak them in water for 30 minutes to prevent them from igniting.
3. Place the chicken and vegetables on the skewers.
4. Grill the kabobs close to the heat for about 6 minutes or broil for about 12 minutes, turning every so often.

Nutritional information
Portion size: 2 skewers. Per serving: 8 g total carbohydrate, 220 cals,
8 g fat, 1 g saturated fat, 2 g fiber, 662 mg sodium.

Turkey Meatballs, Lentils and Mint

■ **COOKING TIME** 55 minutes   ■ **SERVES** 6

The spices give this recipe a very pleasant Middle-Eastern flavor. Serve it over couscous, although there are other suitable starches one can use too.

- 1 lb of ground turkey
- 1 cup of fresh bread crumbs
- 4 cloves of garlic, minced, divided
- 1 cup of dried brown lentils
- ¼ cup of olive oil
- 1 small carrot, peeled and cut into ¼-inch dice
- 1 small onion, cut into ¼-inch dice
- 1 15-oz can of plum tomatoes, drained with juice reserved
- 4 cups of chicken broth, preferably low-salt
- 2 teaspoons of dried mint
- 2 tablespoons of fresh parsley, chopped
- 1 teaspoon of paprika
- ¾ teaspoon of ground cumin
- ½ teaspoon of ground cloves
- ¼ teaspoon of pepper
- ¾ teaspoon of salt or to taste
- ½ teaspoon of pepper

DIRECTIONS:

1. Preheat the oven to 350°F.
2. In a bowl, combine the turkey, bread crumbs, half of the garlic, the mint, parsley, paprika, cumin, cloves, the salt and pepper, and mix well.
3. Divide the mixture into 24 balls, place them on a baking sheet and bake for 10 minutes. Remove from the oven and set aside.
4. Warm the olive oil over a medium heat in a large sauté pan. Add the onion, carrot and remaining garlic and sauté, stirring until the onion is soft, about 10 minutes.
5. Add the lentils, the reserved tomato juice from the canned tomatoes and the chicken stock and simmer gently, uncovered, until the lentils are tender, about 20 minutes longer.
6. Chop up the tomatoes, and add the meatballs and tomatoes to the lentils and simmer for 15 minutes to blend the flavors and finish cooking the meatballs. Season to taste with extra salt and pepper.

> Nutritional information
> Portion size: 1 cup. Per serving: 32 g grain and bean carbohydrate, 40 g total carbohydrate, 424 cals, 18 g fat, 4 g saturated fat, 12 g fiber, 696 mg sodium.

Adapted with permission from "Williams-Sonoma Kitchen Library. Beans and Rice," published by Williams-Sonoma Inc, San Francisco, CA

Turkey-ground Kubbeh

- **SOAKING TIME** 10 minutes
- **COOKING TIME** 21 minutes
- **REFRIGERATOR TIME** 30 minutes
- **SERVES** 13

This is probably as close as one can get to a healthy "hamburger". It tastes good too! The spices give it a very Middle Eastern flavor.

- 1 lb of ground turkey
- $^2/_3$ cup of finely ground bulgur wheat
- 1½ onion, chopped
- $^1/_3$ cup of fresh parsley
- $^1/_3$ cup of pecans, chopped
- 4 or more tablespoons of olive oil
- 1 teaspoon of salt
- ¼ teaspoon of pepper
- 1 teaspoon of paprika
- ½ teaspoon of cinnamon
- ¼ teaspoon of cayenne
- 3 tablespoon of cold water

DIRECTIONS:

1. Heat 2 tablespoons of oil in a skillet over a medium heat. Add 1 chopped onion and sauté for 5 minutes or until it begins to turn golden.
2. Pour 2 cups of cold water over the bulgur wheat. Refrigerate and let soak for 10 minutes (if using medium bulgur soak for 15 to 20 minutes).
3. In a food processor, place half an onion, parsley and spices and chop them fine.
4. In a large bowl, mix the ground turkey and the onion/spice mixture from the food processor. Add the sautéed onions and the chopped pecans and mix well.
5. Drain the bulgur well in a strainer and squeeze out the extra water. Add it to the turkey mixture and mix well.
6. Cover and refrigerate for about 30 minutes.
7. Shape the mixture into small round patties, using ¼ cup for each and flatten them.
8. Heat 4 tablespoons of oil in a large skillet and sauté each cake for 3 to 4 minutes per side or until golden brown and cooked through. Add more oil if necessary.
9. Place on a paper towel to drain. Serve hot or cold.

> Nutritional information
> Serving size: 1 cake. Per serving: 6 g grain and nut carbohydrate, 7 g total carbohydrate, 139 cals, 9 g fat, 2 g saturated fat, 2 g fiber, 214 mg sodium.

Broccoli Quiche

■ **COOKING TIME** 33 minutes ■ **SERVES** 8

This is a dish that will impress everyone. They may not even realize they're eating vegetables!

Crust:
- 1 cup of stone ground whole wheat flour
- 1 cup of white flour
- 1 teaspoon of salt
- ½ cup of canola oil
- 5 tablespoons of ice water

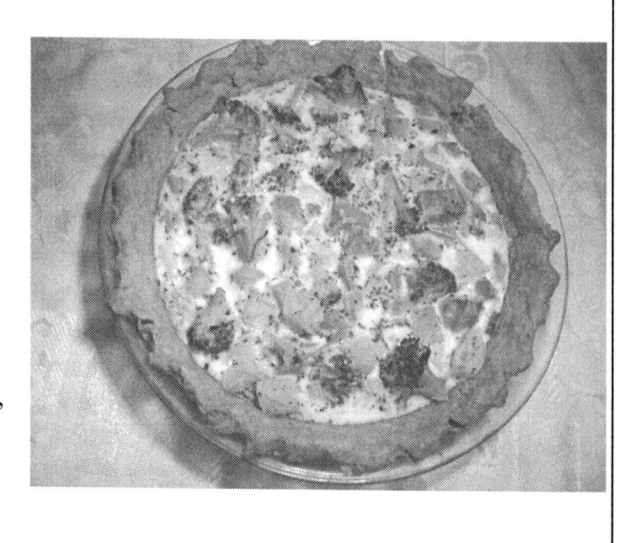

Filling:
- ½ cup of grated cheddar cheese
- 1½ cups of chopped frozen broccoli, defrosted and drained
- 1 medium onion, chopped
- 2 large eggs
- ½ cup of milk
- ½ teaspoon of oregano
- ¼ teaspoon of basil
- 2 tablespoons of stone ground whole wheat flour
- Salt to taste
- Pepper to taste

DIRECTIONS:

1. Preheat the oven to 375ºF.
2. Prepare the pie crust by mixing the flour and salt in a large bowl.
3. In a separate bowl, whisk together the oil and water until the mixture is thick.
4. Stir the mixture into the flour until dough forms.
5. Roll out the dough into a 9-inch pan.
6. Sauté the onion.
7. Sprinkle the crust in this order: cheese, broccoli and sautéed onion.
8. In a separate bowl, mix the eggs, milk, spices, flour and salt and pepper to taste and pour over the filling.
9. Bake at 375ºF for 30 minutes.

Nutritional information (with whole milk)
Serving size: $\frac{1}{8}$th of the pie. Per serving: 28 g total carbohydrate, 306 cals, 18 g fat, 3.0 g saturated fat, 4.0 g fiber, 387 mg sodium.

Spinach Quiche

■ **COOKING TIME** 48 minutes ■ **SERVES** 8

This is another beautiful quiche recipe.

Crust:
- 1 cup of stone ground whole wheat flour
- 1 cup of white flour
- 1 teaspoon of salt
- ½ cup of canola oil
- 5 tablespoons of ice water

Filling
- 1 10-oz package of frozen chopped spinach, thawed, squeezed dry
- 1 medium onion, chopped
- 1 15-oz container of ricotta cheese
- 8 oz of mozzarella cheese, grated
- $\frac{1}{3}$ cup of Parmesan cheese, grated
- 3 large eggs, beaten
- 3 tablespoons of olive oil
- Salt to taste
- ½ teaspoon of pepper
- ¼ teaspoon of nutmeg

DIRECTIONS:

1. Preheat the oven to 375°F.
2. To prepare the pie crust, mix the flour and salt in a large bowl.
3. In a separate bowl, whisk together the oil and water until the mixture is thick.
4. Stir the mixture into the flour until dough forms.
5. Roll out the dough into a 9-inch pan.
6. Sauté the onion in the olive oil in a medium-sized skillet until tender.
7. Mix in the spinach, salt, pepper and nutmeg, and sauté until all the liquid from the spinach evaporates, about 3 minutes.
8. Combine the cheeses in a large bowl.
9. Mix in the eggs.
10. Add the spinach mixture to the large bowl and blend well.
11. Fill the pie crust with the spinach-cheese mixture
12. Bake for about 40 minutes until the filling is set in the center and brown on top.

Nutritional information (using whole milk ricotta cheese)
Serving size: $\frac{1}{8}$th of the pie. Per serving: 35 g total carbohydrate, 503 cals, 33 g fat, 9 g saturated fat, 4 g fiber, 647 mg sodium.

Mushroom Quiche

■ **COOKING TIME** 48 minutes   ■ **SERVES** 8

This is another winning quiche. Take your pick.

Crust:
- 1 cup of stone ground whole wheat flour
- 1 cup of white flour
- 1 teaspoon of salt
- ½ cup of canola oil
- 5 tablespoons of ice water

Filling
- 1 large onion, chopped
- 8 oz of mushrooms, sliced
- 2 tablespoons of olive oil
- 4 eggs
- ½ cup of milk
- 1 cup of shredded cheddar cheese, divided
- ¼ teaspoon of salt
- $\frac{1}{8}$ teaspoon of pepper

DIRECTIONS:
1. Preheat the oven to 375°F.
2. To prepare the pie crust, mix the flour and salt in a large bowl.
3. In a separate bowl, whisk together the oil and water until the mixture is thick.
4. Stir the mixture into the flour until dough forms.
5. Roll out the dough into a 9-inch pan.
6. Sauté the onion, mushrooms in the olive oil, and keep separate.
7. In a bowl, whisk the eggs and milk, and add the salt and pepper.
8. In the unbaked pie shell, layer: ½ cup of shredded cheddar cheese, then the onion/mushroom sauté mixture, and then the remaining ½ cup of shredded cheddar cheese.
9. Pour the egg mixture over all this.
10. Bake at 375°F for 30 minutes

> Nutritional information (with whole milk)
> Serving size: $\frac{1}{8}$th of the pie. Per serving: 27 g total carbohydrate, 399 cals, 23 g fat, 5 g saturated fat, 3 g fiber, 462 mg sodium.

Middle East Vegetable Tacos

■ **COOKING TIME** 10 minutes ■ **SERVES** 12

Whether the vegetables are placed on tacos, over spaghetti, or over other pasta –they taste good!

- 1 tablespoon of olive oil
- 1 medium eggplant, peeled and cut into ½-inch cubes
- 1 medium red bell pepper, cut into ½-inch cubes
- 1 medium onion, cut into ½-inch wedges
- 2 cloves of garlic, minced
- 1 14.5-oz can of diced tomatoes
- ¼ teaspoon of salt or to taste
- ¼ teaspoon of oregano
- 1 10-oz container of hummus
- 12 medium tacos shells

DIRECTIONS:

1. In a 10-inch skillet, heat the oil on a medium-high heat and sauté the eggplant, bell pepper, onion and garlic in oil for 5-7 minutes, stirring occasionally until the vegetables are crisp-tender.
2. Stir in the tomatoes, salt and oregano and reduce the heat to medium. Cover and cook for about 5 minutes or until the eggplant is tender.
3. Spread about 2 tablespoons of hummus inside each taco shell, and spoon the vegetable mixture over the hummus in each shell.

Nutritional information
Serving size: 1 taco. Per serving: 13 gm bean and starch carbohydrate, 18 g total carbohydrate, 140 cals, 7 g fat, 1 g sat fat, 4 g fiber, 346 mg sodium.

Ratatouille Rice

- **COOKING TIME** 30 minutes ▪ **SERVES** 8

This is an easy way for making a colorful and tasty rice dish. It can be used either as a side dish or vegetarian main dish.

- 28-oz can of chopped tomatoes, drained
- 1 small eggplant, peeled, cut in small dice
- 1 medium onion, chopped
- 1 small green pepper, diced
- 1 small red pepper, diced
- ½ lb of zucchini or summer squash, cut into small dice
- 4 large garlic cloves, minced
- 6 tablespoons of olive oil
- 1 teaspoon of dried thyme
- 1 teaspoon of basil
- ¼ teaspoon of salt or to taste
- $^1/_8$ teaspoon of pepper
- 1½ cups of uncooked basmati or other rice

DIRECTIONS:

1. Heat 2 tablespoons of oil in a large skillet. Add the eggplant, salt and pepper and sauté over a medium-high heat for 3 minutes. Transfer to a bowl.
2. Add 2 tablespoons of oil to the pan and heat over medium-high heat. Add onion and peppers and cook for 8 minutes or until the onion is tender but not brown.
3. Add zucchini and cook, stirring for 2 minutes.
4. Return the eggplant to the large skillet. Add the tomatoes, garlic, thyme and basil and heat until sizzling. Cover and simmer over a low heat, stirring occasionally, for 15 minutes or until the vegetables are tender and the mixture is thick.
5. Boil rice as per directions on the package. Drain and rinse with cold water.
6. Heat 2 tablespoons of oil in a large, heavy saucepan. Add the rice and heat over a medium heat, stirring with a fork.
7. Add the hot ratatouille to the rice, and heat, tossing gently, for 2 minutes.

Nutritional information
Serving size: 1 cup. Per serving: 19 g grain and sugar carbohydrate,
26 g total carbohydrate, 177 cals, 7 g fat, 1 g saturated fat, 3 g fiber,
56 mg sodium.

Pasta Primavera

■ **COOKING TIME** 25 minutes   ■ **SERVES** 14

This wonderful family recipe is loaded with tasty vegetables.

- 1 cup of chicken broth, preferably low-salt
- 5 medium-sized carrots, sliced thin
- ½ lb of thin asparagus, trimmed and cut into 2-inch lengths
- 1 large red pepper, seeded and cut into 2-inch long thin strips
- 1 large yellow pepper, seeded and cut into 2-inch long thin strips
- 2 medium-sized zucchini or yellow squash, thinly sliced
- 1½ tablespoon of whole wheat flour, preferably stone-ground
- 1⅓ cups of milk
- 12 oz of uncooked fettuccine
- ½ cup of grated Parmesan cheese
- 3 tablespoons of olive oil
- ½ teaspoons of pepper

DIRECTIONS:

1. Cook the fettuccine according to the package instructions. Keep separate.
2. In a large pot, bring the chicken broth to a boil.
3. Add the carrots, cover and cook over medium heat for 2 minutes.
4. Stir in the asparagus, peppers and zucchini, cover and cook 3 minutes longer, or until the vegetables are crisp tender.
5. In a small bowl, whisk the flour into the milk.
6. Add the milk and flour mixture to the pot and stir until boiling. Simmer, stirring, for 1 to 2 minutes until slightly thickened.
7. Pour this mixture over the pasta in a serving pot. Add the cheese, oil and pepper, and mix well to coat.

> Nutritional information
> Serving size: 1 cup. Per serving: 19 g of grain and dairy carbohydrate, 24 g total carbohydrate, 172 cals, 5 g fat, 2 g saturated fat, 2 g fiber, 90 mg sodium.

Creamy Spaghetti

- **COOKING TIME** 15 minutes   - **SERVES** 6½

You don't need to eat anything else with this spaghetti dish. It's a meal. The leftovers (if there are any) can also be served cold as a spaghetti salad.

- ½ pound fresh broccoli, broken into florets
- 1½ cups of zucchini, sliced
- 1½ cups of fresh mushrooms, sliced
- 1 large carrot, sliced
- 3 tablespoons of olive oil
- 8 oz of uncooked spaghetti
- ¼ cup of onion, chopped
- 3 cloves of garlic, minced
- 2 tablespoons of whole wheat stone ground flour
- 2 teaspoons of chicken bouillon granules
- 1 teaspoon of dried thyme
- 2 cups of whole milk
- ¾ cup of shredded mozzarella cheese

DIRECTIONS:

1. In a large skillet, sauté the broccoli, zucchini, mushrooms and carrots in 1 tablespoon of oil until crisp-tender, about 3 minutes. Remove from the heat and set aside.
2. Cook the spaghetti according to the package directions. Drain and set aside.
3. In another saucepan, sauté the onion and garlic in the remainder of the olive oil until tender.
4. Stir in the flour, chicken bouillon and thyme until blended.
5. Add the milk gradually. Bring to a boil and cook for 2 minutes or until thickened.
6. Reduce the heat to low and stir in the cheese until melted.
7. Add the vegetables and heat through.
8. Toss the spaghetti into the vegetable mixture.

> Nutritional information
> Serving size: 1 cup. Per serving: 29 g grain and dairy carbohydrate, 37 g total carbohydrate, 302 cals, 12 g fat, 3 g saturated fat, 1 g fiber, 264 mg sodium.

Pasta Ratatouille Bake

■ **COOKING TIME** 45 minutes ■ **SERVES** 14

- 8 oz of dry macaroni
- 2 tablespoons of olive oil
- 2 medium onions, chopped
- 1 clove of garlic, chopped
- 1 teaspoon of dried oregano
- 1 teaspoon of dried basil
- 4 medium tomatoes, chopped
- 4 small zucchinis, sliced
- 15-oz (1¼ cups) of cooked white beans, small to large, fresh, frozen or canned
- ½ cup of vegetable stock, either fresh or made from bouillon
- ½ cup of grated parmesan cheese
- 2 teaspoons of salt or to taste

DIRECTIONS:

1. Cook the macaroni according to the package instructions and drain.
2. Preheat oven to 350°F.
3. In a large skillet, heat the oil and cook the onion and garlic until golden.
4. Stir in the herbs, tomato, zucchini, beans, stock and seasoning, and simmer for 5 minutes.
5. Combine the pasta and vegetables in a baking dish and sprinkle the cheese on top.
6. Bake for 35 minutes at 350°F.

Nutritional information
Serving size: 1 cup. Per serving: 15 g grain and sugar carbohydrate, 15 g total carbohydrate, 130 cals, 3 g fat, 1.0 g saturated fat, 3.0 g fiber, 393 mg sodium.

Spinach Lasagna

■ **COOKING TIME** 75 minutes   ■ **SERVES** 12

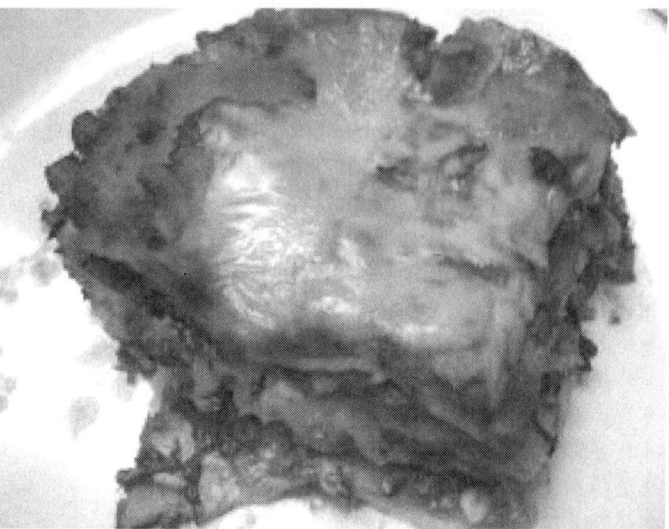

- 1 lb of small curd cottage cheese
- 1½ cup of shredded mozzarella cheese, divided
- 1 egg
- 1 10-oz package of frozen chopped spinach, thawed and drained
- 1 24-oz jar of low salt spaghetti sauce
- 8 oz of dry lasagna noodles
- 1 cup of water
- 1 teaspoon of salt or to taste
- ¾ teaspoon of oregano
- $^1/_8$ teaspoon of pepper

DIRECTIONS:

1. Preheat the oven to 350°F.
2. Grease a 13 x 9-inch pan.
3. In a large bowl, mix the cottage cheese, 1 cup of mozzarella cheese, egg, spinach and spices.
4. Layer ½ cup of spaghetti sauce, $^1/_3$ of the raw noodles, and half of the cheese mixture.
5. Repeat this one more time.
6. Top with the remaining noodles and remaining sauce.
7. Sprinkle with the remaining ½ cup of mozzarella cheese.
8. Pour 1 cup of water around the edges.
9. Cover tightly with foil and bake at 350°F for 1 hour 15 minutes.
10. Let sit for 15 minutes before serving (so it becomes a bit more solid).

Nutritional information
Per serving: Serving size: $^1/_{12}$ th of the pan. 20 g total carbohydrate,
193 cals, 7 g fat, 3 g saturated fat, 3 g fiber, 477 mg sodium.

Baked Pasta Shells with Spinach and Cheese

■ **COOKING TIME** 55 minutes ■ **SERVES** 8

This recipe makes a filling, inexpensive, and always popular supper.

- 12 oz of dry jumbo pasta shells
- ½ lb of fresh or 1 cup of frozen spinach leaves
- 2 cloves of garlic, minced
- ½ lb of ricotta cheese
- ½ lb of mozzarella cheese, grated
- 1 egg
- 1 tablespoon of fresh basil leaves, minced or 1 teaspoon of dried basil leaves
- 2 teaspoons of olive oil
- 1½ cups of low-sodium pasta sauce
- ¼ cup of grated Parmesan cheese
- Salt to taste
- Black pepper to taste

DIRECTIONS:

1. Cook the pasta shells until al dente according to the package instructions.
2. Preheat the oven to 375°F.
3. If using fresh spinach, place the leaves in a pan with a bit of water. Cover and cook over low until the leaves are just wilted. Drain the water from the spinach and chop finely. If using frozen spinach, thaw completely and squeeze all liquid from the spinach. Chop finely.
4. Beat the egg.
5. In a large mixing bowl, blend the spinach, garlic, ricotta and mozzarella cheese, egg, basil, salt and pepper to make the filling.
6. Spread a few tablespoons of pasta sauce on the bottom of a shallow baking dish, large enough to hold the shells in one layer.
7. Fill each shell with about a tablespoon of filling.
8. Arrange the shells in the dish. Pour the remaining sauce over and around the shells.
9. Top the dish with Parmesan cheese.
10. Cover the dish with aluminum foil and bake for about 40 minutes.

Nutritional information
Serving size: 5 shells. Per serving: 32 g grain carbohydrate, 40 g total carbohydrate, 353 cals, 14 g fat, 7 g saturated fat, 3 g fiber, 344 mg sodium.

Veggie Macaroni and Cheese

■ **COOKING TIME** 27 minutes   ■ **SERVES** 9¼

Who doesn't love macaroni and cheese? This is a really good recipe, enhanced even more by the vegetables.

- 12 oz of dry macaroni
- 1½ cups of broccoli florets
- 1 cup of fresh cauliflowerets
- 1½ cups of carrots, thinly sliced
- 1 celery stalk, sliced
- ½ cup of zucchini, sliced
- ½ medium onion, chopped
- ½ tablespoon of olive oil
- ⅛ cup of stone ground whole wheat flour
- ½ cup of milk
- ½ cup of chicken broth, preferably low salt
- 6 oz (about 1¾ cups) of shredded cheddar cheese
- ½ teaspoon of Dijon mustard
- ⅛ teaspoon of salt
- Dash of pepper
- ⅛ teaspoon of paprika

DIRECTIONS:

1. Preheat the oven to 350°F.
2. Cook the macaroni in a medium-sized pot according to the package instructions.
3. In the same pot, for the last 6 minutes of cooking add the vegetables.
4. Transfer the macaroni and vegetables to a 13-in. x 9-in. x 2-in baking dish.
5. In a large frying pan, sauté the onion in the olive oil until tender.
6. Stir in the flour until blended.
7. Stir in the milk and chicken broth.
8. Bring the mixture to a boil, cook and stir for 2 minutes until thickened.
9. Stir in the cheese, mustard, salt and pepper.
10. Pour the cheese mixture over the macaroni and vegetable mixture in the baking dish and stir to coat the macaroni.
11. Sprinkle the dish with paprika.
12. Bake uncovered at 350°F for 15-20 minutes or until heated through.

> Nutritional information (using whole milk)
> Serving size: 1 cup. Per serving: 30 grain and sugar carbohydrate, 35 g total carbohydrate, 262 cals, 8 g fat, 5 g saturated fat, 30 g fiber, 190 mg sodium.

Thin Crust Whole Wheat Pizza

■ **COOKING TIME** 20 minutes ■ **SERVES** 8

A family recipe book would be incomplete without a pizza recipe. Pizza is a tasty way for eating vegetables, but it does have a somewhat high glycemic index. There are ways to reduce it. This recipe uses a mixture of whole wheat flour and white flour.

Pizza dough:
- 2 cups of white flour, with additional flour as needed, about ¼ cup
- 1 cup of stone ground whole wheat flour
- 2 teaspoons of yeast
- ½ teaspoon of salt
- ½ teaspoon of dried basil
- 1 tablespoon of sugar
- 1 cup of water
- 1 tablespoon of olive oil
- $\frac{1}{8}$ teaspoon of garlic powder

Sauce:
- 1 cup of pasta sauce, preferably low salt
- 8 oz of grated Mozzarella cheese

Vegetable topping:
- ½ cup of zucchini, thinly sliced
- ¾ cup mushroom, sliced
- $\frac{1}{3}$ cup of scallion
- ½ of a medium green pepper, cut into small pieces

Garnish:
- ¼ teaspoon of dried basil or dried oregano
- ¼ teaspoon of dried rosemary

DIRECTIONS

1. Preheat the oven to 400°F.
2. In a large bowl, mix the contents of the pizza dough, and knead for about 2 minutes to form the dough.
3. Stretch and roll out the dough to fit a 16-inch pizza pan.
4. Spray the pizza pan lightly with an oil spray (a pizza pan has multiple holes so be careful with what you put underneath!)
5. Spread the pizza sauce onto the dough, up to 1 inch from the end of the dough.
6. Top with cheese.
7. Spread the vegetables onto the sauce.
8. Sprinkle the garnish onto the vegetables.
9. Bake in the oven for 20 minutes at 400°F.

> Nutritional information
> Serving size: $\frac{1}{8}$th of the pizza. Per serving: 52 g total carbohydrate, 350 cals, 10 g fat, 4 g saturated fat, 6 g fiber, 330 mg sodium.

Crunchy Crust Pizza

■ **COOKING TIME** 20 minutes ■ **SERVES** 8

This recipe is made from a mixed grain pizza dough. The crust is mainly white flour, but the whole grains lower the glycemic index somewhat. It's worth the effort.

Pizza dough:
- 3 cups of white flour, with additional flour as needed, about ¼ cup
- ¼ cup of roasted buckwheat (kasha)
- ¼ cup of bulgur wheat
- 1 teaspoon of yeast
- ¼ teaspoon of salt
- ½ teaspoon of dried basil
- 1 teaspoon of sugar
- 1 cup of water
- 1 tablespoon of olive oil

Sauce:
- 1 cup of pasta sauce, preferably low salt
- 8 oz of grated Mozzarella cheese

Vegetable topping:
- ½ onion, coarsely chopped
- ¾ cup mushroom, sliced
- ½ medium green pepper, cut into small pieces
- Black olives (optional)

Garnish:
- ¼ teaspoon of dried basil or dried oregano
- ¼ teaspoon of dried rosemary

DIRECTIONS:

1. Preheat the oven to 400°F.
2. In a large bowl, mix the yeast, whole grains, flour, sugar and salt. Then add the oil and water. Knead the mixture for about 2 minutes to form the dough.
3. Stretch and roll out the dough to the size to fit a 16-inch pizza pan.
4. Spray the pizza pan lightly with an oil spray (note that pizza pans have multiple holes!)
5. In a medium-sized bowl, mix the contents of the pizza sauce.
6. Spread the pizza sauce onto the dough, up to 1 inch from the end of the dough.
7. Spread the vegetables onto the sauce in sections according to taste.
8. Pour the garnish onto the vegetables.
9. Bake in the oven for 20 minutes at 400°F.

Nutritional information
Serving size: ⅛th of the pizza. Per serving: 51g total carbohydrate, 2560 cals, 8 g fat, 4 g saturated fat, 4 g fiber, 256 mg sodium.

Burrito Grande

■ **COOKING TIME** 45 minutes (for the rice) ■ **SERVES** 6½

South America is nowhere near the Mediterranean, but this delicious burrito dish with its mixture of beans and vegetables is very much in the Mediterranean-mode.

- 1 15-oz can of black beans, rinsed and well-drained
- 1 15-oz can of pinto beans, rinsed and well-drained
- 4 oz of frozen whole kernel corn, defrosted
- ½ of a 15-oz can of diced tomatoes and green chilies
- ½ of a medium green pepper, chopped
- 4 scallions, chopped
- 1 garlic clove, minced
- ¼ cup of fresh cilantro, chopped
- 2 tablespoons of lime juice
- $^2/_3$ tablespoon of olive oil
- 1 teaspoon ground cumin
- ½ teaspoon of salt or to taste
- 4 oz of shredded cheddar cheese
- 1 cup of uncooked brown rice

DIRECTIONS:

1. Cook the brown rice according to the package instructions.
2. Combine all the ingredients together and mix well.
3. Serve inside a whole-wheat tortilla.

> Nutritional information (without the tortilla)
> Serving size: 1 cup (sufficient for 1 10" tortilla). Per serving: 35 g total carbohydrate, 262 cals, 8 g fat, 4 g saturated fat, 9 g fiber, 864 mg sodium.

This recipe was kindly provided by Da'Nalis Cafe in Skokie, Illinois.

Roasted Vegetable Chili

■ **COOKING TIME** 30 minutes   ■ **SERVES** 14

- 1 medium butternut squash, peeled and cut into 1-inch pieces
- 2 large carrots, sliced
- 2 medium zucchini, cut into 1-inch pieces
- 2 medium green peppers, diced
- 1 large onion, chopped
- 2 14½-oz cans of diced tomatoes
- 2 15-oz cans of cannelloni or white kidney beans, rinsed and drained
- 3 14½-oz cans of reduced-sodium chicken broth
- 2 tablespoons of olive oil, divided
- 1½ teaspoons of ground cumin
- 1 cup of salsa
- 1 cup of water
- 3 teaspoons of chili powder
- 6 garlic cloves, minced

DIRECTIONS:

1. Preheat the oven to 450°F.
2. Place the squash, carrots, and zucchini in a baking pan.
3. Combine 1 tablespoon of olive oil with the cumin, drizzle over the vegetables and toss to coat.
4. Bake uncovered at 450°F for 25-30 minutes, stirring once.
5. In a large soup pot, sauté the green peppers and onion in the remaining 1 tablespoon of oil for 3-4 minutes until tender.
6. Stir in the broth, tomatoes, beans, water, salsa, chili powder and garlic.
7. Bring to a boil. Reduce heat and simmer uncovered for 10 minutes.
8. Stir in the roasted vegetables.
9. Return to a boil. Reduce heat and simmer uncovered for 5-10 minutes or until heated through.

> Nutritional information (without the tortilla)
> Serving size: 1 cup. Per serving: 15.0 g from beans, 28 g total carbohydrate, 156 cals, 3.0 g fat, 0 g saturated fat, 6.0 g fiber, 251 mg sodium

Stuffed Zucchini or Pepper with Rice

■ **COOKING TIME** 45 minutes ■ **SERVES** 6

The kids will love this tasty recipe. They will also like the way the zucchinis fluff up while they are being cooked. Use either vegetarian meat or lean chopped meat. Don't waste the inside of the zucchinis. They can be used in a soup.

- ½ lb of vegetarian or hamburger meat
- ¾ cup of uncooked basmati or other rice
- 1 onion, chopped (optional)
- 3 medium or large zucchinis, cut in half or thirds crosswise and hollowed out, or use 2 green peppers, cut in half
- 1 egg
- Salt (optional)
- 1 teaspoon of cumin
- ¼ teaspoon of paprika
- 1 tablespoon of bread crumbs
- 1 15-oz can of tomato sauce
- 1 15-oz can of diced tomato
- 3 tablespoons of sugar
- ½ cup of water

DIRECTIONS:

1. Cook the rice in $^3/_4$ cup of water just until the water is absorbed (about 5 minutes).
2. Sauté the onions in a small amount of olive oil.
3. In a large bowl, mix together the meat, egg, fried onion, cumin, salt to taste and bread crumbs.
4. Stuff this mixture into the zucchinis or peppers.
4. In a big pot, bring the tomato sauce, diced tomato, sugar and water to a boil.
5. Put the stuffed vegetable carefully into the sauce. Cover and simmer the sauce for 30-40 minutes, adding more water if it becomes dry.

Nutritional information (not including the meat)
Serving size: ½ zucchini. Per serving: 42 gm total carbohydrate, 185 cals, 1 g fat, 0 g sat fat, 5 g fiber, 539 mg sodium.

Beef Stew with Green Beans

■ **COOKING TIME** 2 hours 17 minutes ■ **SERVES** 5

Steak and meatballs are not what this book is all about. Nevertheless, this recipe deserves to be included, since the combination of vegetables and meat is Mediterranean-style to the core.

- 1½ lbs of green beans, with ends removed
- 1 sweet red, green or yellow pepper, cut in thin strips
- 2 large onions, sliced thin
- 1 14 ½-oz can of stewed tomatoes
- 2 garlic cloves, minced
- 2 beef Bouillon cubes, preferably low-salt
- 2 tablespoons of olive oil
- 1 teaspoon of sweet paprika
- Salt to taste
- ⅛ teaspoon of pepper
- 1 teaspoon of sugar
- 1 cup of water

DIRECTIONS:

1. Sauté the onions in the oil for about 7 minutes on medium-low heat.
2. Add the beef and sauté for another 7 minutes, stirring often.
3. Stir in the garlic, and then add the tomatoes, pepper strips, paprika, salt, pepper and 1 cup of water.
4. Bring to boil, cover and cook over low heat for 1½ hours.
5. Add the green beans and cook for 30 minutes or until the beef and beans are tender, adding a few tablespoons of water from time to time if needed.
6. Add the sugar and mix well.
7. Cook for another 3 minutes.

> Nutritional information
> Serving size: 1 cup. Per serving: 16 g total carbohydrate, 120 cals, 5 g fat, 1 g saturated fat, 5 g fiber, 285 mg sodium.

Free item!

Beef Moussaka

- **COOKING TIME** 45 minutes ■ **SERVES** 6

This delicious meat recipe is also included in this section because the combination of beef and vegetables makes it extremely "Mediterranean-style".

- 1 large eggplant, cut into ½-inch slices
- 1 large onion, sliced
- 1 lb of lean ground beef
- 2 cloves of garlic, minced
- 2 large tomatoes, sliced
- 1 teaspoon of salt
- ½ teaspoon of pepper
- ½ teaspoon of cinnamon
- Dash of paprika

DIRECTIONS:

1. Preheat the oven to 350°F.
2. Wash and liberally salt the eggplant slices and leave for 20 minutes.
3. Rinse off the salt well.
4. Bake the eggplant on a cookie sheet for 10 minutes or until soft.
5. In a medium-sized skillet, sauté the onions and set aside.
6. Sauté the ground beef.
7. Add the seasonings, except for the garlic.
8. In a greased casserole dish, layer the ingredients as follows: half the eggplant with garlic (on the bottom), ground beef, tomatoes, half the garlic, onions and dash of paprika.
9. Bake the ingredients at 350°F for 30 minutes.

Nutritional information
Serving size: $^1/_6$ th of the eggplant. Per serving: 11 g total carbohydrate, 267 cals, 19 g fat, 7 g saturated fat, 4 g fiber, 444 mg sodium.

Vegetable and Wheat Berry Goulash

- **COOKING TIME** $2\frac{1}{4}$ hours   - **SERVES**   11

(The wheat berries should preferably be soaked overnight)

A casserole can be easily made into a tasty Mediterranean-type dish. Plus, it's very satisfying being able to take a meal ready-made out of the oven without having to plan the vegetables, meat and starch separately. This goulash dish uses an unusual starch – wheat berries. Try them. They taste good!

- 1 lb of lean beef
- ¼ cup of stone ground whole wheat flour
- 1 cup of raw wheat berries
- 1 tablespoon of onion soup mix
- 1 large onion, chopped
- 1 clove garlic, minced
- 1 green pepper, sliced
- 1 14-oz can of chopped tomatoes
- 2 tablespoons of olive oil
- water or stock
- 5 medium carrots
- 2 large heads of broccoli
- 1 tablespoon of paprika pepper
- ½ teaspoon of salt
- ½ teaspoon of pepper
- Parsley, chopped, for garnish (optional)

DIRECTIONS:

1. Prepare the wheat berries by soaking them overnight or cooking them in 3 cups of water for 2 hours on low-heat.
2. Preheat the oven to 300°F.
3. Cook the broccoli and carrots and set aside.
4. Add the 2 tablespoons of onion soup mix to the flour.
5. Cut the meat into 1-inch cubes and roll the cubes in the seasoned flour.
6. Fry the meat and onion in a medium-sized skillet until they are lightly browned.
7. Transfer the meat and onion to a casserole dish, and add the tomatoes, garlic, green pepper, paprika, salt and pepper.
8. Add enough water or stock to the casserole dish to cover the meat.
9. Cover the casserole with the lid and cook in the oven at 300°F for about 1½ hours.
10. Add the cooked wheat berries and cooked vegetables and continue cooking in the oven for a further 30 minutes.
11. Garnish with chopped parsley if desired.

> Nutritional information
> Serving size: 1 cup. Per serving: 14 g of starch carbohydrate, 21 g total carbohydrate, 171 cals, 5 g fat, 2 g saturated fat, 2 g fiber, 272 mg sodium

Cauliflower Cheese Pie

■ **COOKING TIME** 55 minutes ■ **SERVES** 8

Crust:
- 1 cup of stone ground whole wheat flour
- 1 cup of white flour
- 1 teaspoon of salt
- ½ cup of canola oil
- 5 tablespoons of ice water

Filling:
- 1 cup of grated cheddar cheese
- 1 medium cauliflower, broken into small flowerets
- 1 garlic clove, minced
- 1 cup of chopped onions
- 3 tablespoons of olive oil
- 2 eggs
- ¼ cup of milk
- Dash of thyme
- ½ teaspoon of basil
- ½ teaspoon of salt
- Dash of black pepper
- $\frac{1}{8}$ teaspoon of paprika

DIRECTIONS:

1. Preheat the oven to 375°F.
2. To prepare the pie crust, mix the flour and salt in a large bowl.
3. In a separate bowl, whisk together the oil and water until the mixture is thick.
4. Stir the mixture into the flour until dough forms.
5. Roll out the dough into a 9-inch pan.
6. In a medium-sized skillet, sauté the onions and garlic in oil until tender.
7. Add the herbs and cauliflower and cook for 10 minutes, stirring occasionally.
8. Spread half the cheese onto the crust, then the sautéed vegetables, followed by the rest of the cheese.
9. Beat the eggs and milk together and pour over the rest of the mixture.
10. Dust with paprika.
11. Bake at 375°F for 35 to 40 minutes until set.

Nutritional information (with whole milk)
Serving size: $\frac{1}{8}$th of the pie. Per serving: 23 gm grain and sugar carbohydrate, 29 g total carbohydrate, 380 cals, 25 g fat, 5 g sat fat, 4 g fiber, 568 mg sodium.

Butternut Squash with Fresh Ginger Casserole

■ **COOKING TIME** 30 minutes   ■ **SERVES** 6

It really is worthwhile going out to the store to buy fresh ginger for this recipe.

- 1 butternut squash
- 2 tablespoons of olive oil
- 1 medium onion, minced
- 1 15½ -oz can of white beans
- 1 cup of canned or frozen corn kernels
- 4 oz of canned diced tomatoes
- 1 tablespoon of peeled gingerroot, minced
- ¼ cup of low-sodium chicken broth or water
- ½ teaspoon of ground ginger
- ¼ teaspoon of sugar (optional)
- Salt to taste
- Pepper to taste

DIRECTIONS

1 Halve the squash and remove the seeds and strings.
2. Put the squash halves cut-side down in a microwave-safe baking dish. Add 2 tablespoons of water and cover with wax paper.
3. Microwave on high power for about 15 minutes or until tender.
4. Remove the squash pulp from the peel and roughly dice the pulp.
5. Heat the oil in a large skillet. Add the onion and sauté over a medium heat for about 7 minutes.
6. Add the minced ginger and sauté over a low heat for 30 seconds.
7. Add the squash pieces, the broth, ground ginger, beans, corn, diced tomatoes, salt and pepper. Cover and cook, stirring often, for about 5 minutes, adding more broth by tablespoons if necessary or until the squash is coated with flavorings and is heated through.

Nutritional information
Serving size: 1 cup. Per serving: 50 g total carbohydrate, 259 cals, 5 g fat, 1 g sat fat, 9 g fiber, 97 mg sodium.

Chapter 9

Experimenting with grains

This is an important chapter, since weaning your family from "white starches" such as potatoes and white rice and onto whole and low-glycemic grains is an essential step in "Going Mediterranean".

Many of the grain recipes here are "pilafs". A pilaf is a Middle Eastern or Central Asian dish in which the grain is often browned in oil and then cooked in a seasoned broth. Depending on the local cuisine, it may contain a variety of meat and vegetables.

Some of the grains used in these recipes may be unfamiliar to you, and a brief description about some of them is included.

Don't get daunted by these unfamiliar grains. Rather, approach this chapter as an adventure in the discovery of new foods. Your attempts may not always be completely on the mark, but you'll be surprised at how often you strike the jackpot!

Rice and Lentil Pilaf (Majedra)

■ **COOKING TIME** 95 minutes ■ **SERVES** 8

This particular pilaf can compete very nicely with potatoes and white rice. It keeps nicely in the fridge incidentally and can therefore be prepared well in advance of a meal – as can many of the dishes in this section.

- 1 cup of uncooked brown rice
- 1 cup of uncooked brown lentils
- 1 teaspoon of mixed dry herbs
- Just over 5½ cups of hot vegetable stock or water
- 3 medium onions, thinly sliced
- 2 tablespoons of olive oil, divided
- ½ cup of almonds, chopped
- 2½ tablespoons of raisins
- 1 teaspoon of salt or to taste
- $^1/_8$ teaspoon of pepper or to taste

DIRECTIONS:

1. Place the rice in a large saucepan with 1 teaspoon of salt, half the dried herbs, and 2½ cups of hot vegetable stock or water. Bring to a boil and simmer gently until all the stock is absorbed (about 45 minutes). Set it aside.
2. Sauté two of the onions in the oil until they are brown.
3. Add the chopped almonds and fry gently for a few minutes.
4. Add the raisins to the onion and nut mixture and set this mixture aside.
5. In a medium-sized saucepan, gently fry the remaining onion in a little oil.
6. Add the lentils, the rest of the herbs, and 3 cups of hot vegetable stock or water to cover them. Bring to the boil and simmer covered until the lentils are soft (about 35 to 40 minutes).
7. Combine the cooked rice that has been set aside and the lentils. Add salt and pepper and bring to a boil again. Simmer on a very low heat until all the liquid has been absorbed.
8. Serve with the onion, almond and raisin mixture piled on top.

Nutritional information
Serving size: 1 cup. Per serving: 39 g total carbohydrate, 259 cals, 8 g fat, 1.0 g saturated fat, 9 g fiber, 295 mg sodium.

Lentils with Tomatoes and Garlic

■ **COOKING TIME**   55 minutes ■ **SERVES**   4

This is not an eye-grabbing dish. However, the kids will love it. It also makes a good cold salad.

- 1 cup of dried lentils
- 5 cloves of garlic, minced
- 8-oz can of diced tomatoes
- 4 tablespoons of olive oil
- 1 tablespoon of lemon juice
- $^{3}/_{4}$ teaspoon of salt or to taste
- 2½ cups of water

DIRECTIONS:

1. In a small frying pan, heat the oil and fry the garlic until it turns lightly brown.
2. Add the tomatoes and cook for about 5 minutes.
3. In a medium pot, add the lentils, water, garlic and salt. Bring to a boil. Cover, lower heat and simmer for about 50 minutes until the lentils are cooked.
4. Add the lemon juice to the cooked lentils.

Nutritional information
Serving size: just under 1 cup. Per serving: 30 g bean carbohydrate,
33 g total carbohydrate, 310 cals, 14 g fat, 2 g saturated fat, 15 g
fiber, 540 mg sodium.

Bulgur Pilaf with Pine Nuts

■ **COOKING TIME** 25 minutes ■ **SERVES** 7

This is another great pilaf. Bulgur is a whole grain made from different wheat species, but mainly durum wheat. The grain is usually parboiled (partially cooked), and then dried. Traditionally, it is also de-branned, but this is not always the case for products available in the stores. Bulgur is not to be confused with cracked wheat, which is made from crushed wheat grains that have not been parboiled. The distinction is important since cooking times are different.

- 1 cup of onion, chopped
- 1½ cups of dry bulgur
- ½ cup of pignoli (pine nuts)
- 1 tablespoon of olive oil
- ¾ cup of celery, chopped
- 3 cups of low-salt chicken broth
- ½ teaspoon of salt or to taste

DIRECTIONS:

1. In a large skillet, heat oil over medium-high heat. Add the onion and celery and cook for about 5 minutes until softened. Remove from the heat and set aside.
2. In a medium saucepan, heat the chicken stock to boiling.
3. Add the bulgur, cover, and reduce the heat to low. Simmer until the liquid is absorbed, about 15 to 20 minutes.
4. Turn off the heat and add the onion and celery.
5. Let the bulgur sit, covered, for abut 10 minutes.
6. Meanwhile, place the pignoli in the pan used for the onions and celery, and sauté over a medium-high heat until the nuts begin to turn golden.
7. Stir into the bulgur mixture and season to taste with salt.

> Nutritional information
> Serving size: 1 cup. . Per serving: 27 g total carbohydrate, 186 cals, 7 g fat, 1.0 g saturated fat, 5.6 g fiber, 418 mg sodium

Orzo Pilaf with Apricots and Cashews

■ **COOKING TIME** 22 minutes ■ **SERVES** 7

Orzo looks like a grain. But it's not. It's a form of pasta. This recipe is also a pilaf because of its chicken soup base. It's simple to make and looks and tastes very gourmet. It can also be served cold as a classy salad.

- 1½ cups of uncooked orzo
- ½ cup of roasted cashews
- 1 medium onion, chopped
- ½ cup of dried apricots, diced
- 3 cups of chicken broth, preferably low salt
- $^1/_3$ cup of parsley, chopped
- 3 tablespoons of olive oil
- 1 teaspoon of ground ginger
- Salt to taste
- Pepper to taste

DIRECTIONS:

1. Sauté the onion in the oil in a medium-size saucepan for 7 minutes or until it begins to turn brown.
2. Add the uncooked orzo to the onion and cook over a low heat for 3 more minutes, stirring.
3. Heat up the chicken broth.
4. Add the diced apricots, heated broth and ground ginger into the mixture and bring to a boil.
5. Cover and cook over a low heat for about 12 minutes or until the orzo is tender.
6. Add the cashews, parsley and seasoning if desired, and stir well. Serve hot or cold.

Nutritional information
Portion size: ¾ cup. Per serving: 37 g carbohydrate, 282 cals, 11.0 g fat, 2.0 g saturated fat, 2.28 g fiber, 58 mg sodium.

Mushroom Kasha Pilaf

PREPARATION TIME 15 minutes ■ **COOKING TIME** 18 minutes ■ **SERVES** 6

This pilaf is made from kasha, which is roasted buckwheat. Buckwheat is a moderately low-glycemic whole grain.

- 1 cup of dry kasha
- 2 cups of chicken broth, preferably low salt
- 1 large onion, chopped
- 3 cups of mushrooms (about 10 oz), sliced
- 6 tablespoons of olive oil, divided
- $^1/_3$ cup of fresh parsley
- ½ teaspoon of salt or to taste
- $^1/_8$ teaspoon of pepper

DIRECTIONS:

1. In a medium saucepan, add 2 tablespoons of oil to the broth and bring to a boil.
2. Add the kasha, salt and pepper to the boiling liquid.
3. Cover and reduce heat to low. Simmer for 10 minutes until most of the liquid is absorbed.
4. In a large skillet heat, heat 4 tablespoons of oil and sauté the onion until tender.
5. Add the mushrooms and sauté until tender.
6. Add the mushroom and onion mixture to the kasha.
7. Add in the parsley.

> Nutritional information
> Serving size: 1 cup. Per serving: 20 g grain carbohydrate, 25.0 g total carbohydrate, 239 cals, 14.0 g fat, 2.0 g saturated fat, 4.0 g fiber, 386 mg sodium.

Brown Rice and Noodle Pilaf

■ **COOKING TIME** 45 minutes ■ **SERVES** 4½

- 1 cup of uncooked brown rice
- 1 oz of dry Angel Hair pasta
- 4 teaspoons of olive oil, divided
- ½ green pepper, diced
- 1 medium onion, diced
- 2 cups of chicken broth, preferably low sodium
- ! cup of water
- ½ teaspoon of salt or to taste
- ¼ teaspoon of pepper

DIRECTIONS:

1. Add the 2 cups of chicken broth to the brown rice. Add an additional 1 cup of water and boil gently for 25 minutes.
2. In the meantime, sauté the pasta, snapped into smaller pieces, in a skillet in 2 teaspoons of oil until it turns partially brown. Place in a bowl.
3. Sauté the pepper and onion in 2 teaspoons of oil in the same skillet and add to the bowl.
4. Add the pasta and vegetables to the rice, add additional water as needed, and cook for another 20 minutes

> Nutritional information
> Serving size: 1 cup. Per serving: 39 g total carbohydrate, 227 cals, 5 g fat, 1 g saturated fat, 2 g fiber, 509 mg sodium.

Rice with Vegetables and Pecan

- **COOKING TIME** 45 minutes   - **SERVES** 12

With this simple winning rice recipe you just can't go wrong.

- 2 cups of uncooked brown or other low-glycemic rice such as Basmati rice, uncooked
- ½ cup of chopped pecans
- 2 cups of broccoli, chopped
- 1 large onion, chopped
- 3 medium carrots, cut into 2-3 inch long strips
- 2 cups of sliced fresh mushrooms
- 2 tablespoons of olive oil
- 3 garlic cloves, minced
- ¾ teaspoon of dried thyme
- ¾ teaspoon of dried basil
- ¾ teaspoon of salt
- ¼ teaspoon of pepper

DIRECTIONS:

1. Cook the rice according to the package instructions (use 2 cups of water for every cup of white rice and cook for about 15 minutes, and for brown rice use 2½ cups of water and cook for about 35 minutes).
2. Cook the broccoli, carrots and onions in a large frying pan for 5-7 minutes.
3. Add the rest of the ingredients, except for the rice and pecans, and cook and stir for 2-3 minutes.
4. Add the rice and pecans and cook for an additional 1-2 minutes.

> Nutritional information
> Serving size: 1 cup. Per serving: 24 gm grain carbohydrate, 29 g total carbohydrate, 186 cals, 7 g fat, 1 g saturated fat, 3 g fiber, 165 mg sodium

Chinese Rice with Vegetables

■ **COOKING TIME** 10 minutes ■ **SERVES** 10½

This can be served as a hot dish or cold salad. It tastes good either way.

- 2 cups of uncooked basmati or other rice
- 1 10-oz package of uncooked frozen peas
- 1½ cups of celery, chopped
- ¼ cup of onion, finely chopped
- ½ cup of olive oil
- 1 tablespoon of soy sauce
- 1 teaspoon of celery salt
- 3 teaspoons of vinegar
- 1 teaspoon of salt
- ½ teaspoon of sugar
- 1 teaspoon of curry powder

DIRECTIONS:

1. Cook the rice according to the package instructions.
2. Add the peas, celery and onion to the cooked rice.
3. Combine the oil, soy sauce, celery, salt, sugar and curry powder in a separate jar. Shake well and toss into the rice mixture.

> Nutritional information
> Serving size: 1 cup. Per serving: 24 gm grain carbohydrate, 29 g total carbohydrate, 186 cals, 7 g fat, 1 g saturated fat, 3 g fiber, 165 mg sodium

Zucchini Pasta

■ **COOKING TIME** 30 minutes ■ **SERVES** 4

This pasta dish is as good as they come.

- ½ pound of dried pasta, such as ziti or penne
- 4 medium zucchinis, cut into ribbons or coins
- 1 large onion, chopped
- 2 tomatoes, in wedges or chopped, with juice
- ¼ cup of extra virgin olive oil
- 1 teaspoon of dried thyme
- Salt to taste
- ¼ teaspoon pepper
- Grated Parmesan cheese or freshly chopped parsley for garnish

DIRECTIONS:

1. In a large skillet, sauté the zucchini, onion and thyme in the olive oil gently, stirring occasionally. Add the salt and pepper and adjust the heat so that the onion and zucchini release their liquid without browning, cooking for about 20 minutes.
2. Add the tomatoes and their liquid to the zucchini and heat the mixture until it bubbles.
3. Bring a large pot of water to boil with salt. Cook the pasta until it is nearly but not quite tender.
4. Drain the pasta and finish cooking it in the sauce.
5. Serve garnished with parsley or Parmesan cheese.

Nutritional information
Serving size: 1½ cups. Per serving: 41 g grain carbohydrate, 47 g total carbohydrate, 357 cals, 15 g fat, 2 g saturated fat, 2 g fiber, 4 mg sodium.

Wheat Berries with Celery and Green Beans

■ **COOKING TIME** 68 minutes   ■ **SERVES** 5

(The uncooked wheat berries are best when soaked overnight)

This is an unusual but nevertheless very tasty starch dish. Cooked wheat berries keep well in the fridge and can be used for this and other recipes as needed.

- 1½ teaspoons of olive oil
- 3 tablespoons of minced shallot
- 2 cups of green beans, frozen or fresh
- 2 stalks of celery, sliced
- 1 cup of uncooked wheat berries
- 1 teaspoon of sesame oil
- ½ teaspoon of salt or to taste

DIRECTIONS:

1. Prepare the wheat berries by soaking them overnight and then boiling for 1 hour. Use 3 cups of water to 1 cup of berries. If not pre-soaked, boil for 2 hours.
2. In a 2-quart saucepan, heat the oil at medium-high heat. Add the shallot and cook, stirring until softened.
3. Add the green beans and celery and cook, stirring until tender-crisp.
4. Stir in the wheat berries and cook, stirring, until heated through.
5. Stir in the sesame oil.

> Nutritional information
> Per serving: 28 g grain and sugar carbohydrate, 32.9 g total carbohydrate, 121 cals, 6.8 g fat, 0.8 g saturated fat, 6.7 g fiber, 255 mg sodium.

Adapted with permission from "Wholesome Harvest. Cooking with the New Four Food Groups - Grains, Beans, Fruits, and Vegetables" by Carol Gelles and published by Little, Brown and Company (Canada) Ltd)

Basil, Mint and Vegetable Couscous

■ **COOKING TIME** 15 minutes   ■ **SERVES** 10

Couscous looks and cooks like a grain, but it's really a form of pasta. Traditionally, it's made from durum wheat, which is the hardest of all forms of wheat. This gives it its moderately low-glycemic index value. This is a healthy dish that can be cooked in a very short time.

- 2 cups of uncooked couscous
- 1 large yellow squash, coarsely diced
- 1 large zucchini, coarsely diced
- 2 cups of tomatoes, coarsely chopped
- 1 cup of onion, chopped
- 1 tablespoon of garlic, chopped
- 3 cups of water or vegetable broth
- 2 tablespoons of olive oil, divided
- 2 teaspoons of dried basil
- 2 teaspoons of dried mint
- Salt to taste
- Pepper to taste

DIRECTIONS:

1. Heat 1 tablespoon of olive oil in a large skillet over medium-high heat. Add the onions and cook until they begin to wilt, about 3 minutes.
2. Stir in the garlic and cook for 1 minute.
3. Add the yellow squash and zucchini and cook stirring for 5 to 8 minutes or until the vegetables are tender.
4. Add the tomatoes, basil and mint. Reduce the heat and cook, stirring, 2 to 3 minutes or until the tomatoes are heated through. Season to taste with salt and pepper. Remove from the heat and reserve.
5. Bring the water or stock to boil. Add the couscous, cover and remove from the heat. Set aside until the liquid has been absorbed, about 5 minutes.
6. Stir in the salt to taste and remaining 1 tablespoon of oil.
7. To serve, label the vegetable mixture over the couscous.

Nutritional information
Portion size: 1 cup. Per serving: 27 g grain carbohydrate, 32 g total carbohydrate, 179 cals, 3.0 g fat, 0.0 g saturated fat, 3.0 g fiber, 23 mg sodium.

Adapted with permission from "Gourmet Grains, Beans and Rice, Simple, Savory and Sophisticated Recipes" by Dorothy Griffith and published by Taylor Publishing Company, Dallas, Texas

Peppers Stuffed with Cinnamon Bulgur

■ **COOKING TIME** 10 minutes ■ **SERVES** 4

- 2¼ cups of water, divided
- ½ cup of carrot, shredded
- ¼ cup of onion, chopped
- 1 teaspoon of instant vegetable or chicken bouillon granules
- ⅛ teaspoon of salt
- ¾ cup of bulgur
- ½ cup of dried cranberries or raisins
- 2 large green peppers
- 2 tablespoons of sliced almonds
- ¾ cup of shredded Muenster or mozzarella cheese
- Dash of ground cinnamon

DIRECTIONS:

1. In a large skillet, stir together 1¾ cups of water, carrot, onion, bouillon granules, salt and cinnamon. Bring to boil, and then reduce heat and simmer, covered, for 5 minutes.
2. Stir in the bulgur and cranberries. Remove from the heat. Cover and let stand for 5 minutes. Drain off excess liquid.
3. Meanwhile, halve the green peppers lengthwise, removing the seeds and membranes.
4. Stir the shredded cheese into the bulgur mixture. Stir this into the sweet pepper halves.
5. Place the green pepper halves in a skillet. Add ½ cup of water.
6. Bring the peppers and water to boil. Reduce heat and simmer, covered for 5 to 10 minutes or until the green peppers are crisp-tender and the bulgur mixture is heated through.
7. Sprinkle the stuffed peppers with nuts.

> Nutritional information
> Serving size: ½ pepper. Per serving: 31 g grain, dried fruit and nut carbohydrate, 37 g total carbohydrate, 257 cals, 9 g fat, 4 g saturated fat, 8 g fiber, 317 mg sodium.

Quinoa and Black Beans

■ **COOKING TIME** 30 minutes   ■ **SERVES** 6

Quinoa? You're in good company if you've never heard of it. Nevertheless, you should definitely try this recipe out. It can be served hot as a starch dish or cold as a salad.

- ¾ cup of uncooked quinoa
- 1 medium onion, chopped
- 3 cloves of garlic, chopped
- 1 cup of frozen corn kernels
- 1 15-oz can of black beans, rinsed and drained
- 1½ cups of vegetable broth, preferably low salt
- 1 teaspoon of olive oil
- 1 teaspoon of ground cumin
- ¼ teaspoon of cayenne pepper
- ½ cup of fresh cilantro
- Salt and pepper to taste

DIRECTIONS:

1. In a medium saucepan, heat the oil and sauté the onion and garlic until lightly browned.
2. Add the quinoa and vegetable broth to the saucepan and season with cumin, cayenne pepper, salt and pepper.
3. Bring the mixture to the boil, cover, reduce heat and simmer for 20 minutes.
4. Stir the frozen corn into the saucepan and continue to simmer for 5 minutes until heated through.
5. Mix in the black beans and cilantro.

Nutritional information
Serving size: 1 cup. Per serving: 38 g carbohydrate, 240 cals, 6 g fat, 1 g saturated fat, 8 g fiber, 80 mg sodium.

Barley Casserole

■ **COOKING TIME** 90 minutes ■ **SERVES** 4½

The mushrooms are a worthwhile addition to this excellent starch side dish.

- 1 cup of uncooked barley
- ½ cup of onion, diced
- 4 cups of chicken broth, preferably low salt
- 4 tablespoons of olive oil
- 2 cups of sliced mushrooms (optional)

DIRECTIONS:

1. In a small skillet, sauté the onion with the olive oil.
2. In a 1½ quart casserole dish, add the barley, chicken broth, salt, mushrooms and sautéed onions.
3. Bake at 350°F uncovered for 1 hour, stirring several times.
4. Cover tightly and bake for another ½ hour.

Nutritional information
Serving size: 1 cup. Per serving: 35 g grain carbohydrate, 38 g total carbohydrate, 241cals, 7 g fat, 1 g saturated fat, 7 g fiber, 38 mg sodium.

Chapter 10
Jazzing up Vegetables

Many families have given up on vegetables. Unfortunately, when vegetables are absent from a meal, starches often take their place, and these are frequently high-glycemic starches. Somehow, veggies have to get back onto the plate.

I have two solutions. The first is make vegetables more attractive by cooking them in ways other than boiling. The second solution is to combine the vegetables with different starches, grains and protein to make tasty combinations. This is termed "Mediterranean-style" cooking in this book. These concepts are illustrated in the first recipe section on "Eating Mediterranean-style" and also in the following section.

Free item!

Winter Roasted Carrots

■ **COOKING TIME** 25 minutes   ■ **SERVES** 6

This is a colorful and tasty way for serving carrots.

- 1 lb of baby carrots, cut into half lengthwise
- 2 small onions, cut into $^{1}/_{8}$'s
- 6 cloves of garlic, minced
- 1 large parsnip, cut into 3-inch strips
- 2 tablespoons of olive oil
- ½ teaspoon of dried thyme
- ¼ teaspoon of salt or to taste
- $^{1}/_{8}$ teaspoon of pepper

DIRECTIONS:

1. Preheat the oven to 450°F.
2. Place the vegetables in a large roasting pan.
3. Drizzle the olive oil over the vegetables and then sprinkle the thyme, salt and pepper.
4. Bake uncovered for 25 minutes, stirring periodically until the carrots begin to brown and are tender when pierced with a knife tip.

Nutritional information
Per serving: 10.8 g total carbohydrate, 86 cals, 4.7 g fat, 0.6 g saturated fat, 2.2 g fiber, 166 mg sodium.

Coated Broccoli

■ **COOKING TIME** 20 minutes   ■ **SERVES** 6

It works like a charm! These vegetables will disappear in no time at all. Cauliflower can also be used instead of broccoli florets.

- 4 cups of broccoli florets
- $^2/_3$ cup of seasoned bread crumbs
- 2 tablespoons of grated Parmesan cheese
- 2 eggs, egg whites, or egg substitute
- 1 tablespoon of milk
- 2 tablespoons of olive oil
- $^1/_8$ teaspoon of salt or to taste

DIRECTIONS:

1. Preheat the oven to 400°F.
2. Prepare 2 sealable plastic bags, one containing the bread crumbs, cheese and salt, and the other containing the eggs and milk. Shake both bags well.
3. Add the vegetables to the bag containing the egg mixture, close and shake to coat the vegetables well.
4. Then add the vegetables to the bag containing the bread crumbs mixture, close and shake to coat well.
5. Lightly coat a 15 x 10-inch baking dish with cooking oil spray. Place the vegetables onto the dish. Drizzle the oil over the vegetables.
6. Bake in the oven at 400°F for about 20 minutes, stirring twice.

Nutritional information
Per serving: 9.5 g grain and sugar carbohydrate, 13.6 g total carbohydrate, 133 cals, 6.4 g fat, 2.8 g saturated fat, 2.1 g fiber, 496 mg sodium.

Oven Roasted Vegetables

■ **COOKING TIME** 30 minutes ■ **SERVES** 4

Vegetables oven-baked in oil are usually tastier and more enticing than boiled vegetables. For this recipe, yellow and red peppers provide a sweeter taste than green ones, as well as adding the important component of color. Other vegetables that can be used are mushrooms (4 oz) and baby eggplant cut into ½ inch cubes. A 30 minute cooking time is appropriate for all these vegetables.

- 1 zucchini, sliced
- 1 yellow squash, sliced
- 1 red bell pepper, cut into broad slices
- 1 yellow bell pepper, cut into broad slices
- 1 red onion, cut into medium sized slices
- 1 pound of fresh asparagus, cut into medium-sized pieces
- 3 tablespoons of olive oil
- ½ teaspoon of salt or to taste
- ¼ teaspoon of black pepper

DIRECTIONS:

1. Preheat the oven to 450°F
2. Place the zucchini, squash, peppers, asparagus and onion in a large roasting pan. Coat with the olive oil, salt and pepper.
3. Cook in the oven uncovered for 30 minutes at 450°F, stirring occasionally, until the vegetables are lightly browned and tender.

Nutritional information
Per serving: 14.1 g total carbohydrate, 155 cals, 10.6 g fat, 1.5 g saturated fat, 5.1 g fiber, 305 mg sodium.

Free item!

Roasted Veggie Medley

- **COOKING TIME** 53 minutes

  - 3 medium carrots, thinly sliced
  - 2 medium yellow summer squash, sliced
  - 2 medium zucchini, sliced
  - 1 small head of cauliflower, broken into florets
  - 2 garlic cloves, minced
  - 4 tablespoons of olive oil, divided
  - 1 cup of chicken broth, preferably low salt
  - 1 teaspoon of salt or to taste
  - ½ teaspoon of white pepper

DIRECTIONS:

1. Preheat the oven to 350°F.
2. In a small saucepan, sauté the garlic in 2 tablespoons of oil for 2-3 minutes. Stir in the broth, salt and pepper.
3. Place carrots, squash and cauliflower in a shallow 3-qt baking dish. Pour a mixture of oil and broth over the vegetables.
4. Cover and bake at 350°F for 50 minutes or until the vegetables are tender.

Free item!

Roasted Cauliflower

■ **COOKING TIME** 15 minutes ■ **SERVES** 4 (if you can stop kitchen thieves from munching them)

This dish is guaranteed to make anyone into a veggie lover. The flowerets taste like a snack food. Try them!

- 1 head of cauliflower, cut into small flowerets
- 4 tablespoons of olive oil
- ½ teaspoon of salt or to taste
- Dash of pepper
- ½ teaspoon of garlic powder
- ½ teaspoon of onion powder
- ½ teaspoon of paprika
- ½ teaspoon of cumin (optional)

DIRECTIONS:

1. In a small bowl, mix the oil and spices.
2. Toss the mixture over the flowerets and stir extremely well.
3. Broil for about 15 minutes, stirring after 10 minutes. For the best taste, the florets should be just slightly burnt.

Nutritional information
Per serving: 4 g total carbohydrate, 108 cals, 10 g fat, 1 g saturated fat, 2 g fiber, 166 mg sodium.

Free item!

Fried Cauliflower with a Taste of Garlic

■ **COOKING TIME** 15 minutes   ■ **SERVES** 4

With a bit of imagination there's a lot one can do with cauliflower. For example, one can make this delightful cauliflower side dish with nothing more than some olive oil, garlic, salt and pepper.

- 1 head of cauliflower, cut into small flowerets
- 4 tablespoons of olive oil
- 2 cloves of garlic, chopped
- ½ teaspoon of salt or to taste
- ¼ teaspoon of pepper
- ¼ cup of black olives (optional)

DIRECTIONS:

1. In a large frying pan, heat the olive oil and sauté the cauliflower for 3 minutes, while sprinkling the salt evenly over the cauliflower.
2. Cover the frying pan, add the garlic and cook over medium-low heat for about 12 minutes.
3. Before serving, add pepper.
4. For an exotic Middle Eastern look add black olives.

Nutritional information
Per serving: 7 g total carbohydrate, 155 cals, 14 g fat, 2 g saturated fat, 3 g fiber, 316 mg sodium.

Free item!

Indian Cauliflower

■ **COOKING TIME** 5 minutes   ■ **SERVES** 4

This is a wonderful spicy dish. The timing is important, so use a timer.

- 1 head of cauliflower
- 4 green onions, sliced into 1-inch pieces
- 1 small red or green pepper, cut into 1-inch squares
- 1 tablespoon of olive oil
- ¼ cup of chicken broth, preferably low salt
- ½ teaspoon of dry mustard
- ¼ teaspoon of turmeric
- ¼ teaspoon of cumin
- $\frac{1}{8}$ teaspoon of coriander
- $\frac{1}{8}$ teaspoon of red pepper

DIRECTIONS:

1. Stir-fry the cauliflower for 3 minutes in large skillet.
2. Add the onions and peppers, and stir-fry for another 1½ minutes.
3. In a small bowl, mix all the spices.
4. Add the spices to the vegetables and cook for a further 30 seconds.
5. Stir in the chicken broth and cook for another 1 minute or until heated through.

Nutritional information
Per serving: 8 g total carbohydrate, 74 cals, 4 g fat, 1 g saturated fat, 4 g fiber, 30 mg sodium.

Cauliflower Patties

- **COOKING TIME** 5 minutes ■ **SERVES** 13

- 1 medium cauliflower
- 1 egg
- 1 cup of breadcrumbs or matzo meal, divided
- ½ teaspoon of oregano
- 4 tablespoons of olive oil
- Salt and pepper to taste

DIRECTIONS:

1. Break the cauliflower into flowerets and cook them in water for about 10-15 minutes until soft.
2. Mash the cauliflower and add the egg, ½ cup of breadcrumbs, oregano, salt and pepper.
3. Mix well and shape into patties.
4. Dip both sides of the patty in the remaining ½ cup of breadcrumbs or matzo meal and sauté on both sides until golden brown.

Nutritional information
Serving size: 1 3"x 2" patty. Per serving: 6 g starch carbohydrate, 8 g total carbohydrate, 85 cals, 5 g fat, 1 g saturated fat, 1 g fiber, 73 mg sodium.

Free item!

Zucchini on the Grill

I have no explanation for why vegetables cooked on the grill often seem tastier than those cooked in other ways. Perhaps it has something to do with family involvement.

- Zucchini, cut into large slices
- Olive oil
- Salt to taste
- Pepper to taste

DIRECTIONS:

1. Lightly coat the vegetables with the olive oil and condiments.
2. Put on the grill until cooked to satisfaction.

Free item!

Microwaved Zucchini Parmesan

■ **COOKING TIME** 5 minutes   ■ **SERVES** 4

Your garden and kitchen are overrun with zucchinis? This is a very tasty way of eating them.

- 3 cups of zucchini, cut into ¼-inch slices (about 1⅓ large zucchini)
- 1 tablespoon of oil
- 2 tablespoons of grated Parmesan cheese
- 1 teaspoon of dried parsley flakes or 1 tablespoon of fresh parsley
- Dash of salt
- Dash of pepper

DIRECTIONS:

1. Lightly oil an 8 to 9-inch round baking dish and place the zucchini slices in the dish.
2. Cover the dish with a plastic wrap and microwave at high for 4-6 minutes or until tender crisp. Drain off the fluid.
3. Combine the cheese, parsley flakes, salt and pepper.
4. Sprinkle the cheese mixture over the zucchini before serving.

Nutritional information
Serving size: ½ cup. Per serving: 1 g total carbohydrate, 45 cals, 4 g fat, 0 g saturated fat, 0 g fiber, 80 mg sodium.

Free item!

Zucchini with Tomato

- **COOKING TIME** 8 minutes

The cumin adds a pleasant Middle Eastern tang to this vegetable dish.

- 3 medium zucchinis, sliced
- 1 15-oz can of chopped tomatoes
- 1 medium onion, diced
- 2 cloves of garlic, minced
- 1 15-oz can of baby corn (optional)
- 1 teaspoon of cumin
- 1 tablespoon of olive oil
- ½ teaspoon of salt or to taste
- $\frac{1}{8}$ teaspoon of pepper

DIRECTIONS:

1. In a large skillet, sauté the onion and garlic on a moderate heat until soft and slightly brown.
2. Add the zucchini and continue cooking until they are cooked but still firm.
3. Add the tomato, condiments, and baby corn and continue heating until all the contents are warm.

Sautéed Zucchini

■ **COOKING TIME** 10 minutes   ■ **SERVES** 4

These zucchinis are simply irresistible.

- 2 medium zucchini
- 2 tablespoons of whole wheat flour
- ½ cup breadcrumbs
- 1 egg or egg substitute
- ¼ cup of olive oil
- ¼ teaspoon salt
- ½ teaspoon of onion powder
- Dash black pepper

DIRECTIONS:

1. Wash the zucchini and cut off the ends. Slice the zucchini lengthwise into ¼-inch thick slices.
2. Stir the salt, onion powder and pepper into the egg.
3. Dip each zucchini piece into the flour, then into the egg with seasoning mixture, and then into breadcrumbs to coat.
4. Gently sauté in oil, turning once, until nicely brown and soft.
5. Drain on a paper towel. Serve warm.

Nutritional information
Serving size: ½ zucchini. Per serving: 13 g grain carbohydrate, 13 g total carbohydrate, 207 cals, 16 g fat, 2 g saturated fat, 1 g fiber, 425 mg sodium.

Stuffed Squash

■ **COOKING TIME** 63 minutes   ■ **SERVES** 4

This gourmet vegetable dish can be used either as a side dish or main course.

- 2 acorn or butternut squash
- 1 large garlic clove, minced
- ½ teaspoon of sage
- ½ teaspoon of thyme
- 3 tablespoons of olive oil
- ½ cup of onion, chopped
- 1 cup of coarsely crumbled whole wheat bread
- ¼ cup of chopped walnuts
- ¼ cup of sunflower seeds
- 1 stalk of celery, chopped
- ½ cup of grated cheddar cheese
- $^1/_8$ teaspoon of salt
- $^1/_8$ teaspoon of pepper
- ¼ cup of raisins (optional)

DIRECTIONS:

1. Preheat the oven to 350°F.
2. Split 2 acorn or butternut squashes lengthwise down the middle. Remove the seeds.
3. Bake the squash face down on an oiled tray for 30 minutes at 350°F.
4. Meanwhile, sauté the onions, garlic, nuts and seeds in butter in a skillet. Add all the remaining ingredients except for the cheese to the skillet, and stirring, cook over a low heat for 5-8 minutes.
5. Remove from the heat and add in the cheese.
6. Pack the ingredients into the baked acorn squash halves.
7. Bake the squash an additional 25 minutes at 350°F.

Nutritional information
Serving size: ½ squash. Per serving: 40 g total carbohydrate, 375 cals, 22 g fat, 5 g saturated fat, 6 g fiber, 262 mg sodium.

Spaghetti Squash Primavera

- **COOKING TIME** 17 minutes   ■ **SERVES** 8

The spaghetti squash gives this dish a pleasant crunchy taste.

- 1 large spaghetti squash
- ¼ cup of carrot, sliced
- ¼ cup of red onion, chopped
- ¼ cup of red sweet pepper, diced
- ¼ cup of green pepper, diced
- 1 garlic clove, minced
- 1 cup of yellow summer squash, thinly sliced
- 1 cup of zucchini, thinly sliced
- 1 14½-can of stewed tomatoes
- ½ cup of frozen corn, thawed
- 2 teaspoons of olive oil
- ½ teaspoon of salt or to taste
- ½ teaspoon of dried oregano
- $\frac{1}{8}$ teaspoon of dried thyme
- 4 teaspoons of grated Parmesan cheese
- 2 tablespoons of minced fresh parsley

DIRECTIONS

1. Cut the spaghetti squash in half and discard the seeds.
2. Place the cut-side up on a microwave-safe plate, cover with waxed paper and microwave on high for 9 minutes or until tender.
3. In a large skillet, sauté the carrot, onion, peppers and garlic in oil for 3 minutes.
4. Add the yellow squash and zucchini and sauté 2-3 minutes longer or until the squash is tender.
5. Reduce the heat and add the tomatoes, corn, salt, oregano and thyme. Cook for 5 minutes longer or until heated thoroughly, stirring occasionally.
6. Separate the spaghetti squash strands with a fork.
7. Spoon the vegetable mixture into the squash.
8. Sprinkle with Parmesan cheese and parsley.

> Nutritional information
> Serving size: 1 cup. Per serving: 6 g spaghetti squash carbohydrate, 15 g total carbohydrate, 76 cals, 2 g fat, 0.7 g saturated fat, 3 g fiber, 194 mg sodium.

Free item!

Sautéed Green Beans

■ **COOKING TIME**   4 minutes   ■ **SERVES**   6

This recipe is a simple way for "jazzing up" otherwise ordinary green beans. It works!

- 1 lb of fresh green beans, trimmed
- 5 teaspoons of olive oil
- ½ teaspoon of garlic powder
- ¼ teaspoon of salt

DIRECTIONS:

1. Heat the oil in a frying pan or wok on high.
2. Add the green beans and stir-fry them over a high heat for 2 to 4 minutes. While frying, add the garlic powder and salt. The beans should be tender-crisp and lightly browned when done.

.

Nutritional information
Per serving: 6 g total carbohydrate, 57 cals, 8 g fat, 0.5 g saturated fat, 3 g fiber, 102 mg sodium.

Green Beans with Tomato

■ **COOKING TIME** 35 minutes ■ **SERVES** 5

This recipe is a tasty blend of green beans and tomato. It can be eaten warm as a side dish or cold as a salad.

- 1 lb of fresh green beans, trimmed
- 1 large onion, chopped
- 2 cloves of garlic, minced
- 1 15-oz can of diced tomatoes
- $^3/_8$ cup of olive oil, divided
- 2 tablespoons of tomato ketchup

DIRECTIONS:

1. In a medium-sized skillet, sauté the onion and garlic in some of the oil until they are just golden.
2. In a large saucepan, place the onion, garlic, green beans, tomatoes, tomato ketchup and remainder of the oil, and bring the mixture to a boil.
3. Simmer the mixture over very low heat for 30 minutes.

Nutritional information
Serving size: ½ cup. Per serving: 13 g total carbohydrate, 204 cals, 16 g fat, 2 g saturated fat, 4 g fiber, 122 mg sodium.

Free item!

Spiced String Beans

■ **COOKING TIME** 30 minutes ■ **SERVES** 6

- 3 lb fresh string beans, washed and trimmed
- 2 tablespoons of olive oil
- $\frac{1}{4}$ teaspoon of turmeric
- $\frac{1}{2}$ teaspoon of cumin
- $\frac{1}{4}$ cup water

DIRECTIONS:

1. Place all the ingredients in a 3 quart saucepan and mix well.
2. Cook, covered, over a small flame for 30 minutes. Serve warm or cold.

Nutritional information
Serving size: ½ cup. Per serving: 13 g total carbohydrate, 204 cals, 16 g fat, 2 g saturated fat, 4 g fiber, 122 mg sodium.

Sautéed Snowpeas with Leek

■ **COOKING TIME** 4 minutes   ■ **SERVES**   4

- 8-oz package of snow peas, frozen
- 1 leek, sliced (use only the white and pale green parts)
- 1 tablespoon of olive oil
- Salt to taste

DIRECTIONS:

1. Sauté the vegetables together in the oil until they are tender, about 4 minutes. Serve either warm or cold.

Nutritional information
Serving size: ½ cup. Per serving: 6 g total carbohydrate, 59 cals, 4 g fat, 0 g saturated fat, 2 g fiber, 6 mg sodium.

Broiled Asparagus

■ **COOKING TIME** 10 minutes   ■ **SERVES** 4

This recipe is much better tasting than boiled asparagus.

- 1 lb bunch of asparagus, with ends removed
- 1 tablespoons of olive oil
- ½ teaspoon of salt or to taste

DIRECTIONS:

1 Place the asparagus in a pan and sprinkle with the oil.
2. Broil for 10 minutes, stirring once.

Nutritional information
Per serving: 4.4 g total carbohydrate, 53 cals, 3.5 g fat, 0.5 g saturated fat, 2.4 g fiber, 293 mg sodium.

Mousakka

■ **COOKING TIME** 80 minutes   ■ **SERVES**   10

Because of its fat content, this dish may fill you more with guilty conscience than eggplant. But there's no reason for this. This delicious dish is full of healthy monounsaturated fat and antioxidant. So enjoy!

- 1 15-oz can of chickpeas (equivalent to 1½ cups of dried chickpeas)
- Approximately 2 cups of olive oil
- 2 medium eggplants
- 3 onions, cut into ¼-inch thick slices
- 1½ teaspoons of salt or to taste, divided
- ½ teaspoon of pepper
- 2 15-oz cans of chopped or crushed tomato
- 1 cup of water

DIRECTIONS:

1. In a heavy skillet, heat about 1 inch of oil until the oil is almost smoking. Drop in the eggplant and stir until all sides are brown, about 2 minutes each side (This can splatter, so you may wish to use gloves and cover all nearby surfaces). Transfer the eggplant to a baking pan.
2. Add more oil as needed. Fry the onions in the oil and cook over a moderate heat until soft and lightly browned.
3. Spread the onions and all the cooking oil over the eggplant in the baking pan. Sprinkle with ¾ teaspoon of salt and pepper.
4. Scatter the chickpeas on top and cover this with the tomatoes. Sprinkle with ¾ teaspoon of salt and more pepper. Add the water.
5. Cover and bake in the lower third of the oven at 400ºF for 1 hour.

Nutritional information
(assuming that all the oil is served)
Serving size: 1 cup. Per serving: 10 g bean carbohydrate, 26 g total carbohydrate, 4874 cals, 44 g fat, 6 g saturated fat, 6 fiber, 742 mg sodium.

Eggplant Parmesan

- **COOKING TIME** 45 minutes ■ **SERVES** 6

I can't think of a more delicious way to eat eggplant and tomatoes.

- 1 medium eggplant, cut into ½-inch circles
- ¼ cup of whole wheat flour, preferably stone ground
- 1 cup of bread crumbs, preferably whole wheat
- 2 eggs
- 12 oz of mozzarella cheese
- Olive oil as needed
- 26-oz jar of pasta sauce, divided approximately into three
- ¼ teaspoon of onion powder
- ¼ teaspoon of garlic powder
- ¼ teaspoon of salt or to taste
- ⅛ teaspoon of pepper

DIRECTIONS:

1. Preheat the oven to 350°F.
2. Put the flour on one plate and the breadcrumbs on another plate.
3. In a small bowl, mix the eggs together with the seasoning.
4. Dip each eggplant in the flour, then the egg mixture, and then the breadcrumbs.
5. In a large skillet, fry both sides of each eggplant circle until golden brown, about 2 minutes each side.
6. In a 9 x 13 inch pan, put $^1/_3$ of the sauce in the bottom of the pan, and then place on top of this half of the eggplant, and then half the cheese. Repeat this sequence. Put the remaining $^1/_3$ of the sauce on top of the cheese.
7. Bake in the oven for 35 minutes at 350°F

Nutritional information
Serving size: $^1/_6{}^{th}$ of the container. Per serving: 37 g total carbohydrate, 396 cals, 18 g fat, 9 g saturated fat, 5 g fiber, 1104 mg sodium.

- 1 medium eggplant, cut into ½-inch slices
- ¼ cup of whole wheat flour, preferably stone ground
- 1 cup of breadcrumbs
- 1 egg
- ¼ teaspoon of garlic powder
- ¼ teaspoon of onion powder
- ¼ teaspoon of salt or to taste
- $\frac{1}{8}$ teaspoon of pepper
- ½ cup of olive oil or as needed

DIRECTIONS:

1. Dip the eggplant slices into the flour until they are covered.
2. In a small bowl, mix the egg, salt, pepper, garlic salt and onion powder.
3. Dip the eggplant slices into the egg mixture.
4. Then dip the eggplant slices in the breadcrumbs.
5. Fry the eggplant slices until golden brown on both sides, about 2 minutes each side.

Nutritional information
Serving size: $\frac{1}{5}^{th}$ of eggplant. Per serving: 20 g starch
carbohydrate, 25 g total carb, 333 cals, 24 g fat, 4 g saturated fat, 4
g fiber, 291 mg sodium.

Free item!

Microwaved Mushrooms

■ **COOKING TIME** 3 minutes   ■ **SERVES** 4

You can't beat this side dish for a quick dinner on the run.

- 8 oz of mushrooms, sliced
- 2 tablespoons of olive oil
- ¼ teaspoon of garlic powder
- ¼ teaspoon of salt or to taste

DIRECTIONS:

1. In a microwave dish, place the mushrooms and sprinkle them with oil, garlic powder and salt to taste.
2. Cover the dish and microwave on High for 2½-3 minutes.

Nutritional information
Per serving: 2 g total carbohydrate, 73 cals, 7 g fat, 1 g saturated fat, 1 g fiber, 148 mg sodium.

Spinach Kugel

■ **COOKING TIME** 40 minutes   ■ **SERVES** 9

This might seem like an unusual way for promoting vegetables, but this is an excellent kugel. A kugel is a sort of solid casserole. Kugels have been cooked in Europe for centuries. The cut-up squares, incidentally, are very handy for packing lunches and snacks.

- ¼ cup of green pepper, chopped
- 1 cup of onion, chopped
- ½ cup of celery, chopped
- 1½ cups of raw carrot, grated
- 10-oz package of fresh spinach, chopped
- 3 tablespoons of olive oil
- ¾ cup of matzoh meal, preferably whole wheat
- 1½ teaspoon of salt

DIRECTIONS:

1. Sauté the green pepper, onion, celery and carrot in the oil for about 10 minutes, stirring occasionally.
2. Cook the spinach until wilted, about 5 minutes, and drain.
3. Combine the vegetables and add the eggs, salt, pepper and matzoh meal.
4. Place the mixture in a greased 9-inch square pan and bake in the oven at 350º F for 30 minutes.
5. Serve as squares either hot or cold.

Nutritional information
Serving size: ¹/₉th of the container. Per serving: 10 g grain and sugar carbohydrate, 16 g total carbohydrate, 88 cals, 2 g fat, 0 g saturated fat, 2 g fiber, 434 mg sodium.

Microwaved Artichoke with Vinaigrette Dip

■ **COOKING TIME** 7 minutes ■ **SERVES** 4

There's something about "doing things" to food that makes it more attractive to kids. Artichokes offer it all – pulling, cutting and dipping. If you're not into making salad dressings, use a ready-made Italian dressing.

- 4 artichokes

Dip
- 6 tablespoons of olive oil
- 2 tablespoons of white wine vinegar
- ½ teaspoon of Dijon mustard
- 1 clove of garlic, minced
- 1 teaspoon of sugar
- ¼ teaspoon of dried oregano
- ⅛ teaspoon of salt
- ⅛ teaspoon of pepper

DIRECTIONS:

1. Wash the artichoke. Cut off the stem and peel off the smallest outer leaves.
2. Place the artichokes in a bowl for microwaving with the artichoke face down in the bowl and cover. Cook on high for 7 minutes and then let stand for 5 minutes with the cover on.
3. Meanwhile, mix the ingredients of the vinaigrette dip and place in a small container.

Braised Cabbage with Tomato

- **COOKING TIME** 28 minutes   ■ **SERVES** 11

There are attractive dishes one can make with cabbage other than coleslaw. This is one of them. Try it!

- 1 medium head of cabbage (about 2 lb), shredded
- 1 large onion, chopped
- 1 green pepper, cut into thin strips
- 1 medium zucchini
- 2 medium tomatoes, sliced or diced (or 1 15-oz can of diced tomatoes)
- 2 cloves of garlic, minced
- $1/_3$ cup of tomato ketchup
- 2 tablespoons of tomato paste
- ¼ cup of olive oil
- ½ cup of water
- ½ teaspoon of basil
- ½ teaspoon of oregano
- Salt to taste
- ¼ teaspoon of pepper or to taste

DIRECTIONS:

1. In a large pot, boil enough water to cover the cabbage.
2. Add the cabbage and a pinch of salt and boil the cabbage for 3 minutes or until tender.
3. Drain the cabbage in a colander and rinse under cold water. Squeeze out the extra water.
4. In a large pot, heat the oil and sauté the onions, garlic, peppers and zucchini for about 5 minutes.
5. Add the shredded cabbage and sauté for another 5 minutes.
6. Mix the tomato paste with some water and add to the pot along with the tomato, tomato ketchup and seasonings.
7. Cover and cook the cabbage mixture over a low heat, stirring often, for 15 minutes or until the cabbage is tender.
8. Add salt and pepper to taste.

Nutritional information
Serving size: ½ cup. Per serving: 10 g total carbohydrate, 86 cals, 5 g fat, 1 g saturated fat, 3 g fiber, 111 mg sodium.

Chapter 11

Classy Cold Salads

Salads are of considerable importance in this program. Particularly if you are trying to control or lose weight, eating a salad is an excellent way for keeping the edge off your hunger.

Salads containing no grains and no more than a small amount of sugar are regarded as "free items".

This is not a low-fat diet and there is no reason to use low-fat salad dressings. For reasons discussed in the chapter "Clogging and Unclogging Arteries", I regard salad dressings containing olive oil or canola oil to be more healthful than those made with corn oil.

Vinaigrette

I highly recommend keeping a good vinaigrette at hand. With this available, a few cut-up vegetable can become an enticing salad in a matter of minutes. This is a vinaigrette with a subtle taste.

- 6 tablespoons of olive oil
- 2 tablespoons of white wine vinegar
- ½ teaspoon of Dijon mustard
- 1 clove of garlic, minced
- 1 teaspoon of sugar
- ¼ teaspoon of dried oregano
- $^1/_8$ teaspoon of salt
- $^1/_8$ teaspoon of pepper

Fresh Garden Salad

This salad can be made in a few minutes. Add a sprinkle of lemon juice and it will keep in the fridge for several days. The English don't peel their "English cucumbers". Leaving the skin on also makes the salad colorful and crunchy.

- ½ English cucumber, unpeeled, sliced
- 3 medium tomatoes, sliced
- 1 Romaine lettuce, cut into bite size pieces
- ¼ cup of black olives, halved
- Sprinkle of lemon juice (optional)
- Shredded carrot (optional)

DIRECTIONS:

1. Mix the ingredients together in a salad bowl.
2. Add lemon juice if the salad is not being used immediately or part of it is going to be left for later use.
3. Garnish with shredded carrot if desired.
4. Serve with a vinaigrette or salad dressing.

Mandarin Orange Salad

■ **COOKING TIME** 2 minutes   ■ **SERVES** 9

- 1 large head of leaf lettuce, cut into bite-sized pieces
- 1 cup of celery, sliced
- 4 green onions, chopped
- 1 tablespoon of fresh parsley, chopped
- ¼ cup of slivered almonds
- 2 fresh mandarin oranges or 1 11-oz can of mandarin oranges in light syrup, drained

Dressing:
- ¼ cup of olive oil
- 2 tablespoons of red wine vinegar
- ¼ teaspoon of tarragon
- ½ teaspoon of salt or to taste
- 2 tablespoons of sugar

DIRECTIONS:

1. In a small skillet, toast the almonds until very lightly browned.
2. In a small bowel, mix the oil, vinegar, tarragon, salt and sugar.
3. Pour the dressing over the vegetables, fruit and almonds just before serving, and toss the salad.
4. Serve chilled.

Nutritional information
Per serving: 8 g total carbohydrate, 100 cals, 8 g fat, 1 g saturated fat,
2 g fiber, 145 mg sodium.

Free item!

Mediterranean Salad

A plate of tomatoes, cucumbers and peppers is wholesome, but nothing to get too excited about. However, chop these vegetables into small pieces and add some lemon juice, salt and pepper and you have an extraordinarily tasty salad.

- 1 cucumber
- 3 medium-size tomatoes
- 1 green pepper
- 2 scallions
- 3 cloves of garlic, minced
- ½ cup of fresh parsley

Dressing:
- 2 tablespoons of lemon juice
- ½ teaspoon of salt or to taste
- ⅛ teaspoon of pepper or to taste

DIRECTIONS:

1. Cut all the vegetables into small dices no larger than ½ inch, and mix together.
2. Add the parsley, oil, lemon juice, salt and pepper.

Free item!

Seven Layer Salad

■ **SERVES** 13

The kids will love digging into this great salad.

- 1 iceberg lettuce, shredded
- 1 green pepper, chopped
- 1 10-oz box of frozen peas, defrosted
- 1 red onion, finely sliced
- 4 carrots, shredded
- 2 stalks of celery, finely chopped
- Approximately 1 cup of healthy mayonnaise, e.g. canola-based

DIRECTIONS:

1. In a large serving dish, put each of the vegetables in layers.
2. Cover the salad with the mayonnaise.
3. Cover the entire salad with the shredded carrots.

Nutritional information
Serving size: 1 cup. Per serving: 7 g total carbohydrate, 155 cals, 14 g
fat, 1 g saturated fat, 2 g fiber, 148 mg sodium.

Free item!

Apple Feta Salad

■ **COOKING TIME** 18 minutes ■ **SERVES** 11

This is the queen of salads.

- 1 head of romaine lettuce, torn into bite-sized pieces
- 1 head of leaf lettuce, torn into bite sized pieces
- 1 medium red apple, chopped
- 1 medium green apple, chopped
- 4 oz of feta cheese
- 2 tablespoons of olive oil
- 1 cup of walnut halves
- 1 tablespoon of sugar
- $\frac{1}{8}$ teaspoon of pepper

Dressing
- 6 tablespoons of olive oil
- 2 tablespoons of white wine vinegar
- 2 tablespoons of onions, very finely chopped
- 1½ teaspoons of Dijon mustard
- 2 cloves of garlic, minced
- ½ teaspoon of sugar
- ¼ teaspoon of dried oregano
- $\frac{1}{8}$ teaspoon of dried parsley flakes
- $\frac{1}{8}$ teaspoon of pepper

DIRECTIONS:

1. Preheat the oven to 350°F.
2. In a medium skillet, fry the walnuts over medium heat. Sprinkle with sugar and pepper and stir until the walnuts are well coated.
3. Spread the walnuts onto a baking sheet and bake at 350°F for 15 minutes, stirring every 5 minutes. Cool on a wire rack.
4. In a large bowl combine the romaine, red lettuce, apples and feta cheese. Set aside.
5. In a small bowl, mix the dressing ingredients.
6. Drizzle the dressing over the salad.
7. Sprinkle the salad with the sugared walnuts and serve immediately.

Nutritional information
Serving size: 1 cup. Per serving: 7 g total carbohydrate, 154 cals, 14 g fat, 4 g saturated fat, 2 g fiber, 137 mg sodium.

Portabella Mushroom Salad

■ **COOKING TIME** 7 minutes   ■ **SERVES** 9½

This salad won't hang around for long - guaranteed!

- ½ cup of a homemade vinaigrette (see beginning of this section) or Italian dressing
- 6 portabella mushrooms, sliced
- 4 cups of Romaine or leaf lettuce, cut into bite-sized pieces
- ½ cup (2 oz) of feta cheese
- 4 medium tomatoes, sliced

DIRECTIONS:

1. Set oven control to broil. Spray broiler pan rack with cooking spray.
2. Brush the Italian dressing on both sides of each mushroom, and leave the remaining for a dressing. Broil the mushrooms 2 to 4 inches from the heat for 4 minutes. Turn and broil for 3 minutes or so longer until the mushrooms are tender.
3. Crumble the cheese and mix with the greens, tomatoes and mushroom.
4. Drizzle the remaining dressing over the salad.

> Nutritional information
> Serving size: 1 cup. Per serving: 5 g total carbohydrate, 82 cals, 6 g fat, 1 g saturated fat, 2 g fiber, 287 mg sodium.

Free item!

Avocado with Citrus Salad

■ **SERVES** 12

This is a tasty and classy salad. Highly recommended!

- 6 cups of torn salad greens
- 1 medium grapefruit, peeled and sectioned
- 2 navel oranges, peeled and sliced
- 1 ripe avocado, peeled and sliced
- ¼ cup of slivered almonds

Dressing:
- ½ cup of olive oil
- 3 tablespoons of sugar
- 3 tablespoons of vinegar
- 2 teaspoons of poppy seeds
- 1 teaspoon of finely chopped onion
- ½ teaspoon of ground mustard
- ½ teaspoon of salt

DIRECTIONS:

1. Prepare the salad ingredients in a large bowl.
2. Prepare the salad dressing in a small bowl.
3. Mix the two together and chill before use.

Nutritional information
Serving size: 1 cup. Per serving: 4 gm of sugar carbohydrate, 10 g total carbohydrate, 151 cals, 13 g fat, 2 g saturated fat, 2 g fiber, 100 mg sodium.

Spanish Orange and Avocado Salad

■ **SERVES** 7½

This salad and the previous one are somewhat similar, but each has its own unique taste.

- 1 bunch of romaine lettuce, torn into bite-size bits
- 3 tangerines or Spanish Clementine oranges, peeled and separated into sections
- 2 small avocados or 1 large avocado, peeled and diced
- 1 small red onion, very thinly sliced (slice the red onion extremely thin, otherwise it will dominate the rest of the salad).

Dressing:
- 2 teaspoons of lemon juice
- 1 teaspoon of Dijon-style mustard
- ½ teaspoon of sugar
- ½ teaspoon of salt or to taste
- ¼ teaspoon of black pepper
- Just under ¼ cup of olive oil

DIRECTIONS:

1. In a small bowl, combine the lemon juice, mustard, sugar, salt and pepper. Slowly whisk in the olive oil until the dressing is thick and forms an emulsion (this dressing can be prepared in advance).
2. Just before serving, combine the lettuce, oranges, avocado and red onion.
3. Add the dressing and toss well to coat.

Nutritional information
Serving size: 1 cup. Per serving: 16.7 g total carbohydrate, 208 cals, 16.3 g fat, 2.3 g saturated fat, 4.6 g fiber, 183 mg sodium.

Cucumber Salad

■ **SERVES** 7

- 2 large cucumbers, peeled and sliced, or 1 seedless English cucumber, unpeeled
- ¾ cup of onion, thinly sliced
- 1½ teaspoon of salt

Dressing:
- ½ cup of boiling water
- ½ cup of white vinegar
- ½ cup of sugar

DIRECTIONS:

1. Layer the cucumber and onion in a large bowl and sprinkle each layer liberally with salt. Leave it to sit for 30 minutes.
2. Rinse the vegetables with plenty of water and drain well.
3. Mix the water, sugar and vinegar in a small bowl until the sugar dissolves.
4. Pour the dressing over the vegetables.
5. Chill before serving.

Nutritional information
Serving size: ½ cup. Per serving: 18 g total carbohydrate, 75 cals, 0 g fat, 0 g saturated fat, 1 g fiber, 2 mg sodium.

Health Salad

This is a colorful salad that will keep nicely in the fridge for days. This salad is obviously not sugar-free, but much of the sugar-containing dressing remains behind when served.

- 1 carrot
- 1 green pepper
- 1 medium cabbage
- 1 onion
- 1 cucumber

Dressing:
- ½ cup of sugar
- ¾ cup of vinegar
- $^{1}/_{2}$ cup of olive oil
- $^{1}/_{4}$ cup of water
- 2 teaspoons of salt or to taste

DIRECTIONS:

1. Slice all the vegetables thinly (this step is most conveniently done with a food processor).
2. In a small bowl, mix the sugar, vinegar, oil, water and salt, and dissolve the mixture in the microwave.
3. Make sure that it is cool, and pour it over the vegetables.

Nutritional information
Serving size: 1 cup. Per serving: 10 g sugar carbohydrate, 12 g total carbohydrate, 142 cals10 g fat, 1 g saturated fat, 1 g fiber, 449 mg sodium.

Free item!

Hearts of Palm Salad

■ **SERVES** 11

- 4 avocados, peeled, pitted and diced
- 1 14-ounce can of hearts of palm, drained and sliced
- ½ cup of red onion, finely chopped
- 2 cups of grape or cherry tomatoes, halved
- 1 heaping tablespoon of mayonnaise, for example canola-based
- Juice from half of a lemon or 4½ teaspoons of lemon juice
- Salt to taste
- Pepper to taste

DIRECTIONS:

1. Combine the ingredients in a large bowl.

Nutritional information
Serving size: $^3/_4$ cup. Per serving: 12 g total carbohydrate, 161 cals, 12 g fat, 2 g saturated fat, 7 g fiber, 168 mg sodium.

Sumi Salad

- **COOKING TIME** 13 minutes   - **SERVES** 14

This is a salad with a beautifully crunchy and satisfying taste.

- ¼ cup of sliced almonds
- ¼ cup of sesame seeds
- 8 oz of angel hair pasta, broken in thirds
- 1 head of red cabbage, shredded
- 6 scallions, sliced
- 1 8-oz can of sliced water chestnuts
- ½ teaspoon of olive oil

Dressing:
- ¼ cup of sugar
- 1 teaspoon of salt or to taste
- 1 teaspoon of pepper
- 1 cup of olive oil
- ¼ cup of cider vinegar

DIRECTIONS:

1. Cook the pasta according to the packet instructions. Rinse with cold water.
2. In a small skillet, toast the almonds and sesame seeds in oil. Set them aside.
3. Combine the pasta with the cabbage, scallions and water chestnuts.
4. In a small bowl, combine the dressing ingredients and pour the dressing over the pasta and cabbage mixture.
5. Chill the salad for a few hours.
6. Before serving the salad, sprinkle the almonds and sesame seeds on top.

Nutritional information
Serving size: ½ cup. Per serving: 16 g grain, sugar and nut
carbohydrate, 26 g total carbohydrate, 273 cals, 18 g fat, 2 g saturated
fat, 3 g fiber, 188 mg sodium.

Asian Spaghetti Salad

- 12-oz of thin spaghetti, uncooked
- 1 big bok choy, chopped
- 5 spring onions, chopped
- ¼ cup of sesame seeds
- ¾ cup of slivered almonds

Dressing:
- ¼ cup of vinegar
- ½ cup of sugar
- ¼ cup of soy sauce
- ½ cup of olive oil

DIRECTIONS:

1. Cook the spaghetti according to the package directions.
2. Brown the sesame seeds without any oil for about 2 minutes.
3. Brown the slivered almonds with 1 teaspoon of oil for about 2 minutes.
4. Sauté the bok choy and onions with a small amount of oil until the bok choy is just beginning to wilt, about 3 to 4 minutes.
5. Mix the spaghetti, sesame seeds, almonds and sautéed bok choy and onion together.
6. Mix the dressing in a small bowl. Pour over the salad and mix well.

Nutritional information
Serving size 1 cup. Per serving: 27 g grain and sugar carbohydrate,
30g total carbohydrate, 262 cals, 14 g fat, 2 g saturated fat, 2 g fiber,
270 mg sodium

Noodle with Peanuts Salad

■ **COOKING TIME** 13 minutes ■ **SERVES** 14

This is a sumptuous noodle salad that will get eaten very quickly.

- 1½ lb of spaghetti
- 6 scallions, sliced thin
- 1 cup of chopped cilantro
- 1½ cups of lightly salted dry roasted peanuts, coarsely chopped

Dressing:
- ¼ cup of sesame oil
- ¼ cup of soy sauce
- 2 tablespoons of sugar
- 1½ tablespoons of balsamic vinegar
- 1 teaspoon of salt

DIRECTIONS:

1. Cook the spaghetti according to the package instructions.
2. Add the scallions, cilantro and peanuts to the spaghetti.
3. Prepare the salad dressing in a small bowl, mix well and pour over the salad.
4. Toss the salad to coat thoroughly.

> Nutritional information
> Serving size: 1 cup. Per serving: 42 g carbohydrate, 317 cals, 12 g fat,
> 2 g saturated fat, 3 g fiber, 407 mg sodium.

Spinach Orzo Salad

■ **COOKING TIME** 9 minutes   ■ **SERVES** 8½

Your family will be pleasantly surprised how nicely the spinach sets off this salad. Orzo is a form of pasta and can be found in the noodle section in the supermarket. Unlike many green leaf salads, this one will keep well in the refrigerator for a few days.

- 8 oz of dried orzo
- ¾ lb of fresh spinach, torn into bite-sized pieces
- ⅓ cup of red onion, finely diced
- 1 small tomato, diced
- ¼ lb of feta cheese, coarsely crumbled
- ¼ cup of olive oil
- 1½ teaspoon of lemon juice
- ½ tablespoon of pepper
- ½ tablespoon of salt or to taste

DIRECTIONS:

1. Boil the Orzo with 3 cups water and 1 teaspoon of salt for 9 minutes.
2. Allow the Orzo to cool somewhat and mix it with the vegetables.
3. Mix the oil, lemon juice, salt and pepper in a small bowl and add to the salad.
4. Place the feta cheese as a garnish on the salad.

Nutritional information
Portion size: 1 cup. Per serving: 20 g grain carbohydrate, 23 g total carbohydrate, 260 cals, 166 g fat, 4 g saturated fat, 2 g fiber, 320 mg sodium.

Tabouli

■ **SERVES** 10

This tasty Middle Eastern salad is easy to make and it's just oozing with health- promoting ingredients! Bulgur wheat is low-glycemic; the lemon juice, tomatoes and olive oil are full of antioxidants; and the olive oil contains monounsaturated fat.

- 1 cup of dry bulgur wheat
- ½ cup of chopped scallions (include the green)
- 3 medium tomatoes, finely diced
- 1 cup of fresh parsley
- 1½ cups of boiling water
- 2 teaspoons of salt or to taste

Dressing:
- ¼ cup of lemon or lime juice
- 1 heaping teaspoon of crushed garlic
- ½ teaspoon of dried mint
- ¼ cup of olive oil

DIRECTIONS:

1. Combine the bulgur, boiling water and salt in a bowl. Cover and let stand for 15-20 minutes or until the bulgur is chewable.
2. Make sure most of the water is absorbed by the grain. If not, dry with a paper towel.
3. Add the lemon juice, garlic, oil and mint to the bulgur and mix thoroughly.
4. Refrigerate the bulgur for a few hours.
5. Just before serving, add the vegetables and mix gently.
6. This salad can also be garnished with feta cheese and olives.

Nutritional information
Portion size: ½ cup. Per serving: 11 g grain carbohydrate, 12 g total carbohydrate, 104 cals, 6.0 g fat, 1 g saturated fat, 3 g fiber, 473 mg sodium.

Bulgur with Leek, Cranberries and Almonds

- **COOKING TIME** 19 minutes ■ **SERVES** 11

If you like healthy salads and also have a sweet tooth, this is the salad for you.

- 1½ cups of dry bulgur wheat
- 1½ cups of leeks, chopped (use only the white and pale green parts)
- ⅓ cup of dried cranberries
- ⅓ cup of sliced almonds
- 3 tablespoons of olive oil
- 2½ cups of chicken broth, preferably low salt
- Salt and pepper to taste

DIRECTIONS:

1. In a large saucepan, sauté the chopped leaks until tender, about 12 minutes.
2. Add the chicken broth and bring to a boil. Stir in the bulgur and boil for 5 minutes.
3. Add the dried cranberries.
4. Remove from the heat, cover and let stand for 15 minutes.
5. Season with salt and pepper to taste.

Nutritional information
Serving size: ½ cup. Per serving: 20 g total carbohydrate, 141 cals, 6 g
fat, 1 g saturated fat, 4 g fiber, 22 mg sodium.

Fruited Rice Salad

■ **COOKING TIME** 45 minutes　　■ **SERVES** 8

With this recipe you will appreciate the crunchiness of the rice in combination with the sweetness of the fruit. Incidentally, wild rice is not really rice but the seed of an aquatic grass.

- 1 cup of uncooked wild rice
- 2 Golden Delicious apples, chopped
- 1 cup of seedless red grapes, halved
- 1 cup of fresh parsley
- 1 cup of chives or green onions
- 1 cup of pecans, halved

Dressing:
- ¼ cup of olive oil
- $^{1}/_{3}$ cup of orange juice
- 2 tablespoons of honey
- 1 teaspoon of lemon juice

DIRECTIONS:

1. Cook the wild rice in 3½ cups of water with 1 teaspoon of salt for 45 minutes. Allow to cool-
2. In a small bowl, combine the ingredients for the salad dressing.
3. In a large salad bowl, combine the salad ingredients and pour over the dressing.
4. Chill for a few hours before serving.

> Nutritional information
> Serving size: 1 cup. Per serving: 22 g grain, nut and sugar carbohydrate, 34 g total carbohydrate, 284 cals, 16 g fat, 2 g saturated fat, 4 g fiber, 9 mg sodium.

Sopa Seca Salad

■ **COOKING TIME** 50 minutes   ■ **SERVES** 12

This is another great-tasting and filling salad.

- 1 15½ -oz can of chick peas, rinsed and drained (or 1½ cups of dried chick-peas soaked overnight in 2 cups of water)
- 3 tablespoons of olive oil
- 2 onions, chopped
- 2 cloves of garlic, minced
- 1 green pepper, chopped
- 1 cup of uncooked basmati or other rice
- 1 cup of boiling water
- 1 14 ½-oz can of chopped tomatoes, with juice
- ¼ teaspoon of oregano
- ½ teaspoon of chili powder
- 1 teaspoon of salt or to taste
- ¼ teaspoon of pepper
- ¼ cup of raisins
- ¼ cup of sliced almonds

DIRECTIONS:

1. If using dried chicken peas, simmer them uncovered in water to cover for 30 minutes, and then drain.
2. Meanwhile, heat the olive oil in a large skillet. Sauté the onions, garlic, green pepper and rice until browned.
3. Add the boiling water, tomatoes, chick peas and spices to the skillet. Cover and simmer for 40 minutes.
4. Stir in the raisins and cook for 5 minutes longer.

Nutritional information
Serving size: ¾ cup. Per serving: 21 g bean and grain carbohydrate, 28 g total carbohydrate, 168 cals, 5 g fat, 1 g saturated fat, 3 g fiber, 221 mg sodium.

Red Cabbage Salad

■ **SERVES** 14

Crunchy. Colorful. Tasty.

- 1 16-oz bag of shredded purple cabbage or approximately half of a medium cabbage, shredded
- $\frac{1}{3}$ cup of scallions, chopped
- $\frac{1}{3}$ cup of pine nuts
- 1 8-oz bag of shredded carrot or 4 medium carrots, shredded
- 1 11-oz can of mandarin oranges (some of the juice is used for the salad dressing)
- $\frac{1}{8}$ cup of Craisins (sweetened dried cranberries)

Dressing:
- 4 tablespoons of brown sugar
- ½ teaspoon of pepper
- ¼ teaspoon of salt
- 4 tablespoons of wine vinegar
- ½ cup of olive oil
- Dash of garlic powder
- 1 teaspoon of chicken bouillon granules
- 1 tablespoon of mandarin juice (from the opened can)

DIRECTIONS:

1. Mix everything together in a large bowl.
2. Serve chilled. (This salad will keep well in the fridge for a few days).

Nutritional information
Serving size: ½ cup. Per serving: 12 g total carbohydrate, 138 cals, 10 g fat, 1 g saturated fat, 1 g fiber, 145 mg sodium.

Free item!

Middle Eastern Carrot Salad

- **COOKING TIME** 10 minutes
- **SERVES** 9½

- 2 lb of carrots, sliced

  Dressing:
- 5 cloves of garlic, minced
- 1½ teaspoons of cumin
- 2 teaspoons of paprika
- Juice from 2 lemons, or 6 tablespoons of lemon juice
- ¼ cup of olive oil
- ¼ cup of fresh parsley, chopped
- Salt to taste

DIRECTIONS:

1. Cook the carrots until they are tender but crisp.
2. Cool the carrots.
3. Pour the salad dressing over the cooled carrots.

Nutritional information
Serving size: ½ cup. Per serving: 10 g total carbohydrate, 94 cals, 6 g fat, 1 g saturated fat, 3 g fiber, 69 mg sodium.

Free item!

Baby Carrot Salad

■ **COOKING TIME** 12 minutes ■ **SERVES** 4

- 1 lb of baby carrots
- 6 cloves garlic, minced
- 1½ cups of water
- ¼ cup of balsamic vinegar, divided
- 1 teaspoon of salt
- 1 teaspoon of dried mustard
- 2 tablespoons of honey
- 4 teaspoons of dried dill

DIRECTIONS:

1. In a medium-sized pot, bring to a boil the water, 2 tablespoons of vinegar, salt, mustard and honey and stir until they dissolve.
2. Add the carrots, garlic and dill and lower heat to a simmer.
3. Cook uncovered for about 10 minutes or until the carrots are as tender as you like them.
4. Cool to room temperature and add the remaining 2 tablespoons of vinegar.
5. Transfer to a container and chill.

Nutritional information (including liquid contents)
Serving size: ½ cup. Per serving: 22 g total carbohydrate, 89 cals, 0 g fat, 2 g fiber, 686 mg sodium.

Carrots with Raisins

■ **SERVES** 5

This salad beats carrot sticks any day.

- ½ lb of carrots, finely grated
- ½ cup of raisins
- ¼ cup of sunflower seeds
- 2 tablespoons of healthy mayonnaise, e.g. canola-based

DIRECTIONS:

1. Grate the carrots finely using a food processor.
2. Mix the contents of the salad together.

> Nutritional information
> Serving size: ½ cup. Per serving: 13 g seed and dried fruit
> carbohydrate, 17 g total carbohydrate, 124 cals, 6 g fat, 1 g
> saturated fat, 2 g fiber, 75 mg sodium.

Free item!

Fried Eggplant Salad

■ **SERVES** 7

This salad exudes the Middle East. It's one of my favorites.

- 1 large eggplant, cut into ½ inch slices
- Olive oil for frying
- 6 cloves of garlic, minced
- ½ cup of parsley, chopped
- ½ teaspoon of salt or to taste
- ½ teaspoon of black pepper
- 1 teaspoon of paprika
- ½ teaspoon of cumin
- ¼ cup of lemon juice
- ¼ cup of white vinegar
- ½ cup of water
- Black olives (optional)

DIRECTIONS:

1. Liberally salt the eggplant and put in a colander to drain. After 1 hour, rinse the salt off and dry the eggplant with paper towels.
2. Deep-fry the eggplant slices in hot oil on both sides over medium heat until slightly brown.
3. After frying, put the eggplant on a paper towel to absorb the extra oil.
4. In a medium-sized bowl, mix together all the ingredients other than the oil and eggplant.
5. Dip the slices in this mixture and put them aside.
6. In a salad bowl, pour the rest of the mixture over the eggplant slices.
7. Cool in the fridge.
8. Garnish with black olives if desired.

> Nutritional information (including liquid contents)
> Serving size: 2 slices. Per serving: 6 g total carbohydrate, 31 cals, 1 g fat, 0 g saturated fat, 3 g fiber, 171 mg sodium.

Four Bean Salad

■ **COOKING TIME** 5 minutes   ■ **SERVES** 10

This is one of the better tasting four-bean salads. It's also extremely easy to make. Just open the cans and pour them into the salad bowl - except for the green beans which you will need to cook.

- 1 16-oz can of chick peas, rinsed and drained
- 1 16-oz can of kidney beans, rinsed and drained
- 16 oz of frozen green beans
- 8 oz of frozen corn
- ½ of a large red onion, finely chopped
- 1 red pepper, chopped
- ½ cup of vinegar
- ¼ cup of canola oil (tastes better than olive oil for this salad)
- 1 teaspoon of oregano
- 1 teaspoon of crushed garlic
- ½ teaspoon of salt or to taste
- ¼ teaspoon of pepper

DIRECTIONS:

1. Cook the green beans for 5 minutes in ½ cup of water, according to the package instructions.
2. Combine the ingredients in a large bowl.
3. Serve chilled.

> Nutritional information
> Portion size: $^2/_3$ of a cup. Per serving: 13 gm of bean carbohydrate, 23 g total carbohydrate, 173 cals, 7 g fat, 0 g saturated fat, 6 g fiber, 316 mg sodium.

Colorful Pepper Salad

■ **COOKING TIME** 18 minutes ■ **SERVES** 4

- 3 red, yellow or orange peppers, sliced lengthwise
- 1 tablespoon of olive oil
- 1 tablespoon of white vinegar
- Salt to taste

DIRECTIONS:

1. Sauté the peppers in the olive oil.
2. Cover the pan and cook the peppers for 15 minutes, stirring occasionally.
3. Drain the peppers on paper towel.
4. Put the peppers in a serving bowl and add the vinegar and salt to taste.

Cesar Salad with Croutons

■ **COOKING TIME** 20 minutes   ■ **CROUTONS SERVE** 16

This is a very family-friendly salad - in other words it will get eaten very quickly. With the croutons and salad dressing, it also makes a filling snack. Note that the croutons will get soggy if left on the salad too long.

- 4 stalks of Romaine lettuce
- 4 cloves garlic, crushed
- ¾ cup of healthy mayonnaise, e.g. canola-based
- 1 tablespoon of lemon juice
- 1 teaspoon of Worcestershire sauce
- 1 teaspoon of Dijon mustard
- Salt to taste
- Pepper to taste

Homemade Croutons:

- 6 slices of whole wheat bread, cut into small cubes
- ¼ cup of olive oil
- ¼ cup of healthy mayonnaise, e.g. canola-based
- 1 tablespoon of green onion, finely chopped
- 1 garlic clove, minced
- ¼ cup of Honey Dijon Mustard
- ¾ teaspoon of dried oregano

DIRECTIONS:

1. To make the croutons, preheat the oven to 350°F.
2. Heat the olive oil in a large pan, and whisk in all the other ingredients until they are all well combined.
3. Add in the bread cubes and toss until they are well coated.
4. Transfer to a baking sheet and cook in the oven for 15-20 minutes.
5. Allow the croutons to cool before serving. They can also be stored in a container or frozen.
6. Mix the contents of the salad in a large bowl.
7. Serve chilled.
8. Add the croutons just before serving.

> Nutritional information for the croutons
> Serving size: 10 croutons. Per serving: 6 g total carbohydrate, 85 cals, 7 g fat, 1 g sat fat, 12 g fiber, 110 mg sodium.

Tuna Salad with Grapes and Almonds

■ **COOKING TIME** 3 minutes   ■ **SERVES** 5

This is an incredibly delicious salad. Case closed.

- 10-oz can of tuna in spring water, drained
- $^1/_3$ cup of chopped scallions
- 1 cup of grapes, cut in quarters
- ½ cup of celery, chopped
- 3 tablespoons of healthy mayonnaise, for example canola-based
- 1 teaspoon of lemon juice
- $^1/_4$ teaspoon of salt
- $^1/_8$ teaspoon of pepper
- $^1/_4$ cup of slivered almonds

DIRECTIONS:

1. Toast the slivered almonds in a small dry skillet for a few minutes until they are just turning golden.
2. Set aside 1 tablespoon of almonds.
3. Combine all the ingredients in a bowl and mix well.
4. Sprinkle the reserved almonds on top of the salad.

Nutritional information
Serving size: $^1/_2$ cup. Per serving: 8 g total carbohydrate, 177 cals,
11 g fat, 1 g saturated fat, 1 g fiber, 438 mg sodium.

Chapter 12

Breakfast – an Essential Meal

Breakfast should be an important meal for everyone. Many kids have gotten into the habit of skipping breakfast and rolling directly from bed into the school bus. Scientific studies have repeatedly shown, however, that children who miss breakfast are more prone to obesity and do worse on learning tasks at school.

Unfortunately, most of the popular breakfast cereals found in the stores have a high or moderately high glycemic index. Therefore, why not make your own breakfast cereal? There's plenty of scope for creativity with home-made cereals. One can add different nuts and dried fruit to the basic recipe and the cereal can be topped with berries and fresh fruit, such as strawberries, blueberries and apple slices.

Other easy and healthful breakfast suggestions, besides the recipes here, include plain yogurt topped with berries, fruit or granola, and whole grain toast with a non transfat-containing margarine, cheese or peanut butter. Eggs also make a filling breakfast.

Crunchy Granola

■ **COOKING TIME** 25 minutes ■ **SERVES** 8

There's nothing like a home-made granola for breakfast. Add berries and fresh fruit such as blueberries, strawberries, slices of apple and banana and it tastes even better. Vary the fruit and nuts and you have a different breakfast each day!

- 2 cups of Old Fashioned rolled oats
- ½ cup of shredded coconut
- ½ cup of wheat germ
- ½ cup of hulled sunflower seeds
- ¼ cup of honey
- ¼ cup of olive or canola oil
- 1 teaspoon of vanilla extract
- ½ cup of raisins

Variations: Add ½ cup of peanuts, chopped pecans, walnuts, or slivered almonds before roasting or dried fruit after roasting.

DIRECTIONS:

1. Preheat the oven to 325°F.
2. Spray a cookie sheet well with an oil spray, or even better place parchment paper on the cookie sheet (the ingredients of this recipe become very sticky).
3. In a large mixing bowl, mix all the solid ingredients except for the raisins.
4. In a measuring cup, add the oil, honey and vanilla, and then work this mixture into the dry ingredients.
5. Spread the granola onto the cookie sheet and roast at 325°F for a total of 20-30 minutes.
6. Stir after 15 minutes or so, and add the raisins for the last 5 to 10 minutes of roasting.
7. When the mixture comes out the oven, it is still very pliable. Dried fruit can be added as a finishing touch at this time.
8. When the granola has cooled completely, store in an airtight container.
9. Serve in a bowl with milk.

Nutritional information (without added milk)
Portion size: ½ cup. Per serving: 35 g total carbohydrate, 259 cals, 12 g fat, 3.0 g saturated fat, 4.0 g fiber, 4 mg sodium.

Maple Nut Granola

■ **COOKING TIME** 60 minutes   ■ **SERVES** 12

This is another wonderful granola recipe. If you like variety, alternate it with the granola recipe on the previous page.

- 3 cups of Old Fashioned rolled oats
- 1 cup of walnuts, coarsely chopped
- ½ cup of almonds, sliced or slivered
- ¼ cup of stone ground whole wheat flour
- Pinch of salt
- ½ teaspoon of cinnamon
- ½ cup of maple syrup
- $^1/_3$ cup of canola or olive oil
- 1 teaspoon of vanilla
- ¼ cup of raisins

Variations: Add sunflower seeds, sesame seeds, coconut or cashews. Use dried dates instead of raisins.

DIRECTIONS:
1. Preheat the oven to between 300° to 350°F.
2. In a mixing bowl, combine all the dry ingredients except for the raisins.
3. Add the liquid ingredients and mix until the dry ingredients are well-coated.
4. Spread the mixture on a large oiled baking tray.
5. Bake for 45 minutes at 300° to 350°F.
6. Stir the granola occasionally.
7. Add the raisins to the hot or cold granola.
8. Serve in a bowl with milk.

> Nutritional information (without added milk)
> Portion size per serving: ½ cup. Per serving: 31 g total carbohydrate,
> 264 cals, 14 g fat, 1 g saturated fat, 3.0 g fiber, 16 mg sodium.

Muesli

■ **SERVES** 6

This is an incredibly good Muesli. It's also extremely simple and quick to make. Serve it with either milk or yogurt and put berries or fruit on top. As with the previous granola recipes, there's plenty of scope for varying the ingredients and toppings to produce new and exciting tastes.

- 2 cups of Old-Fashioned rolled oats
- ¼ cup of wheat germ
- ¼ cup of wheat bran
- ½ cup of raisins
- ¼ cup of brown sugar
- ¼ cup of chopped walnuts
- ¼ cup of raw sunflower seeds

DIRECTIONS:

1. In a large mixing bowl, combine all the ingredients and mix well.
2. Store the muesli in an airtight container. (It can easily keep for up to 2 months at room temperature).
3. Serve with milk, with or without fresh berries or sliced fresh fruit. For a smoother texture, allow the milk to soak into the cereal for ½ hour or so before serving.

Nutritional information (without added milk)
Portion size: ½ cup. Per serving: 32 g carbohydrate, 227 cals, 9 g fat,
1 g saturated fat, 5 g fiber, 4 mg sodium.

Spanish Omelet

■ **COOKING TIME** 10 minutes   ■ **SERVES** 4

Strictly speaking a Spanish omelet is a thick omelet stuffed with fried potato and fine cut onion that have been fried in olive oil. It can also include cheese and ham. In this recipe, high-glycemic potato has been replaced by lower glycemic corn, and other vegetables have been added. It's as good as the original and perhaps even better!

- 4 eggs
- ¼ cup of milk
- ¼ of a large green pepper, chopped
- ½ of a large onion, chopped
- 1 celery stalk, chopped
- 2 oz of frozen corn
- 1 tablespoon of olive oil
- ¼ teaspoon of salt or to taste
- ¼ teaspoon of pepper

DIRECTIONS:

1. Sauté the vegetables in the oil until softened. Transfer to a bowl.
2. Mix well the eggs, milk, salt and pepper, and fry until the mixture becomes slightly firm.
3. Add the vegetable mix to the eggs and continue cooking until the eggs are the appropriate consistency.

> Nutritional information (using whole milk)
> Serving size: 1 egg. Per serving: 1 g of carbs from milk, 10 g total carbohydrate, 149 cals, 9 g fat, 2 g saturated fat, 1 g fiber, 232 mg sodium.

Strawberry Banana Smoothie

■ **SERVES** 2

A smoothie is a great breakfast for a teenager on the run. Put it in a container and it can be finished on the bus. Especially if made with full-fat yogurt, it can be quite filling. The texture is best when the fruit is frozen before being added to the smoothie, but fresh banana also works well.

- ½ cup of plain yogurt
- ½ cup of orange juice
- 1 cup of frozen strawberries
- 1 cup of frozen banana (1½ bananas)
- 1 teaspoon of sugar

DIRECTIONS:

1. Puree all the ingredients in a blender until fully mixed.
2. Served chilled.

Nutritional information
Serving size: just over 1 cup. Per serving: 34 g total carbohydrate,
164 cals, 3 g fat, 1 g saturated fat, 3 g fiber, 30 mg sodium.

Shadowbox Egg

- **SERVES** 1

This is a very kid-friendly way of introducing different types of breads.

- 1 egg
- 1 slice of mixed grain or whole wheat bread
- 1 tablespoon of olive oil

DIRECTIONS:

1. Make a large hole in a slice of bread. If the slice of bread is big enough, use the edges of a glass cup.
2. Add the oil to a small skillet, place the bread in the skillet and a whole egg in the hole.
3. Fry the bread and egg until the egg is just beginning to turn white and then flip the egg-bread combination.
4. Continue frying until the egg is cooked to your satisfaction.
4. Fry the bread taken from the hole in any remaining oil.

Nutritional information
Serving size: 1 slice of bread and 1 egg. Per serving: 12 g total carbohydrate, 258 cals, 19 g fat, 4 g saturated fat, 2 g fiber, 197 mg sodium.

Chapter 13

Snacking to Health!

There are many nutritionists who encourage snacking, since there may be some health advantages in eating small meals throughout the day. I don't recommend it though. The problem is that popular snacks these days are crackers, pretzels, cookies, and potato chips. These are all weight-inducing high-glycemic starches, and there is no health advantage to eating such foods throughout the day. Many kids also use breakfast cereal as a snack food. These also are often high in sugar and highly-refined carbohydrate and are high-glycemic.

Snacking on healthy snacks, however, is certainly permitted. I admit that preparing appetizing snacks containing whole grains, vegetables and fruit can be a challenge, but with a bit of thought it can be achieved. This section will provide you with ideas.

A sandwich makes an attractive snack and some novel sandwich fillings are included in this section. As discussed in chapter 6, my preference for bread is a mixed grain bread, with whole grain, rye, pumpernickel and sourdough bread a second choice. A whole wheat pita can also be useful, since it's easier to fill with salad and vegetables than a sandwich. White pita bread has the same glycemic index as white bread, but the glycemic index of whole wheat pita is quite a bit lower at 56.

Raw vegetables can be made extremely tasty with a good dip. Many dip recipes are heavy on sour cream and mayonnaise, but Middle Eastern foods such as hummus, tahini and babaganoush make excellent dips and can be bought in small containers.

Making sure that your family uses the right type of drinks is extremely important. Regular soda and other sugar-containing drinks such as power drinks and fruit punch are obviously not part of this plan. Even such juices as apple juice, grape juice and mango juice provide an unnecessary amount of sugar and fructose, even though their sugars are natural ones. Orange juice and grapefruit juice contain natural antioxidants and seem to provide health benefits not available from many other juices, so that one to two cups a day of these citrus juices is quite appropriate.

There is good scientific evidence that cola-containing drinks, both diet and regular cola, leach out calcium from one's bones, probably due to their content of phosphate. The effect from one drink will be small but over time it does add up. Bones that are low in calcium in adolescence increase the risk for fractures in youth and for developing osteoporosis in old-age.

Milk is a wonderful accompaniment for a snack. Unfortunately, people are drinking less milk than they used to in the past, and many individuals are no longer meeting their requirements for calcium. Children and teenagers especially need to be encouraged to drink an adequate amount of milk. Three glasses a day is usually sufficient.

This table below shows the recommended amount of elemental calcium for children and adults:

Age	Recommended daily elemental calcium intake
1 to 3 years	500 mg
4 to 8 years	800 mg
9 to 18 years	1,300 mg
Adults 19 to 50 years	1,000 mg
Adults 50 plus	1,200 mg

An 8-oz cup of milk provides 300 mg of elemental calcium, 1 8 oz-cup of calcium-fortified orange juice about 300 mg, 8 oz of yogurt 350-400 mg, and 1 oz of cheese 175-275 mg. A few non-dairy foods such as spinach contain calcium, but the amount is rather small. Therefore if your dairy intake is low, you are probably not meeting your requirements for calcium.

A useful exercise is to add up the amount of elemental calcium in your family's diets and see whether it reaches the age-appropriate figure in the table. If it's far from these recommendations they would probably benefit from a calcium supplement, and this should be discussed with their health provider.

Homemade Trail Mix

■ **SERVES** 10

Nuts are high on our list of healthy foods. Plus, there's no reason to pay out a lot of money for a small packet of fruit and nuts when you can make the same thing yourself at much lower cost. Obviously, there's a lot of scope for innovation here.

- ½ cup of whole shelled (unpeeled) almonds
- ½ cup of unsalted, dry-roasted peanuts
- ½ cup of white raisins
- ½ cup of chocolate chips
- 4 oz of dried apricots or other dried fruit

Nutritional information
Size per serving: ¼ cup. Per serving: 18 g total carbohydrate, 161 cals, 9 g fat, 3 g saturated fat, 2 g fiber, 3 mg sodium.

Cream Cheese and Vegetable Wraps

- **SERVES** 4

A wrap is an attractive way for getting family members to eat more vegetables. Experiment with different vegetables to find the combinations they like. Be aware that many tortillas are quite high in salt.

- 4 10" mixed grain tortilla wraps
- 6 tablespoons of cream cheese
- 1 small carrot
- ¼ red onion
- 12 black olives
- ½ red pepper
- ¼ cucumber

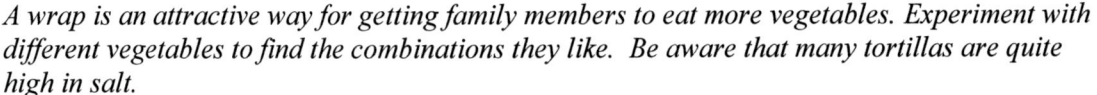

DIRECTIONS:

1. Cut all the vegetables into very thin slices.
2. Spread the cream cheese thinly onto the wrap.
3. Place the vegetables in the form of a line on the wrap as shown above.
4. Fold over the wrap and cut into desired lengths. Each wrap should contain a selection of all the vegetables.

Nutritional information
Serving size: 1 tortilla. Per serving: 27 g grain and sugar carbohydrate, 31 g total carbohydrate, 225 cals, 10 g fat, 2 g saturated fat, 6 g fiber, 608 mg sodium.

Vegetable Focaccia

■ **COOKING TIME** 15 minutes   ■ **SERVES** 12

The kids will love this pizza-like dish.

- 1¼ cups of bread or white flour
- 1 cup of whole wheat flour
- 1 package of quick-rise yeast (2 teaspoons)
- 1 teaspoon of salt
- 1 cup of warm water
- 1 tablespoon of canola or olive oil

Topping:
- 3 medium tomatoes, chopped
- 5 fresh mushrooms, sliced
- ½ cup of chopped green peppers
- ¼ cup of chopped onion
- 3 tablespoons of olive oil
- 2 tablespoons of red wine vinegar
- ¾ teaspoon of salt
- ¼ teaspoon of garlic powder
- ¼ teaspoon of dried oregano
- ¼ teaspoon of pepper
- 2 teaspoons of cornmeal
- ½ cup of sliced black olives (optional)

DIRECTIONS:

1. Preheat the oven to 475°F.
2. In a large mixing bowl, combine the flour, yeast and salt. Add the water and the oil and beat until smooth. Stir in enough remaining flour to form a soft dough.
3. Turn onto a floured surface and knead until smooth and elastic.
4. Cover and leave for 15 minutes.
5. In a bowl, combine all the topping ingredients except for the cornmeal.
6. Coat a 15 x 10 x 1-inch pan with nonstick cooking spray.
7. Sprinkle with cornmeal.
8. Press the dough into the pan. Prick the dough generously with a fork.
9. Bake at 475° for 5 minutes.
10. Cover with the vegetable mixture.
11. Bake for 8-10 minutes longer or until the crusts are golden.

> Nutritional information
> Portion size: ¹/₁₂ of the focaccia. Per serving: 17 g grain carbohydrate, 24 g total carbohydrate, 155 cals, 5 g fat, 1 g saturated fat, 4 g fiber, 360 mg sodium.

Broiled Portabella Mushroom Sandwich

■ **COOKING TIME** 10 minutes   ■ **SERVES** 4

This is one of those "wow, what's that?" sandwiches. It's as good as or even better than a hamburger. The sandwich is best served warm – either freshly cooked or warmed in the microwave. Preferable to a bought Italian dressing would be to make your own vinaigrette (see Cool Salad section).

- 4 fresh portabella mushrooms
- 1 medium onion, cut into ¼" slices
- 4 tomato slices
- 8 slices of mixed grain or whole wheat bread
- 4 teaspoons of Italian dressing

DIRECTIONS:

1. Brush the mushrooms and onion slices liberally with Italian dressing.
2. Broil the mushrooms and onion for 10 minutes, turning the mushroom over after 5 minutes.
3. Fill the sandwich with the mushroom, onion and slices of tomato.

> Nutritional information
> Portion size: 1 sandwich with 2 slices of bread. Per serving: 24 g grain carbohydrate, 28 g total carbohydrate, 161 cals, 3 g fat, 1 g saturated fat, 4 g fiber, 336 mg sodium.

Tuna Salad in a Pita

■ **SERVES** 6

This tuna salad goes well inside a whole wheat pita. Put extra vegetables on top, such as a Mediterranean Salad (see Cool Salad section),

- 2 6-ounce cans of tuna in spring water, well drained
- $^1/_4$ cup of a canola-based mayonnaise or salad dressing
- 1 medium onion, finely chopped
- 2 stalks of celery, chopped
- Pita

DIRECTIONS:

1. Combine the tuna, mayonnaise, onion and celery.
2. Fill half a pita with the tuna salad.

Nutritional information (including the pita)
Serving size: ½ of a whole pita. Per serving: 18 g starch
carbohydrate, 20 g total carbohydrate, 227 cals, 9 g fat, 1 g saturated
fat, 3 g fiber, 440 mg sodium.

Falafel

For a change of pace, try falafel in a pita. Falafel balls are fried balls made from spiced fava beans or chickpea. You can make them from scratch, but it's much easier to use a ready-made mix. When served in a (preferably) whole-wheat pita they make an excellent snack. There is plenty of scope for originality here. Besides the Mediterranean salad, consider additional fillings such as sauerkraut or a cut-up pickle. In the Middle East, a hot spice sauce is often dripped on top. If you really want to get into this seriously, look for falafel with hot sauce recipes on the web.

- Falafel balls (made from falafel mix)
- Whole wheat pita
- Mediterranean salad (see under Cool Salads recipe section)
- Tahini (a paste made of ground sesame seeds) or hummus dip (a spread made from cooked mashed chickpeas and other ingredients)

DIRECTIONS:

1. Fry the falafel balls in olive oil as per the instructions on the package.
2. Place 2 falafel balls in each half pita and fill top to the top with vegetables.
3. Spread tahini or hummus liberally on top of the vegetables.

Free item!

Guacamole

■ **SERVES** 2

Serve this wonderful snack with corn tortilla chips. Corn tortilla chips are a low-glycemic starch. If you can find them, stone ground corn tortilla chips would be even better.

- 2 ripe avocados, mashed
- 2 tablespoons of lemon juice
- 2-3 garlic cloves, minced
- $1/4$ teaspoon of salt or to taste
- ¼ teaspoon of chili powder
- Black pepper to taste

DIRECTIONS:

1. In a large bowl, mash the avocados well and combine the remaining ingredients.
2. Mix thoroughly until smooth.
3. Chill the guacamole but use it fairly soon after preparation, as it keeps poorly beyond 24 hours.
4. Serve with corn tortilla chips (preferably low-salt)

Nutritional information (not including the tortillas)
Serving size: ½ plate. Per serving: 10 g total carbohydrate, 155 cals, 13 g fat, 2 g saturated fat, 6 g fiber, 305 mg sodium.

Roasted Chickpeas

- **COOKING TIME** 20 minutes ■ **SERVES** 7

This recipe tastes like a snack food, so be sure to prepare enough as your child's friends will probably want to share them! They make a great addition to a lunch or snack.

- 1 large 20-oz can of chickpeas
- 3 tablespoons of olive oil
- ½ teaspoon of salt or to taste
- ½ teaspoon of black pepper
- ¾ teaspoon of chili powder or to taste
- $^1/_8$ to ¼ teaspoon of red pepper to taste

DIRECTIONS:

1. Preheat the oven to 400°F.
2. Rinse and drain the chickpeas thoroughly, and shake them until they are fairly dry.
3. In a large baking pan, combine the chickpeas, olive oil, salt and pepper.
4. Bake the chickpeas as a single layer for 15 minutes or until they begin to brown. Stir twice to make sure they brown evenly.
5. Remove from the oven and season with chili powder and red pepper to taste.
6. Bake an additional 5 minutes until they are dark golden red.

> Nutritional information
> Per serving: 23 g total carbohydrate, 182 cals, 6 g fat, 1 g saturated fat, 1 g fiber, 173 mg sodium.

Adapted with permission from "Good Carb, Better Carb Cookbook," published by Publications International Ltd, Lincolnwood, IL

Tuna Noodle Salad

■ **COOKING TIME** 8 minutes   ■ **SERVES** 4

- 8 oz of dried Rotini noodles or other pasta
- 1 5-oz can of chunk light tuna in water
- ¼ cup of red onion, finely diced
- 1 medium celery stalk, diced
- 2 tablespoons of canola-based mayonnaise
- ⅛ teaspoon of pepper
- ¼ teaspoon salt or to taste

DIRECTIONS:

1. Cook the pasta according to the package directions.
2. In a large bowl, combine all the ingredients together.

Nutritional information
Serving size: 1 cup. Per serving: 44 g total carbohydrate, 307 cals, 7 g
fat, 1 g saturated fat, 1 g fiber, 328 mg sodium.

Farfalle and Artichoke Salad

■ **COOKING TIME** 11 minutes   ■ **SERVES** 14

Prepare the full recipe. It will disappear rapidly.

- 16-oz packet of farfalle or bow-tie pasta
- 1 jar of pimentos, drained
- ½ cup of red onion, finely chopped
- ½ cup of parsley, chopped
- 1 14-oz can of artichoke hearts, cut into quarters

Dressing:
- $^{1}/_{3}$ cup of olive oil
- ¼ cup of red wine vinegar
- 1 teaspoon of salt or to taste
- $^{1}/_{8}$ teaspoon of pepper

DIRECTIONS:

1. Cook the farfalle according to the package instructions. Allow to cool for 10 minutes.
2. Mix the salad dressing ingredients together
3. Add the pimento, artichokes, red onion and parsley to the salad dressing and pour onto the farfalle. Mix well.
4. Cool before serving.

Nutritional information
Serving size: 1 cup. Per serving: 23 g grain carbohydrate, 26 g total carbohydrate, 178 cals, 6 g fat, 1 g saturated fat, 2 g fiber, 265 mg sodium.

Quick Chili

■ **COOKING TIME** 25 minutes   ■ **SERVES** 11

This is a very versatile dish. It tastes equally good cold as a salad, as a filling in a pita or taco, or served warm as a vegetarian main or side dish. As a pita or taco filling, cover it with grated cheese, vegetables such as lettuce and chopped tomatoes, and pour a taco dressing on top.

- 1 tablespoon of olive oil
- 3 onions, chopped
- 1 carrot, chopped
- 2 cloves of garlic, minced
- 3-4 teaspoons of chili powder
- 1 teaspoon of ground cumin
- 1 28-oz can plus 1 14-oz can of chopped tomatoes, with juice
- 1 teaspoon of brown sugar, packed
- 2 15-oz cans of red kidney beans, drained and rinsed (equivalent to $1^1/_3$ cups of dried beans)
- $^1/_3$ cup of bulgur

DIRECTIONS:

1. Heat the oil over medium heat in large saucepan. Add the onions, carrots, garlic, chili powder and cumin, and sauté for 5-7 minutes or until the onions and carrots are soft.
2. Add the tomatoes with their juice and the brown sugar, and cook for 5 minutes over high heat.
3. Stir in the beans and bulgur and reduce heat to low.
4. Simmer the chili uncovered for 15 minutes or until thickened.

> Nutritional information
> Serving size: ¾ cup. Per serving: 15 g bean and grain carbohydrate, 25 g total carbohydrate, 132 cals, 2 g fat, 0 gm sat fat, 6 g fiber, 519 mg sodium.

Chicken Wraps

■ **COOKING TIME** 22 minutes   ■ **SERVES** 8

Your family will rave about this recipe. It's very filling and makes an excellent snack or meal.

- 3 boneless skinned chicken breasts halved
- ¼ cup of red onion, chopped
- ½ cup of healthy mayonnaise, e.g. canola based
- 6 tablespoons of honey mustard
- 2 celery ribs, thinly sliced
- ½ cup of chopped cashews
- 1 tablespoon of red wine vinegar
- ¼ teaspoon of salt
- Dash of pepper
- 8 6-inch whole wheat tortillas

DIRECTIONS:
1. Boil the chicken in enough water to cover for about 20 minutes, until no longer pink inside.
2. In a bowel, combine the mayonnaise, mustard, vinegar, salt and pepper. Stir in the chicken, celery and cashews.
3. Spoon the mixture into each of the tortillas and roll up the tortilla.
4. Warm the tortillas for a few minutes in the oven.

Nutritional information
Serving size: 1 tortilla. 33 g total carbohydrate, 344 cals, 23 g fat, 3 gm sat fat, 5 g fiber, 773 mg sodium.

Chapter 14

Satisfying Soups

Home-made soups are the perfect way for increasing your family's intake of vegetables. They are also very filling, especially if they are thick or contain whole vegetables. This is not just my opinion. Scientists have studied the matter and it is indeed the case.

If your family is unsatisfied with the portion sizes you are giving them and are frequently requesting doubles, start a meal with a soup course. If they like the soup – give them seconds. It often works. Home-made soups also make wonderful between-meal snacks.

For the purposes of this diet, clear soups containing vegetables but no grains are considered "free items". For thick soups, the entire carbohydrate content is counted.

Split Pea and Barley Soup

■ **COOKING TIME** 70 minutes ■ **SERVES** 9

This soup is irresistible - kids and adults will love it. It's also very filling.

- 1½ cups of dried split peas
- ½ cup of uncooked barley
- ½ medium onion, chopped
- 1 large carrot, peeled and diced
- 1 stalk of celery, diced
- 1 large clove of garlic, diced
- 7 cups of chicken broth, preferably low-sodium, divided
- 1 cup of water (or more if needed)
- ¼ teaspoon of oregano
- Salt to taste
- White pepper to taste

DIRECTIONS:

1. In a large saucepan, combine the split peas, onion, carrot, celery, garlic and 6 cups of broth and bring the ingredients to a boil.
2. Reduce the heat to low, and simmer the mixture in an uncovered pan for 1 hour, stirring it occasionally. If the liquid gets too low, add more water to prevent scorching.
3. Meanwhile, in a small covered saucepan, cook the barley in the remaining 1 cup of broth plus 1 cup of water over a low heat for 40 to 60 minutes or until the barley is tender.
4. When the vegetable mixture is done, puree it using an immersion blender.
5. Return the puree to the saucepan, and stir in the barley, herb seasoning and white pepper.
6. Heat the soup over a low heat, stirring it often before serving it.

> Nutritional information
> Serving size: 1 cup. Per serving: 25 g total carbohydrate, 156 cals, 2 g fat, 0 g saturated fat, 9 g fiber, 66 mg sodium.

Zucchini-Tomato Soup

■ **COOKING TIME** 20 minutes　　■ **SERVES** 6

This is a very tasty, easy-to-make, fairly low-carb soup.

- 1 medium onion, chopped
- 2 cloves of garlic, minced
- 2 medium zucchinis, chopped
- 1 medium potato, sliced
- 2 cups of chicken broth, preferably low-sodium, divided
- 1 large tomato, chopped
- 1 cup of milk, rice milk or soy milk
- ¾ teaspoon of basil
- ½ teaspoon of salt or to taste
- ¼ teaspoon of pepper

DIRECTIONS:

1. In a large pot, combine the onion, garlic, zucchini, potato, and 1½ cups of broth. Bring to a boil, and then cover and simmer for 15 minutes.
2. Add the tomato and simmer for 5 minutes longer.
3. Partially puree the mixture with an immersion blender only enough to leave chunks of vegetable remaining.
4. Add the milk, basil, salt, pepper and remaining broth.

Nutritional information (with whole milk)
Serving size: just over 1 cup. Per serving: 14 g total carbohydrate, 80 cals, 2 g fat, 1 g saturated fat, 2 g fiber, 405 mg sodium.

Free item!

Easy Vegetable Soup

- **COOKING TIME** 40 minutes
- **SERVES** 8½

You can't beat a soup like this for encouraging your family to eat more vegetables.

- 3 cups of chicken broth, preferably low salt
- 1 cup of water
- 2 cups of canned diced tomatoes
- 1 onion, coarsely chopped
- 1 large or 2 small cloves of garlic, finely chopped
- 2 stalks of celery, finely chopped
- 2 carrots, peeled and sliced
- 1½ cups of fresh or thawed frozen corn kernels
- 3 medium zucchini, sliced
- 2 tablespoons of fresh parsley, chopped
- ½ teaspoon of chili powder
- Pinch of cayenne
- ¼ teaspoon of salt or to taste
- $\frac{1}{8}$ teaspoon of pepper
- (Variations: sliced turnips, broccoli, asparagus or green peppers can be added with the zucchini).

DIRECTIONS:

1. In a large soup pot, combine the broth, water, tomatoes, onion, garlic, celery, carrots and seasonings. Bring to a boil, cover and simmer for 30 minutes.
2. Add the corn, zucchini and parsley and continue to simmer for an additional 10 minutes.

Nutritional information
Serving size: 1 cup. Per serving: 15 g total carbohydrate, 72 cals, 1 g fat, 0 g sat fat, 3 g fiber, 370 mg sodium

Tangy Vegetable Soup

■ **COOKING TIME** 20 minutes   ■ **SERVES** 7

This vegetable soup has a wonderfully tangy taste. It's also very easy to make.

- 1 medium onion, diced
- 3 stalks of celery, diced
- ½ cup of green beans, frozen or fresh
- ½ cup of peas, frozen or fresh
- 2 carrots, diced
- 1 leek, diced
- 1 14½-oz can of diced tomatoes
- 1 tablespoon of olive oil
- 1½ tablespoon of tomato puree or tomato ketchup
- 2 oz of dried pasta
- ⅛ teaspoon of pepper
- ¼ teaspoon of salt or to taste
- 1½ teaspoon of Italian seasoning
- 4½ cups of boiling water

DIRECTIONS:

1. In a large skillet, heat the oil and fry the onions, leeks and celery gently for 5 minutes, stirring if required.
2. Add the can of tomatoes, tomato puree, beans, carrots and frozen peas. Bring to the boil and add the pasta, herbs, salt and pepper.
3. Reduce the heat and simmer for 15 minutes or so until the pasta is cooked.

Nutritional information
Serving size: 1cup. Per serving: 6 g pasta carbohydrate, 20 g
total carbohydrate, 110 cals, 2 g fat, saturated fat 0 g fiber, 381
mg sodium.

Red Lentil Soup

- **COOKING TIME** 30 minutes   - **SERVES** 7

This is another tasty soup.   Appearances are important, so use red lentils and red pepper for the best color effect.

- 1½ cups of uncooked red lentils
- 6 cups of water
- 3 bay leaves
- 4 cloves of garlic, chopped
- 2 slices of fresh ginger, each about the size of a quarter
- 2 medium carrots, grated
- 1 cup of canned chopped tomatoes, un-drained, or 1 large fresh tomato, chopped
- 1 small sweet red or green pepper, finely chopped
- 1½ cups of onion or 1 large onion, finely chopped
- 2 tablespoons of olive oil
- 1½ teaspoons of ground cumin
- 1½ teaspoons of ground coriander
- Pinch of cayenne pepper
- 2 tablespoons of fresh lemon juice
- ½ teaspoon of salt or to taste
- Pepper to taste

DIRECTIONS:

1. In a skillet, sauté the onions and garlic in the olive oil for about 10 minutes or until browned.
2. Add the cumin, coriander and cayenne and sauté for another minute.
3. In a large pot, combine the water, lentils, bay leaves, garlic, ginger, carrots, tomatoes and pepper. Bring to a boil, stir, and then simmer covered for 20 minutes until the lentils are tender.
4. Remove the bay leaves and ginger from the soup.
5. Stir in the onions and lemon juice.
6. Add salt and pepper to taste.

Nutritional information
Serving size: just over 1 cup. Per serving: 33 g total carbohydrate, 212 cals, 5 g fat, 6 g fiber, 193 mg sodium.

Sweet Potato Soup

- **COOKING TIME** 45 minutes ■ **SERVES** 12

- 4 large sweet potatoes, unpeeled but quartered (care with the fingers!)
- 1 large onion, chopped
- 3 cups of carrots or 6 large carrots, peeled and chopped
- 1 cup of celery stalks or 2 stalks, chopped
- 5 cups of chicken broth, preferably low sodium
- 1 tablespoon of olive oil
- ½ teaspoon of dried oregano
- ½ teaspoon of dried thyme
- 1 pinch of nutmeg
- ½ teaspoon of ground cumin
- 1 teaspoon of salt or to taste
- $1/8$ teaspoon of pepper or to taste

DIRECTIONS:

1. Fill a large pot with enough water to cover the quartered sweet potatoes and add 1 teaspoon of salt to the water. Bring to a low boil and cook until tender.
2. Drain the potatoes and water from the pot.
3. When the potatoes have cooled, remove the potato skins by hand and put aside the sweet potato.
4. Sauté the carrots, onions and celery in a large (or the same) pot.
5. Add the broth, sweet potatoes and seasonings. Bring to a full boil and simmer for 40 minutes. You may need up to add 1 cup of water if the consistency is too thick.
6. With an immersion blender, puree the soup until it is almost smooth.

Nutritional information
Serving size: 1 cup. Per serving: 15 g total carbohydrate,
83 cals, 2 g fat, 0 g sat fat, 3 g fiber, 277 mg sodium.

Pumpkin and Corn Soup

- **COOKING TIME** 15 minutes ■ **SERVES** 6

This has been voted a yummy soup.

- 2 tablespoons of olive oil
- 1 small onion, minced
- 1 10-oz package of frozen whole kernel corn
- 1 16-oz can of pumpkin
- 1½ cups of water
- 1 tablespoon of sugar
- 1 teaspoon of salt or to taste
- ⅛ teaspoon of ground cinnamon
- 2 chicken-flavored bouillon cubes, preferably low-salt
- 2 cups of milk
- 1 tablespoon of chopped parsley for garnish

DIRECTIONS:

1. Cook the onion in the olive oil until tender over a medium heat.
2. Add the frozen corn and cook for 2 to 3 minutes until the corn is just tender.
3. Stir in the pumpkin, water, sugar, salt, cinnamon and bouillon until blended and mixture begins to boil. Cook for 5 minutes to blend the flavors.
4. Stir in the milk and heat through. (Do not boil after adding the mix or the mixture will curdle).
5. Serve and garnish with chopped parsley.

> Nutritional information (with whole milk)
> Serving size: 1 cup. Per serving: 26 g total carbohydrate, 185 cals, 87 g fat, 3 g saturated fat, 4 g fiber, 436 mg sodium.

Pumpkin Soup

■ **COOKING TIME** 25 minutes   ■ **SERVES** 6

Don't throw that pumpkin away after Halloween. There are things one can do with it - make a great soup for example!

- 1 lb of pumpkin, peeled, seeded and cut into 1-inch cubes
- 3 cups of chicken broth, preferably low salt
- 1 medium potato, peeled and diced
- 1 medium onion, peeled and chopped
- ¼ teaspoon of nutmeg
- $\frac{1}{8}$ teaspoon of white pepper
- $\frac{1}{8}$ teaspoon of salt

DIRECTIONS:

1. In a large saucepan, combine the pumpkin, broth, potato and onion. Bring to a boil, reduce the heat, cover the pan and simmer the vegetables for 20 minutes.
2. Puree the mixture using an immersion blender.
3. Heat the puree just to boiling point.
4. Add the nutmeg, pepper and salt.

Nutritional information
Per serving: 21.8 g carbohydrate, 110 cals, 1.2 g fat, 5.8 g fiber, 441 mg sodium.

Chickpea and Green Bean Soup

■ **COOKING TIME** 35 minutes   ■ **SERVES** 8

This soup has a special flavor all of its own. It usually doesn't last long..

- 1 15-oz can of chickpeas
- 2 cups or 1 large sweet potato, peeled and chopped
- 1 cup of frozen green beans
- ½ cup of celery, chopped
- 3 cups of chicken broth, preferably low-salt
- 2 cloves of garlic, minced
- 2 cups or large onion, chopped
- 1 14½-oz can of diced tomato or 1 cup of fresh tomatoes, chopped
- ¾ cup of sweet peppers, chopped
- 3 tablespoons of olive oil
- 1 tablespoon of soy sauce
- 2 teaspoons of paprika
- 1 teaspoon of basil
- 1 teaspoon of salt
- 1 teaspoon of turmeric
- 1 bay leaf
- Dash of cinnamon
- Dash of cayenne pepper

DIRECTIONS:

1. In a large saucepan, sauté the onions, garlic, celery and sweet potatoes in olive oil for 5 minutes.
2. Add the seasonings and chicken broth, and simmer covered for 15 minutes.
3. Add the remaining vegetables, chickpeas and soy sauce, bring to the boil, and simmer for another 10 minutes until the vegetables are tender.

> Nutritional information
> Serving size: 1 cup. Per serving: 19 g bean and potato carbohydrate,
> 27 g total carbohydrate, 184 cals, 6 g fat, 1 g saturated fat, 5 g fiber,
> 423 mg sodium.

Cold Beet Soup

■ **COOKING TIME** 75 minutes   ■ **SERVES** 8

Beet soup may not be on the top of your list of soups to try out. But this soup is well worth the experiment. It has a refreshing sweet taste.

- 2 lb of beets, peeled and cut into 1-inch pieces
- 1 cup of chopped onion
- 2 cups of thinly sliced celery
- 2 tablespoons of olive oil
- 2 teaspoons of sugar
- Pepper to taste
- 1-2 tablespoons of red vinegar to taste
- 4 cups of chicken broth, preferably low-salt

DIRECTIONS:

1. Sauté the onion and celery together with the sugar and pepper for about 10 minutes until soft.
2. In a large soup pot, add the beets, vinegar and broth and simmer covered for 1 to 1¼ hours until the beets are very tender.
3. Puree the soup mixture.
4. Cover, refrigerate and serve cold.

Nutritional information
Serving size: 1 cup. Per serving: 7 g total carbohydrate, 75 cals, 4 g fat, 1 g saturated fat, 1 g fiber, 77 mg sodium.

Gazpacho

This is a refreshing cold soup that's chock full of natural antioxidants. It's ideal for a hot summer day.

- 4 cups of tomato juice, preferably with no added salt
- 1 small onion, diced
- 2 cups of fresh tomatoes, diced
- 1 green pepper, diced
- 1 teaspoon of honey
- 1 clove of garlic, crushed
- 1 cucumber, diced
- 2 scallions, chopped
- ¼ cup of parsley, chopped
- Juice of ½ lemon or 1½ tablespoons of lemon juice
- Juice of 1 lime or 1½ tablespoons of lime juice
- 2 tablespoons of wine vinegar
- 1 teaspoon of tarragon
- 1 teaspoon of basil
- Dash of cumin
- ½ teaspoon of salt
- $^1/_8$ teaspoon of pepper
- Dash of Tabasco sauce (optional)

DIRECTIONS:

2. Combine all the ingredients.
3. Blend the ingredients with an immersion blender, leaving enough solid vegetables for a chunky consistency. (Make sure to keep the blender vertical, otherwise the gazpacho will splash all over you)
4. Chill for at least 2 hours.

> Nutritional information
> Serving size: 1 cup. Per serving: 6 g sugar carbohydrate (tomato juice), 12 g total carbohydrate, 52 cals, 0 g fat, 2 g fiber, 187 mg sodium.

Chapter 15

Encouraging Fish

Fish, and particularly fatty fish, are an extremely healthy food because of their high omega-3 fat content. From a health perspective, fish is many times better than meat. However, for many American families, fish has to be approached in the same way as vegetables. It has to be packaged in a tasty and attractive way, otherwise it just won't get eaten.

A word of caution is appropriate. Fish, and this is particularly the case for fatty fish, is susceptible to contamination with pollutants and heavy metals such as mercury. Nevertheless, for most people the health benefits of eating fish outweigh by far the theoretical risk of slight contamination. However, if you eat a lot of local freshwater fish, you would be advised to check on its source and status. Also, young children, and pregnant and breast-feeding women are advised to avoid large predatory fish such as shark, tilefish and king mackerel, and to limit their intake of albacore tuna. To be on the safe side, the government advises pregnant women and young children to limit their intake of tuna to less than 12 oz a week.

Honey Salmon

■ **COOKING TIME** 25 minutes   ■ **SERVES** 2

It can be difficult sometimes to get non-fish lovers to change their ways. This quick and easy recipe has almost a 100% success rate!

- 1 lb of fresh salmon
- 1½ tablespoons of honey mustard
- 1 tablespoon of honey

DIRECTIONS:

1. Preheat the oven to 350ºF.
2. Cover the top of the salmon with the honey mustard and honey.
3. Place in the oven at 350ºF and bake for 25 minutes.

Nutritional information
Serving size: 6 oz salmon steak. Per serving: 11 g sugar carbohydrate, 11 g total carbohydrate, 458 cals, 25 g fat, 5 g saturated fat, 0 g fiber, 202 mg sodium.

Salmon Pie

■ **COOKING TIME** 35 minutes   ■ **SERVES** 8

This recipe is one of our family favorites. The first part of the recipe is for a 2 crust pie.

Pie crust:
- 1 cup of stone ground whole wheat flour
- 1 cup of white flour
- 1 teaspoon of salt
- ½ cup of canola oil
- 5 tablespoons of ice water

Filling:
- 1 14^3/$_4$-oz can of pink salmon, drained, broken into pieces
- 2 tablespoons of canola oil
- ¾ cup of frozen peas
- 2 tablespoons of stone ground whole wheat flour
- 1 cup of milk
- 1 egg yolk, slightly beaten, or egg substitute
- 1 teaspoon of salt or to taste
- ¼ teaspoon of pepper
- 4-oz can of pimentos, coarsely chopped

DIRECTIONS:

1. In a large bowl, combine the flour and salt for the pie crust. Whisk together the oil and ice water until it has the appearance of whipping cream.
2. Add the dry ingredients. Mix well with a fork or pastry cutter.
3. Divide into two parts. Roll between two pieces of wax paper. (Hint: the wax paper will stay on the counter if the counter is made wet. The wax paper sometimes needs to be torn off the dough in strips.)
4. Line the pan with half of the pastry dough.
5. For the filling, melt the butter in a 2-quart saucepan. Blend in the flour and milk. Cook until thick, stirring constantly. Stir in the salmon, pimentos, peas and seasoning.
6. Pour the filling into the pastry-lined pan.
7. Cover with the remaining dough and seal the edges. Cut slits for the steam to escape.
8. Bake at 450°F for 10 minutes and then at 400°F for 20-25 minutes until golden brown.

> Nutritional information
> Serving size: ^{1}/$_8$th of the pie. Per serving: 26 g grain and sugar carbohydrate, 27 g total carbohydrate, 375 cals, 22 g fat, 3 g saturated fat, 3 g fiber, 350 mg sodium.

Salmon Pasta

■ **COOKING TIME** 6 minutes   ■ **SERVES** 4

This is a delicious and very Mediterranean-style dish that's easy and quick to make. Highly recommended!

- 8 oz of uncooked linguine
- 2 salmon fillets (16 oz), cut into 1-inch cubes
- 1 teaspoon of minced fresh rosemary or ½ teaspoon of dried rosemary
- 5 tablespoons of olive oil, divided
- 2 medium-sized tomatoes, chopped
- 5 garlic cloves, minced
- ½ teaspoon of salt or to taste
- $^1/_8$ teaspoon of pepper

DIRECTIONS:

1. Cook linguine according to the package directions. Drain the linguine and place in a bowl.
2. Cut the salmon into small 1-inch cubes, peeling off any skin.
3. In a large skillet, sauté the salmon cubes and rosemary in 2 tablespoons of oil for 5 minutes or until the salmon flakes easily with a fork.
4. Add the tomatoes, garlic, salt and pepper to the salmon and cook for 1 minute.
5. Add the linguine to the salmon mixture and toss gently.
6. Drizzle the remaining 3 tablespoons of oil over the mixture (if you find this too oily, use only 2 tablespoons of oil).

Nutritional information
Serving size: ¼ of the dish. Per serving: 30 g grain carbohydrate, 34 g total carbohydrate, 519 cals, 30 g fat, 5 g saturated fat, 2 g fiber, 380 mg sodium.

Free item!

Microwaved Poached Salmon with Sour Cream Sauce

- **COOKING TIME** 14 minutes   - **SERVES** 2

This is a classy recipe.

- 4 6-oz salmon steaks
- 1½ cups of hot water
- 2 peppercorns
- 1 lemon, thinly sliced
- 1 bay leaf
- 1 teaspoon of instant minced onion
- 1 teaspoon of salt or to taste
- ⅓ cup of dry wine (optional)

Sauce:
- ½ cup of sour cream
- 1 tablespoon of finely chopped parsley
- 1 teaspoon of lemon juice
- ½ teaspoon of dill weed
- Pinch of white pepper

DIRECTIONS:

1. In an oval microwave baking dish, pour the water and wine. Add the peppercorns, lemon, bay leaf, onion and salt.
2. Microwave on High for approximately 5 minutes or until it reaches a full boil.
3. Carefully place the salmon steaks in the hot liquid. Microwave, covered with plastic wrap, on High for approximately 2 to 3 minutes or until the fish becomes opaque.
4. Let the steaks stand for about 5 minutes to finish cooking.
5. To prepare the sauce, mix all the ingredients in a small bowl. Cook on 80% power for 3 to 4 minutes or until hot.
6. Drain the salmon and serve with the heated sauce.

Nutritional information
Serving size: 6 oz salmon steak. Per serving: 1 g total carbohydrate, 75 cals, 7 g fat, 4 g saturated fat, 0 g fiber, 20 g sodium.

Baked Salmon with Herbs and Rice

■ **COOKING TIME** 40 minutes   ■ **SERVES** 4

- 1 cup of brown rice, dried
- 1½ cups of water
- 1 lb of salmon fillets
- ¼ cup of orange juice
- 1 teaspoon of dried dill weed
- 1 teaspoon of dried rosemary
- 1 teaspoon of dried basil
- 1 teaspoon of ground mustard
- 1 teaspoon of lemon pepper

DIRECTIONS:

1. In a small saucepan, bring 2½ cups of water to boil. Add the rice and stir. Reduce heat, cover and simmer for 20 minutes. Set aside.
2. Preheat the oven to 350°F.
3. In a large baking pan, add enough water to just cover the bottom of the pan. Lay the salmon fillet in the pan, pink side up. Place cooked rice around the outside of the fish. Sprinkle the orange juice over the fish and rice.
4. In a small bowl, combine the dill weed, rosemary, basil, mustard, lemon pepper and sprinkle over the fish and rice.
5. Cover with aluminum foil.
6. Bake in the preheated oven for 30-40 minutes or until the salmon is tender and flaky.

Nutritional information
Serving size: ¼ of the dish. Per serving: 39 g total carbohydrate, 346 cals, 9 g fat, 1 g saturated fat, 2 g fiber, 53 mg sodium.

Grilled or Baked Salmon with Vinaigrette

- **COOKING TIME** 20 minutes   - **SERVES** 4

Salmon is such a versatile fish in terms of how one can cook it. This is an easy, very gourmet recipe. If you want to skip the fanciness, leave out the spinach and orange slices.

- 4 6-oz salmon fillets
- 2 tablespoons of lemon juice
- 1 teaspoon of pepper
- 6 oz of fresh spinach
- 4 oranges, sliced

Vinaigrette:
- ¼ cup of orange juice
- 2 tablespoons of olive oil
- 2 tablespoons of balsamic vinegar, preferably rice vinegar
- ½ teaspoon of honey mustard
- ½ teaspoon of pepper
- 1 clove of garlic, minced

DIRECTIONS:

1. Drizzle the lemon juice over salmon and sprinkle with the pepper.
2. Grill or bake until done.
3. Arrange 4 plates with the spinach, orange slices and salmon and pour the dressing on top.

Nutritional information
Serving size: 6 oz salmon steak. Per serving: 3 g sugar carbohydrate, 30 g total carbs, 426 cals, 18 g fat, 3 g saturated fat, 8 g fiber, 117 g sodium.

Salmon Patties with Spinach

■ **COOKING TIME** 10 minutes   ■ **SERVES** 13

- ½ cup of dried couscous
- $^2/_3$ cup of orange juice
- 1 14¾ -oz can of red salmon, drained
- 1 10-oz package of frozen chopped spinach - thawed, drained and squeezed dry
- 2 egg yolks, beaten
- 2 cloves garlic, crushed
- 3 tablespoons of olive oil
- 1 teaspoon of ground cumin
- ½ teaspoon of ground black pepper
- ½ teaspoon of salt or to taste

DIRECTIONS:

1. Prepare the couscous according to the package directions, but instead of water use $^2/_3$ cup of orange juice.
2. In a bowl, combine all the ingredients except for the olive oil and form into patties.
3. In a large skillet, heat the olive oil over medium heat and fry the patties until golden brown for about 8 to 10 minutes, turning once.

> Nutritional information
> Serving size: 1 pattie (2½"x ½"). Per serving: 6 g sugar and grain carbohydrate, 8 g total carbohydrate, 120 cals, 6 g fat, 1 g saturated fat, 1 g fiber, 132 mg sodium.

Tuna Patties

■ **COOKING TIME** 5 minutes   ■ **SERVES** 10

This fish recipe is a good one for kids.

- 15-oz can of canned tuna in water
- ½ onion, chopped fine
- ½ cup of whole wheat flour, preferably stone-ground, divided
- 1 egg or egg substitute
- 3 to 5 tablespoons of olive oil for frying

DIRECTIONS:

1. Mix the ingredients together with ¼ cup of the flour.
2. Make into patties.
3. Cover each patty with the remaining flour.
4. Fry in olive oil until slightly brown.

Nutritional information
Serving size: 1 patty. Per serving: 5 g total carbohydrate, 121 cals,
8 g fat, 1 g saturated fat, 1 g fiber, 188 mg sodium.

Microwaved Tuna Casserole

■ **COOKING TIME** 12 minutes ■ **SERVES** 4

Even if tuna is overplayed in your house, you should try this recipe. It's really good served over rice.

- 2 tablespoons of butter
- 2 tablespoons of whole wheat flour, preferably stone ground
- ½ teaspoon of salt or to taste
- ¼ teaspoon of dry mustard
- $\frac{1}{8}$ teaspoon of pepper
- 1 cup of milk
- ½ cup of shredded Cheddar cheese
- 1 6½-oz can of chunk light tuna, drained
- 1 stalk of celery, thinly sliced
- ¼ cup of onion, chopped
- ½ a medium green pepper, cut into ¼ x 1-inch strips
- 1 cup of basmati or other rice, uncooked
- 1 4-oz can of mushroom stems and pieces, drained (optional)
- ¼ cup of sliced almonds (optional)

DIRECTIONS:

1. Cook the rice according to the package instructions.
2. In a 1-quart casserole dish, melt the butter in the microwave on high for 30 to 45 seconds.
3. Blend in the flour, salt, mustard and pepper. Stir in the milk.
4. Microwave for 4½ to 7 minutes, or until thickened, interrupting the microwaving to stir every minute.
5. Stir in the cheese until melted. Add the tuna, and mushrooms if desired.
6. In a 2-quart casserole dish, place the celery, onion and green pepper and cover the dish.
7. Microwave for 2½ to 3½ minutes on high or until tender-crisp.
8. Stir in the cheese sauce.
9. Microwave uncovered for 2½ to 3½ minutes on high or until thoroughly heated.
10. Sprinkle with almonds (optional).
11. Serve over the rice.

> Nutritional information (with whole milk)
> Serving size: ¼ of the dish. Per serving: 43 g grain and milk carbohydrate, 44 g total carbohydrate, 395 cals, 15 g fat, 8 g saturated fat, 1 g fiber, 598 mg sodium.

Free item!

Fish Cheese Puff

■ **COOKING TIME** 30 minutes   ■ **SERVES** 4

Cheese and fish might seem an unusual combination, but they go well together in this recipe.

- 1 lb of fillet (e.g. sole or flounder), with skin removed
- ½ cup of milk
- ½ cup of shredded Cheddar cheese
- 2 eggs, with the white and yolks separated
- 1 tablespoon of onion, finely chopped
- ¼ teaspoon of salt or to taste

DIRECTIONS:

1. Heat oven to 350 °F.
2. Grease an 11 x 7 inch baking dish. Arrange fillets, slightly overlapping. Set aside.
3. In a large mixing bowl, combine the milk, cheese, egg yokes, onion and salt. Set aside.
4. In a medium mixing bowl, beat the egg whites with a mixer at high speed until stiff but not dry.
5. Gently fold the egg whites into the milk mixture. Spread the mixture evenly over the fillets.
6. Bake at 350ºF for 25 to 30 minutes, or until the fish is firm and opaque and just begins to flake and the puff is light golden brown.

Nutritional information
Serving size: 4 oz fillet of fish. Per serving: 1 g total carbohydrate, 135 cals, 6 g fat, 3 g saturated fat, 0 g fiber, 333 mg sodium.

Spanish Style Fish

■ **COOKING TIME** 40 minutes ■ **SERVES** 6

There's no "fishy taste" about this dish. It's a winning recipe even for kids.

- 6 fillet of fish (e.g. sole or flounder)
- ¼ cup of olive oil
- 1 large onion, chopped
- 1 green pepper, chopped
- 1 clove garlic, finely chopped
- ¼ cup of stone ground whole wheat flour
- 2 cups of tomato juice, preferably low salt
- Salt to taste
- Pepper to taste

DIRECTIONS:

1. Preheat the oven to 350°F.
2. Place the fish in a 9 x 13 inch pan.
3. In a medium-size skillet, sauté the onion, pepper and garlic in the olive oil.
4. Add the flour, tomato juice, salt and pepper.
5. Pour this mixture over the fish.
6. Bake the fish in the oven for 30-40 minutes at 350°F.

Nutritional information
Serving size: 1 4-oz fillet. Per serving: 11 g total carbohydrate, 356 cals, 13 g fat, 2 g saturated fat, 2 g fiber, 237 mg sodium.

Rolled Fish

■ **COOKING TIME** 50 minutes ■ **SERVE** 4

One way to make fish attractive to non-fish-eating families is to make the dish different from preconceived notions of what a fish dish should be like. With the toothpicks and tomato sauce, this often does the trick.

- 1 lb fillet of fish (e.g. sole or flounder)
- 1½ cups of celery, chopped
- 1 large onion, chopped
- $\frac{1}{3}$ cup of seasoned bread crumbs
- 8-oz can of tomato sauce
- Salt to taste
- Pepper to taste
- 8 oz of mushroom (optional)

DIRECTIONS:

1. Preheat the oven to 350°F.
2. Sauté the celery, onion and mushroom together in a small skillet until they are soft.
3. Remove from the heat. Add bread crumbs and season to taste.
4. Spread the mixture over the fillets. Roll up the filets and place in a toothpick to hold them in shape.
5. Place the fish in a dish and pour the tomato sauce over the fish.
6. Bake at 350°F for 45 minutes.

Nutritional information
Serving size: 1 4-oz fillet. Per serving: 15 g total carbohydrate, 171 cals, 3 g fat, 1 g sat fat, 2 g fiber, 575 mg sodium.

Chapter 16

Tasty Desserts!

Including desserts in a health book might seem a contradiction in terms, especially if they contain a hefty measure of sugar and are loaded with calories. Clearly, for those trying to lose weight these items should be avoided, but for everyone else occasional cakes and cookies are a part of life.

Nevertheless, an important point is being made in this section, namely that even cakes and cookies can be made in a way that minimizes non-healthful high-glycemic ingredients and maximizes healthful ones, such as nuts, whole wheat flour and whole grains. If your family is sneaking from the cookie jar, at least make sure the cookies are as healthy as you can make them!

Even with the best of intentions, though, one does come up against reality. It would be nice, for example, if one could use whole wheat flour instead of white flour for baking cakes, but unfortunately they usually do not rise well when made like this and one often has to use a mixture of white and whole wheat flour instead. It would also be nice if one could substitute canola oil for butter, margarine and shortening, but this also doesn't work well a lot of the time.

My own opinion is that if one keeps to an otherwise low-glycemic Mediterranean-style meal plan most of the time, butter and cream for occasional desserts are fine. The French have been eating like this for years and have far less heart disease than Americans. A moderate amount of eggs should also present no problem to individuals who have normal cholesterol levels and are not at high-risk for coronary disease.

Nutty Fruit Salad

■ **COOKING TIME** 3 minutes   ■ **SERVES** 4

I can think of two ways for encouraging your family to eat more fruit. One is to hand them some fruit. But if you find this doesn't work (and even if it does), making a fruit salad is a wonderful alternative. There are as many variations in this recipe as there are fruit and berries in the store, but this is a good one to out start with. Branch out from here!

- 1 cup of grapes, halved
- 2 oranges, cut into pieces
- 1 banana, sliced
- 2 kiwis, sliced
- $1/3$ cup of walnuts, broken into small bits
- $1/3$ cup of orange juice
- ¼ teaspoon of cinnamon
- $1/8$ teaspoon of nutmeg

DIRECTIONS:

1. In a small skillet toast the walnuts (without any oil) until they are just turning brown.
2. Mix all the ingredients in a large bowl, including the walnuts.
3. Serve chilled.

Nutritional information
Serving size: 1 cup. Per serving: 3 g sugar and nut carbohydrate, 31 g total carbohydrate, 183 cals, 7 g fat, 1 g saturated fat, 5 g fiber, 3 mg sodium.

Bran Muffins with Raisins

- **COOKING TIME** 20 minutes
- **SERVES** 12 muffins

Nothing much is achieved by leaving a meal feeling hungry. It's just an invitation for after-meal snacking. This is where a tasty muffin can be extremely handy if it's full of quality and filling grains. Like this muffin for example.

- 1½ cups of 100% bran cereal
- 1 cup of milk (or 1 cup of rice milk plus 1 tablespoon of white vinegar for a dairy-free recipe)
- 1 egg
- ¼ cup of canola oil
- ½ cup of whole wheat flour, preferably stone ground
- ½ cup of white flour
- 2½ teaspoons of baking powder
- ½ teaspoon of baking soda
- ½ cup of raisins
- ½ cup of granulated sugar

DIRECTIONS:

1. Preheat the oven to 400°F.
2. Mix the bran cereal and milk (or milk substitute) and let stand for 5 minutes. (If the bran does not at least partially dissolve, then find another form of bran.)
3. Add the egg and oil.
4. To this mixture, add the flour, sugar, baking powder, baking soda and raisins.
5. Fill about 12 muffin cups to a bit below the top of the cup and bake for 20 minutes at 400°F.

> Nutritional information
> Serving size: 1 cupcake: 28 g total carbohydrate, 164 cals, 6 g fat, 1 g saturated fat, 4 g fiber, 190 mg sodium.

Banana Muffins

- **COOKING TIME** 25 minutes   ■ **SERVES** 12 muffins

The picture might look the same, but these taste very different from the previous recipe.

- ½ cup of whole wheat flour, preferably stone ground
- ½ cup of white flour
- 2 teaspoons of baking powder
- ½ teaspoon of salt
- $^1/_3$ cup of granulated sugar
- ¼ teaspoon of cinnamon
- 1 cup of 100% bran cereal
- 1 cup of milk (or 1 cup of rice milk plus 1 tablespoon of white vinegar for a dairy-free recipe)
- 1 large mashed banana
- 1 egg or egg substitute
- 3 tablespoons of canola oil
- ½ cup of walnuts
- ½ cup of raisins (optional)

DIRECTIONS:

1. Preheat the over to 350°F.
2. In a large bowl, mix the beaten egg, bran, milk, mashed banana, and oil. Let the mixture soak for 5 minutes.
3. Add the flour, sugar, baking powder, salt and cinnamon.
4. Add the walnuts and raisins (if desired).
5. Fill about 12 muffin cups to a bit below the top of the cup.
6. Bake at 350°F for 25 minutes.

Nutritional information (without the raisins)
Serving size: 1 cupcake: 22 g total carbohydrate, 158 cals, 8 g fat, 1 g
saturated fat, 3 g fiber, 207 mg sodium.

Apple Muffins

■ **COOKING TIME** 20 minutes   ■ **SERVES** 12 muffins

- ¾ cup of milk (or ¾ cup of rice milk with ¾ tablespoon of vinegar for a dairy-free recipe)
- ½ cup of maple sugar
- 2 egg whites, eggs or egg substitute
- 1 tablespoon of canola oil
- ½ cup of grated tart apple
- ½ cup of shredded carrot
- ¾ cup of whole wheat flour, preferably stone ground
- ½ cup of wheat bran
- ¼ cup of all-purpose flour
- 3 tablespoons of granulated sugar
- 1 teaspoon of baking powder
- 1 teaspoon of baking soda
- ½ teaspoon of salt
- ½ teaspoon of ground cinnamon

DIRECTIONS:

1. Preheat the oven to 375°F.
2. In a large bowl, beat the milk, syrup, eggs and oil until smooth.
3. Stir in the apple and carrot.
4. Combine the dry ingredients, and stir them into the milk mixture just until moistened.
5. Coat the muffin cups with nonstick cooking spray and fill until two-thirds full.
6. Bake at 375°F for 20 minutes.

Nutritional information
Serving size: 1 cupcake: 23 g total carbohydrate, 2 g fat, 0 g saturated fat, 270 cals, 2 g fiber, 233 mg sodium.

Pear Muffins

■ **COOKING TIME** 20 minutes ■ **SERVES** 18 muffins

Each of these muffin recipes is a treat.

- 4 large pears, peeled and cored
- 1 cup of sugar
- ½ cup of canola oil
- 2 large eggs, beaten
- 2 teaspoons of vanilla extract
- 2 cups of stone ground whole wheat flour
- 2 teaspoons of baking soda
- 2 teaspoons of ground cinnamon
- 1 teaspoon of ground nutmeg
- 1 teaspoon of salt
- 1 cup of raisins
- 1 cup of chopped walnuts

DIRECTIONS:

1. Preheat the oven to 375ºF.
2. Mix the pears and sugar in a medium bowl.
3. Blend the oil, eggs and vanilla in a large bowl.
4. Combine the flour, baking soda, cinnamon, nutmeg and salt in another medium bowl.
5. Stir the pear mixture into the egg mixture, and mix in the dry ingredients. Add the raisins and walnuts.
6. Coat the muffin cups with nonstick cooking spray and divide the batter among the prepared cups.
7. Bake for about 30 minutes.

> Nutritional information
> Serving size: 1 cupcake: 36 g carbohydrate, 249 cals, 11 g fat, 1 g saturated fat, 279 mg sodium.

Oatmeal Cookies

■ **COOKING TIME** 10 minutes ■ **YIELD** 5 dozen cookies

- 1½ cups of whole wheat flour, preferably stone ground
- 2 cups of rolled oats
- ½ teaspoon of baking soda
- 1 teaspoon of salt
- ½ teaspoon of ground cinnamon
- ½ teaspoon of ground nutmeg
- 1 cup of butter
- ¾ cup of granulated sugar
- ¾ cup of brown sugar
- 2 eggs, beaten, or egg substitute
- 1 cup of chopped nuts
- 1 cup of raisins

DIRECTIONS:

1. Preheat the oven to 350°F.
2. Place the raisins in hot water for 5 minutes. Drain.
3. In a large bowl, cream the butter with the sugar.
4. Add the remainder of the ingredients.
5. Drop the mixture onto a cookie sheet (keep the cookies small and separate as they tend to expand a bit).
6. Bake at 350°F for 10 minutes.

> Nutritional information
> Serving size: 1 2" diameter cookie. Per serving: 11 g total carbohydrate, 88 cals, 5 g fat, 2 g saturated fat, 1 g fiber, 46 mg sodium.

Fruit-Almond Crisp

■ **COOKING TIME** 50 minutes ■ **SERVES** 12

Topping:
- ½ cup of whole wheat flour, preferably stone ground
- 1 cup of old-fashioned oats
- ⅓ cup of firmly packed brown sugar
- ¼ teaspoon of salt
- 1 teaspoon of ground ginger
- ½ teaspoon of ground cinnamon
- ½ cup of canola oil
- 1 cup of sliced almonds

Filling:
- ¾ cup of granulated sugar
- 2 tablespoons of quick cooking tapioca or cornstarch
- 1 teaspoon of ground ginger
- pinch of salt
- 2½ lb of apricots or nectarines, pitted and diced

DIRECTIONS:

1. Preheat the oven to 350°F.
2. To make the topping, in a medium bowl, stir together all the topping contents.
3. To make the filling, in a small bowl stir together the sugar, tapioca, ginger and salt.
4. Place the apricots or nectarines in a large bowl and sprinkle with the sugar mixture and toss to distribute evenly.
5. Spread the fruit mixture in a greased 9 x 13-inch or 12-inch oval baking dish. Sprinkle the topping evenly over the fruit.
6. Bake until the topping is crisp and golden brown and the fruit-filling bubbles slowly, about 50 minutes at 350 F.
7. Serve warm or cold.

> Nutritional information
> Serving size: 1/12th of pan. Per serving: 40 g total carbohydrate, 290 cals, 14 g fat, 1 g saturated fat, 4 g fiber, 52 mg sodium.

Adapted with permission from "Williams-Sonoma Fruit Desserts" by Simon and Schuster and published by Williams-Sonoma Inc, San Francisco, CA)

Apple-Cranberry Crisp

■ **COOKING TIME** 50 minutes ■ **SERVES** 9

- 2 lb of apples, peeled, cored and thinly sliced
- ¾ cup of fresh cranberries
- ¼ cup of sugar
- 3 teaspoons of ground cinnamon
- 1 teaspoon of ground nutmeg
- $\frac{1}{3}$ cup of old fashioned rolled oats
- $\frac{1}{3}$ cup of stone ground whole wheat flour
- ½ cup of packed light brown sugar
- ¼ cup of butter or margarine, cut into pieces
- ½ cup of chopped pecans

DIRECTIONS:

1. Preheat the oven to 375°F.
2. Grease an 8-inch square baking dish.
3. In a large bowl, mix together the apples, cranberries, white sugar, cinnamon and nutmeg. Place this mixture evenly into the baking dish.
4. In the same large bowl that you used previously, combine the oats, flour and brown sugar. Then mix in the butter with a fork until the mixture is crumbly.
5. Stir in the pecans.
6. Sprinkle this over the apple mixture.
7. Bake in the oven at 375°F for 40-50 minutes or until the topping is golden brown.

Nutritional information
Serving size: $\frac{1}{9}$th of serving pan. Per serving: 49 g total
carbohydrate, 279 cals, 10 g fat, 4 g saturated fat, 5 g fiber, 2 mg

Baked Banana

■ **COOKING TIME** 1½ minutes   ■ **SERVES** 1

This is a great way for using leftover bananas that are starting to go brown.

- 1 banana
- ½ teaspoon of canola oil
- Pinch of cinnamon

DIRECTIONS:

1. Spread the cinnamon and oil on the banana.
2. Heat the banana in the microwave on High, about 1½ minutes for one banana (2½ minutes for 2 bananas) until soft and mushy.

Nutritional information
Serving size: 1 banana. Per serving: 27 g total carbohydrate, 125 cals, 3 g fat, 0 g saturated fat, 3 g fiber, 1 mg sodium.

Chapter 17

References for the Scientifically Bold

1. Why Changing Carbohydrate is so Important

1. Slyper AH. The pediatric obesity epidemic: causes and controversies. Journal of Clinical Endocrinology and Metabolism 2004;89:2540-2547

This paper covers the science on which much of this chapter is based. For many years I was intrigued by the fact that many of my obese pediatric patients didn't seem to be overeating. Either they were lying (which I really didn't believe) or something else was going on. It turns out that the government has been keeping nutritional data for decades. So I plotted it out. I found that caloric intake in kids has remained reasonably constant throughout the years, despite a marked increase in obesity. Only recently has food and caloric intake been increasing. However, if caloric intake hasn't changed, then something else must have changed. What has changed is that kids are eating less fat, more carbohydrate, and more high-glycemic carbohydrate than in years previously. They may also be exercising less, although I'm not convinced that this has been that influential in influencing the population's weight. The full article is available on line at http://jcem.endojournals.org/cgi/content/abstract/89/6/2540

2. Chaput J-P, Tremblay A, Rimm EB et al. A novel interaction between dietary composition and insulin secretion: effects on weight gain in the Quebec Family Study. American Journal of Clinical Nutrition 2008;87:303-309

276 adults who had had a baseline glucose tolerance test with insulin levels were restudied after 6 years. At the 6-year time point, body weight and waist circumference were not related to the amount of fat these subjects were eating. However, the 30-minute insulin level on the baseline glucose tolerance test was strongly related to body weight and waist circumference, especially for subjects consuming lower-fat diets. Insulin levels at 120 minutes on the baseline glucose tolerance test were inversely related to these end points, i.e. the higher the insulin level, the lower were body weight and waist circumference. The insulin level at 30 minutes is a proxy measure of insulin secretion, whereas the insulin at 120 minutes is a measure of insulin resistance. This study has therefore demonstrated a relationship between the amount of insulin that people secrete and weight gain 6 years later. The authors discuss that this may have a lot to do with the glycemia of their diet.

See also: Ludwig DS. The glycemic index – physiological mechanisms relating to obesity, diabetes, and cardiovascular disease. Journal of the American Medical Association (JAMA) 2002;287:2414-23

For those interested in the mechanisms whereby high-glycemic diets can lead to obesity and insulin resistance, this is an invaluable article. Interestingly, in the study by Chaput et al discussed above (i.e. reference 2), hypoglycemia occurring towards the end of the glucose tolerance test (known as reactive hypoglycemia) was strongly related to weight gain, especially among those in the low dietary fat group. This fits nicely into Ludwig's hypothesis that the hormonal response to a high-glycemic diet can induce insulin resistance. A low-fat diet increases the possibility that this will happen.

3. Slyper AH. The pubertal timing controversy in the USA, and a review of possible causative factors for the advance in timing of onset of puberty. Clinical Endocrinology 2006;65:1-8

Girls are maturing earlier than in the past, and early maturing girls are more likely to become obese in adolescence and adulthood. Early development of pubic hair has also become common in girls and boys and many of these children are hyperinsulinemic (even if not obese). As these girls mature, many are at risk of developing polycystic ovarian syndrome. In this paper I hypothesize that pubertal onset is

influenced by hyperinsulinemia. If this is the case, then insulin resistance may be a lot more common than previously recognized (since girls are maturing earlier than they did in the past).

4. de Lorgeril M, Salen P, Martin JL et al. Mediterranean diet, traditional risk factors, and the rate of cardiovascular complications after myocardial infarction. Final report of the Lyon Diet Heart Study. Circulation 1999:99;779-785

I've always been fascinated by the Lyon Diet Heart Study. It made quite a splash when it first came out. This report provides the final data for 4-year cardiovascular events. The "Mediterranean diet" tested was very similar to that used by Greeks in Crete, while the control or comparison diet was almost comparable to an American Heart Association "Step 1 Diet". In a Step 1 Diet, total fat is reduced to 30% and saturated fat to 10% of total calories. In actuality, fat reduction for subjects on the Mediterranean diet was a bit lower than in a Step 1 Diet, whereas dietary fat for the control subjects was cut back to only 32.7 % of total calories and saturated fat to 11.7%, so that subjects were not quite on a Step 1 Diet. It is of interest that the benefits of the Mediterranean diet had nothing to do with LDL cholesterol levels or any other blood lipid for that matter, since lipid levels were the same at the end of the study for both groups.

5. Mitrou PN, Kipnis V, Thiebaut ACM et al. Mediterranean dietary pattern and prediction of all-cause mortality in a US population. Archives of Internal Medicine 2007;167(22):2461-2468

Most people don't think of diet as having much to do with cancer. But think again. This very large 5-year prospective study used a 9-point system to assess conformity to a Mediterranean dietary pattern. A Mediterranean dietary pattern was associated with reduced mortality from all causes, including cardiovascular disease and cancer.

6. Ludwig DS, Majzoub JA, Al-Zahrani A, Dallal GE, Blanco I, Roberts SB. High glycemic foods, overeating, and obesity. Pediatrics 1999;103:E26

The investigators gave three types of breakfast and lunch to kids: high-glycemic, low-glycemic and something in between. They then let them eat however much food they wanted, and measured how hungry they felt and how much food they ate after lunch. The investigators found that hunger and food intake depended entirely on the glycemic index of the breakfast and lunch. With high-glycemic food the kids ate more and felt hungrier, and the opposite was the case with low-glycemic food. With the intermediate food, the situation was in between. The message is clear – if you want to control hunger during the day, start with a low-glycemic breakfast. In actuality, the results of this study are nothing new. Numerous studies have demonstrated that high-glycemic food influences appetite. However, this study demonstrated this in a very elegant way.

7. Simopoulos AP. The Mediterranean diets: what is so special about the diet of Greece? The scientific evidence. Journal of Nutrition 2001;31:3065S-3073S

This review article points out that the term "Mediterranean diet" is a misnomer. There is not one but many Mediterranean diets. Of all Mediterranean countries, Greece had the lowest rate of cancer and heart disease until 1960, when its diet started to become more Western. However, this diet is still eaten in Crete, and has been the subject of scientific study (see reference 4). The Crete diet has a high content of fruit, vegetables, nuts, cereals (mainly in the form of sourdough, which is a low-glycemic starch), olive oil, olives, cheese, fish, and wine, but is low in milk and meat. It's moderately high in fat (37% of total calories), with a lot of this fat being omega-3 fat. For comparison, the average adolescent in the US is eating about 32% of his or her calories from fat. Hence, it's not so much the amount of fat one eats that's important in preventing heart disease but the type of fat.

8. Slyper AH, Jurva J, Gutterman D et al. The influence of dietary constituents and glycemic load on HDL cholesterol in youth. American Journal of Clinical Nutrition 2005;81:376-379

In this study, I looked at the diets of adolescents and young adults, some of whom had high cholesterol levels. I found a strong relationship between the percentage fat in their diets and its "glycemic load". This was because many of these individuals had cut back on dietary fat (because of their high cholesterol levels), and as a result were eating more carbohydrate. This in turn was lowering their HDL cholesterol levels.

9. Harding AH, Warcham NJ, Bingham SA et al. Plasma vitamin C level, fruit and vegetable consumption, and the risk of new-onset type 2 diabetes mellitus. Archives of Internal Medicine 2008;168(14):1493-1499

In this large 12-year prospective study, blood vitamin C levels were used as a biomarker of fruit and vegetable intake. Many fruits and vegetables have a high content of antioxidant. The study found that higher vitamin C levels, and to a lesser degree fruit and vegetable intake, were associated with a substantially reduced risk for diabetes. The investigators suggest that their findings support the notion that even a small quantity of fruit and vegetables may be beneficial, and that protection against diabetes increases progressively with the quantity of fruit and vegetables consumed.

Nevertheless, the antioxidant hypothesis is still just that – an hypothesis. I think it's an attractive one and it's getting an increasing amount of press. One of the major objections to the antioxidant hypothesis is the demonstration that long-term administration of vitamin C and vitamin E (both of which are antioxidants) fails to protect against coronary artery disease. If antioxidants are beneficial how could this be? Does it not negate the entire antioxidant hypothesis? May be…. or maybe not. It could be that long-term administration of high dose antioxidants has a different effect on blood vessels than intermittent exposure to antioxidants. It's even possible that long-term antioxidant therapy down-regulates normal antioxidant production. This is about as much as one can say at the moment.

10. Snowling NJ, Hopkins WG. Effects of different modes of exercise training on glucose control and risk factors for complications in type 2 diabetic patients. A meta-analysis. Diabetes Care 2006;29:2518-2527.

This paper contains a meta-analysis. A meta-analysis is an analysis that uses statistical methods to combine the results of many similar studies and is able to reach a conclusion more reliable than that obtained from one study alone. 27 studies that looked at the effect of exercise on type 2 diabetes are summarized. Aerobic exercise produced a decrease in BMI of only 1.5%. However, it did produce a 28% decrease in insulin sensitivity, a 20% decrease in fasting insulin, and an 11% reduction in abdominal fat. Bottom line? The metabolic improvement obtained from exercise is a lot more impressive than the weight loss.

See also the front cover article of Time Magazine August 17, 2009, "The Myth about exercise. Of course it's good for you, but it won't make you lose weight. Why it's what you eat that really counts." This article by John Cloud explains why exercise alone can't make you thin. From a scientific perspective this is not a very impressive article. However, it's fun reading and the message is on target.

2.   Go Mediterranean and Control Body Weight!

1. Ebbeling CB, Fledman HA, Osganian SK et al. Effects of decreasing sugar-sweetened beverage consumption on body weight in adolescents: a randomized, controlled pilot study. Pediatrics 2006;117:673-680

103 adolescents who regularly consumed sugar-sweetened beverages were randomly assigned to 2 groups for 25 weeks; one of the groups decreased their consumption of sugar-sweetened drinks and the other group made no change. For the study patients overall, the intervention made no difference. However, when the investigators looked at the adolescents with a higher BMI (those in the upper third), there was a marked change in BMI between the intervention and control groups. This difference was *not* related to a decrease in energy intake as a result of drinking less sugar-sweetened drinks. In some way, the heavy adolescents seemed more sensitive to cutting back on sugar-sweetened drinks.

   See also: Palmer JR, Boggs DA, Krishnan S et al. Sugar-sweetened beverages and incidence of type 2 diabetes mellitus in African American women. Archives of Internal Medicine 2008;168(14):1487-1492

In this large 10-year prospective study of African American women, the incidence of type 2 diabetes mellitus was higher with a higher intake of sugar-sweetened soft drinks and fruit drinks. This study is worth discussing because it implicated both soft drinks *and* fruit juices in the etiology of diabetes. Interestingly, orange and grapefruit juice were not implicated.

2. Stanhope Kl, Griffen SC, Bair BR et al. Twenty-four hour endocrine and metabolic profiles following consumption of high-fructose corn syrup-, sucrose-, fructose-, and glucose-sweetened beverages with meals. American Journal of Clinical Nutrition 2008a;87:1194-1203

There is a substantial amount of evidence in experimental animals that a high-fructose diet produces obesity, insulin resistance, glucose intolerance and abnormal blood lipids, but the evidence in humans is sparser. In this study, investigators compared beverages of pure glucose, pure fructose, high-fructose corn sweetener and sucrose (sugar). The intake of these sugars was higher than the average person would consume but within the range for a heavy soda drinker. Fructose, sugar and high-fructose corn sweeteners led to almost identical post-meal triglyceride levels, but triglyceride levels for all 3 fructose-containing drinks were significantly higher than for pure glucose. Biochemists can get carried away with this, figuring out how fructose pathways in the liver can lead to the accumulation of triglyceride in the liver, increased production of VDLD particles and eventually increased insulin resistance.

3. Heaton KW, Marcus SN, Emmett PM, Bolton CH. Particle size of wheat, maize, and oat test meals: effects on plasma glucose and insulin responses and on the rate of starch digestion in vitro. The American Journal of Clinical Nutrition 1988;47:675-682

The glycemic indices of wheat, maize and oats were lower in the form of whole grains than in the form of cracked grains. The glycemic indices for cracked grains were lower than for coarse flour, and the glycemic indices for coarse flour lower than for fine flour.

4. Jenkins DJ, WessonV, Wolever TM et al. Wholemeal versus wholegrain breads: proportion of whole or cracked grain and the glycaemic response. The British Medical Journal 1988;297:958-960

By "wholemeal" bread, the authors mean bread containing wholegrain flour, whereas a "wholegrain" bread is one containing intact kernels of grain within the bread. I agree this is confusing – but that's how it is. This study found that the glycemic indices of the breads were a function of the quantity of whole grains relative to flour - the more whole grains, the lower the glycemic index.

5. Ludwig DS, Majzoub JA, Al-Zahrani A et al. High glycemic index foods, overeating, and obesity. Pediatrics 199;103:e26

This is not the first study to show that high-glycemic foods lead to hunger, but it illustrates the effect rather nicely.

6. Rampersaud GC, Pereira MA, Girard BL et al. Breakfast habits, nutritional status, body weight, and academic performance in children and adolescents. Journal of the American Dietetic Association 2005;105:743-760

Between 10-30% of children and adolescents skip breakfast. This study summarizes 47 cross-sectional studies. In general, breakfast-eaters consume more daily calories and yet are less likely to be overweight, although some studies were unable to show this effect. Breakfast-eaters also have superior nutritional profiles than their breakfast-skipping peers. Memory and test grades are also improved by eating breakfast. Again, not at all studies found this effect, but a lot more did than didn't.

Also: Gleason PM, Dodd AH. School breakfast program not school lunch program participation is associated with lower body mass index. Journal of the American Dietetic Association 2009;109:S118-S128)

This cross-sectional study looked at the association with BMI of having either a school breakfast or a school lunch. Participation in school breakfast was associated with a modest but significantly lower BMI than not having school breakfast, but this was not shown for school lunch. This effect was not related to total daily calories. One can't make any causal inferences from this study, since it's possible that the school breakfast and lunch participants differed from each other in ways not picked up by the study (which did nevertheless control for numerous variables).

7. Flood JE. Rolls BJ. Soup preloads in a variety of forms reduce meal intake. Appetite 2007;49:626-634

Eating a vegetable soup before a meal reduced the energy intake of that meal by 20%. This study showed that it made no difference whether the soup was chunky or pureed. However, at least one other study has shown that it does make a difference, and that food intake is significantly less following a chunky vegetable soup than a strained vegetable soup. (Himaya A, Louis-Silvestre J. The effect of soup on satiation. Appetite 1998;30:199-210)

3. Control Carbs and Lose Weight!

1. Slyper AH. The pediatric obesity epidemic: causes and controversies. Journal of Clinical Endocrinology and Metabolism 2004;89:2540-2547

Is it possible that the amount and type of carbohydrates one eats has more influence on body weight than calories? Or to put the question another way, is the body no more than a combustion engine and all that matters are the calories in and the calories out?

Quite frankly, there's not much evidence either way, since most scientists haven't even thought of the question! Nevertheless, the above paper presents suggestive evidence from studies using low-glycemic and low-carb diets that there's more to body weight than just calories.

For example: Sondike et al found that adolescents using a low-carb diet lost more weight than those on a low-fat diet, even though they were eating more calories. Thus, either there is more to weight loss than calories alone or these investigators added up the calories incorrectly. Most nutritional experts would hold the latter, and feel that the success of low-carb diets is due solely to eating less calories. Of course, eating less carbs does lead to eating less calories – but I'm not convinced that this is the entire answer.

See Sondike et al. Effects of a low-carbohydrate diet on weight loss and cardiovascular risk factors in overweight adolescents. Journal of Pediatrics 2003;142:253-258

2. Halton TL, Willett WC, Liu S et al. Low-carbohydrate-diet score and the risk of coronary heart disease in women. New England Journal of Medicine 2006;355:1991-2002

This study posed the following question - are chronic low-carb diets associated with an increased risk of coronary heart disease? Low-carb diets are often high-protein diets, which could theoretically be associated with an increase in coronary risk. The investigators looked at 20-year follow-up data from 2,802 women in the Nurses' Health Study to find the answer. The investigators found no increase in coronary risk for women on a low-carb diet compared to those who ate more carbohydrate. However, they also found that if the carbohydrate was replaced with vegetable sources of protein and fat rather than animal protein and fat this was associated with a moderate *reduction* in risk for coronary disease. This is not the study to end all debate – but it's a good start. Low-carb diets high in animal fat and animal protein don't decrease coronary risk, whereas vegetable protein and fat do. This study found no deterioration in kidney function with a high protein diet, but we know from other studies that this can be a concern for those who already have abnormal kidney function. Bottom line – stick to vegetables!

See also: Philips SA, Jurva JW, Syed AQ et al. Benefit of low-fat over low-carbohydrate diet on endothelial health in obesity. Hypertension 2008;51:376-382

The assumption has always been that weight loss is beneficial to health, however it's achieved. Hence the popularity of high-fat low-carb diets. This study compared the effect of two weight-loss diets on blood vessel health - an Atkins-type high-fat diet and a low-fat diet. Blood vessel function improved on the low-fat diet but worsened on the high-fat diet. So much for that assumption. The reality is that deterioration in vascular health would not be a big deal if this were only for a few weeks. However, obesity doesn't disappear so easily however great the diet, so that one has to regard these diets as being long-term. The bottom line? A long-term low-calorie high-fat diet is not an effective way for improving one's vascular health.

3. Pereira MA, Swain J, Goldfine AB et al. Effects of a low-glycemic load diet on resting energy expenditure and heart disease risk factors during weight loss. Journal of the American Medical Association 2004;292:2482-249

This study examined 39 obese young adults who were placed on either a low-fat or low-glycemic weight-loss diet. The amount of energy they expended at rest was tested before and after 10% weight loss.

Resting energy expenditure fell significantly less with the low-glycemic diet compared to the low-fat diet. The authors conclude from these results that dietary composition does affect how the body adapts to weight loss. One might also speculate from the results of this study that it might be a little bit easier to lose weight and keep that weight off with low-glycemic dieting than with low-fat dieting.

4.   Lee A, Griffin B. Dietary cholesterol, eggs and coronary heart disease risk in perspective. British Nutrition Foundation Nutrition Bulletin 2006;31:21-27

Dietary cholesterol raises blood cholesterol in 20 to 30% of people. However, this review article points out that no study has been able to show that this translates into an increased risk for heart disease except in diabetics. One study looked at data from 1 million subjects and found no difference in cardiovascular disease risk between those who ate less than one egg a day compared to those who ate more than one egg a day. There are not too many studies in the literature with this number of subjects! Eggs lead to a 50% greater satiety than common breakfast foods such as breakfast cereal and white bread. I think these authors are onto something.

See also: Chan W. Egg consumption and endothelial function: a randomized controlled crossover trial. International Journal of Cardiology 2005;99(1):65-70

49 healthy adults were assigned to either 2 eggs a day or to oats for 6 weeks and then switched over after a 4-week washout period. The eggs had no effect on total or LDL cholesterol levels, whereas the oats lowered total and LDL cholesterol levels. Endothelial function, which is a measure of vascular health, remained stable during both treatment branches.

4.   Dubois L, Girard M, Kent MP et al. Breakfast skipping is associated with differences in meal patterns, macronutrient intakes and overweight among pre-school children. Public Health Nutrition 2008;12(1):19-28

A number of studies in adolescents and school children (although not all) have shown a positive association between skipping breakfast and increased weight. This study found that pre-school children who skip breakfast have lower dietary quality and a higher consumption of energy-containing carbohydrate snacks in the afternoon and evening. However, their total caloric intake is not increased. This is another small bit of suggestive evidence that in terms of gaining weight it's not how much you eat but what you eat that's really important.

5.   McManus K, Antinoro L, Sacks F. A randomized controlled trial of a moderate-fat low-energy diet compared with a low fat, low-energy diet for weight loss in overweight adults. International Journal of Obesity 2001;25:1503-1511

101 overweight men and women were randomized over 18 months to a moderate-fat Mediterranean diet (35% of energy as fat) or a standard low-fat diet (20% of energy as fat). Subjects on the Mediterranean diet lost weight (4.1 Kg) whereas those on the low-fat diet gained weight (2.9 Kg). Also, a lot more participants gave up on the low-fat diet than the Mediterranean diet (54% versus 20%).

See also: Shai I, Schwarzfuchs D, Henkin Y et al. Weight loss with a low-carbohydrate, Mediterranean or low-fat diet. New England Journal of Medicine 2008;359:229-241

This 2-year trial compared three weight loss diets – low-fat, Mediterranean and low-carbohydrate. Average weight loss was 2.9 Kg for the low-fat, 4.4 Kg for the Mediterranean, and 4.7 Kg for the low-carb diet. The low-carb diet achieved a greater initial weight loss but this was followed by a gradual regain of weight. The diabetics did better on the Mediterranean diet. This study's conclusion was that a Mediterranean and a low-carb diet offer an effective alternative to a low-fat diet for weight loss.

4. Clogging and Unclogging Arteries

1. Hooper L, Summerbell CD, Higgins JPT, Thompson RL, Clements G, Capps N, Davey Smith G, Riemersma R, Ebrahim S. Reduced or modified dietary fat for preventing cardiovascular disease (Review). Cochrane Library 2009, issue 4, published by John Wiley and Sons, Ltd

This meta-analysis showed that people at high risk for coronary disease do obtain a small benefit from a low-fat diet in terms of coronary events. However, there is no effect on morbidity. For people at low risk for coronary disease there is no significant benefit.

2. McManus K, Antinoro L, Sacks F. A randomized control trial of a moderate-fat, low-energy diet compared with a low fat, low-energy diet for weight loss in overweight adults. International Journal of Obesity 2001;25:1503-1511

This large 18-month interventional study compared two weight-loss diets - a moderate-fat Mediterranean-type diet and a low-fat diet. Subjects on the moderate-fat diet increased their fat intake to 35% of total calories while the low-fat group decreased their fat intake initially to 28% and subsequently to 30% of total calories. At 18 months, the moderate-fat group had lost 4.1 Kg while the low-fat group had *gained* 2.9 Kg. By the end of the study, only 20% of the subjects in the low-fat group were participating in this study versus 54% for the moderate-fat group. Their conclusion: low-fat dieting is difficult and rarely successful.

3. Hu FB, Stampfer MJ. Nut consumption and risk of coronary heart disease: a review of epidemiologic evidence. Current Atherosclerosis Reports 1999;1:204-209

This review article discusses five studies that have shown that diets containing a lot of nuts have a favorable influence on cardiovascular disease. The authors suggest that nuts deserve a more prominent position in the Food Pyramid. It's hard to argue with that conclusion.

4. Natoli S, McCoy P. A review of the evidence: nuts and body weight. Asia Pacific Journal of Clinical Nutrition 2007:16(4):588-597

This review discusses five large longitudinal studies that examined the relationship between nut consumption and body weight. Three of them found nut consumption to be associated with a lower body weight while one did not. The results were less impressive when nuts were part of a weight-loss diet. In only one of four interventional studies was there a greater weight loss with nuts than without, while in one study there was a slight weight gain. Clearly, if you eat too many nuts you will gain weight, but as a replacement for other weight-inducing food items they are a good choice.

5. Simopoulos AP. The importance of the omega-6/omega-3 fatty acid ratio in cardiovascular disease and other chronic diseases. Experimental Biological Medicine 2008;233:674-688

The writings of this author are not mainline thinking, but I like his suggestions a lot (which is why I quote them). He suggests that an abnormal ratio of dietary omega-6/omega-3 fatty acids promotes cardiovascular disease, cancer, inflammatory disease and autoimmune disease and he provides evidence (although not a whole lot) to support his theory. Most people's diets in this country have a ratio of omega-6/omega-3 of about 15:1, which is quite high. In actuality, administration of omega-3 fat has not been found to be the cure-all for most of these diseases, although this does not negate his hypotheses. However, as the Lyon Heart Study found out, omega-3s are very helpful for preventing cardiovascular disease. The author also points out that there are interesting interactions in the body between fats. Olive oil, for example, increases the incorporation of omega-3 fat into cell membranes, whereas omega-6 from corn oil prevents omega-3 incorporation. In other words, omega-6 crowds out omega-3. I find this and the author's other papers on this subject sobering reading in that it's very easy to ignore how various nutrients interact with each other within the body and how modern agricultural practices have impacted on the fatty acid composition of the food we eat.

6. Mozaffarian D, Katan M, Ascherio A et al. Trans fatty acids and cardiovascular disease. New England Journal of Medicine 2006;354:1601-1613

At the time this paper was published, the average intake of trans fat in the American population was 2 to 3% of total calories. Harmful effects are possible even at these low levels. The authors advise complete or near-complete avoidance of industrially produced trans fat.

7. Elwood PC, Pickering JE, Hughes J, Fehily AM, Ness AR. Milk drinking, ischaemic heart disease and ischaemic stroke II. Evidence from cohort studies. European Journal of Clinical Nutrition 2004;58:718-724

This is an often quoted paper. The authors analyzed ten studies that looked at the relationship between milk intake and coronary disease and stroke. Taken together, they show no increase in risk for coronary disease and possibly a small benefit in terms of stroke. This review article also points out that most of these studies were completed before the full impact of the low-fat milk campaign, so that many, if not most, of the participants in these studies would have been drinking whole milk.

8. Slyper AH, Huang W-M. Milk, dairy fat, and body weight in Pediatrics: time for reappraisal. Infant, Child and Adolescent Nutrition 2009:148-159

With only a few exceptions, pediatric cross-sectional and prospective studies from across the globe have demonstrated *negative* associations between dairy/milk intake and body mass index or body fat; in other words, the more milk you drink the less you weigh. Howeve, it's difficult to know whether this is a true cause and effect relationship. Four pediatric studies looked specifically at the influence of the fat content of milk and none were able to implicate whole or 2% milk as being more weight-inducing than lower-fat milk.

For more scientific reviews of this nature, see my website eatforhealth.org

206355LV00001B/93/P

LaVergne, TN USA
27 November 2010

SPHINX® PUBLISHING ORDER FORM

Qty	ISBN	Title	Retail	Ext.
		GEORGIA TITLES		
_____	1-57248-340-7	How to File for Divorce in GA (5E)	$21.95	_____
_____	1-57248-180-3	How to Make a GA Will (4E)	$21.95	_____
_____	1-57248-341-5	How to Start a Business in Georgia (3E)	$21.95	_____
		ILLINOIS TITLES		
_____	1-57248-244-3	Child Custody, Visitation, and Support in IL	$24.95	_____
_____	1-57248-206-0	How to File for Divorce in IL (3E)	$24.95	_____
_____	1-57248-170-6	How to Make an IL Will (3E)	$16.95	_____
_____	1-57248-247-8	How to Start a Business in IL (3E)	$21.95	_____
_____	1-57248-252-4	The Landlord's Legal Guide in IL	$24.95	_____
		MARYLAND, VIRGINIA AND THE DISTRICT OF COLUMBIA		
_____	1-57248-240-0	How to File for Divorce in MD, VA and DC	$28.95	_____
		MASSACHUSETTS TITLES		
_____	1-57248-128-5	How to File for Divorce in MA (3E)	$24.95	_____
_____	1-57248-115-3	How to Form a Corporation in MA	$24.95	_____
_____	1-57248-108-0	How to Make a MA Will (2E)	$16.95	_____
_____	1-57248-248-6	How to Start a Business in MA (3E)	$21.95	_____
_____	1-57248-209-5	The Landlord's Legal Guide in MA	$24.95	_____
		MICHIGAN TITLES		
_____	1-57248-215-X	How to File for Divorce in MI (3E)	$24.95	_____
_____	1-57248-182-X	How to Make a MI Will (3E)	$16.95	_____
_____	1-57248-183-8	How to Start a Business in MI (3E)	$18.95	_____
		MINNESOTA TITLES		
_____	1-57248-142-0	How to File for Divorce in MN	$21.95	_____
_____	1-57248-179-X	How to Form a Corporation in MN	$24.95	_____
_____	1-57248-178-1	How to Make a MN Will (2E)	$16.95	_____
		NEW JERSEY TITLES		
_____	1-57248-239-7	How to File for Divorce in NJ	$24.95	_____
		NEW YORK TITLES		
_____	1-57248-193-5	Child Custody, Visitation and Support in NY	$26.95	_____
_____	1-57248-351-2	File for Divorce in NY	$26.95	_____
_____	1-57248-249-4	How to Form a Corporation in NY (2E)	$24.95	_____
_____	1-57248-095-5	How to Make a NY Will (2E)	$16.95	_____
_____	1-57248-199-4	How to Start a Business in NY (2E)	$18.95	_____
_____	1-57248-198-6	How to Win in Small Claims Court in NY (2E)	$18.95	_____
_____	1-57248-197-8	Landlords' Legal Guide in NY	$24.95	_____
_____	1-57071-188-7	New York Power of Attorney Handbook	$19.95	_____
_____	1-57248-122-6	Tenants' Rights in NY	$21.95	_____

Qty	ISBN	Title	Retail	Ext.
		NORTH CAROLINA TITLES		
_____	1-57248-185-4	How to File for Divorce in NC (3E)	$22.95	_____
_____	1-57248-129-3	How to Make a NC Will (3E)	$16.95	_____
_____	1-57248-184-6	How to Start a Business in NC (3E)	$18.95	_____
_____	1-57248-091-2	Landlords' Rights & Duties in NC	$21.95	_____
		OHIO TITLES		
_____	1-57248-190-0	How to File for Divorce in OH (2E)	$24.95	_____
_____	1-57248-174-9	How to Form a Corporation in OH	$24.95	_____
_____	1-57248-173-0	How to Make an OH Will	$16.95	_____
		PENNSYLVANIA TITLES		
_____	1-57248-242-7	Child Custody, Visitation and Support in PA	$26.95	_____
_____	1-57248-211-7	How to File for Divorce in PA (3E)	$26.95	_____
_____	1-57248-358-X	How to Form a Corporation in PA	$24.95	_____
_____	1-57248-094-7	How to Make a PA Will (2E)	$16.95	_____
_____	1-57248-357-1	How to Start a Business in PA (3E)	$21.95	_____
_____	1-57248-245-1	The Landlord's Legal Guide in PA	$24.95	_____
		TEXAS TITLES		
_____	1-57248-171-4	Child Custody, Visitation, and Support in TX	$22.95	_____
_____	1-57248-172-2	How to File for Divorce in TX (3E)	$24.95	_____
_____	1-57248-114-5	How to Form a Corporation in TX (2E)	$24.95	_____
_____	1-57248-255-9	How to Make a TX Will (3E)	$16.95	_____
_____	1-57248-214-1	How to Probate and Settle an Estate in TX (3E)	$26.95	_____
_____	1-57248-228-1	How to Start a Business in TX (3E)	$18.95	_____
_____	1-57248-111-0	How to Win in Small Claims Court in TX (2E)	$16.95	_____
_____	1-57248-355-5	the Landlord's Legal Guide in TX	$24.95	_____

SUBTOTAL THIS PAGE _____

SUBTOTAL PREVIOUS PAGE _____

Shipping— $5.00 for 1st book, $1.00 each additional _____

Illinois residents add 6.75% sales tax _____

Connecticut residents add 6.00% sales tax _____

TOTAL _____

To order, call Sourcebooks at 1-800-432-7444 or FAX (630) 961-2168 (Bookstores, libraries, wholesalers—please call for discount)
Prices are subject to change without notice.
Find more legal information at: **www.SphinxLegal.com**

SPHINX® PUBLISHING ORDER FORM

BILL TO:		SHIP TO:	
Phone #	Terms	F.O.B. Chicago, IL	Ship Date

Charge my: ☐ VISA ☐ MasterCard ☐ American Express

☐ **Money Order or Personal Check**

Credit Card Number

Expiration Date

Qty	ISBN	Title	Retail	Ext.	Qty	ISBN	Title	Retail	Ext.
		SPHINX PUBLISHING NATIONAL TITLES				1-57248-169-2	The Power of Attorney Handbook (4E)	$19.95	
	1-57248-238-9	The 529 College Savings Plan	$16.95			1-57248-332-6	Profit from Intellectual Property	$28.95	
	1-57248-349-0	The Antique and Art Collector's Legal Guide	$24.95			1-57248-329-6	Protect Your Patent	$24.95	
	1-57248-148-X	Cómo Hacer su Propio Testamento	$16.95			1-57248-344-X	Repair Your Own Credit and Deal with Debt (2E)	$18.95	
	1-57248-226-5	Cómo Restablecer su propio Crédito y Renegociar sus Deudas	$21.95			1-57248-350-4	El Seguro Social Preguntas y Respuestas	$14.95	
	1-57248-147-1	Cómo Solicitar su Propio Divorcio	$24.95			1-57248-217-6	Sexual Harassment: Your Guide to Legal Action	$18.95	
	1-57248-166-8	The Complete Book of Corporate Forms	$24.95			1-57248-219-2	The Small Business Owner's Guide to Bankruptcy	$21.95	
	1-57248-229-X	The Complete Legal Guide to Senior Care	$21.95			1-57248-168-4	The Social Security Benefits Handbook (3E)	$18.95	
	1-57248-201-X	The Complete Patent Book	$26.95			1-57248-216-8	Social Security Q&A	$12.95	
	1-57248-163-3	Crime Victim's Guide to Justice (2E)	$21.95			1-57248-221-4	Teen RIghts	$22.95	
	1-57248-251-6	The Entrepreneur's Internet Handbook	$21.95			1-57248-335-0	Traveler's Rights	$21.95	
	1-57248-346-6	Essential Guide to Real Estate Contracts (2E)	$18.95			1-57248-236-2	Unmarried Parents' Rights (2E)	$19.95	
	1-57248-160-9	Essential Guide to Real Estate Leases	$18.95			1-57248-218-4	U.S. Immigration Step by Step	$21.95	
	1-57248-254-0	Family Limited Partnership	$26.95			1-57248-161-7	U.S.A. Immigration Guide (4E)	$24.95	
	1-57248-331-8	Gay & Lesbian Rights	$26.95			1-57248-192-7	The Visitation Handbook	$18.95	
	1-57248-139-0	Grandparents' Rights (3E)	$24.95			1-57248-225-7	Win Your Unemployment Compensation Claim (2E)	$21.95	
	1-57248-188-9	Guía de Inmigración a Estados Unidos (3E)	$24.95			1-57248-330-X	The Wills, Estate Planning and Trusts Legal Kit	&26.95	
	1-57248-187-0	Guía de Justicia para Víctimas del Crimen	$21.95			1-57248-138-2	Winning Your Personal Injury Claim (2E)	$24.95	
	1-57248-103-X	Help Your Lawyer Win Your Case (2E)	$14.95			1-57248-333-4	Working with Your Homeowners Association	$19.95	
	1-57248-164-1	How to Buy a Condominium or Townhome (2E)	$19.95			1-57248-162-5	Your Right to Child Custody, Visitation and Support (2E)	$24.95	
	1-57248-328-8	How to Buy Your First Home	$18.95			1-57248-157-9	Your Rights When You Owe Too Much	$16.95	
	1-57248-191-9	How to File Your Own Bankruptcy (5E)	$21.95				**CALIFORNIA TITLES**		
	1-57248-343-1	How to File Your Own Divorce (5E)	$26.95			1-57248-150-1	CA Power of Attorney Handbook (2E)	$18.95	
	1-57248-222-2	How to Form a Limited Liability Company (2E)	$24.95			1-57248-337-7	How to File for Divorce in CA (4E)	$26.95	
	1-57248-231-1	How to Form a Nonprofit Corporation (2E)	$24.95			1-57248-145-5	How to Probate and Settle an Estate in CA	$26.95	
	1-57248-345-8	How to Form Your Own Corporation (4E)	$26.95			1-57248-336-9	How to Start a Business in CA (2E)	$21.95	
	1-57248-224-9	How to Form Your Own Partnership (2E)	$24.95			1-57248-194-3	How to Win in Small Claims Court in CA (2E)	$18.95	
	1-57248-232-X	How to Make Your Own Simple Will (3E)	$18.95			1-57248-246-X	Make Your Own CA Will	$18.95	
	1-57248-200-1	How to Register Your Own Copyright (4E)	$24.95			1-57248-196-X	The Landlord's Legal Guide in CA	$24.95	
	1-57248-104-8	How to Register Your Own Trademark (3E)	$21.95			1-57248-241-9	Tenants' Rights in CA	$21.95	
	1-57248-233-8	How to Write Your Own Living Will (3E)	$18.95				**FLORIDA TITLES**		
	1-57248-156-0	How to Write Your Own Premarital Agreement (3E)	$24.95			1-57071-363-4	Florida Power of Attorney Handbook (2E)	$16.95	
	1-57248-230-3	Incorporate in Delaware from Any State	$24.95			1-57248-176-5	How to File for Divorce in FL (7E)	$26.95	
	1-57248-158-7	Incorporate in Nevada from Any State	$24.95			1-57248-356-3	How to Form a Corporation in FL (6E)	$24.95	
	1-57248-250-8	Inmigración a los EE.UU. Paso a Paso	$22.95			1-57248-203-6	How to Form a Limited Liability Co. in FL (2E)	$24.95	
	1-57071-333-2	Jurors' Rights (2E)	$12.95			1-57071-401-0	How to Form a Partnership in FL	$22.95	
	1-57248-223-0	Legal Research Made Easy (3E)	$21.95			1-57248-113-7	How to Make a FL Will (6E)	$16.95	
	1-57248-165-X	Living Trusts and Other Ways to Avoid Probate (3E)	$24.95			1-57248-088-2	How to Modify Your FL Divorce Judgment (4E)	$24.95	
	1-57248-186-2	Manual de Beneficios para el Seguro Social	$18.95			1-57248-144-7	How to Probate and Settle an Estate in FL (4E)	$26.95	
	1-57248-220-6	Mastering the MBE	$16.95			1-57248-339-3	How to Start a Business in FL (7E)	$21.95	
	1-57248-167-6	Most Val. Business Legal Forms You'll Ever Need (3E)	$21.95			1-57248-204-4	How to Win in Small Claims Court in FL (7E)	$18.95	
	1-57248-360-1	Most Val. Personal Legal Forms You'll Ever Need (2E)	$26.95			1-57248-202-8	Land Trusts in Florida (6E)	$29.95	
	1-57248-098-X	The Nanny and Domestic Help Legal Kit	$22.95			1-57248-338-5	Landlords' Rights and Duties in FL (9E)	$22.95	
	1-57248-089-0	Neighbor v. Neighbor (2E)	$16.95				*Form Continued on Following Page*	**SUBTOTAL**	

To order, call Sourcebooks at 1-800-432-7444 or FAX (630) 961-2168 (Bookstores, libraries, wholesalers—please call for discount)

Prices are subject to change without notice.

Find more legal information at: **www.SphinxLegal.com**

Sphinx® Publishing's National Titles
Valid in All 50 States

Legal Survival in Business

The Complete Book of Corporate Forms	$24.95
The Complete Patent Book	$26.95
The Entrepreneur's Internet Handbook	$21.95
How to Form a Limited Liability Company (2E)	$24.95
Incorporate in Delaware from Any State	$24.95
Incorporate in Nevada from Any State	$24.95
How to Form a Nonprofit Corporation (2E)	$24.95
How to Form Your Own Corporation (4E)	$26.95
How to Form Your Own Partnership (2E)	$24.95
How to Register Your Own Copyright (4E)	$24.95
How to Register Your Own Trademark (3E)	$21.95
Most Valuable Business Legal Forms You'll Ever Need (3E)	$21.95
Profit from Intellectual Property	$28.95
Protect Your Patent	$24.95
The Small Business Owner's Guide to Bankruptcy	$21.95

Legal Survival in Court

Crime Victim's Guide to Justice (2E)	$21.95
Grandparents' Rights (3E)	$24.95
Help Your Lawyer Win Your Case (2E)	$14.95
Jurors' Rights (2E)	$12.95
Legal Research Made Easy (3E)	$21.95
Winning Your Personal Injury Claim (2E)	$24.95
Your Rights When You Owe Too Much	$16.95

Legal Survival in Real Estate

Essential Guide to Real Estate Contracts (2E)	$18.95
Essential Guide to Real Estate Leases	$18.95
How to Buy a Condominium or Townhome (2E)	$19.95
How to Buy Your First Home	$18.95
Working with Your Homeowners Association	$19.95

Legal Survival in Personal Affairs

The 529 College Savings Plan	$16.95
The Antique and Art Collector's Legal Guide	$24.95
Cómo Hacer su Propio Testamento	$16.95
Cómo Restablecer su propio Crédito y Renegociar sus Deudas	$21.95
Cómo Solicitar su Propio Divorcio	$24.95
The Complete Legal Guide to Senior Care	$21.95
Credit Smart	$18.95
Family Limited Partnership	$26.95
Gay & Lesbian Rights	$26.95
Guía de Inmigración a Estados Unidos (3E)	$24.95
Guía de Justicia para Víctimas del Crimen	$21.95
How to File Your Own Bankruptcy (5E)	$21.95
How to File Your Own Divorce (5E)	$26.95
How to Make Your Own Simple Will (3E)	$18.95
How to Write Your Own Living Will (3E)	$18.95
How to Write Your Own Premarital Agreement (3E)	$24.95
Inmigración a los EE. UU. Paso a Paso	$22.95
Living Trusts and Other Ways to Avoid Probate (3E)	$24.95
Manual de Beneficios para el Seguro Social	$18.95
Mastering the MBE	$16.95
Most Valuable Personal Legal Forms You'll Ever Need (2E)	$26.95
Neighbor v. Neighbor (2E)	$16.95
The Nanny and Domestic Help Legal Kit	$22.95
The Power of Attorney Handbook (4E)	$19.95
Repair Your Own Credit and Deal with Debt (2E)	$18.95
El Seguro Social Preguntas y Respuestas	$14.95
Sexual Harassment:Your Guide to Legal Action	$18.95
The Social Security Benefits Handbook (3E)	$18.95
Social Security Q&A	$12.95
Teen Rights	$22.95
Traveler's Rights	$21.95
Unmarried Parents' Rights (2E)	$19.95
U.S. Immigration Step by Step	$21.95
U.S.A. Immigration Guide (4E)	$24.95
The Visitation Handbook	$18.95
The Wills, Estate Planning and Trusts Legal Kit	$26.95
Win Your Unemployment Compensation Claim (2E)	$21.95
Your Right to Child Custody, Visitation and Support (2E)	$24.95

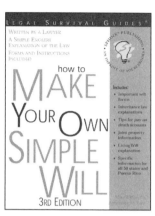
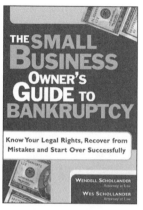